In the years when our Country

was in mortal danger

who served

gave generously of his time and

powers to make himself ready

for her defence by force of arms

and with his life if need be.

*George R.I.*

# THE HOME GUARD

# THE
# NORTHAMPTONSHIRE
# HOME GUARD
## 1940–1945

His Majesty King George VI, Colonel-in-Chief, The Home Guard
who has been graciously pleased to accept a copy of this volume

# THE
# NORTHAMPTONSHIRE HOME GUARD
## 1940-1945

---

## A History

of the services of men and women of Northamptonshire who in the world
war of 1939-45 forsook their rest and leisure to rally in defence
of the Homeland and defiance of the invader

*Editor*

## B. G. HOLLOWAY
ZONE H.Q. INTELLIGENCE AND PUBLIC RELATIONS OFFICER

*Collaborator*

## H. BANKS
A COMPANY, 12TH (NORTHAMPTON) BATTALION

**The Naval & Military Press Ltd**

*Published by*

**The Naval & Military Press Ltd**
Unit 10 Ridgewood Industrial Park,
Uckfield, East Sussex,
TN22 5QE England

Tel: +44 (0) 1825 749494
Fax: +44 (0) 1825 765701

www.naval–military-press.com
www.nmarchive.com

TO THOSE COMRADES WHO,

DURING DUTY WITH THE NORTHAMPTONSHIRE HOME GUARD,

PASSED TO THE HIGHER SERVICE,

AND TO THOSE WHO,

GRADUATING TO THE REGULAR FORCES,

MADE THE SUPREME SACRIFICE IN THE CAUSE OF FREEDOM,

THIS HISTORY IS PROUDLY AND GRATEFULLY DEDICATED

# FOREWORDS

15 May 1940

*To*

*Col. the Most Hon. the Marquess of Exeter, K.G., C.M.G., T.D.,*
*Burghley House, Stamford*

I AM sure that we may count on your co-operation and help in connection with the Local Defence Volunteer Force which, as I announced last night, the Government have decided to raise and as to which instructions have been issued to local military authorities including the area commanders who will be primarily concerned with the detailed arrangements.

ANTHONY EDEN

## BY HIS MAJESTY'S LORD LIEUTENANT OF NORTHAMPTONSHIRE
### (Colonel the Marquess of Exeter, K.G., C.M.G., T.D.)

IT is a far cry back to the night of 14 May 1940 when we heard Mr. Anthony Eden's call to arms and his announcement of the formation of the Local Defence Volunteer Force.

Within a few weeks this country was standing alone against the forces of evil, and it behoved every man capable of bearing arms to stand ready to defend his homeland.

From these beginnings grew the Home Guard, a title which will for ever be honoured in this country.

Though never called upon to repel invasion, the Home Guard did undoubtedly, by its very existence, play no small part in deterring the German High Command from launching an attempt.

The response in Northamptonshire was magnificent, not only in the immediate surge of recruits at the first call, but in the continued enthusiasm and keen efficiency displayed throughout the long years of war.

Such a record is one of which the County may justly be proud.

BURGHLEY HOUSE,                                                                    EXETER
        STAMFORD.

## BY MAJOR-GENERAL SIR HEREWARD WAKE, Bt., C.B., C.M.G., D.S.O., D.L., J.P., C.A.
### (First County Commander, Northamptonshire Home Guard)

FOR this historical work Northamptonshire owes a debt of gratitude to the author, Mr. B. G. Holloway, and to his collaborator, Mr. H. Banks. Both served during the 1914–18 war, and in May 1940 joined the Local Defence Volunteers. Mr. Holloway subsequently became Intelligence and Public Relations Officer at Home Guard County Headquarters, duties which kept him in close touch with all battalions up to the end of the war. Readers will find this history an interesting and very complete record of our County's contribution to Home defence during the 1939–45 war.

The story shows how Northampton responded to the call to arms at the most critical time in England's history; how the original six "divisions" of Local Defence Volunteers grew, in two or three months, into the Home Guard of fourteen (later fifteen) battalions with a total strength of over 15,000, every parish producing its volunteers; how red tape was thrown to the winds and all were ready to act without waiting for orders.

In the early days invasion was imminent and weapons were few. But Dunkirk and all it might mean had aroused a spirit—who did not feel it?—of fierce determination; of over-confidence, perhaps, for I believe many of the men *wanted* the Germans to come. And, if they had, there were many vital duties for the Home Guard, armed or not, and all proceeded to find out what these tasks were and to learn how to do them.

Let it be remembered that the Home Guardsman carried out his training and military duties in his spare time. The duties involved much night work. All had their civilian jobs which had to be carried on. Training and construction of defences took place on Saturday afternoons and on Sundays.

The County Home Guard owed much, as I had reason to know, to the leadership of the Lord Lieutenant, the Marquess of Exeter. I would also add that, without the active co-operation and support of the local authorities and, indeed, the whole of the people of the County, and not least of the veterans of the British Legion, little could have been achieved.

This volume will be read with pride by future generations. May they never be faced with similar dangers!

HEREWARD WAKE

COURTEENHALL,
NORTHAMPTON.


By COLONEL P. LESTER REID, C.B.E., D.L., J.P.

(Zone Commander and Sub-District Adviser, Northamptonshire Home Guard)


As I served from the first day to the last of the Home Guard, as Volunteer, Battalion Commander, Zone Commander, and Sub-District Home Guard Adviser, I think I got a better picture than anybody else of the Home Guard of Northamptonshire.

I am sure that on D-Day we a had most useful fighting force, built up by the loyal co-operation of officers and other ranks.

There is no doubt that every member had a right to be proud of the result.

THORPE MANDEVILLE MANOR,
BANBURY, OXON.

P. L. REID

# PREFACE

No history of the fifteen battalions of the Northamptonshire Home Guard could claim to be complete.

Even did the prescribed limits of the present work permit, it would be impossible to compile such a history seeing that most of the finest service performed by the Home Guard was unobtrusively rendered by individuals, singly or in small groups, far beyond the orbits of either official or unofficial records.

At the same time, every endeavour has been made to present as comprehensive a picture as possible of the Home Guard scene in Northamptonshire, during four memorable years, and of the grim and glorious national background against which it was set.

No attempt has been made to record all important events, exercises, and so on, in individual battalions. Such selections of these items have been made as are considered typical of all, exceptions being made only in such cases as special merit has demanded.

As much detail as was not necessitated by historical accuracy has also been excised and, apart from a few sections in which completeness, to permit of readier reference, was to be preferred to chronological sequence, events and developments are recorded in the order in which they occurred.

If to rising and future generations this record conveys some measure of the credit due to those of whom it tells, its purpose will have been achieved.

NORTHAMPTON.

B. G. H.
H. B.

---

## NOTE

The designation of units and the rankings of personnel in letterpress and captions to illustrations are, with a few exceptions, those held by the units, officers and other ranks at the dates of the references or of the taking of the photographs.

# CONTENTS

# ACKNOWLEDGMENTS

The authors gratefully acknowledge the ready and courteous co-operation of all who have assisted in a hundred ways in the preparation, collation, production, and publication of this history.

Special thanks are due to the following:

*H.M. the King (Colonel-in-Chief).* For gracious permission to reproduce a studio portrait as frontispiece and for acceptance of a copy of the volume.

*Col. the Marquess of Exeter and Major.-Gen. Sir Hereward Wake* for the contribution of forewords.

*Col. P. Lester Reid* for the initiation, planning, and organization of the history, much personal assistance in its production and the contribution of a foreword.

*All senior officers* for assistance in the collection of material and records and for the passing of proofs.

*Lt.-Col. O. K. Parker, M.C.,* and the staff of the Northamptonshire T.A.A. for access to their records.

*Lt.-Col. L. E. Barnes (ex-C.O. 12th (Northampton) Battalion)* for permission to reproduce extracts and pictures from his history of the 12th Battalion.

*Major T. C. Shillito* for the supply of information relating to early internal organization and records.

*Mr. C. Graves and Messrs. Hutchinson & Co.,* author and publishers of *The Home Guard of Britain,* for extracts therefrom.

*The Editors* of the *Northampton Chronicle and Echo,* the *Northampton Independent,* the *Kettering Leader,* and the *Peterborough Advertiser and Citizen,* and Mr. G. Turnill (Stamford) for the use of many illustrations and for much helpful publicity.

*Messrs. Rylee, Ltd.,* Sheepcote Street, Birmingham, for the use of cartoons.

*The officers and members of Northamptonshire British Legion* for readily rendered assistance in the publicizing and distribution of the history.

*Messrs. Jarrold and Sons, Ltd., Norwich,* for much technical assistance and valuable suggestions in printing and production.

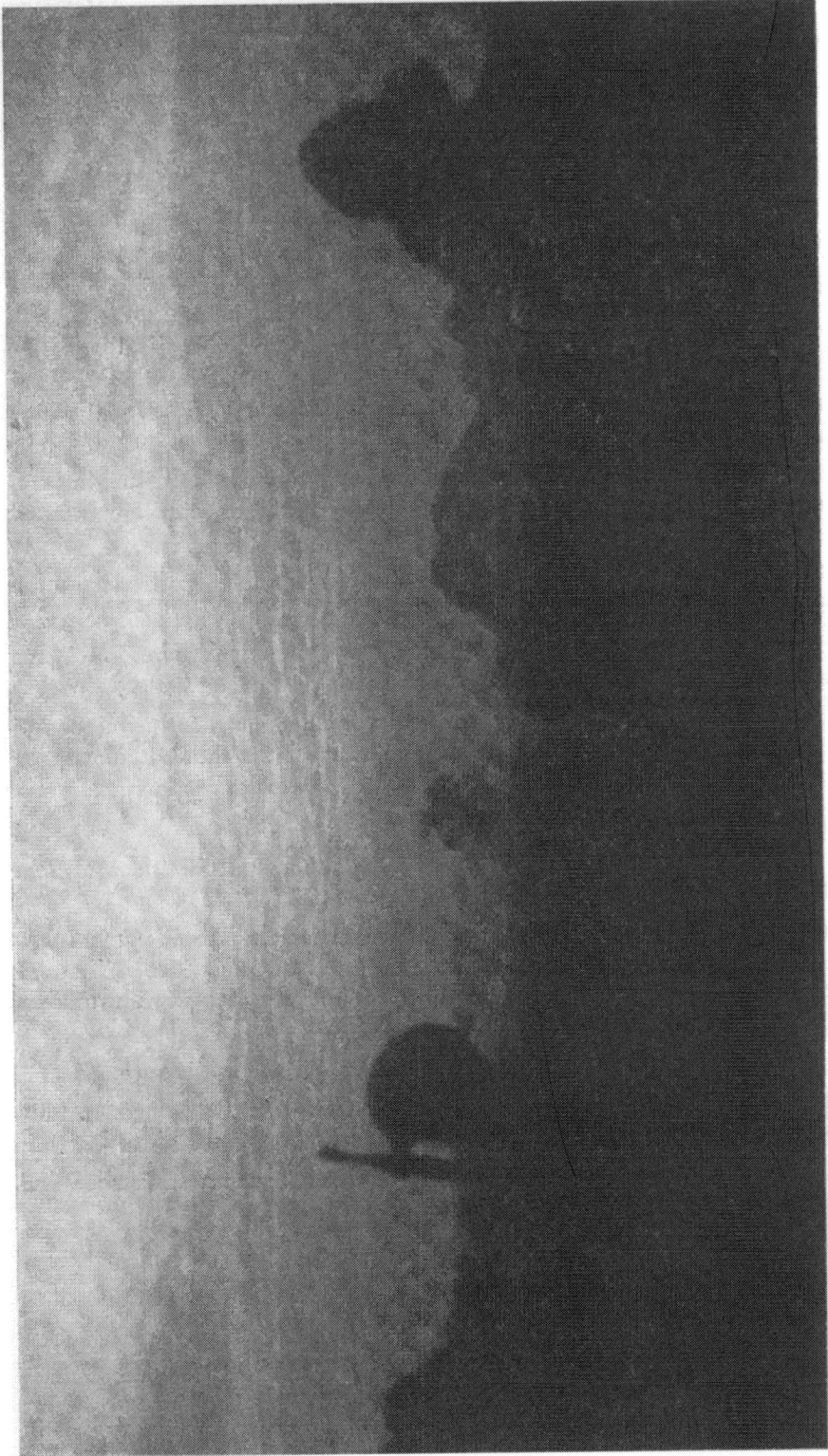

Waiting, Watching, Ready. (A dawn picture at Weston Favell, Northampton.)

[*Photo: J. Wright.*

## Chapter I

## THE CALL TO ARMS

I have nothing to offer but blood, toil, tears, and sweat . . . We have before us many, many months of struggle and suffering. You ask "What is our policy?" . . . It is to wage war by sea, land, and air with all our might, and with all the strength that God can give us . . . against a monstrous tyranny never surpassed in the dark, lamentable catalogue of human crime. That is our policy . . . Come, then, let us go forward together with our united strength.

THOSE fateful words, spoken by Mr. Winston Churchill, Prime Minister of Great Britain, on Monday, 13 May 1940, are now part of history—the history of the greatest and most evil menace with which Britain has ever been threatened, and of the supremely magnificent effort whereby the menace was repelled and, finally, crushed.

The British people did go forward together—every man, woman, and child "under arms" whether in battle by sea, land, or air, or on the Home Front, in defiant defence and in ceaseless, unremitting toil.

The story recorded in these pages tells of but one section of that vast Home Front army—a section bounded by the County of Northamptonshire and the ranks of the County's Home Guard, but it is a story that, for its reflexion of the national spirit during the crisis of 1939–45 and for the benefit of those succeeding generations who may seek to divine it, should be told.

It is difficult enough even at the time of writing, much less at a distance of decades, fully to appreciate the proportions of the national peril amid which the Home Guard was born.

Indeed, it was just as well that, beyond inner circles with fuller official information, the general rank and file of the people were unable to make a true assessment of the position, for even the stoutest of nations might have been forgiven for quailing in the face of it.

The facts were that relatively nothing stood between the German forces and the British homeland in May 1940.

After conquering Poland, and, with the aid of parachute troops and traitorous agents, later to be known as "fifth columnists" and "quislings", occupying Norway and Denmark, Hitler's mechanized hordes, by air and land, had crashed into Holland and Belgium, the great French army was disintegrating in incredulous disorder and the British Expeditionary Force was being driven to the Channel ports by overwhelmingly superior forces.

### AN EXULTANT ENEMY

Meanwhile, the Nazi newspapers and radio stations screamed daily in exultant anticipation of imminent triumph. Here are but four typical extracts:

Forty-five million Englishmen are facing the final phase of war. They have no hope . . . (Radio Zeesen.)

There is no prospect of Britain finding an escape from her present situation of air inferiority, either in the coming months of 1940, or in the years 1941 or 1942, or even later (Radio Zeesen.)

It is certain that the British are about to surrender. The settlement with England will be terrible. The British will be exterminated. London will only be the prelude. No stone will be left standing on the other in the Island Empire. (*Voelkischer Beobachter.*)

The legend of British self-control and phlegm is being destroyed. . . . The population is seized by fear—hair-raising fear. . . . The English have lost their wits and do not know how to defend their ports or their capital. (Radio Paris.)

It was not surprising that the situation precipitated a political upheaval of almost unprecedented magnitude. On 10 May the Prime Minister, Mr. Neville Chamberlain,

## MR. ANTHONY EDEN'S BROADCAST

And so, after a day of hectic conferences, the call went forth in the form of a broadcast appeal on 14 May by the Secretary of State for War, Mr. Anthony Eden.

His words, spoken in a tone of deadly earnestness at 9 p.m., were heard, and weighed in equally earnest silence, in every British home.

Here is Mr. Eden's broadcast, reproduced in full, because, of all the many

Adolf Hitler pictured at his mountain retreat at Berchtesgaden.

resigned, and was succeeded by Mr. Winston Churchill, who at once proceeded to form a united government of all parties.

By 11 May it was obvious in high quarters that it was only a matter of days before the Expeditionary Force must be annihilated, captured, or—evacuated.

Simultaneously came information from Norway verifying the success of the Germans' use of parachute troops in the invasion of that country.

What, then, of Britain?

The reply was the same that was flung at Napoleon by the Fencibles of 1803. Every Briton who could bear arms of any sort was to be ready, in the words of Mr. Winston Churchill, spoken a month later, to fight the invader "on the beaches, the landing grounds, in the fields, in the streets, and on the hills".

utterances relating to the Home Guard, this was the most momentous:

I want to speak to you to-night about the form of warfare which the Germans have been employing so extensively against Holland and Belgium—namely the dropping of troops by parachute behind the main defensive lines. Let me say at once that the danger to us from this particular menace, though it undoubtedly exists, should not be exaggerated. We have made preparations to meet it already.

Let me describe to you the system under which these parachute raids are carried out. The troops arrive by aeroplane, but let it be remembered that any such aeroplane seeking to penetrate here, would have to do so in the teeth of the anti-aircraft defences of this country.

If such penetration is effected, the parachutists are then dropped—it may be by day, it may be by night. These troops are especially armed and equipped and some of them have undergone specialized training. Their function is to seize important points such as aerodromes, power stations, villages, railway junctions, and telephone exchanges—either for the purpose of destroying them at once, or of holding them until the arrival of reinforcements. The purpose of the parachute attack is to disorganize and confuse, as a preparation for the landing of troops by aircraft.

The success of such an attack depends on speed. Consequently the measures to defeat such an attack must be prompt and rapid. It is upon this basis that our plans have been laid. You will not expect me to tell you, nor the enemy, what our plans are; but we are confident that they will be effective. However, in order to leave nothing to chance, and to supplement, from sources as yet untapped, the means of defence already arranged, we are going to ask you to help us, in a manner which I know will be welcome to thousands of you.

Since the war began, the Government have received countless inquiries from all over the Kingdom from men of all ages who are, for one reason or other, not at present engaged in military service and who wish to do something for the defence of their country. Well, now is your opportunity.

We want large numbers of men in Great Britain, who are British subjects and between the ages of seventeen and sixty-five, to come forward now and offer their services in order to make assurance doubly sure. The name of the new force which is now to be raised will be "The Local Defence Volunteers". This name describes its duties in three words. It must be understood that this is, so to speak, a spare-time job, so there will be no need for any volunteer to abandon his present occupation.

Part-time members of existing civil defence organizations should ask their officers' advice before registering under the scheme. Men who will ultimately become due for calling up under the National Service (Armed Forces) Act may join temporarily and will be released to join the army when they are required to serve.

Now a word to those who propose to volunteer. When on duty you will form part of the armed forces, and your period of service will be for the duration of the war. You will not be paid, but you will receive uniform and you will be armed. You will be entrusted with certain vital duties for which reasonable fitness and a knowledge of firearms is necessary. These duties will not require you to live away from home.

A "Home Guard" of the last century. The 5th Earl Spencer is seen demonstrating "the kneeling position". The photo was shown at an exhibition of old photographs at Northampton in 1942.

In order to volunteer, what you have to do is to give in your name at your local police station; and then, as and when we want you, we will let you know. This appeal is directed chiefly to those who live in country parishes, in small towns, in villages, and in less densely inhabited suburban areas. I must warn you that for certain military reasons there will be some localities where the numbers required will be small, and others where your services will not be required at all.

Here, then, is the opportunity for which so many of you have been waiting. Your loyal help, added to the arrangements which already exist, will make and keep our country safe.

## AN ELECTRIC RESPONSE

In Northampton and its shire, as throughout the length and breadth of the

United Kingdom, the reception of this broadcast was as electric as it was stupendous.

Men of all types and classes literally flocked to the police stations or to their village institutes, and here let the highest tribute be paid to the police of Northampton town and county for their unreserved and invaluable aid in compiling the first registers. Thereby they first demonstrated a whole-hearted co-operation with the Home Guard which endured to the end.

Within a very short time S O S demands were going out for more and more supplies of enrolment forms which had, accordingly, to be reproduced upon any sort of duplicating machines the harassed provisional commanders could beg or borrow.

The Local Defence Volunteer force had captured overnight the imagination and desire to serve in a combatant arm of thousands of Northamptonians. Here was a call appealing to their traditional fighting spirit—a spirit reflected in the records of their famous County Regiment, Yeomanry and Territorials, and in the service in the old volunteer forces of their forefathers, over centuries past.

### COUNTY COMMANDER'S APPOINTMENT

Within forty-eight hours (16 May 1940) a special meeting was held at the Territorial Army Association Headquarters, the Drill Hall, Clare Street, Northampton, to consider local organization of the Local Defence Volunteers.

Among those attending were Colonel the Marquess of Exeter, K.G., C.M.G., T.D. (Lord Lieutenant of the County), Major-Gen. Sir Hereward Wake, Bt., C.B., C.M.G., D.S.O., D.L. (Chairman of Northamptonshire Territorial Army Association), Major G. T. Lemon, O.B.E., V.D. (Assistant Liaison Officer), Lt.-Col. A. St. G. Coldwell (Commanding Depot North-amptonshire Regiment), and Mr. A. A. Ferguson (Chief Constable of the County).

The meeting expressed the opinion that the Territorial Army Association should be responsible for administration of the Northamptonshire Local Defence Volunteers, and Sir Hereward Wake then accepted a unanimous invitation to be its leader.

Thus was placed at the head of the Northamptonshire force a distinguished and capable soldier of the King's Royal Rifle Corps with the right class of infantry experience that the control of the new army demanded.

Educated at Eton and at the Royal Military College, Sandhurst, Sir Hereward was in the early twenties when he went out to the South African war with the King's Royal

Major-General Sir Hereward Wake.

Rifles. He went through some of the stiffest battles of the campaign, was wounded, mentioned in dispatches four times, received the Queen's Medal with five clasps, and the King's Medal with two clasps. In addition he received the D.S.O.

During the 1914–18 war he again greatly distinguished himself, was mentioned in dispatches, promoted to rank of colonel, and awarded the C.M.G. He was advanced to the rank of brigadier-general in 1917, commanded the 4th Battalion King's Royal Rifles from 1920 to 1923, and became a C.B. in 1933. From 1928–9 he commanded the East Midland Territorial Infantry Brigade, was A.D.C. to the King during 1931–2, commanded the 12th Infantry Brigade at Dover from 1929–32, and from 1932, when he became a major-general, he commanded the 46th North Midland Division of the Territorial Army until he retired in 1937. A year later he was made

Colonel Commandant of the 1st Battalion K.R.R.C., the old 60th, and, in 1942, President of the Midland Area of the British Legion.

In addition to his military decorations Sir Hereward received the bronze medal of the Royal Humane Society for saving life from drowning.

It is interesting to note that since Sir Hereward Wake's Home Guard command

appeared to those pioneers it needs little imagination to realize.

However, Sir Hereward began to grapple with them while his subordinates throughout the county were equally absorbed in the endeavour to weld motley assortments of men of all classes, ages, sizes, and abilities into some semblance of military units.

Sir Hereward established his headquar-

A mufti parade of a section of the Northampton Gaslight Co. Platoon, with Platoon Commander N. C. Batten (*left*) and Deputy Platoon Commander F. Cole at the head (Sept. 1940).

embraced the Peterborough district he thus took charge of the original Hereward the Wake's own country, round about the cathedral city, where, if we are to believe Charles Kingsley, his immortal ancestor made the last and very nearly successful stand against the Norman invader.

Having appointed a County Commander the L.D.V. formation meeting then decided to appoint three Sub-Commanders, held that 2,000 rifles should be provided for the county (little did those present imagine that the issue would eventually total four or five times that number) and then plunged into details of expenditure, transport, uniforms, ammunition, etc.

Just how baffling these items must have

ters at the Clare Street Drill Hall in Northampton, and his staff included Col. G. Hobson, Capt. P. Y. Atkinson, Capt. G. T. Lees, and others; with Lt.-Col. Raynsford in charge of administration.

The plan of organization was soon issued. The county was divided into six "Divisions" according to area and population. The town of Northampton formed a Division, the City and Soke of Peterborough another; the remaining four were Kettering, Wellingborough and Towcester, and Northampton district, including the rural districts around these towns. Each Division was sub-divided into "Groups" of parishes, each parish providing one or more "Sections", and in the towns industrial and similar concerns provided complete Sections or Groups. The military terms and titles were not permitted at this stage.

## STRANGE SCENES AT FIRST PARADES

Well may the members of Northamptonshire's general public have smiled, if good-naturedly, at the strange spectacles

A typical specimen of a German parachute soldier firing, from the hip, his machine pistol which could also be fired from the shoulder by means of an ingenious extension stock.

the early parades of those units presented, and memorable to every one of the participants was the infinity of "chaff" to which each subjected the other.

The great thing, however, was that everyone *was* smiling and at a time when it seemed more than probable that every man of them would be a casualty, killed, wounded, or captured within an almost measurable time.

For that was the situation of England in May 1940.

To the thoughtful seniors of those early units, who had had some previous experience of war, there was something infinitely inspiring, and yet saddening, in the contemplation of any one of those parades.

"What possible chance," these leaders asked themselves, "can these fine fellows stand against the full force of a well-trained and thoroughly equipped mechanized army?"

But they did not say so.

Meanwhile, from Sir Hereward Wake's headquarters there came a succession of orders, and always they were characteristically brief, pertinent, and sound:

"The volunteers will not be paid. Training will be carried out in the evenings and on Saturday afternoons and Sundays. Volunteers should live close to their Unit H.Q. so that they can reach it in a few minutes after an alarm. The most favourable time for enemy parachute landings is between sunset and an hour or so after dawn. Air Raid Precautions organization is not to be interfered with . . .", and so on.

## PART OF THE ARMED FORCES

Then on 18 May came some form of official directive in the shape of a War Office letter.

Its most determinate and, to the rank and file, most gratifying passage was that in which it was laid down that the L.D.V. would "form part of the armed forces of the Crown and be subject to Military Law". For, whatever stern implications were contained in the latter edict, the new civilian army were proud to be recognized, officially, as "real soldiers".

In the next paragraph, however, the War Office indulged in some rich, unconscious

THE FIRST PARADE!

humour, which was only apparent in the light of subsequent events.

Thus all ranks may well smile in reading now that it was "the intention of the Army Council that outstanding features of the administration would be simplicity, elasticity, and decentralized control plus a MINIMUM OF REGULATIONS AND FORMALITIES"! ! ! (The capitals are ours.)

The letter then proceeded:

of enrolment form. Casualties of a serious nature will be notified by County Commander to next-of-kin.

Arms and uniforms will be issued under Command arrangements to areas, who will be responsible for storage, distribution, and safeguarding. The utmost care is to be taken in the selection of suitable stores.

Instructions regarding arms, ammunition, uniform, travelling allowances, petrol issues, etc., will be issued separately.

Early days in E Co. 12th (Northampton) Battalion. Sub-Section Leaders parade for orders. On left is C.S.M. G. Quartermain, D.C.M., M.M., and, on right, Capt. R. J. Marfleet (second-in-command).

There will be no Establishment, no officers or N.C.O.s in the ordinary Army sense, and no pay or emoluments. Engagement will be for a period not exceeding the present emergency— but may be terminated at any time by giving fourteen days' notice on both sides.

Volunteers will be formed into Sections, and Sections grouped into Platoons and Companies, according to local requirements. Normal size of a Section—ten men, but rigid adherence to this is not necessary. . . .

No records, no pay, no organization, and no forms other than enrolment forms are contemplated at present.

Casualties or appointments to be reported to Company Commanders and entered on back

Claims for compensation to be dealt with under regulations at present in force. These regulations provide for the same terms in case of death or permanent disablement as are applicable to private soldiers and their dependants.

The Commander-in-Chief Home Forces is responsible for operational control, organization, and training of the L.D.V. Force.

That gave the still very loosely knit units something to work on in point of the broader aspects of constitution, but, while prohibiting officers and N.C.O.s in the "ordinary army sense", it did not say what was to replace them.

Thus, by some sort of rough vote and tacit understanding, leaders of companies, platoons, and sections were gradually appointed but no one seemed to know whether their unit belonged to a battalion and who was its commander!

Most leaders were chosen by virtue of experience in the war of 1914–18, and though they had then just nothing in the way of equipment, their knowledge of drill, discipline, and service organization was invaluable in welding almost completely "raw" bodies of widely assorted men into some semblance of military cohesion and order.

### "HIDEOUS APPARATUS OF AGGRESSION"

If during those first five days of the L.D.V.'s existence any one of its members or of the civilian public had entertained any doubts of the necessity for the formation of the force or of the deadly threat that it had to face, those doubts were finally scattered by a broadcast speech by the Prime Minister delivered on 19 May.

Said Mr. Churchill:

I speak to you for the first time as Prime Minister in a solemn hour of the life of our country and Empire. . . . A tremendous battle is raging in France and Flanders. The Germans have broken through the French defences north of the Maginot Line . . . and strong columns are ravaging the open country.

They have penetrated deeply and spread alarm and confusion in their tracks. Behind them are now appearing infantry in lorries, and behind them again masses are moving forward.

The regrouping of the French armies has been proceeding for several days, largely assisted by the magnificent efforts of the Royal Air Force. . . .

It would be foolish to disguise the gravity of the hour. It would be still more foolish to lose heart and courage. . . . In the air, often at serious odds, we have been clawing down

three or four to one of our enemies, and the relative balance of the British and German Air Forces is now considerably more favourable to us than at the beginning of the battle. . . .

We must expect . . . the bulk of that hideous apparatus of aggression which gnashed Holland into slavery and ruin in a few days will be turned upon us . . . we are ready to face and endure it, and to retaliate against it to any extent that the unwritten laws of war permit. . . .

Is not this the appropriate time for all to make the utmost exertions in their power? . . . We must have quickly more aeroplanes, tanks, shells, guns. There is imperious need for these vital munitions. . . .

Our task is not only to win the battle but the war. . . . After this battle will come the battle for our island, for all that Britain is or means. . . . Interests of property, hours of labour, are nothing compared with the struggle for life and honour, for right and freedom. . . .

We have differed and quarrelled in the past, but now one bond unites us all, to wage war until victory is won, and never surrender ourselves to servitude, and shame, whatever the cost and agony may be. This is one of the most awe-striking periods in the history of France and Britain. It is also beyond doubt the most sublime.

Side by side, unaided except by their kith and kin in the great Dominions and by the wide Empires which rest beneath their shield, the British and French peoples have advanced to rescue not only Europe but mankind from the foulest and most soul-destroying tyranny which has ever darkened and stained the pages of history. . . .

To-day is Trinity Sunday. Centuries ago words were written to be a call and spur to the faithful servant of truth and justice:
Arm yourselves, and be ye men of valour . . .

### AN UNARMED ARMY

The L.D.V. heard and proceeded to redouble their efforts to be worthy of the nation and empire that stood alone.

Gradually the senior commands emerged

and on 22 May it was announced by the Area Organizer of the South Midland Area that the following had been appointed L.D.V. (Company) Division Commanders in Northants:

Kettering Division.—Lt.-Col. H. Burditt, M. C., T.D.

Northampton County Division.—Lord Braye, J.P.

Towcester Division.—Lt.-Col. Lester Reid, O.B.E., J.P.

Wellingborough Division. — Brig.-Gen. A. F. H. Ferguson, D.L., J.P.

Peterborough (City and Soke) Division. —Col. A. H. Mellows, T.D., D.L.

Northampton Borough Division.—Major T. E. Manning.

"Appointments of Group Commanders in each Division," the announcement added, "is proceeding, and parish etc. sections are being enrolled."

Blithely the message added that "rifles, ammunition, and clothing are being issued to-morrow"!

The junior commanders heard of this announcement and were heartened, but they heard no more and certainly saw no rifles, ammunition, or clothing. They carried on in hope while keeping a watchful inventory of the number of shot-guns, .22 rifles, air-guns, scythes, and pitchforks in their section areas!

The next directive came from a "high-up" military command which shall be nameless.

Dated 23 May 1940 it is eloquent of the "growing pains" from which the L.D.V. suffered. Consider these extracts and the

Britain has always raised its "home guard" when threatened with invasion. We may hope, however, that the guard of 1796 was not quite so ludicrous as here depicted by Gillray. Note the tailors, barbers, cobblers, masons and artists in the ranks still bearing the tools of their trades.

immediate and obvious questions (in brackets) they evoked among the L.D.V. leaders to whom they were addressed:

In view of the uncertainty which appears to exist as to the duties of the L.D.V. the following instructions are issued:

1. The duty of the L.D.V. is local—as the name implies—whether it be their factory, village, or town. [What duty?]
2. In case of factories, these should be so organized that they can take up arms without interfering with their work. [What arms?]
3. In case of localities, the duties are:
   To prepare road blocks. [What with?]
   Defend them. [What with?]
   To use petrol bombs from behind hedges or windows. A simple form of bomb is a bottle of petrol. [Whose petrol?]
   To arrange warning systems on notification by police by which L.D.V. can be called out to man posts. [What systems?]
   In case of attack to defend posts to last man. [That's understood, but what with?]

The military command concerned could not be blamed for such orders. Everybody was feeling their way almost blindly in an unprecedented situation.

Some orders, of some sort, had to be given and they were given, but, at this stage, it soon became apparent to the junior commands, with or without officers or N.C.O.s, that something had got to be done and done quickly.

Accordingly, at all levels in Northamptonshire commands, improvisation became the watchword—the same improvisation which the L.D.V. found it necessary to invoke, not merely for a few weeks, as was then expected, but for months, and even, in some cases, for years.

Thus, each commander set himself and his subordinates to the task of surveying and organizing his area, and, as he devised and tested ideas, conveyed them to County Headquarters with the fourfold purpose of keeping the senior command posted, of inviting criticism, of making suggestions, and of asking questions.

Typical of such reports was that from Division Commander Major T. E. Manning (Northampton) on 24 May 1940.

It records that he had divided the borough into four groups, north, south, east, and west, and each group into three companies, equalling the twelve wards. Company leaders had been appointed and a parade of volunteers who had done prior service was to be held on the following Sunday for organization purposes. Over five hundred were expected on parade, and another five hundred had volunteered with no previous army experience, and would be dealt with later.

Those figures and the phrase "no previous army experience" serve eloquently to exemplify the tough problems with which the early commands throughout the county were faced.

But, the figures convey no impression of those parades in point of the general scene presented by motley crowds of men loosely drawn up in nondescript, unsized, parade order on town squares or village greens, wearing all colours of suits, all shapes of hats, and all types of expressions.

They were, nominally, equipped with rifles, bayonets, and steel helmets, but these remained imaginary. How could they be when, in point of fact, there were then no more than seventy odd thousand rifles available in the whole country?

However, they did have one outward and visible sign of their official military status though it consisted of nothing more than a khaki armlet upon which the letters L.D.V. had been hurriedly stencilled, with an addition of blue bars to indicate leaders.

Another document of this date summarizes the duties of the L.D.V. as follows:

1. Maintain observation by outpost, and patrols.
2. Oppose parachute landings. [That word "oppose" was a gem of non-committal generalization.]
3. Give warning of such to police.

Section of the Northampton Platoon of a Post Office company on an armlet parade in August 1940. In the forefront are: Platoon Commander W. R. Morton (centre), with Section Commanders W. J. Dean (left), and J. S. Duke (right). In the smaller picture (at top) the Guards are seen receiving musketry instruction from an Army sergeant.

4. Maintenance of a continual watch to listen-in to B.B.C. [No names of the heroes thus detailed are unfortunately on record.]
5. Provide system of messengers, i.e. cyclists and/or Boy Scouts.

After revealing that four hundred rifles had been allocated to Northamptonshire, of which fifty had been sent to Corby, the summary added: "shot-guns are not to be used since they would contravene the Geneva Convention".*

Sir Hereward Wake, for reasons which will be detailed later, agreed with this restriction, but the majority of his subordinates, with, perhaps, more recklessness than discretion, very warmly disagreed.

Thus, when the prohibition order was issued, they either turned upon it the Nelsonic eye, with which they were all equipped, or else passed the order along to their units with the consoling and sure knowledge that, Convention or no

* It may now be revealed that these 400 rifles were withdrawn (by the Police) from Wellingborough School O.T.C. armoury.

Convention, orders or no orders, every shot-gun, blunderbuss, and flint-lock in the county was well and truly "in commission" and ready for any intruder by air, land, or sea.

Happily, a few days later the order came through Central Midland Area that shot-guns *could* be used and that an endeavour was to be made to get some cartridges.

So that was that, though for the time being the County Commander suggested that, against enemy landings, rifles were more effective.

In most company areas commanders made early contact with as many local military and air units as possible and also liaised with the Observer Corps, of which, at this time, there were about twenty posts in the County.

Thus, they were able to beg or borrow sundry items of arms and equipment with which some semblance of practical training could begin, and parade orders at this time included tuition in handling firearms, observation, and patrolling, in addition to perfecting warning arrangements.

In the first months the chief duty was to give warning of an enemy landing, which in Northamptonshire could only be made by air. In daylight no special watch was necessary, but during the hours of darkness and early dawn Observation Posts were manned (usually on the church tower) in every parish, and patrols provided to watch remote areas. In small parishes with perhaps less than a dozen volunteers this duty became very arduous and one night in three out of bed not unknown. In one parish, Courteenhall, the women came forward to ease the strain and "manned" the church tower for two or three nights a week.

## CHURCH BELLS WARNING SYSTEM

Frequent reference has been made to the duty of giving alarm in case of airborne enemy landings, and it can be claimed that the early warning system eventually adopted by the greater part, if not the whole, of the country was originated by Northamptonshire's County Commander, Sir Hereward Wake.

That this was so is indicated by a letter to Sir Hereward from the G.H.Q. Home Forces, dated 26 June 1940, as follows:

The system of church bell warning in this county is as follows:

The Commander-in-Chief, Home Forces, was told at a meeting of L.D.V. Commanders, held yesterday in Lincolnshire, that you had evolved a system of warning by the ringing of church bells. General Ironside would be most grateful if you could let him have details of this system.

To this Sir Hereward replied on the following day:

1. The alarm bell is only rung on definite information of an enemy landing or the presence of the enemy in the parish concerned or in a neighbouring parish.

2. The L.D.V. section commander or his nearest senior present, gives the order to sound the alarm, but on real emergency anyone may sound it.

3. The next parish also sounds the alarm, but only on receipt of definite information (to prevent its spreading all over the place unnecessarily).

4. The alarm is one bell rung twice, again and again, with short pauses, for ten minutes (a little practice is required and the bell has to be tied up in a certain way).

5. The "All Clear" is one bell rung for ten minutes at quarter-minute intervals.

There are nine counties bordering on Northamptonshire and they have different signals; I think it would be a good thing if one method of ringing could be laid down for the whole country; mine may not be the best. I don't think any other county has an "All Clear" signal and this seems to me very necessary.

In this connection, an amusingly significant reply to a report from Peterborough's Divisional Commander was made by Sir Hereward on 26 May.

In the course of other inquiries the Peterborough Commander wrote: "Is the use of church bells prohibited by the War Office?"

Sir Hereward replied: "No truth in rumour about not using church bells—probably started by the bishop!"

### "MUCH ADO . . ."

Soon after midnight on the night of 4 June church bells rang out and the L.D.V. stood to arms over all England, except Northamptonshire. This is the story:

The War Office had issued a Secret Order that the word "Cromwell" sent by telephone would mean "Enemy has landed" and all L.D.V. would at once stand to arms. On the night in question a junior officer at Headquarters Home Forces received a report that a landing had taken place on the coast. Without further investigation he sent out the dread word "Cromwell" with the result above. And the bells went on ringing all the rest of the night! For some unknown reason Northamptonshire had never received the secret code so no one knew what it meant, but the bells ringing all round the county could only mean invasion and the clamour was reported to County Headquarters from every part of the border.

Now the order issued to the County Commander was that bells were not to be rung unless the near presence of the enemy was definitely reported. This was to avoid unnecessary disturbance. So the bells rang on, but Northamptonshire slept through it, and we heard no more about it. Whether the other counties received an apology was never heard, but the good discipline of the Northamptonshire L.D.V. on the county

borders in rather trying circumstances was proved. The County Commander, who slept on a sofa near his telephone in those times, had a sleepless night.

One amusing incident must be recorded. A certain division commander was out when the telephone rang and a sepulchral voice uttered to his wife the word "Cromwell". She did not know what it meant, but the sender told her to tell her husband directly he came in. He'd know! But he did not. So they went to bed.

The church bells remained as a general alarm until 10 September when G.H.Q. Home Forces ordered that church bells would *not* be rung as alarm for turning out the Home Guard in case of *invasion*, but only as a warning that parachutists were in the neighbourhood. "The signal," added the order, "will *not* be taken up by other localities where parachutists have not actually been seen."

At this stage we will leave the Northamptonshire scene for that of London to note a close Northamptonshire association with the first big effort to place the L.D.V. on a nationally organized basis.

### DRAMATIC HOURS IN LONDON

The association was made through the person of a Northamptonian, Lt.-Gen. Sir John Brown, K.C.B., D.S.O., then Deputy Adjutant-General (T.).

Mr. Charles Graves in his book *The Home Guard of Great Britain* (Hutchinson) relates:

The response of the L.D.V.s was so staggering that, despite the most brilliant improvisation, the movement became rapidly unwieldy. As the lovely summer days of May drew to a close, Great Britain teemed with still more eager volunteers.

Those were the days of the Lords Lieutenants' armies, dozens of them. . . .

The day came when it was absolutely necessary to try to co-ordinate the various armies, and late on 30 May Major-Gen. (later Lieut.-Gen.) Sir John Brown, K.C.B., D.S.O., Deputy Adjutant-General (T.), received a telephone call in his office at Victoria Street, S.W.1.

The caller was Major-Gen. Macdougall, C.G.S. Home Forces, and he requested Sir John Brown and his Military Assistant, Major Underhill, to see him immediately at his headquarters outside London.

Lieut.-General Sir John Brown.

On arrival, Sir John Brown was asked whether he and the Territorial Associations would be responsible for the organization and administration of the L.D.V. Sir John Brown agreed.

Major-Gen. Macdougall said "Gen. Malden will be responsible for the training." [Gen. Malden was D.M.T.—Director of Military Training.]

"What does it entail?" asked Sir John Brown.

"It means organizing the forces *and getting ready to fight in a fortnight!*"

"Can I have any papers you have got on it?"

Lt.-Col. R. M. Raynsford.

Major-Gen. Macdougall handed over the files and added: "I'll send the rest to you to-morrow."

Sir John Brown and Major Underhill returned to the flat they shared in Sloane Street, and went through the files. Even a cursory examination lasted until 2 a.m. Both men realized that it was a huge job, and that they must have assistance.

They promptly telephoned, in the small hours of the morning, to Col. Sir Harold Wernher and Col. Sir Walter Craddock to come and help them. Both arrived just after breakfast—one from Rutland and the other from Gloucestershire.

At 11 a.m. a nonchalant taxi-cab arrived at the office in Victoria Street with over two thousand unopened letters and the rest of the files. It became immediately clear that all welfare work in which Sir John Brown's staff was engaged would have to cease at once while they sifted the mass of material.

An urgent postal telegram had already been sent that day to all Commands to say that the administration and general organization of the

Lt.-Col. O. K. Parker.

L.D.V.s had been taken over by the Deputy Adjutant-General (T.), telephone number VIC 9125, and that no further inquiries should be addressed to G.H.Q. Home Forces.

It was added that the operational control of the L.D.V.s would remain under commands, but that training would be arranged by the D.A.G. (T.), in consultation with the D.M.T.

This was circulated for information (but not for action) to all Territorial Army Association secretaries on the day following.

Thus it was that the L.D.V. passed under the wing of the Territorial Army Association by whom it was administered, and very efficiently and loyally administered, for the remainder of its service, in the Northamptonshire Association, first with Lt.-Col. R. M. Raynsford, D.S.O., and then with Lt.-Col. O. K. Parker, M.C., as secretary.

## Chapter II

## THE "DENIM DAYS"

No single factor in the early days did more to implement the L.D.V.'s confidence and to confirm the military status of the force than the issue of denim battledresses, which began to trickle through towards the end of May.

These travesties of military uniform were comic in their lack of even the elementals of style, cut, fit, or quality, indeed the biggest laughs of the L.D.V.'s life marked their distribution, particularly when it was found that many men had, perforce, to wear a tunic one or two sizes larger, or smaller, than their trousers, or vice versa, simply because "someone, somewhere" had failed to send along the proper proportions of matching garments.

But, whatever their shortcomings, the denims *were* the King's uniform and with the aid of patient womenfolk or local "odd-jobbing" tailors, pieces were taken out here or inserted there, and hooks and eyes were ingeniously introduced to hold together the looser sections, so that eventually they bore some remote resemblance to regulation battledress.

Cleverest of all in the matter of devices were, naturally, the "old sweats" who, apart from the fact that the inward demands of previous military training just had to be satisfied, felt it incumbent on them to do whatever was possible to render their uniform worthy of the several ribbons—sometimes rows of them—which they were now able to "put up".

Best of all, the L.D.V. was authorized

**ISSUING BATTLE DRESS**

later (5 June 1940) to wear the badge of their county infantry or yeomanry regiment, as desired, with the consent of the colonels concerned, so that thenceforth

Denim Days. Sgt.-Instructor J. Kerr (Northamptonshire Regt.) taking a section of the Northampton Gaslight Co. Platoon in rifle drill in September 1940.

difficulties attending the distribution of these and other stores and equipment as they gradually trickled through, we cannot do better, at this stage, than take a brief

Still "In the Rough". A Home Guard section on the march in 1940.

even the humblest Northamptonshire L.D.V. section paraded with the proud badge of the Northamptonshire Regiment in its caps.

**A TOUR OF THE DIVISIONS**

To gain some idea of the administrative

"tour" of some of the divisional areas to see what was being done and who was doing it.

At this date (29 May 1940) the groups and their commanders were listed as follows:

| Division | Sub-Division | Group | Commander |
|---|---|---|---|
| Wellingborough | North | 1 | Major R. D. Pendered |
| | | 2 | Capt. Berridge |
| | | 3 | Lt. Harvey |
| | South | 9, 10 | Major R. D. Pendered |
| | | 11 | Capt. V. H. Sykes |
| | | 12, 13, 14 | Lt. R. Chamberlain |
| | | 21 | Lt.-Col. H. G. Sotheby |
| | | 22, 23 | Mr. C. J. Chouler |
| Kettering | | 4 | Capt. Lucas |
| | | 5 | Mr. R. Ginns |
| | | 6 | Canon Grimes |
| | | 7 | The Rev. G. Holborow |
| | | 8 | Capt. B. Wright |
| | | 15 | Major N. S. Regnart |
| | | 16 | Capt. R. Saville |
| | | S. & Lloyds | Mr. Menzies-Wilson |
| Northampton District | North | 17 | Lt.-Col. G. Middleton |
| | | 18 | Capt. J. D. Houison-Crauford |
| | | 19 | Capt. A. T. Page |
| | | 20 | Major G. S. Watson |

| Division | Sub-Division | Group | Commander |
|---|---|---|---|
| Northampton District | West | 27 | Mr. E. B. Forwood |
| | | 28 | Major P. Nickalls |
| | | 29 | Major K. B. Joynson |
| | | 30 | — |
| | | 31 | Capt. G. Meredith |
| | | 32 | Brig.-Gen. K. Knapp |
| | | 24 | Capt. W. J. Penn |
| | | 25 | Major J. A. Knight |
| | | 26 | Mr. H. Glover |
| Towcester | | 33 | Mr. F. C. Kench |
| | | 34 | Mr. A. E. S. Guinness |
| | | 35 | Capt. Dacre Smith |
| | | 36 | Lt.-Col. F. Douglas Pennant |
| | | 37 | Capt. P. Y. Atkinson |
| | | 38 | Major N. Furlong |
| | | 39 | Mr. J. F. Blakiston |
| | | 40 | Mr. E. C. Lessen |
| | | 41 | Capt. J. R. Guinness |
| Northampton Borough | | 1 | Mr. N. P. Andrews |
| | | 2 | Mr. W. Care |
| | | 3 | Mr. A. Macfarlane |
| | | 4 | Major R. Manning |
| | | L.M.S. | Capt. E. W. H. Powell |

## THE CATHEDRAL CITY

Taking Northamptonshire from north to south the tour begins in the area of what was later to become the 1st (City of Peterborough) Battalion.

It says much for the patriotism of the cathedral city that over four hundred men, including twenty-six ex-officers and fifty-two ex-N.C.O.s, were enrolled in Peterborough within two days of Mr. Eden's appeal, many applications coming from men outside both the age limits of seventeen and sixty-five.

A week later saw the Peterborough unit in being, with Col. A. H. Mellows in command, and Capt. Crowden as second-in-command, and by 22 May well over a thousand men were enrolled.

The following appointments were made:

Group Commander, Capt. R. J. C.-Crowden, M.C. (also second-in-command of the Division).

Assistant Group Commander and Adjutant, Mr. G. Baker.

Transport Officer, Sir Arthur Craig.

Assistant Transport Officer, Mr. A. Wilson.

Liaison Officer, Mr. A. F. Percival.

Records Officer, Mr. W. B. Buckle.

Quartermaster, Mr. H. P. E. Dawson.

Company Leaders:

City No. 1—Mr. D. C. Banks.

City No. 2—Major H. H. Staton.

City No. 3—Mr. H. A. Goodacre

Soke No. 1—Mr. H. L. Samson.

Soke No. 2—Mr. H. Elliot.

Soke No. 3—Vice-Admiral A. H. Alington.

Regimental Sgt.-Major, Mr. Atkinson.

Q.-M. Sgt, Mr. J. L. Jones.

Former N.C.O.s were also provisionally allotted to companies.

It will be noted that a vice-admiral was in command in one company. Unofficial battalion records relate that he took his turn carrying a .22 saloon rifle, and declined to perform the duty in a vice-admiral's full dress uniform, or to direct operations from the deck of a fen barge!

The unit's first regular quarters were

made in the Horse Repository in Lincoln Road, where the commanding officer addressed his first battalion parade, standing on a truss of hay.

The armoury and magazine were at the county jail (long since disused for the purposes of criminal detention), but for six weeks there was only one rifle for every ten men, though others made a brave show with 12-bore shot-guns, pistols from the last war, and even a German Mauser rifle with one clip of S.A.A.!

It was on 24 May 1940 that Peterborough received one hundred and twenty .303 S.M.L.E. rifles and two hundred and eighty came on 5 July. The joy of possession of these weapons was, however, short-lived, for on 8 August they were replaced by one thousand .300 American rifles.

These, too, did not remain long in the Battalion's custody, for they were replaced at a later date by the Ross .303.

All of these arms had to be carefully cleaned, and Northamptonshire Home Guards who remember the thick grease in which they were packed will agree that it was "some job". There is still a legend going the round in North Northants that new rifles were only sent to Peterborough to be cleaned for other units!

On 27 May 1940, fifty-seven suits of denim battledress arrived and those responsible had the infinitely difficult—and

No. 2 Company of the 1st (City of Peterborough) Battalion leaving Peterborough Cathedral after attending the Day of National Prayer Service, 8th September 1940.

diplomatic—task of allocating them between a thousand men!

Fortunately a second consignment of four hundred arrived on 5 July so that approximately every other man was now able to parade in uniform.

From the onset the Peterborough L.D.V. undertook to provide seventy-two men per night to patrol the city's sectors on an air raid alert sounding, and at all times during the night to stand by at their platoon headquarters.

The entire Battalion also placed itself at the service of the city authorities in air raids, provided it was not otherwise engaged in military duties.

This service received some stern tests, notably when bombs fell on the L.N.E.R. Locomotive Works in Bridge Street, Bishops Road, the Minster Precincts, Peterborough North Station, Cowgate, and Priestgate.

Sixty Home Guard shooting teams participated in a shooting competition at a Red Cross Fête at Lilford in September 1940.

In one instance, members of the 1st Battalion saved a garage full of cars, and in another rescued from destruction all of the engineer's plans of the L.N.E. Railway system.

Very early on the 1st Battalion became the envy of its fellows for soon after formation it was presented with instruments for a military band by Mrs. F. Smith of Peterborough.

The players were soon found and on its first performance the band raised over £200 for the local hospital.

Later the band was in continuous

1st Northants (City of Peterborough) Home Guard Battalion Regimental Band, under Bandmaster B. V. Powé. (Instruments were presented to the Battalion by Mrs. F. Smith, of Peterborough.)

1st Northants (City of Peterborough) Home Guard Battalion Dance Band under Cpl. F. Meakin.

Royal Guard of Honour. H.R.H. The Duchess of Gloucester inspecting the guard of honour provided by the 1st (City of Peterborough) Battalion when on June 26, 1941, she visited Peterborough to receive, on behalf of the city, a magnificent ambulance presented, at the hands of Mrs. Summerville Smith, by residents of Peterborough, New Hampshire, U.S.A. Accompanying H.R.H. are the Battalion C.O. (Lt.-Col. R. J. C. Crowden, M.C.), and in centre, at rear, the Lord Lieutenant, Col. the Marquess of Exeter, K.G.

demand, not only for battalion and sector parades, but for civic purposes, notably the visits of the Duchess of Gloucester and the Princess Royal, and all Savings Campaign opening ceremonies, as well as for numerous inspections by high-ranking officers, including the Lord Lieutenant of the County (Colonel the Marquess of Exeter), Major-Gen. Sir Hereward Wake, Major-Gen. Johnson, V.C. (Inspector-General of the Forces), Viscount Lord Bridgeman (Director-General of the Home Guard), the General Officers commanding Eastern Command, and the Sub-District Commanders, etc.

### THE FENLAND "PARACHUTIST"

One richly humorous event in the Peterborough district's early days occurred shortly after the issue of the first rifles and before the men had been trained in loading and unloading.

A parachutist was said to have been seen landing on the fenlands to the east of the city. News quickly spread, and "A" Company turned out rapidly in civilian clothes with arms and ammunition, eager to defend the city at all costs.

Rifles were loaded, and the troops deployed in Padholm Road, when suddenly from the east arrived a fast-moving car which was stopped at the point of the bayonet.

The driver proved to be the Commanding Officer, complete with straw hat, breeches, leggings and revolver.

One volunteer was heard to say, "Blimey, it's the old man!"

The postmistress at the end of the road half swooned into the arms of the officer in command (Capt. C. J. Thompson, D.C.M.) and only recovered on being assured that the battalion would willingly lay down their lives in her defence. The story does not end there, however.

Having got their rifles loaded, only a very few volunteers knew how to eject the rounds without firing, and to save the face of the Battalion, the officer in charge took the men into a side street and personally unloaded all the rifles in the dark and in the rain.

The men then "fell in", proceeded to Company Headquarters, and fought the battle over again over beer. Then, like well-trained soldiers, they cleaned their rifles and returned home feeling satisfied that their duty had been well and truly done.

No one knows to this day, however, who started the parachutist alarm and the volunteers concerned are still wondering if one of themselves was not the perpetrator of a joke which, harmless and funny as it happened, might not have proved so funny if an accident had ensued.

The Peterborough district, later to become the 2nd (Soke of Peterborough) Battalion put up a no less worthy start.

Following Mr. Eden's broadcast, a meeting of ex-officers and N.C.O.s was called and held at the Drill Hall, Lincoln Road, Peterborough on the 22 May.

A list of enrolments was obtained from the police authorities, and the volunteers were sorted out into four groups based on their home addresses.

At that period the Commander was Mr. H. L. Sampson, who had for his second-in-command Capt. H. W. A. Elliott.

### THE OUNDLE AND THRAPSTON DISTRICT

Moving on into the Oundle and Thrapston District (later the 3rd Battalion) we enter another area which was fortunate enough to be able to produce an ideal leader "overnight".

He was Lieut.-Col. F. R. Berridge, D.S.O., M.C., of Barnwell, who won distinguished military spurs in the war of 1914–18 as Intelligence Officer of the 7th

Battalion Northamptonshire Regiment and later Brigade I.O. He was a comrade of Lt.-Col. Edgar Mobbs, D.S.O., and was in fact in the action at Shrewbury Forest in the Ypres Salient in which that famous Northamptonshire soldier-sportsman made the supreme sacrifice on 31 July 1917.

Lt.-Col. Berridge personally called the first meeting in this District immediately following the L.D.V. call, and with Brig.-Gen. A. F. H. Ferguson (Polebrook), Major R. A. Muntz (Achurch), Capt. C. E. Harvey (Thorp Achurch), Capt. E. A. Barnes (Adjutant of the Oundle School J.T.C.) and several others, formed a committee to undertake the weapon training, and to secure a suitable leader in every village who was also on the telephone, to get local sections going.

Capt. Harvey, himself, signed on no fewer than 185 volunteers in a single morning.

The next problem was the general one of training. Cars were secured from farmers and others to travel to Oundle at night time and to take out squads of the senior boys of the School O.T.C., who held Certificate "A", with their rifles to instruct village members in arms and musketry.

Oundle School boys may therefore claim to have been responsible for the original training of the L.D.V. in the School area. This invaluable work was performed under Capt. Barnes, and R.S.M. Cottingham, the School Armourer.

In addition, ex-Servicemen at Oundle were trained as instructors and the battalion was again fortunate in gaining the use of the School's grounds, equipment and rifle range.

The then Headmaster (Dr. K. Fisher, J.P.) himself volunteered and gave the local men the full use of every available facility.

As more equipment became available, Major R. K. Yeld, who served in the 1914–18 war, undertook the joint posts of Adjutant and Quartermaster of the Oundle L.D.V. As such his car was "endlessly" used in travelling to Northampton to secure rifles and Lewis guns, etc., and then in taking them round to the villages.

He was assisted nobly by Mrs. Spragg, wife of Major F. F. Spragg, commander of the Oundle Company of the 3rd Battalion from its inception.

Major Yeld continued his good work until Regular adjutants were appointed, and it is still recalled with appreciation throughout the area.

### KETTERING TOWN'S FLYING START

Coming south to Kettering Town it is not surprising to discover that this always "go-ahead" centre claimed something of a record in point of recruiting speed.

It is on reliable record that within ten minutes of the end of Mr. Eden's broadcast, Kettering Police Station was besieged by volunteers—a state of affairs which went on for days.

Soon afterwards a conference of potential officers was called by Col. H. Burditt, M.C., T.D., and the Rector of Kettering, the Rev. G. Holborow, was chosen as Commanding Officer.

Lt.-Col. G. Holborow.

Lt.-Col. Holborow, as he later became, began his service in the 1914–18 war at the Royal Military College, Sandhurst, in October 1914.

Proceeding to France in 1915 he served there successively as Captain and Adjutant 19th Divisional Train. R.A.S.C.; Intelligence Officer 56th Infantry Brigade, and Captain 5th Battalion The Connaught Rangers, continuing in the Army of Occupation in Germany until July 1919.

Lt.-Col. Holborow's second-in-command was Councillor G. D. Howard.

It was decided to form four companies, No. 1, Mr. H. R. Newbould (the then Sports Editor of the *Kettering Evening Telegraph*); No. 2, Mr. H. Bellows; No. 3, Mr. A. J. Shepherdson (Headmaster of St. Mary's School), and No. 4, Councillor A. E. Tutty.

On Friday 24 May 1940 the first parade was called on the lawn of the Rectory when the first allocation to companies took place.

No. 1 consisted of men from the west side of the town, No. 2 the south side, No. 3 the east and No. 4 the north.

Patrols began that same night, though the Kettering men were no better and no worse off than all the other L.D.V.s in point of available weapons.

Nevertheless, the Kettering companies set about their new and unaccustomed duties with all the good will which characterized the force from its enrolment to the Stand Down.

The meagre supplies of arms and equipment as they arrived were shared equally between the companies, and gradually organization improved as further supplies became available.

### KETTERING DISTRICT ORGANIZED

Meanwhile in the Kettering District Col. H. Burditt, M.C., T.D., of Desborough, was similarly engaged in organizing the villages with Lt.-Col. Sir Frederick Robinson, M.C., as his second-in-command.

Col. Burditt was hardly raw at the task of military organization for he gained his earliest experience as a member of the old Volunteers and Territorials from 1901 to 1932, during which time he held every rank from volunteer to colonel.

In the 1914–18 war he was promoted from the ranks in January 1915 when he was serving with the 1/4th Northamptonshire Regiment which he had joined in 1914. He served in Egypt, Palestine and Gallipoli as well as in France and gained the Military Cross for meritorious service in the second battle of Gaza, and also the Territorial Decoration for long service.

Colonel
H. Burditt.

Col. Burditt began his L.D.V. plans by calling a meeting at Kettering, at which Group Commanders were appointed and the forming of village sections began.

The first rifles came on 25 May and distribution was carried out with a lorry bearing an armed man seated beside the driver and led by Col. Burditt in his own car.

Numbers were almost comically inadequate. Thus, Desborough itself, with over 100 volunteers, received four rifles.

However, on the following day, drilling began, watched by large crowds of spectators, dusk and dawn patrols were out and around every village area. They were mainly armed with shot-guns and got around on cycles. The attitude of the police and other residents varied in different villages. Thus some volunteers were summoned for riding bicycles without lights, and one local parson objected to the appointment of a certain village commander because the nominee was in the habit of calling at the village inn!

The spirit of the largely rural personnel of the 5th District was typical. Major Ginns (B Company) recalls visiting a post at Brampton Ash on a cold and blustery night. He found it manned by two elderly farm labourers armed with shot-guns. These men had been working in the fields until dusk and would be out again at daybreak, but they were cheerfully standing watch all night and were ready with their challenge to "visiting rounds" at 0200 hours.

Like their fellow battalions the Kettering district laboured manfully and with infinite ingenuity in devising and erecting road blocks on all main roads. For a time members also examined the papers of all motorists, who were held up every few miles. Volunteers performed the duty with gusto, but the motorists hardly appreciated this precautionary duty and, after the first "electric" period, road blocks were opened and road block checks were eased.

Quite early tactical exercises in conjunction with the A.R.P. were held and so great was the public curiosity that there were often more spectators than troops!

During May the Kettering district staged a practice alarm and there was a fine turn-out in reasonable time.

Meanwhile close co-operation between the L.D.V. and local searchlight units was arranged, and the training of instructors was generously undertaken by the 3rd County of London Yeomanry, then stationed at Rushton Hall.

## HOW "STEELTOWN" RALLIED

The Corby district (later the 6th Battalion) had very good reason to be on its mettle following the *débâcle* in France and the threat of invasion. Northamptonshire's steel town was indeed a "V.P." (vulnerable point) in capital letters!

But, apart from that fact, the men of Corby were men of iron in every sense, and no sooner had the call gone forth than Messrs. Stewarts and Lloyds, owners of the giant steel works, were inundated with appeals from employees to organize and arm them for the purpose of protecting Corby and Islip.

A total of 2,843 men were enrolled, including 924 ex-Servicemen and organized into a battalion consisting of headquarters staff with eight full companies and two half-companies.

The operational area covered by the unit comprised the following:

1. Corby Steel Works area.
2. The Lancashire and Corby Steel Manufacturing Co. Ltd.
3. The Mines and Quarries area at Corby.
4. The Islip Works area and Quarries.

The Corby Steel Works area was made into more or less a fortress surrounded by barbed wire entanglements, covering a distance of $5\frac{1}{2}$ miles.

The protection of this area was entrusted to seven full companies drawn from within the works.

The eighth company was drawn from the personnel of the mines and quarries area and they were responsible for the defence of all the plant and machinery in this area.

One half-company was enrolled from the Lancashire and Corby Steel Manufacturing Company's Works and was responsible for the defence of that area.

The other half-company was enrolled from the Islip Works mines and quarries area and was responsible for the defence of those works.

Drill and discipline soon started, and in addition to the erection of barbed wire defences and barricades previously mentioned, trees were felled, lopped, and dragged to fields where hostile aircraft might have landed.

Bangalore torpedoes and Molotov cocktails were made out of tubes and bottles, while pikes and other primitive weapons were made by members of the unit themselves for use until, later, they were armed with shot-guns and loaned sporting rifles.

The Town L.D.V. was under the command of Mr. G. F. Satow, and the Works Unit under the command of Mr. J. R. Menzies-Wilson.

### O.T.C. CADETS OPERATE AT WELLINGBOROUGH

So on to Wellingborough Town (later 7th Battalion).

Here L.D.V. history records that operations began with a visit by Brigadier A. F. H. Ferguson to Capt. Frank Barron, whom he asked to organize the L.D.V. for the town. At this interview Major R. D. Pendered was suggested as commanding officer and subsequently accepted the command.

One of his first actions was to ask Capt. H. L. Allsopp, commanding the School O.T.C., if, until he had some organization in being, senior cadets of the School O.T.C., being armed and relatively trained, would undertake the duty of locating and containing the enemy if and where necessary. He offered to find them transport. With the approval of the then Headmaster and parents a "flying squad" of some forty senior boys was immediately enrolled for this purpose.

Major Pendered then called a meeting of his proposed company leaders, who met on 31 May at the Old Drill Hall, Great Park Street.

Those present were Major R. D. Pendered, Capt. H. L. Allsopp, Capt. Barron and Messrs. E. E. Jones, A. H. Bull, H. J.

Major-Gen. Sir Hereward Wake (Zone Commander), Lt.-Col. H. G. Sotheby (Group Commander), and Capt. (later Lt.-Col.) H. L. Allsopp, pictured at an inspection by Sir Hereward of a 7th (Wellingborough) Battalion church parade in October 1940. He is here passing along the ranks of the Wellingborough School Platoon.

Crane, C. C. Worster, T. Smillie, J. Bennie, J. R. Gammidge, A. H. Minney, T. R. Curtis and A. E. S. Bayley.

At this inaugural meeting it was decided to form companies as follows:

"A" Company, Wellingborough West Ward, Mr. E. E. Jones.

'B" Company, Wellingborough North Ward, Mr. A. H. Bull.

"C" Company, Wellingborough East Ward, Mr. C. C. Worster.

"D" Company, Wellingborough South Ward, Mr. H. J. Crane.

"F" Company, Finedon, Mr. J. R. Gammidge.

"H" Company, Harrowden, Isham, Orlingbury, and Hardwick, Mr. J. Bennie.

"I" Company, Irthlingborough and the Addingtons, Mr. T. R. Curtis.

"L" Company, Wellingborough Iron Works, Mr. W. D. Holton.

"M" Company, Wellingborough L.M.S. Railway, Mr. A. E. S. Bayley, M.C.

"P" Company, Wellingborough Iron Company, Thingdon Mines, Mr. R. R. Partridge.

"S" Company, Wellingborough School O.T.C., Capt. H. L. Allsopp.

Capt. Allsopp was to be group second-in-command and Capt. Barron administrative assistant. (Actually there were two groups, Nos. 9 and 10, but these were combined.)

Major Pendered announced that he had received forty-two rifles and fifteen suits of denims, allowing four rifles to each company except "M" and "P". which received six and twelve respectively, and the School, who had sufficient to give each of the enrolled cadets one per man.

Meanwhile, some four hundred invitations to a general meeting of all those enrolled in Wellingborough and not in a

"works" company, had been issued, and at this gathering on 1 June, the four town companies were formed. Major Pendered issued some twenty rifles and ammunition, and the fifteen suits of denims. Organization began in the office on that evening while R.S.M. J. J. Atkins, Instructor of the School O.T.C., gave instruction in the main Hall.

Training had already started before this on the School field and miniature range, where men of the L.M.S. Railway were the first to appear as a "unit". This field, on those first Sunday mornings and afternoons —as well as on week-nights—was literally thronged with hundreds learning or refreshing their weapon training, generally under O.T.C. officers or senior cadets, while firing went forward on the miniature range at the rate of over three hundred per week. Parallel progress was going on in the out-town and works companies.

Once the new company commanders had sorted out their men, ex-Servicemen were selected for training as instructors, the Tower Hamlets Rifles, temporarily stationed at Wellingborough, giving valuable assistance, and the O.T.C. had less to do. The cadets were, however, allotted important "guard duties" and also represented enemy paratroops in exercises run by Major Pendered during June. Eight picked men were selected from each town company to form a new flying squad, and when Capt. Allsopp took over command of these Lt. J. A. S. Taylor succeeded to the command of the School L.D.V.

Unfortunately, the Drill Hall was requisitioned for the use of regular troops at the end of June, and in view of the acute lack of accommodation, the School field and range continued to be used for the remainder of the summer, but gradually the companies found their own quarters and built their own ranges in some cases, to such good effect that not only were there, in August, open rifle meetings at Harrowden and Irthlingborough, but the Wellingborough Iron Works companies brought back shooting trophies from farther afield. Moreover, the Wellingborough Group was the first of the L.D.V. units to be able to make use of Sywell Rifle Range (so well known later to hundreds of Home Guards); it was fortunate that the O.T.C. had not only rifles but plenty of ammunition wherewith companies could blaze away, not to mention R.S.M. J. J. Atkins, an old Small Arms School instructor, whose valuable experience and assistance were at their disposal morning, noon, and night, and who could later look back on having assisted personally in the construction of at least four miniature ranges which afterwards did very good service.

Were Wellingborough envied? Were they!

Lt.-Col. H. L. Allsopp.

On 12 July 1940 Major Pendered resigned his command, and Capt. Allsopp then became the battalion's commanding officer. Lt.-Col. H. L. Allsopp, O.B.E., T.D., was first commissioned Second-Lieutenant in the Territorial Army for service with Wellingborough School O.T.C. in 1922. In 1924 he was promoted Lieutenant, and in 1926, Captain. From 1927 to 1935 he held various staff appointments on Brigade Headquarters at O.T.C. annual camps, and in 1935 assumed command of Wellingborough School O.T.C. (now J.T.C.).

Lt.-Col. Allsopp later regularly commanded the annual camps of Northamptonshire Army Cadet Force, being appointed in September 1944 to command a cadet battalion with the acting rank of Lieutenant-Colonel, T.A. He was awarded the Territorial Decoration in 1942 and the O.B.E., for H.G. work, in 1944.

## RUSH OF RECRUITS IN WELLINGBOROUGH DISTRICT

The men of Wellingborough Town's brother battalion (later 8th) provided another memorable demonstration of readiness for service in 1940.

Within a matter of minutes of the end of Mr. Eden's broadcast men of Rushden and Higham Ferrers and surrounding villages were offering themselves for enrolment in hundreds, and a distinguished soldier in Lt.-Col. H. G. Sotheby, M.V.O., D.S.O., of Ecton, readily accepted an invitation to become the group's first commander.

Meanwhile, operatives, bakers, shop assistants, and so on, some veterans of the last war, others but youths in their 'teens, walked, drove, or cycled to join up.

This went on for days, and then on Sunday, 26 May, they were called to a conference at Rushden Legion Hall, and nearly nine hundred responded.

Mr. Bob Denton, Chairman of the local British Legion, and Capt. C. Clark (Chief A.R.P. Warden of Rushden) gave out the latest news of organization of the L.D.V.

The enthusiasm was enormous, but, alas, once again the supply of equipment was woefully small! A public appeal was immediately launched for such items as binoculars as part of patrolling and observation equipment.

First arrangements provided for Mr. R. Chamberlain (Higham Ferrers) to command all L.D.V.s (popularly known as "parashooters") in Rushden, Higham Ferrers, and Irchester, with Mr. R. Tarry as second-in-command, and Mr. A. F. Weale as adjutant.

Mr. Chamberlain joined the Royal Navy shortly afterwards, however, and Mr. A. D. Denton took his place.

Rushden platoons were formed under Messrs. A. J. Sturgess, V. H. Partridge, C. King Woods, and J. S. Parker, and at Higham Ferrers the leader was Mr. Leo Claridge.

On 3 June sections were formed and more specific duties allocated, though some patrol work had already been carried out.

Then, armed with borrowed sporting-guns and plenty of optimism, Wellingborough District L.D.V. proceeded on their guard duties over bridges, stations, and factories, or patrolled all high ground, scanning the skies for invading aircraft.

None appeared, but there is a local story about a black bullock with a white face which tested the nerves of some of the watchers, and another story concerning the precarious position of two leaders who found themselves one night at the wrong end of a gun!

The local units began to take shape and became No. 12 Company of the Wellingborough and District Home Guard Battalion. It was a clumsy arrangement as platoons were almost at company strength, but it had to suffice for the time being.

At that time Rushden had four platoons, and Higham Ferrers, Newton Bromswold, and Irchester one each.

No. 12 Company worked keenly and combined their long hours of guard and patrol duties with much technical training.

No. 11 Group was formed on 27 May 1940 at a public meeting called and addressed by Capt. V. H. Sykes in the Church of England School at Raunds—and the first Company Orders were issued for the week beginning 3 June 1940.

Next let us look at the Brixworth district.

## BRIXWORTH ANTICIPATED THE EDEN BROADCAST

There is a document which has been carefully filed in the archives of the 9th Brixworth District Battalion which proves that this command was a "live one", even in its infancy.

This records that in the area the enrolment of the Local Defence Volunteers was anticipated at least a week before Mr. Eden's broadcast when a meeting was called to discuss the emergency by Mr. G. S. Watson, later to become commanding officer of the battalion and still later a sector commander with the rank of colonel.

Col. G. S. Watson.

Subsequently Major (as he then was) Watson was requested by Sir Hereward Wake (County Commander) to take command of No. 20 Group Local Defence Volunteers, and thus was born the 9th (Brixworth) Battalion.

Col. Watson, its commander, was first commissioned in the Loyal North Lancashire Regt. in August 1914. In the following November he went to France with the famous 6th Division. He fought in the

No. 3 Platoon (Boughton) of D Co. of the 9th (Brixworth District) Battalion after an evening lecture at their headquarters in November 1940. The commander was Lt. Hugh Willett with 2nd Lt. J. J. Cowieson as his deputy.

A unit of the East Haddon Home Guard. In front is the Platoon Commander, Lt. S. Allen, D.C.M., M.M. His deputy was 2nd Lt. W. Jones.

The Brington Platoon of 1940. Led by Lt. R. M. Day of Great Brington Grange, the ages of the personnel ranged from 18 to 65 years of age.

A parade of Hardingstone Platoon of B Co. of the 11th (Hardingstone District) Battalion in October 1940. In front is Lt. H. D. Wraith (Platoon Commander) and, on left centre, his second-in-command, 2nd Lieut. A. H. Clay. Subsequently Lieut. Clay was promoted to the platoon command as Lieutenant with 2nd Lieut. J. Downie as his second. On left of front rank is Capt. Dacre Smith, who was the 11th Battalion's first Adjutant.

second battle of Ypres and the battle of Hooge, and was promoted Lieutenant in December and Captain in June of the following year. He served through the Somme battle and then, in December 1916, was wounded at Ypres. Upon recovery he was posted to the reserve battalion of his regiment and was appointed Adjutant and later Brigade Major while serving in Ireland. His next appointments were to the General Staff of the 64th Division in East Anglia, and then to Brigade-Major of No. 2 Sub-District of the Southern Command in Ireland, a post he held until demobilization in 1919.

At the outset the Brixworth District Battalion formed part of the Northamptonshire Central Group, together with the Hardingstone and Daventry District Battalions, and the Northampton Borough Battalion.

Group Headquarters were at the Drill Hall, Clare Street, Northampton.

The Administrative Assistant (a designation which was afterwards changed to that of Adjutant) was Capt. R. Dickens. There were four companies commanded by Capt. C. G. Middleton, Capt. J. D.

Houison-Crauford, Major G. P. Lankester, and Major J. T. H. Pettitt.

Later, E Company was added under the command of Capt. C. M. Newton.

So the same wonderful story of an English shire rising to arms continues as we proceed through the areas of Daventry (later the 10th Battalion), Hardingstone (later the 11th Battalion), and the Towcester and Brackley Group formed and commanded by Col. P. Lester Reid (Thorpe Mandeville) and later to become respectively the 13th (Towcester) and 14th (Brackley) Battalions.

## THE FIRST TOWCESTER AND BRACKLEY GROUP

At this period the Towcester and Brackley Group was organized as follows:

*Group and Action H.Q.*—Territorial Club, High Street, Towcester.

*Commander.*—Lt.-Col. P. Lester Reid, O.B.E., Thorpe Mandeville, Banbury.

*Administrative Assistant for both Battalions.*—Capt. G. Meredith.

*Towcester Battalion.*—C.O., Lt.-Col. F. Douglas Pennant, Sholebroke Lodge, Towcester.

A November 1940 parade of a section of the Duston Platoon which claimed a D.C.M. and a M.M. in its ranks, and was one of the largest platoons in the 11th Battalion.

*Action H.Q.*—Territorial Club (as above).

*Action H.Q.*—Territorial Club (as above).

*Brackley Battalion.*—C.O., Brig.-Gen. W. Allason, D.S.O., Chacombe Priory, Banbury.

*Battalion and Action H.Q.*—Drill Hall, St. Peter's Street, Brackley.

To the old Towcester and Brackley Group L.D.V. belongs the honour of providing, in the person of Col. Reid, a subsequent Zone Commander whose succession to Major-Gen. Wake is recorded later.

Finally, we view the L.D.V. scene in the county town of Northampton, which provided the 12th Battalion and later the 15th Battalion.

## THE COUNTY TOWN'S RALLY

Responding to a unanimous invitation, Major T. E. Manning undertook to become the first Officer Commanding of Northampton's Groups, and thus added another page to a notable military career which began when he was gazetted Second Lieutenant in the Northamptonshire Yeomanry as far back as 1905. Major Manning served in

North Company of the Northampton Town Home Guard led by Company Commander N. P. Andrews and Platoon Commander G. H. Oates, marching to a church parade at Holy Trinity, Northampton, in November 1940.

the regiment throughout the 1914–18 war, going to France with the rank of Captain in 1914, as second-in-command of A Squadron. Later he commanded the Squadron from 1916–18 before demobilization with the rank of Major in 1919.

Lt.-Col. T. E. Manning.

Major Manning selected as his first staff officers Major L. E. Barnes (later to command the 12th) and Mr. A. W. Gardner (later to become Quartermaster of the 12th). Headquarters were located at 4, The Arcade, Northampton, and a first parade was called at the Drill Hall, Clare Street, on 26 May 1940.

Nearly five hundred volunteers turned out, most of them "old sweats" of the 1914–18 war.

From these it was not difficult to select group and company leaders, and in this respect it may be noted that three of these original officers retained their offices throughout. They were Major A. MacFarlane, Major W. R. Morton, and Lt. L. W. Lucas.

On the following day the first observation posts were manned. All of the sentries were in civilian clothes and some of them carried umbrellas, though not in any Munich spirit!

By the 30th of the month, so great was the tidal wave of eager recruits, the strength had risen to 2,109, comprised as follows:

| | | |
|---|---|---|
| Headquarters Group | - | - | 618 |
| North Group | - | - | 436 |
| East Group | - | - | 320 |
| South Group | - | - | 264 |
| West Group | - | - | 206 |
| L.M.S. Group | - | - | 265 |

Here is their organization, including the original commanders and headquarters:

| Division Commander | Major T. E. Manning | |
| Second-in-command | Major L. E. Barnes | |

**North Group**

| Group Commander | N. P. Andrews | Duncan House |
|---|---|---|
| Second-in-command | P. Hutton | St. George's Avenue |
| No. 1 Company (Kingsley) Leader | R. E. Corsby | Jordan's Yard, Chestnut Rd. |
| No. 2 Company (Kingsthorpe) Leader | J. V. Collier | Cock Hotel |
| No. 3 Company (St. George's) Leader | H. G. Oates | 18, Junction Road |

**East Group**

| Group Commander | Major H. St. J. Browne | 21, The Drive |
|---|---|---|
| Second-in-command | S. H. Barber | |
| No. 1 Company (Weston) Leader | F. W. Freestone | Library, Lindsay Avenue |
| No. 2 Company (St. Michael's) Leader | C. C. Oakey | Little House, The Headlands |
| No. 3 Company (St. Crispin's) Leader | H. St. J. Browne | Drill Hall, Clare Street |

**South Group**

| Group Commander | A. McFarlane | 37, Ardington Road |
|---|---|---|
| Second-in-command | O. J. Hargrave | Chamber of Commerce Club |
| No. 1 Company (Delapre) Leader | L. W. Lucas | Warwick Arms, Bridge St. |
| No. 2 Company (South) Leader | P. C. Williams | Angel Hotel |
| No. 3 Company (St. Edmund's) Leader | H. G. Beers | King of Denmark Inn |
| No. 4 Company (Stimpson's) Leader | S. B. Patrick | Abington Mill |

**West Group**

| Group Commander | Major R. Manning | Naylands, Dallington |
|---|---|---|
| Second-in-command | A. S. Baxter | |
| No. 1 Company (Castle) Leader | J. S. Mennell | Semilong W.M. Club |
| No. 2 Company (Spencer) Leader | P. A. Jones | The Warren, Harlestone Rd. |
| No. 3 Company (St. James') Leader | C. Phillipson | Franklin's Gardens |

*Detached Companies under Division Headquarters*

| | | |
|---|---|---|
| Company Commander | Capt. F. H. Holder | Northampton Electric Light Company |
| Second-in-command | Lt. H. L. C. Jennings | Bridge Street |
| Company Commander | Capt. N. C. Batten | Northampton Gaslight Company |
| Second-in-command | F. Cole | Works, Tanner Street |
| Company Commander | Insp. F. T. Lea, C.S.M. | Northampton Borough Transport |
| Second-in-command | H. Cattell | St. James' Road |
| Company Commander | L. H. Brown | Northampton Borough Water Dept. |
| Second-in-command | R. Reynolds | Fish Street |
| Company Commander | V. Amberg | The Express Lift Company |
| Second-in-command | F. H. Salter | Weedon Road |
| Company Commander | W. R. Morton | G.P.O. Company |
| Second-in-command | J. S. Hulse | General Post Office |

Among these groups will be noted companies composed of members of the Northampton Borough Transport Department and the Northampton Borough Water Department. These, however, were disbanded after a few weeks as it became obvious that, in the event of emergency, their prior duties would be in their respective departments maintaining essential services.

While they existed the Water Department platoon put in some good work as guards of the borough's water supplies, notable at Ravensthorpe Reservoir, with its important power-house and other essential works. The members of the Northampton Borough Water Department who worked at Ravensthorpe and Hollowell reservoirs were retained as detached Sections and transferred to the 9th Battalion for special duties, in whose area the reservoirs were situated.

6 Platoon of B Company of the 12th (Northampton) Battalion pictured at their first annual supper. Sitting left to right at rear are Deputy Platoon Commander W. Evans, Company Commander A. Macfarlane, Platoon Commander K. Thornton, and Deputy Platoon Commander O. J. Hargreaves. (February 1941.)

# Chapter III

## COMMANDERS' EARLY ANXIETIES

RETURNING to County Headquarters at the Territorial Hall, Clare Street, Northampton, we may now the better view Northampton's home defence development through the media of communications which vividly, often divertingly, reflect the resource, determination, and ingenuity with which the district commands, at all levels, were carried on during the ensuing months, and, in many districts, the very serious work and gallant duty that were being done.

Suggestions for the training and organization of the L.D.V. poured in from all and sundry.

Here is a typical specimen of the *right* variety of communication, submitted to Col. A. H. Mellows (Peterborough) by Major J. W. Goddard, M.C. (R.F.A. retired), Park Corner, Peterborough, in June 1940.

How sound remains most of this veteran's advice even to-day!

Every member of the section should know every other member and the two men on *each* flank should know the two men on the flank of the section next to them, so that if a message is being passed, either verbally or in writing (avoid verbal if possible) the receiver will know the message is genuine.

During the 1914–18 war many English *posts* were given away by officers and men acting on the messages brought to them by Germans.

The volunteer, when once allotted to a beat, should not be changed more often than is absolutely necessary and he should immediately familiarize himself with every hedge, wall, house, ditch, or any other cover which affords a place for observation or hiding.

Neglect of this precaution may cost the volunteer his life.

Where a beat is near a wood, only men of the keenest intelligence should be placed there.

Find the distance from point to point, in yards, this will enable accurate fire at once to be opened.

To find a range quickly—Extend the right arm to its fullest extent, pointing to the object. Raise the thumb. Close the left eye. Look at the object over the left side of the thumb with the right eye. Close the right eye and open the left eye, the line of sight will then be to the right of the object. Estimate the distance in yards from the new line to the object, multiply by ten and this will give the range. Tracer ammunition should be used as much as possible to give the volunteer an idea where his shot has gone.

Aim at the centre of the body, this will allow for error in elevation.

Rapidity of fire is essential and the volunteer should practise opening and closing the breech without taking the rifle from the shoulder.

Much of such counsel was not only adopted by the commanders who received it but was also passed along for possible distribution to other commands.

### REGULAR GUARDS IMPOSSIBLE

Equally eloquent of another L.D.V. aspect is the answer of County Headquarters to a commander who in June 1940 suggested that Regular soldiers might be detailed to guard two particularly vital points —an important bridge and a large petrol depot—in his area.

Ran the County Commander's reply:

As regards getting Regular army guards for vital points, e.g. —— bridge and petrol depot at ——, I think this is impossible. Every regular soldier in the country should be either on his way to France or training hard to go there.

Another revealing communication was that from Lt.-Col. Mellows to the County Commander. He wrote on 26 June:

I feel I must draw attention to my position in this area under present conditions. Groups 2, 3, and 4 have eighteen rifles each, together with a limited number of shot-guns without ammunition. The bulk of the remainder of the rifles has been issued for the purpose of guarding vulnerable points within the City of Peterborough.

It is clear to me that my Group Commanders can undertake no offensive or defensive action of any military value with the limited number of weapons under their control.

I have at present informed them that as many rifles as possible should be concentrated on the defence of road blocks in the event of the approach of enemy troops. It will, however, be appreciated that the only duty which they can possibly be expected to discharge at this time is observation together, of course, with report.

In the event of a landing from the air they will automatically warn the nearest searchlight section and also the police.

As regards military aid, under present orders they have to warn the Infantry Training Depot at Northampton, and I understand that the police are doing the same thing.

## AMMUNITION ONLY

Finally, consider in the light of any military experience at all, a letter from Capt. (later Lt.-Col.) V. H. Sykes, 8th Battalion, to the County Commander, dated 29 May 1940.

After dealing with other matters Capt. Sykes added: "the following equipment is required—aiming disks, targets, dummy ammunition, .22 rifles and ammunition".

Sir Hereward Wake replied on 31 May 1940: "We have no aiming disks, no tripods, no dummy ammunition, and no .22

Earls Barton started its War Weapons Week in February 1941 with a combined service, and the Home Guard formed part of the procession to the church.

rifles, but we have some ammunition and can send you 150 rounds".

These letters were typically reflective of the anxieties and deficiencies which L.D.V. commanders, both senior and junior, "took to bed with them" nightly while preserving an outward semblance of calm confidence and coolness.

## ROAD BLOCKS FROM JUNK

And, over and above all the items here detailed, there was the further big "head-ache" provided by the necessity, not only of setting up road blocks at all key points on important highways, but of finding the blocks themselves to set up.

In this connection we may effectively quote from the history of the 12th (North-ampton) Battalion by Lt.-Col. L. E. Barnes, M.B.E.

After the experience of France [he writes] where the enemy armoured columns were allowed to roam at will on the roads, and where not a single civilian thought of stopping the enemy tanks from obtaining petrol from the various wayside filling stations, the denial of the English highways to the enemy was deemed of paramount importance in 1940, so there appeared on our roads at selected sites the most marvellous collection of old junk that has ever been seen.

Sir Hereward Wake, the County Commander, suggested the following as suitable ob-structions:

> Logs of timber, gates, iron railings;
> Farm carts, wagons, lorries, old cars;
> Wire netting, and pig netting;
> Wire to tie materials together.

It was reckoned that some of these which were too old for use could be assembled at once, and others should be located for use if required. One of the primary objects of the road blocks was to impose delay upon the enemy and put his time-table out of gear. A little delay here, a few minutes delay there, and we hoped that his plans would be upset. It was evident that the majority of these blocks would have been of little practical use against enemy tanks, but if they had been ineffective against these they would certainly have been a hind-rance to light cars, dispatch riders, etc. Be-sides, the L.D.V. were doing something which gave them confidence, a confidence that was shared by the general public, and a spirit of confidence was very necessary in those days. Knife-rests were also quickly made and assembled at the blocks.

In addition it was necessary to site railway blocks so that approach to towns could not be made by the railway lines. Most of these blocks were sited at railway bridges.

In the summer of 1941 an improved road obstacle came into being in the form of steel rails which were fitted into specially made holes in the road and which it was hoped would be strong enough to withstand enemy tanks. With the appearance of these rails, practices were held on each of these positions, and the Home Guard felt more confident than ever of stopping enemy armoured fighting vehicles.

## THE SHADOW OF DUNKIRK

There was no doubt about it, the situa-tion in 1940 was serious, deadly serious. All ranks of Northamptonshire's L.D.V. had seen the tragic, if glorious, return of members of the British Expeditionary Force from France, miraculously evacua-ted from Dunkirk on 12 May 1940 and following days.

The L.D.V. talked with these men—tired, dog-tired, men. All their gallant attempts at cheerfulness failed to conceal the depression that had seized them during an evacuation under ceaseless bombing, shelling, and machine-gunning on open beaches—a brilliant retreat, but still a retreat.

Moreover, hundreds of members of the British Expeditionary Force were the sons of Northamptonshire's L.D.V., to whom they confided the worst details of the whole terrible *débâcle* in France.

Then, on 10 July, Italy entered the war on the side of the enemy.

No wonder the L.D.V. commanders and their subordinates pondered long and deeply and redoubled their efforts to be ready for the next stage in the German onslaught.

Yet what could they do? We have just referred to a communication to County Headquarters from Peterborough. Sir Hereward Wake could only reply on 28 June:

"You will, I hope, get 180 more rifles next week and 10 rounds per rifle. This will bring your Division well above the average in weapons."

"Ten rounds per rifle . . . well above the average"! And yet it was so, for Peterborough was an area that in view of the invasion possibilities of the Wash estuary and the East Anglian flat-lands had to receive priority consideration.

### WHEN THEY LAUGHED

*The officers of the 6th (Corby Works) Battalion took turns as orderly officer during the night. On one occasion the second-in-command, after going the rounds with the Sergeant-Major, was challenged by the sentry on returning to Battalion Headquarters. The Sergeant-Major replied "Friend", to which the sentry replied, "That's all right, Sergeant-Major, I know you, but who's that little —— standing behind you?"*

## Chapter IV

# DID HITLER INTEND TO INVADE?

Two questions were regularly addressed to ex-Home Guards for years after the cessation of the war. They were "Did Hitler ever really intend to invade Britain?"—and "Was there any real likelihood of the Home Guard ever going into action in the homeland?"

These questions need to be weighed in this history if justice is to be done to Northamptonshire's Home Guards and their fellows throughout the United Kingdom.

A German official who attended all of the Hitler-Mussolini meetings claimed that Hitler never had the slightest intention of attempting an invasion of Britain.

That may have been true, for Britain had previously been invaded no fewer than fifty-four times, and the results of those attempts may well have made Hitler hesitate. He also maintained a profound respect for the British and made no effort to disguise the fact from his intimates.

Thus addressing a meeting of his commanders in his study at the Reich Chancellery on 23 May 1939 he referred to England as "the driving strength against Germany", adding: "The British themselves are proud, courageous, tenacious, firm in resistance, and gifted as organizers."

### ENEMY'S INVASION MAPS

Nevertheless, addressing his generals soon after the invasion of Poland, he said that his decision was unalterable:

I shall attack France and Britain [he said] at the most favourable moment. The breach of neutrality of Belgium and Holland is meaningless. No one will question it when we have won.

Without attack the war cannot be ended victoriously. The question whether the attack will be successful no one can answer. Everything depends on the favourable moment.

Moreover, that he had made long-term and careful preparations for the possibility of invasion was proved by the subsequent discovery of maps of all areas of England on which all the vulnerable points and those of military significance had been meticulously indicated by red lines and symbols.

Typical of these are maps of Northamptonshire from which a section of the county town is reproduced opposite.

Significantly the caption reads: "Town plan of Northampton. To be worked according to the plan laid down on 1.8.1941."

That, of course, post-dates the Dunkirk period by fifteen months, but it shows that the invasion idea was still in being.

Hitler's first definite intimation of his invasion intention took the form of a directive.

It opened with a statement of which Englishmen may for ever be proud that

Since England, despite her military hopeless situation, shows no signs of willingness to come to terms, I have decided to prepare a landing operation against England, and if necessary to carry it out.

The aim is [the directive continued] to eliminate the English homeland as a base for the carrying on of the war against Germany. The preparations for the entire operation must be completed by mid-August.

Those preparations were completed and, on 17 August 1940, a warning order was sent out from the German G.H.Q. in

# Stadtplan von Northampton

Mil.-Geo.-Bearbeitung nach den bis zum 1.8.1941 vorhandenen Unterlagen

Die

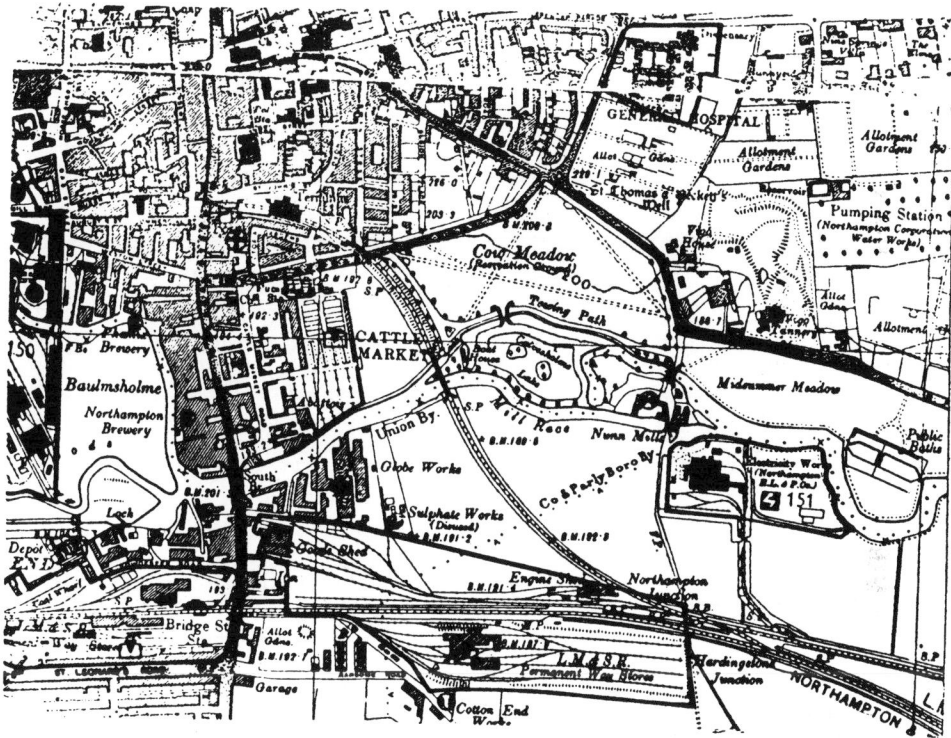

Berlin to the 16th Army though no D-Day date was indicated. "The date," it said, "will be set later."

Under this order the Germans planned to strike at southern and south-east England with twenty-two divisions. Seventeen

GB 8, BB 18, Nr. 14: Nene-Viadukt bei Peterborough (Northamptonshire).
Eisenbahnbrücke der London and North Eastern Railw. über den River Nene zwischen Peterborough und Manton. Vollwandige Blechträger, 4 m über dem Flußspiegel. Gesamtlänge 100 m; erbaut 1924.

Another illustration from the enemy's "guide-book" to Britain, prepared for their invading forces.

additional divisions were to have been in reserve.

The attack was to be carried out by the 16th and 9th German armies forming Army Group "A", and was to concentrate on the South Coast between Margate and Portsmouth.

Meanwhile, airborne landings were to be made just north of the Romney Marshes between Folkstone and Hastings, on the South Downs behind Brighton, and on Beachy Head east of Brighton.

The German invading army was to be armed with a, then, "secret weapon", their six-barrelled "Nebelwerfer" mortar.

British and Canadian forces were to be smashed in the hedgerow country of Kent, Sussex, and Surrey, and London was then to be cut off and strong mobile forces were to break through to occupy important coastal towns and industrial areas in the Midlands.

The code name for the invasion was to be "Sea Lion".

### INVASION H.Q. IN NORTHANTS

Another invasion plan came to light at Cherbourg among other "top secret" enemy documents. This revealed that, in the event of an invasion of Britain via East Anglia, first G.H.Q. was to be established at Willow Hall, near Thorney.

Elaborating the reasons for their selection it was stated that this farm was of the necessary size and yet had unique cover from view both from land or air.

Another factor in the Nazi mind was that the vast area of flat land around it could readily have been converted into an aerodrome.

GB **8**, BB 23, Nr. 55: Bahneinschnitt bei Blisworth (Northamptonshire).

This German illustration of Roade railway cutting was included in the important and vulnerable points in Britain pictured and described in a top secret "guide-book" to Britain prepared by the enemy for the use of their invading and occupation forces. Note the identification numbers.

With Willow Hall as the nerve centre of a drive across the middle of England, London, it was said, could have been cut off from the industrial North.

The capture of the important railway junction of Peterborough was determined as the first main objective.

## ENGLISHMEN TO BE SLAVE LABOURERS

What was to happen after the completion of the invasion and occupation is just as relative to the picture of the situation as the invasion itself.

For the answer to this question we cannot do better than refer to one of the German High Command's most secret documents titled "The Military Administration of England".

This shows that when Hitler had conquered Britain he intended to seize all of the wealth of the country for German use and transport to the Continent, as slave labourers, all of the male population between the ages of seventeen and forty-five.

It also shows that Hitler planned to complete the occupation of England before 9 September 1940, some fourteen weeks after Dunkirk.

On the orders of Field-Marshal von Brauchitsch, the C.-in-C. of all the German Forces, the male British population were to be deported to the Continent as soon as possible after the conquest, in order to prevent sabotage.

In their place, German workers were to be rushed here to transform Britain into Germany's main workshop, turning out all kinds of weapons for the battle against Russia.

This "blue-print" for Britain in defeat was mapped out by administration experts under the direct guidance of von Brauchitsch and Gen. Halder, Nazi Chief of Staff.

These are some of the regulations outlined, the first one having a particularly "interesting" significance for Home Guards:

Any person impeding the German war effort in Great Britain by taking up arms will be treated as a guerrilla and shot.

Hostages will be taken as a "security" measure.

The country's state of health will be considered important only as a safeguard for the resources of the country.

There will be compulsory acceptance of German State bank notes and coins. The rate of exchange will be 9.6 marks to the pound [the pound would thus have been debased to the value of 13s. 6d. according to pre-war exchange rates].

Business concerns, including banks, must be kept open. Closing without adequate reason will be severely punished.

German soldiers can buy whatever they desire. Instead of cash payment in many cases, they can issue certificates admitting the value of the goods.

For sabotage, concealment of harvest products or concealment of arms, the death penalty will be decapitation by the axe or guillotine.

A curfew will be imposed from sunset to sunrise.

The following commodities will be requisitioned: Agricultural products of all kinds, ores, mica, asbestos, precious and semi-precious stones, all kinds of fuel and rubber, textiles, leather and timber.

To complete this economic enslavement of Britain, the document stated that an army economic staff would be installed in all harbours and industrial centres, and would have charge of transporting raw materials and war equipment.

## HITLER TAKES COMMAND

The first invasion date was finally fixed for 15 September 1940 but this was put off for two days and then postponed again to 22 September.

At this time Hitler had taken over command and overrode his generals who preferred an assault on Britain to an assault on Russia.

Field-Marshal von Brauchitsch wanted to invade Britain, but Hitler would not agree until Goering assured him of air superiority.

To this von Brauchitsch replied that they could invade despite the lack of air superiority and Goering then promised superiority in the air but not the overwhelming superiority Hitler demanded.

Another preparation for invasion—one that was carried out—was the movement of large bodies of troops to Norway and their concentration there in an effort to fox the British High Command that the invasion was to come from Norway across to the Wash.

Other diversions were the bombing of East Anglia and the sowing of magnetic mines with which Hitler had hoped to gain the mastery of the seas and the immobilization of the Royal Navy.

Nevertheless, just before 22 September arrived, it was decided to make another postponement until the spring of 1941, and preparations went on all through the winter of 1940 with invasion of England still in view.

But, when the spring came, Hitler was even more undecided, mainly owing to the gloom of Goering and his fears of Russia, and the invasion of Britain was abandoned in favour of that of Russia.

Even that decision did not remove the threat of invasion for Hitler was convinced that a quick victory could be gained over Russia and then, presumably, the plan laid down for 1 August 1941, previously referred to in connection with the detailed maps of England, was to operate.

Why it never did is now history.

## COUNTERING AIRBORNE LANDINGS

None of these facts was, however, to be known to the British command, still less to the Northamptonshire Home Guard patrolling their towns or villages at all hours of the night searching the skies for parachutes, immobilizing unattended cars, mounting tedious guards at V.P.s and, meantime, still training in every available hour to fit themselves to be tough field soldiers.

They took not the slightest chance, knowing full well that they had a tough enemy in prospect led by a command that was reckless of sacrifice either of men or material.

Though they knew that an invasion of England would probably have cost Hitler a million men, they knew also that this would not be reckoned with.

They remembered the report of a deputation of Luftwaffe officers who went to see Goering shortly before the war and complained that his rigorous training methods had caused the accident rate among recruits to rise rapidly. Goering sneered at them: "Tell the men," he replied, "that they are being trained to die. The sooner they learn it the better for them."

They remembered, too, that the primary danger in the initial stages of an invasion lay in the air, from which the Nazi command might be expected to launch airborne advance armies on any and every landing ground.

Thus the Home Guard combined in rendering every possible landing area as "uncomfortable" as possible for aircraft likely to select it for alighting, and in this process they received the whole-hearted co-operation of local farmers.

Generally speaking, any field (grass or arable) which provided a runway of 300 yards or more was regarded as a potential landing ground and was obstructed.

For the obstructions almost "any old thing" served so long as it was substantial and at least four feet high—old farm carts or other farm implements, strong posts planted firmly in the ground; anything likely to damage a plane on landing.

Troop-carrying planes were known to be especially susceptible to damage from such obstructions, and it was imperative to ensure that no such plane should be in a condition to make a second journey.

**KEEN SHORTAGE OF MAPS**

In all of these early operations the Home Guard suffered from a serious lack of one of a soldier's essential needs—comprehensive and up-to-date maps of their operational area.

The County Commander was well enough aware of this lack but he had, perforce, to keep up morale by glossing over it.

Thus on 13 June 1940 he issued the following instruction:

Applications for purchase of maps are being received for use of L.D.V. sections. A general issue would involve great expense and cannot be authorized. Further, it is considered inadvisable to use them. Men know their own parish and the position of surrounding villages, and are only confused by trying to read maps. It is sufficient if they know the points of the compass. . . .

Note-books and pencils should be purchased and charged to stationery account.

Maps hung up outside garages should be removed. L.D.V. to see to this.

Far from receiving maps it was, ironically enough, the job of the L.D.V. to remove what maps there were.

What Sir Hereward really thought of these omissions and the possibilities they left open, with the gravest potential consequences, was recorded in a confidential letter he forwarded to the Lord Lieutenant

(The Marquess of Exeter) on 22 June 1940:

We now have over 15,000 L.D.V. in the county [he wrote] with 990 rifles, less than one to fifteen men, and about 20 rounds of ammunition per rifle. I was told to-day by Area that we cannot expect any more weapons in immediate future and I know the reason, but there is a growing uneasiness among the L.D.V. about their position if and when they face the enemy with hardly any arms and no uniforms and with L.D.V. sewn on their sleeves.

In certain places men have declined to enrol till they get rifles and ammunition. They are reported to be beginning to say that they may expect to be shot off-hand by the Germans if they oppose them in plain clothes . . . whereas if in uniform they would be treated as P.O.W.s. . . . They are perfectly right.

I have met nearly all my fifty group commanders in the last ten days . . . splendid people. They go so far as to say that though all L.D.V. have their "tails up" the present position is beginning to have a demoralizing effect.

I have told them to tell the men that we shall shortly have uniforms for all (this was promised by C.-in-C. Home Forces) and that we shall get rifles and ammunition and that we are not asking L.D.V. to fight a well-armed enemy without these things. . . .

In a neighbouring county L.D.V. have been ordered to use knives, axes and bludgeons if they have no better weapons—but this ignores several unpleasant facts.

I wrote privately to Sir E. Grigg, Under Secretary for War, at the end of May doubting the wisdom of using shot-guns against the Germans . . . which would give them the excuse they wanted for reprisals. . . .

He replied that shot-guns are legal under The Hague Convention and that "the Germans will in any case need no excuse for every form of brutality".

If so . . . at the first news that the Germans are shooting every L.D.V. off-hand and burning his village, every L.D.V. within knowledge would take off his armlet and put his shot-gun in the ditch, if he has no uniform, and no exhortation of the people to "stay put" will in my view prevent a general flight. . . .

Although we have been assured that the L.D.V. are part of the Army, the pamphlets issued by the Government on Invasion Advice refer to the Army, Air Force and L.D.V. as though the latter were quite separate, and they insist on calling the officers "organizers" instead of commanders, which rubs in the difference.

What I think should be done—

1. Issue uniforms at once.
2. L.D.V. armlets should not be worn while in uniform, nor any other armlet distinguishing the force from soldiers, so that the enemy will treat them as soldiers.
3. Armlet with plain clothes is useful for police duty—but should be removed if there is any chance of capture.
4. Give officers local and temporary army rank.

It was hardly coincidence that no more

than two days later (24 June 1940) an Army Council Instruction was issued laying it down that the L.D.V. would adopt the usual Army organization of battalions (1,500 men), companies, platoons, and sections.

## REORGANIZATION OF UNITS

The County Command directed that the organization of the County would remain as it was except that the nine divisions and sub-divisions would be renamed battalions; the commanders, battalion commanders; Stewarts and Lloyds would be a separate battalion under orders of the Kettering Division commander; where sections were more than twenty-five strong, platoons of two or more sections might be formed; platoons and sections might be grouped in companies, when qualified commanders were available; every unit should have a second-in-command.

## WHEN THEY LAUGHED

*During a weapon demonstration in the 4th (Kettering Town) Battalion, several 20-lb. A.T. Spigot mortar shells had been fired and two had missed the target and had failed to explode. They were left to be located and destroyed later. Imagine the feelings of the C.O. when a sergeant walked up to the second-in-command carrying one of the shells under his arm, saying, "I've found one, sir, shall we fire it again?"*

"PLATOONS WERE FORMED"

## Chapter V

# FULL MILITARY STATUS

AND so the L.D.V. gained its first proper military status, a status which was further confirmed when it was laid down that, in all towns and villages in which no Army unit or detachment was stationed, the L.D.V. officer was to become the Military Commander and that when an Army unit left a town or village the O.C. was to hand over his defence scheme to the senior L.D.V. officer.

This was recognition of the highest order and the L.D.V. rose to it but, necessarily, some weeks elapsed before the new battalion reorganization could be completed.

In the meantime, despite their heavy preoccupation with the planning of the new system, all ranks put in their full duty.

This rarely ended with the dismissal of a parade or a relief from guard mounting.

Indeed, apart from the endless hours spent at home studying military manuals, cleaning equipment, and so on, there were also many instances of individual acts of courage and resolution performed while, officially, outside "orders".

### REMOVAL OF BOMBS

Typical of these was that credited to C.S.M. Orton of what was later to be "E" Company of the 7th (Wellingborough Town) Battalion, who won a Good Service Certificate for a piece of cool action combined with keen observation.

C.S.M. Orton, while driving his railway engine through some sidings in June 1940, noticed that some unexploded bombs dropped by an enemy raider had lodged in the truck of a stationary goods train on the next track.

Forthwith, he stopped his engine, clambered aboard the truck, removed the bombs to a place of safety, well away from the line, and then reported their whereabouts before proceeding on his journey.

C.S.M. Orton also received a Certificate of Merit for his action.

### P.M.'S MESSAGE TO FORCES

The national situation remained as tense as ever—how tense, an extract from a message to all Forces issued by the Prime Minister on 4 July 1940 serves to indicate.

On what may be the eve of an attempted invasion or battle for our native land [ran the message] the Prime Minister desires to impress upon all persons holding responsible positions in the Government, in the fighting services, or in the civil departments, their duty to maintain a spirit of alert and confident energy. . . .

The Royal Air Force is in excellent order and at the highest strength it has yet attained. The German Navy was never so weak, nor the British Army at home so strong as now. The Prime Minister expects all His Majesty's servants in high places to set an example of steadiness and resolution. They should check and rebuke expressions of loose and ill-digested opinion in their circle or by their subordinates. . . .

Another message issued hereabouts reveals the co-operation the L.D.V. officers were receiving at this time.

It was sent by Sir Hereward Wake to the Northamptonshire branches of the British Legion as follows:

I wish to express to the Legion in the county and in the Soke of Peterborough my deep appreciation of the efforts made by every branch and every member to assist in the organization of the L.D.V. We are now 18,000 strong. . . . I thank the Legion for their support and assistance on which I shall always rely.

## OFFICIAL NIGGARDLINESS

It was as well such assistance, and much more from all varieties of agencies, was forthcoming, for the niggardliness of officialdom towards the L.D.V. was, at first, as extreme as it was disconcerting.

On 19 July 1940 we find the County Commander issuing this instruction:

VILLAGE L.D.V. CLUBS. Cases have occurred where public subscriptions have been asked for on patriotic grounds by L.D.V. leaders towards expenses incurred by the L.D.V. Certain allowances are granted by the War Office, but the provision of rooms for local headquarters has been left to private generosity. No responsibility can be accepted for establishment of village L.D.V. clubs. They are a luxury, not a necessity. . . .

SUBSISTENCE ALLOWANCE, now amended.
5 to 10 hours continuous duty 1s. 6d.
Over 10 hours continuous duty 3s.

Five to ten hours *continuous* duty for eighteen pennies was surely good value for England.

The L.D.V. accepted with cheerfulness the principle that volunteers should not demand payment for their services, but they did expect some sort of reasonable allowances towards their expenses. They did not get them.

Nor was any account taken of the depreciation of Home Guards' personal effects.

Wrote the County Commander to the E.M. Area on 9 September 1940:

No boots yet received for this County. Thousands of H.G. wear their own boots which rapidly fall to pieces if used for military purposes. Demand is becoming serious and men may be forced to resign if boots promised

are not soon issued. Alternative suggestions—give men permission to purchase locally Army boots at Army prices or make H.G.s a personal allowance in lieu of boots.

The appeal fell on deaf ears and Home Guards' civilian boots continued to "fall to pieces".

In the beginning H.G.'s expenses were laid down as "half a crown per group per rifle" (whatever that may have meant) plus the munificent sum of £10 to Zone Organizers. Having made these princely gestures, the donors warned those responsible for the disbursements that no expenditure on clerical assistance would be met from public funds.

It became a matter of burning the midnight oil after having supplied one's own paraffin.

These grants were stretched to the uttermost farthing. It might have been said of those penurious days, that never in the field of financial grants had so little been given to so many by so few.

Things improved a little later on, but right up to the Stand Down it can be said that no more economical force ever proceeded on its multifarious duties.

There was a keen controversy following the order that Home Guard officers must travel third class, while all other Services officers automatically travelled first class.

This slight not only aroused the rancour of the commissioned ranks, but, with a loyalty that was admirable, that of the rank and file as well.

The absurdity of the anomaly was well illustrated by a story of a Northamptonshire Home Guard officer who was travelling third class to a course and was accosted by a military policeman, who told him that as an officer he must travel first.

Though protesting, the officer duly changed to a first-class compartment, and had hardly settled down in it, when he was

# DAVENTRY VOLUNTEERS.

At a MEETING of the COMMITTEE, held at the
WHEAT SHEAF INN, in *DAVENTRY*,

The FIFTEENTH Day of JUNE, 1797.

CAPTAIN CLARKE, in the CHAIR,

*The following* RULES *for the* REGULATION *of the* CORPS
were unanimously adopted.

*First.* THAT each Member do immediately furnish himself with such
Uniform, Arms, and Accoutrements, as directed by the Officers of the
Corps.

*Second.* THAT *Monday* in each Week being appointed by the Officers to be
the Field Day, each Member do, on that Day, appear on the Parade, in
full Uniform, and under Arms, exactly at NINE o'Clock; fifteen Minutes
after which the Roll shall be called, and each Absentee, unless sufficient
Cause be by him shewn to, and allowed by the Commanding Officer, shall
be fined *One Shilling*.

*Third.* THAT Commissioned Officers, if absent on Field Days, without good
Cause, do forfeit *Two Shillings* and *Six-pence*.

*Fourth.* THAT each Member who does not on the Field Days appear on the
Parade clean, his Hair powdered, and neat in Person, Dress, Arms, and
Accoutrements, as becoming a Soldier, shall forfeit *One Shilling*.

*Fifth.* THAT no Member do talk or behave in any Manner unsteadily, whilst
under Arms, under the Penalty of *One Shilling*.

*Sixth.* THAT if any Member shall withdraw himself from the Corps, without
such Reason as shall prove satisfactory to the Officers and the Committee,
he shall forfeit *Five Guineas*.

*Seventh.* THAT if any Substitute shall withdraw himself from, or be deemed by
the Committee improper to be continued in the Corps, the Principal shall
provide another Substitute, or be subject to the Fine imposed by the preceding Rule.

*Eighth.* THAT the Sum of *Five Shillings* be paid by each Member on his Admission into the Corps, for the Purpose of defraying such extraordinary Ex-
pence as may occur, and that such Subscription shall be repeated as may
by the Committee be hereafter judged necessary.

*Ninth.* THAT the Fines be collected once in each Month, and paid into the
Hands of the Commanding Officer, to be applied to the Service of the
Corps.

*Signed by the Chairman, and the Members of the Corps.*

EDM. BURTON, Sec.

Block by courtesy of the Editor, The Northamptonshire Regimental Journal]
THE "10th (DAVENTRY) BATTALION" OF 150 YEARS AGO
(See caption opposite.)

challenged by a ticket inspector for travelling in a first-class compartment with a third-class ticket.

The bewildered officer tried to explain, but the ticket inspector remained adamant, and what is more insisted on collecting three shillings and threepence excess fare, which, in terms of Home Guard finance, was slightly more than a day's subsistence allowance.

**WHAT WAS "WEAR AND TEAR"?**

Again, the issue of uniform brought with it its own peculiar difficulties.

As the Home Guard was an unpaid force there could be no question of "stoppages" for careless treatment of kit and accoutrements, and the black looks focused on the few offenders by harassed quartermaster-sergeants had little effect.

Then there arose the practically insoluble problem of what was really "fair wear and

**DIGGING REQUIRES STRONG (ARMY) BOOTS**

An interesting reminder of the Napoleonic Wars is provided by Rules of the Daventry Volunteers, dated June 15, 1797, a photograph of which appears opposite. In that year England stood alone in the war against France, whilst the whole of Europe was being overrun by the victorious Bonaparte. It is difficult to compute the present-day equivalent of the fines provided for by these rules, but there is no doubt that misbehaviour was an expensive business, and for this reason, if no other, it is probable that the discipline of the Corps was very high.

The original of the notice now hangs in the Officers' Mess of the 585 (Northamptonshire) S.L. Regiment, R.A. (T.A).

tear". Some of the damage was as incredible as the stories told to account for it.

How, for example, army boots could get their uppers practically charred away in the course of any conceivable Home Guard duties was a matter which no explanations could possibly cover.

The only reasonable solution was a train of events which began at one end with warriors anxious to warm their cold feet, and concluded at the other with a practically red-hot stove.

### LINK WITH THE CHANNEL ISLANDS OCCUPATION

It was in July 1940 that there came to the Northamptonshire Home Guard a link with the enemy occupation of the Channel Islands (30 June 1940) in the person of Major T. C. Shillito.

Major
T. C. Shillito.

Capt. Shillito, as he was then, had retired from the Army to live in Guernsey but, rather than submit to the humiliation of remaining in the island under a German garrison, he determined to forsake his home and to risk the loss of all his belongings, other than those he could carry. Thus he and his family left by the first available boat when the occupation became imminent.

Arrived in England, Capt. Shillito at once set about discovering ways and means whereby he could serve the British war effort and to this end contacted Sir Hereward Wake, his former Colonel in the K.R.R.C., in which he himself had served since 1897.

In that period, among other campaigns, he had served in the South African War (1899–1902), including the Defence of Ladysmith, and in the 1914–18 war in Egypt, France, Belgium, and India, being commissioned from R.S.M. in 1914 "for service in the field".

It was not surprising when Sir Hereward Wake learned that Capt. Shillito's services were available, that he at once offered him a post at Zone Headquarters of the Northamptonshire Home Guard.

Accepting it, Capt. Shillito became Zone Administrative Officer and filled the post with an exemplary efficiency, worthy of his regiment and record, both under Sir Hereward and his successor in the Zone Command (Col. P. Lester Reid).

Regularly combining with his staff duties those of exercise umpire and adjudicator of field ambulance and other tests, Capt. Shillito also prepared and produced a valuable little training handbook under the title of *A Hundred and One Questions for the Home Guard.*

Capt. Shillito received well-deserved promotion to Major in June 1941.

# Chapter VI

## "L.D.V." BECOMES "HOME GUARD"

### ALARMS AND EXCURSIONS

As was to be expected at a time when the enemy was continually seeking to infiltrate spies, saboteurs, and agents, the whole countryside had waxed "parachute conscious" and there were inevitably many strange occurrences and many false alarms in Northamptonshire, as elsewhere.

Into the former category fell an alarm sounded in the 9th (Wellingborough) Group L.D.V. when on Friday evening, 5 July 1940, a report was received that "two white objects" had been seen in the sky at 8 p.m. near Finedon Railway Station.

Fifty members of the L.D.V. were turned out from Wellingborough, Finedon, and Isham, but nothing was discovered.

There was, however, a sequel to this affair which nearly ended in tragedy for the unknown man concerned in it.

Two days later Mr. S. Challenger, sub-section leader in charge of the guard at Brookfield Pumping Station (Wellingborough U.D.C. Water Works) reported to his Company Commander (Mr. A. H. Bull) that one of his men (Eason) had stopped a man at the golf course gate between 10.15 and 10.20 p.m.

The man produced an identity card with nothing on it but his name, and rather surprisingly was allowed to proceed.

At about 12.30 a.m. another guard (Hocking) reported that an aeroplane, flying very low, had just gone over, presumably to land at Sywell.

### MYSTERIOUS LIGHTS

A few minutes afterwards, while Challenger and Hocking were standing discussing the matter, they saw a red light flash followed by a white one, which flashed several times and then went out.

A few minutes later a plane came over, flying high, and made in the direction from which the lights had flashed. This was in the direction of Mears Ashby. Mears Ashby was too far to reach, so it was decided to log the matter and report it later.

Challenger then went for a patrol round the inside of the waterworks and, hearing a noise behind the hedge outside, thought it was his guard making contact, and went outside to meet him.

He saw a man coming down the hedge side and gave the agreed signal with his torch, whereupon the intruder turned and bolted.

The guard was turned out, while Challenger reported to his headquarters by telephone, and also informed the police.

The police were on the spot inside ten minutes, and Challenger went to meet them.

As he did so, he heard a movement in the hedge, and discovered that the intruder had got across the golf links and was making across Mr. Dac's field.

He shouted to him to halt, and as he did not obey, Challenger opened fire, but in the dark missed him.

Nothing was subsequently found of the mysterious intruder except several traces of his presence.

His identity must, therefore, remain a mystery, and Mr. Challenger may well have regretted for years afterwards that the darkness and the swiftness of his moving target combined to spoil what would undoubtedly have been the "shot of his lifetime".

### "MUCH BETTER CALLED THE HOME GUARD"

The L.D.V. got their full meed of praise for such services and a particularly big thrill of satisfaction rippled through the ranks when on 14 July 1940 the Prime Minister delivered another memorable broadcast.

Any plans [he said] which Hitler made for invading Britain must have had to be entirely recast in order to meet our new position.

Two months ago, nay, one month ago, our first and main effort was to keep our army in France . . . but now we have got it all at home. Never before, in the last war or in this, have we had in this island an army comparable in quality, equipment, or numbers to that which stands here on guard to-night.

We have a million and a half men in the British Army under arms to-night. . . . No praise is too high for the officers and men, aye, and civilians who have made this vast transformation in so short a time.

Behind these soldiers of the Regular Army, as a means of destruction for parachutists, airborne invaders, and any traitors that may be found in our midst . . . we have more than a million of the L.D.V., or as they are much better called, the Home Guard.

These officers and men, a large proportion of whom have been through the last war, have the strongest desire to attack and come to close quarters with the enemy wherever he may appear. Should the invader come to Britain there will be no placid lying down of the people in submission before him, as we have seen, alas, in other countries. We shall defend every village, every town, and every city.

Mr. Churchill had used the phrase "They are much better called the Home Guard", and the hint was taken.

On 23 July 1940 the title Local Defence Volunteers was dropped and that of the Home Guard replaced it with the unanimous approval of all ranks. "Home Guard" was stronger, it was shorter, and it was ideally appropriate both in the national and local sense.

"Proud to serve as privates now . . ." A cartoon of July 1941.

Coincidentally, the War Office sanctioned the use of blue shoulder stripes to denote officers' ranks—three for battalion commanders, two for company commanders, and one for platoon commanders—and laid it down that henceforth the Home Guard was entitled to all the privileges as well as the responsibilities of a soldier.

Finally, and this was perhaps one of the most welcome pieces of news the Home Guard received, it was decreed that, in future, the ranker was to be designated "Private" instead of "Member" or "Volunteer".

While the term "Private" has always seemed a misnomer (for goodness knows there is precious little privacy in the life of a private soldier) it was a happier appellation than that of "Member"—which seemed to have a dubious parliamentary ring about it.

It was also a vast improvement on the term "Guardsman" which, while perhaps more obvious, was a little too pretentious.

### THE "BROOMSTICK" ARMY

Upon all these progressive measures Goebbels, Germany's "ace" propagandist, made a characteristic comment. "Churchill has spoken of Home Guards under arms," he said. "We ask—under what arms? Broomsticks or the arms of the local pub, with pots of beer and darts in their hands?"

Nevertheless, the generally awaited invasion did not break, which was the best compliment Hitler could pay to the British fortress, and its defending forces, not excluding the "broomstick" army whose members only waxed more alert than ever, and also waxed so numerous that recruiting had temporarily to be suspended, although names continued to be registered.

## WHEN THEY LAUGHED

*A Brigadier happened to pass a Home Guard sentry post and recognized the sentry— his own solicitor, who promptly turned out the guard. They were all elderly, and most of them wore a good many Service ribbons. He asked one man, "What were you before you joined the Home Guard?" "A Rear-Admiral, sir." He passed to the next, "And what were you?" "A Major-General, sir." He moved somewhat hurriedly to the third man. "You are wearing some decorations that I don't seem to recognize at all. Foreign, I suppose?" "I was an ambassador, sir." After that the Brigadier decided, very discreetly, to dismiss the guard.*

## Chapter VII

# THE BATTALIONS REVIEWED (1)

**FIRST MEDICAL SERVICE ORGANIZED**

IT soon became evident that, whatever else the L.D.V. lacked, there was no reason why it should be denied at least one of the essentials of a fighting force—a field ambulance and medical service.

How this was eventually organized on a regular basis is told later, but it should here be set down that the genesis of the service was dated 15 July 1940, when the Secretary of the Central Medical War Committee, in a letter to the Secretary of State for War, offered, on behalf of the medical profession, initial first-aid treatment to members of the Local Defence Volunteers who became casualties while on duty.

The Army Council gratefully acknowledged this offer and copies of the correspondence were received by the Northamptonshire Territorial Association with a request that full advantage be taken of this offer of medical assistance.

That advantage *was* taken by all units goes without saying and the Home Guard will always recall with appreciation the services of the medical men, ranging from eminent specialists down to the humblest "G.P.s" who repaired the sundry physical hurts they sustained on duty during those early days.

Since in the further review of battalions which immediately follows the names of battalion medical officers, for convenient reference, are included, it will be well if we here forsake chronological sequence to pursue the L.D.V. medical organization into 1941 when the M.O.s were first authorized.

It was Col. W. C. Harthill, O.B.E., M.C., Medical Adviser, G.H.Q. Home Forces, who drafted the original scheme for a Home Guard Medical Organization.

This was discussed between War Office, G.H.Q. Home Forces, Ministry of Health, Ministry of Home Security, and the British Medical Association, and on 2 April 1941, the Army Council authorized a "Medical Organization" within Home Guard units based on a modification of that of an infantry battalion.

The main provisions were:

(*a*) A medical officer (Major) to be appointed for each Battalion Home Guard.

(*b*) Stretcher-bearer squads and medical orderlies to be trained.

(*c*) Training as a stretcher bearer not to affect liability to be trained in the use of weapons or to be called upon to use them.

(*d*) A regimental aid post, if required, to be established at Battalion Headquarters.

(*e*) Arrangements for evacuation of casualties were to be reviewed having regard to the requirements of local defence schemes.

(*f*) A scale of medical equipment was authorized for each platoon of approximately one hundred men.

**ANOTHER REVIEW OF BATTALIONS**

At this point with the formation of battalions taking shape we will revert to July 1940 to take another look at the county areas.

In the 1st (City of Peterborough) Battalion spirits were soaring mainly because late in July they had received a further 1,000 American rifles.

ROUTE MARCH

In the same month the Ordnance Department notified the battalion that 1,700 denim blouses, 1,700 pairs of trousers, and the same number of caps and buckles, together with a huge number of buttons, were being dispatched.

To issue this quantity in time for a week-end march which the Commanding Officer said must take place without fail, the Q. Branch sweated and toiled for days.

### PETERBOROUGH GROUP DIVIDED

In the end the distribution took place in bulk to companies, who then had the job of doing the individual fitting out—a job which produced some novel effects, especially among those whose trousers chafed them under the arm-pits!

Still, the job was done, the route march took place, and Peterborough had the first real glimpse of its defenders in new, if not gorgeous, uniforms.

The band which led the march was hardly of the Wellington Barracks order, it consisted of "potted music" supplied by an amplified gramophone, but it served.

It was on 17 July 1940 that a Battalion Order was published notifying the splitting up of the Peterborough Group into two battalions—the 1st (City of Peterborough) Battalion and the 2nd (Soke of Peterborough) Battalion.

Col. A. H. Mellows, T.D., assumed command of the 1st Battalion, with Capt. R. J. C. Crowden, M.C., as his second-in-command. The Adjutant was Capt. G. Baker, and the Quartermaster, Capt. H. P. E. Dawson.

Col. Mellows was commissioned in the Huntingdonshire Cyclist Battalion in April 1914, and was duly mobilized on the outbreak of the 1914–18 war.

Leaving the Battalion in England, Col. Mellows then served from 1916 to the end of 1918 in Mesopotamia, first in a Stokes

Mortar Brigade, later on the Staff in Baghdad, and finally as an Observer in 30 Squadron, Royal Air Force. He was twice mentioned in dispatches.

Lt.-Col. A. H. Mellows.

After the war Col. Mellows was one of the original officers who joined the 5th (Huntingdonshire) Battalion Northamptonshire Regiment at its birth in 1920. He joined with his demobilization rank of Captain and served with the 5th from 1920 to 1934, commanding it from 1928 to 1934.

He was gazetted Lieutenant-Colonel on assuming command, and Brevet-Colonel in 1932.

As his intelligence officer in City of Peterborough Home Guard Battalion Col. Mellows had Vice-Admiral A. H. Alington, and the Battalion fortunately retained the services of R.S.M. Atkinson and Q.M.S. Jones.

The whole of Peterborough City was organized into defence localities, and not a post of danger was left unwatched. The operational area of the 1st Battalion lay within a perimeter enclosing, on the west, the entrance to Thorpe Hall, on the north along the line of the L.N.E. Railway and the Midland and Great Northern Joint Railway to the Paxton crossing, on the east to the Newark and Edgley drain, and on the south the river and sewerage farm, thence due west on the river line including the town rail-road bridges, thence along the towing-path to a point south of Thorpe Park.

The flanking battalions were—on the east, the 1st Cambridge (Isle of Ely), on the south, the 1st Hunts., and, on the north and west, the 2nd (Soke of Peterborough).

It was significant that, at a conference held in Northampton on 16 July 1940, the Peterborough Division's importance was again underlined and the opinion expressed that it should have priority for equipment.

The reasons were obvious, for, at one point, the Soke of Peterborough is within twenty miles or so of the sea, where the waters of the Wash flow far inland.

This low-lying land has always been regarded as the most likely point of attack by an invader, with its large, level tracts, and few natural obstructions.

It was for the greater part of this vulnerable area that the 2nd Battalion now became responsible. It covered some eighty square miles and apart from its invasion possibilities was spanned by vital main roads and railways, such as the Great North Road, and the main line of the L.N.E. Railway.

The right flank of the Battalion rested on Peterborough, and the left flank on Stamford—where, in both cases, the strength was greatest.

## 2ND BATTALION'S HEAVY RESPONSIBILITY

The role assigned to the 2nd Battalion by Eastern Command was particularly onerous, being nothing less than that of a Communications Battalion with the prior duty of keeping open lines of communication. These ran from north to south along the Great North Road, and from Lincoln to Peterborough.

In addition there were the Stamford to Spalding roads running east to west as well as the road from Leicester to Wisbech.

Along these important lines it was the duty of the 2nd to harass and delay the enemy, deny him his lines of communication, and, of course, wherever possible, destroy him.

Like other battalions, the 2nd also had its own special problems and responsibilities— among them being the Wittering, Kingscliffe and Westwood aerodromes, the works of P. Brotherhood & Co., the Royal Army Ordnance Depot at Walton, and the Wansford viaduct on the Great North Road.

The Battalion Commander at this time is shown as Lt.-Col. H. L. Samson, with Battalion Headquarters at the Cock Inn, Werrington.

His Administrative Assistant was Capt. R. P. Carter, whose Action Headquarters were the Milton Estate Offices, 25 Priestgate, Peterborough.

There were four companies, A, B, C, and D, with Action Headquarters at the Riding School, Castor, The Cock Inn, Werrington (B and C Companies), with D Company at the Manor House, Dogsthorpe.

Later, Lt.-Col. A. H. Mellows, who had been previously Group Commander of the Peterborough Group, became Commanding Officer of the 2nd, and Capt. R. J. C. Crowden, M.C., was promoted to the command of the 1st.

Lt.-Col. Crowden, as he now became, served during the 1914–18 war with the 1st/4th (T.) Battalion Lincolnshire Regiment in France and Egypt and, promoted

1st Northants (City of Peterborough) trio. Left to right, Capt. C. L. Pilley, Lt.-Col. R. J. C. Crowden, M.C. (Commanding Officer), and Battalion second-in-command, Major H. J. Farrow.

1st Northants (City of Peterborough) Home Guard Battalion Officers' Mess Night, May 1941. Lt.-Col. R. J. C. Crowden, M.C., and officers of Battalion and honoured guests—the Mayor of Peterborough (Alderman Major H. J. Farrow, J.P.) in centre. Major Farrow was second-in-command of the Battalion.

to Captain, gained the Military Cross and was also mentioned in dispatches.

Lt.-Col. R. J. C. Crowden

In the latter part of the war he was seconded to the 138th Brigade staff.

Coincident with this change of command there was added to the 2nd Battalion's territory the Borough of Stamford and the parishes of Uffingham and Tallington. These were all in Lincolnshire!

## OUNDLE DIVIDED INTO SIX COMPANIES

The 3rd (Oundle) Battalion (Lt.-Col. F. R. Berridge) was well in step with the new regularization. It now divided into six companies, with the area reaching from Denford and Addington in the south to Easton on the Hill in the north, and from Lutton in the east to Brigstock and Deene in the west.

A Company (Kingscliffe) was originally commanded by Major F. J. Lenton, M.C., who later became the Battalion's second-in-command. He was succeeded by Major Simpson, a farmer, and a veteran of the 1914–18 war.

B Company at Bulwick was commanded by Major G. Le Mare, of Messrs. Stewarts and Lloyds.

C Company (Barnwell area) was originally under Capt. Harvey, but his work as a farmer and a Government lecturer all over the country made it necessary for him to hand over to Major H. P. Hewett, a house-master at Oundle School and another 1914–18 veteran.

D Company (Thrapston) was first under Major Llewellyn Richards and when he left the district came under the command of Capt. E. St. Clair Gainer. However, as the Government decided that doctors should not command companies, he handed his command to Major C. R. Jones of the National Provincial Bank.

E Company was the Oundle School Boys' Company. They volunteered to form a company which comprised boys over seventeen, commanded by Major P.

The 3rd (Oundle) Battalion used old petrol tins in connection with training in house clearing. On right is a First Aid Party being inspected. At rear, left to right, are Lt.-Col. L. D. B. Cogan Zone M.O.), Sgt. W. G. Wright (Instructor), and Major E. I. White, Battalion M.O.

Priestman, Commander of the J.T.C. They were used throughout as a Mobile Company and were always exceedingly keen and efficient.

F Company (later Headquarters Company) was the Oundle Company commanded by Major F. F. Spragg.

Two more companies, making eight in all, were added later. They were G and H Companies, and were offshoots of D Company, which became too unwieldy.

Major R. H. Ward took over G Company and Major T. W. W. Smith assumed command of H Company.

Three adjutants in all assisted the 3rd Battalion—Capt. Sharpe, Major H. K. F. Nailer, and Capt. J. H. Heard (of Oundle), a repatriated prisoner of war from Germany.

The 3rd Battalion Specialist Officers were as follows:

Medical Officer, Major E. I. White (Thrapston); Chief Guide, Capt. G. E. Bellville (Brigstock); Transport Officer, Capt. P. G. Cooms (Oundle); Ammunition Officer, Capt. J. M. Branfoot (Oundle); Liaison Officer, Lt. R. K. Yeld (Oundle); Signals Officer, Lt. D. L. Venning (Oundle); Camouflage Officer, Lt. T. Freeman (Denford); Weapon Training Officer, Capt. E. Barnes (Oundle); and Intelligence Officer, Lt. D. J. L. Simpson of Warmington.

When the Battalion strength reached 2,000 Capt. P. J. Wootton was appointed Administrative Officer. He was formerly a Regimental Sergeant-Major in the Lancashire Fusiliers and was of great assistance, as also were the two permanent staff instructors.

### KETTERING'S CONCENTRATED TASK

When the 4th (Kettering Borough) Battalion shed its L.D.V. label Lt.-Col. Holborow retained the command, and had as second-in-command Major J. Baker.

A Company was then commanded by Major H. R. Newbould (who retained this command throughout the life of the unit), B Company by Major G. D. Howard, C Company by Major A. J. Shepherdson, and D Company by Major A. Burns. E Company was commanded by Major J. W. Watt, G Company by Major A. Johnson, and the Headquarters Company by Major A. Russell.

Major J. Baker had previously been acting as Adjutant until he assumed the role of second-in-command, when he was succeeded by Capt. H. Davis as Battalion Adjutant. Capt. Davis had previously commanded H Company, the Works Company. He was joined later by Capt. H. J. Maidment as Quartermaster.

Later, Capt. Davis was transferred to the 8th Battalion, and was succeeded by Capt. J. H. Banks.

Lt.-Col. A. R. Russell.

When later Lt.-Col. Holborow relinquished his command, Major Russell was promoted to Lieutenant-Colonel and took over command of the Battalion.

Lt.-Col. Russell spent the whole of his military career with the Northamptonshire Regiment. At the age of sixteen he joined the 2/4th Battalion in 1914 and, promoted Corporal, went to France with the 2nd Battalion and performed gallant service with them on the Somme until he returned to England for hospital treatment. Returning to the Battalion, he fought with them at Ypres and Passchendaele and returned to England to join an officer cadet battalion of Artists Rifles preparatory to a commission, which he received eight months later. He was then posted to the 4th Battalion and remained with them until "demobbed" in 1919.

In the L.D.V., Lt.-Col. Russell formed the Kettering Electricity Works Platoon, and in 1941 became second-in-command of H Company of the 4th (Kettering Town) Battalion, which company he next commanded with the rank of Major until transferred to the command of Headquarters Company of the 4th.

Major Burns became Lt.-Col. Russell's second-in-command, and thus, with the retirement of Major Shepherdson, three company changes were involved. In each case the company second-in-command was promoted—Capt. Issett to C Company, Capt. Davenport to D Company, and Capt. Bell to Headquarters Company.

Prior to this, Major Green had succeeded Major Johnson in the command of the Railway Company (G).

The 4th Battalion Specialist Officers, all of Kettering, were as follow:

Medical Officer, Major W. Shirkey; Chief Guide, Capt. H. C. Langham; Intelligence Officer, Capt. H. C. Langham; Ammunition Officer, Lt. C. A. Davidson; Gas Officer, Lt. T. H. Watson, Signals Officer, Lt. L. Plowright; Transport Officer, Lt. C. D. W. Andrews; Liaison Officer, Lt. F. E. Francis; and Contact Officer, Lt. A. Green.

The operational area of the 4th was, as its name implies, the Borough of Kettering.

Battalion Headquarters and the Headquarters Company were located at the Rectory, A Company Headquarters were at Trafalgar Road, B Company at Avenue House, Rockingham Road, C Company in Stamford Road, D Company at the Brickyard, London Road, E Company at the Royal Hotel, and G Company at the L.M.S. Railway Station.

The strategic role of the Battalion underwent several changes as the war progressed, but the central idea remained static. This was to deny the town and main roads to the enemy, and at the same time to permit of passage of our own regular troops.

The general nature of the Battalion area was urban. It was closely built up with main road junctions, and would have been far from a simple matter to defend.

There were many V.P.s, including the L.M.S. main line which ran along the Battalion's western boundary, the Petroleum Store, the Post Office, the Electricity Generating Station, the Gas Works, and many munition factories.

The 5th (Kettering District) Battalion linked up all round, with the 6th and 7th Battalions.

Cameraderie was a primary feature of life in the 4th. Discipline was maintained, but all ranks "swung in" together. Thus is was not uncommon for fatigue parties to be made up of about six officers, ten N.C.O.s, and two privates!

### IN THE KETTERING DISTRICT

Meanwhile, in the Kettering town's sister battalion, the 5th (Kettering) District Battalion, Col. H. Burditt continued in command with Sir Frederick Robinson, Bt., M.C., as his second-in-command.

Lt.-Col. Sir F. V. L. Robinson.

Later, Sir Frederick Robinson took over the command, Col. Burditt being promoted commander of No. 1 Group —later No. 1 Sector— comprising the 3rd, 4th, 5th, and 6th Battalions.

Lt.-Col. Sir Frederick Robinson was commissioned in the Northamptonshire Regiment during the South African war and joined the 2nd Battalion in the field in time to take part in the operations of 1902, gaining the Queen's S.A. Medal with two clasps. He was promoted Captain in 1909 and retired two years later and at the same time was appointed Captain 3rd Battalion. He rejoined the Northamptons (1st Battalion) in the 1914–18 war and served as Assistant Provost-Marshal with the 25th Division. Twice wounded and mentioned in dispatches, he won the Military Cross for his conspicuous courage in action, also the French Croix de Guerre, the Mons Star, and two other war medals.

The organization of the 5th differed from that of the 4th. The area of the 5th was widely scattered, and included Corby, Desborough, Rothwell, Burton Latimer, Welford, and Naseby. Lt.-Col. Sir Frederick Robinson continued in command throughout, and his second-in-command was Major B. Wright, M.C., who formerly commanded D Company.

There were six companies.

A Company (Corby) was originally commanded by Capt. G. P. Lucas of Corby, then by Major G. F. H. Satow of Corby, and later by Major G. C. S. Oliver of Weldon.

In 1942 this Company was transferred *en bloc* to the 6th (Corby Works) Battalion for operational reasons.

A new A Company was then formed by splitting B Company into two.

The new A Company was placed under Major J. S. Chawner of East Carlton.

B (Desborough and District) Company was formerly commanded by Major Colvin, M.B.E. When this officer left the district in February 1943, B Company was split up as above, and the new B Company was then commanded by Major R. Ginns of Desborough.

Here it may be mentioned that it was Lt. Tailby's platoon of the Company which won Col. Burditt's Cup for the Battalion Battle Platoon Competition in 1943, and that Capt. H. Barratt (second-in-command of this Company) was awarded the Good Service Certificate in June 1944.

C (Rothwell and District) Company was originally commanded by Canon (later Archdeacon) Grimes of Thorpe Malsor, who was also second-in-command of the Battalion until February 1941, when the command was taken over by Major A. E. Sarjeant of Rothwell.

In 1943, owing to increased work, part of D Company was transferred to C Company, making the two companies of approximately equal size.

D (Burton Latimer District) Company was commanded by Major B. Wright, M.C., until April 1942, when he was appointed Battalion second-in-command, and Major R. W. Waterfield (Headmaster of Broughton School) was appointed Company Commander.

E (East Farndon and Clipston Area) Company was commanded successively by Major Pelley of Sibbertoft, Major Regnart of Clipston, and Major Hankey of Sibbertoft. Then in December 1941 Major R. M. C. Sanderson of Oxenden Hall took over.

Lt. Levett's platoon of this Company won the Sector Battle Platoon Competition of 1944 and also Col. Burditt's Cup.

F (Welford and Naseby) Company was commanded by Major R. R. L. Savil from its inception.

The 5th Battalion Headquarters (originally at Rushton Road, Desborough) was moved to 75 London Road, Kettering, in April 1941, and later to 17 The Grove, Kettering.

Lt. S. Gillard was the commander of the Headquarters Platoon.

In April 1941 Capt. F. H. Butler (General List), formerly with A Company of the 4th Battalion, was appointed Adjutant and Quartermaster. Later (June 1942), as duties increased, a separate quartermaster (Capt. L. C. Jackson) was appointed.

The 5th Battalion Specialist Officers were as follows:

Medical Officer, Major G. F. P. Gibbons; Chief Guide, Capt. S. Wallis; Transport Officer, Lt. T. Wallis; Weapon Training Officer, Capt. E. F. Towell; Intelligence Officer, Lt. N. Lloyd; Ammunition Officer, Lt. F. C. Harris; Signals Officer, Lt. W. E. Blamire; Gas and P.A.D. Officer, Lt. E. Bull; and Camouflage Officer, 2nd Lt. M. A. James.

Two permanent staff instructors were attached for training— C.S.M. E. White, Leicester Regiment (late Coldstream Guards) and C.S.M. W. R. Murdin, Northamptonshire Regiment. Both were excellent instructors, and as popular as they were invaluable.

### IMPORTANT "V.P.s"

The general nature of the Battalion's area was rural. It included, however, the small industrial towns of Rothwell, Desborough, and Burton Latimer, also the vulnerable points of Sterling Metals of Burton Latimer and the airfields at Grafton Underwood, Desborough, Harrington, and Sulby.

The companies responsible for these V.P.s maintained a strict liaison with their static defence units throughout the war.

The strategy of the Battalion varied during the course of the war, but was generally based on a series of defended localities at Cottingham and Stoke Albany (A Company), Desborough (B Company), Rothwell (C Company), Geddington, Cranford, and Burton Latimer (D Company), the cross-roads at Kelmarsh (E Company), and Welford and Naseby (F Company).

Each Company had a trained mobile battle platoon for use in its own area, and ready also, if required, to join a mobile battle company which was based on Rothwell.

The operational role of the Battalion was to deny main roads to the enemy, with particular regard for the protection of the road and railway systems converging on Kettering.

### "PARACHUTES" AT ISHAM

No less than other battalions the 5th had its share of "parachute" landing alarms at this period. Thus on 5 July 1940 a report was received that parachutes had been sighted at Isham at 2030 hours.

All volunteers stood by until 0030 hours on 6 July and there was also activity at Kettering, where L.D.V., police, and military were out searching.

The parachutes were subsequently alleged to have been two swans alighting on a lake in Wicksteed Park, Kettering, but this was never confirmed.

The 5th also took a full part in the July road block "scramble". On 6 July a dispatch rider arrived with orders for sites to be chosen for road blocks on every road leading to every village. Blocks were to be constructed by local councils.

Much work was done in selecting suitable sites, but when this had been completed the Rural Council stated that they were unable to co-operate and that in any case neither material nor labour was available.

Hundreds of these blocks would have been needed in the area.

Later the Group was ordered to construct them, with no materials, no transport, no petrol, and no money!

A compromise was made by earmarking farm vehicles, etc., near to sites, to be rushed into position if necessary.

Also one-inch wire cables given by the Sheepbridge Iron Company were set aside to be fastened to steel rails set in concrete.

One end was made fast and the other was to be fastened by a blacksmith volunteer detailed for the job.

One block was actually constructed by Desborough Urban District Council, only later to be rammed by a car carrying the local Company Commander engaged on a night operation!

### THE NEW DEFENCE OF CORBY

Following battalion reorganization in the 6th (Corby) Battalion area, Major G. F. Satow took over the command of the Corby Company of the 5th Battalion (in 1941 this was merged with the 6th) and Lt.-Col. J. R. Menzies-Wilson, O.B.E., became Battalion Commander of the 6th (Corby Works) Battalion, with Major W. C. Bell (Steel Works Manager) as second-in-command, and Capt. J. Woolley, M.C., a re-employed regular officer, as Adjutant. All three held their appointments throughout.

The Battalion Commander, Lt.-Col. J. R. Menzies-Wilson, was first gazetted 2nd Lieutenant, R.E., on 5 August 1914. Serving abroad as Lieutenant, he commanded a cable section of the Signal Service at the Suvla Landing on Gallipoli. In

1916 he was classified unfit for further foreign service, and on his return became

Lt.-Col. J. R. Menzies-Wilson.

Adjutant of Hitchin Signal Service Depot. Demobilized as Captain, he was awarded the O.B.E. (Mil. Div.) for his meritorious service.

From the original formation of seven companies the Battalion was telescoped twice.

The original formation was: A Company, Mr. W. L. Opie; B Company, Mr. D. C. Hendry; C Company, Mr. T. Rutherford; D Company, Mr. H. Oldale; E Company, Mr. D. J. Bell; F Company, Mr. W. Houston; Headquarters Company, Mr. G. A. Hunter.

On the second formation, Capt. Opie retained A Company, Capt. Bell took B Company, Capt. Oldale D Company, and Lt. J. W. Hill the Headquarters Platoon.

The final change saw Capt. Opie with A Company (which command he retained throughout), Capt. Houston B Company, Capt. J. Glen C Company, while Headquarters was in command of Capt. C. G. Jeavons.

Headquarters Company had auxiliary units—Bomb Disposal (Capt. B. M. Harris) and the "Y" Light Anti-Aircraft Troop under Capt. D. Bell.

Originally there were two senior company commanders, Messrs. R. B. Beilby, M.C., and D. Wingate, M.C., who later acted as the officers commanding the right and left halves of the Battalion with the rank of Major.

The Specialist Officers of the 6th were as follow:

Medical Officer, Major J. Irving; Assistant Medical Officer, Capt. W. Wilson; Intelligence Officer, Lt. J. C. Alexander; Transport Officer, Lt. N. Biddle; Ammunition Officer, Lt. R. M. Chadwick; Bomb Disposal Officer, Capt. B. M. Harris; Signals Officer, Lt. J. Dunn; Gas Officer, Lt. G. L. Jones; and Camouflage Officer, Lt. H. T. Dawson.

The duties of all these officers were carried out at Corby.

The operational area of the Battalion was bounded on the north by the village of Gretton, on the east by the village of Weldon, south-east by the village of Stanion, south-west by the villages of Great and Little Oakley, and north-west by the village of Rockingham.

Headquarters were as follows:

Battalion Headquarters, Corby Works; A Company Headquarters, Gretton Brook; B Company Headquarters, Corby and District Water Company Offices; C Company Headquarters, Corby Works.

The primary operational role of the Battalion was the defence and protection of Corby Steel Works. They were also to be called upon to mop up and destroy parachute troops who might be dropped sporadically for nuisance purposes; to hold and contain airborne troops within certain defined areas until such times as the army in the field could bring up reinforcements;

in the event of a full-scale invasion to deny the enemy forces the use of roads and passage through the Battalion area and to keep open road and rail communications within the Battalion area for the passage of our own forces and supply columns.

The whole of the Battalion's operational area in the north-west sector lay within the Welland Valley.

**GOOD COVER FOR AIRBORNE ENEMY**

The central area, around the town of Corby, is occupied by industrial works which are surrounded on the north, east, and south sides by ironstone quarries and devastated areas, but beyond these the area is, generally speaking, lightly wooded and the remainder agricultural land.

The quarry areas and devastated lands could not have been used by ordinary road vehicles, which would have had to stick to the highways in order to pass through this area.

The mining areas would, however, have provided good cover for airborne forces had Corby Works and Corby Town proved an immediate objective.

The Works area, which was the counterpart of a keep in rural battalions, was, as previously stated, heavily surrounded by barbed wire entanglements.

The 6th Battalion's vulnerable points were as numerous as they were vitally important.

The works area included ancillary works at Corby and district.

Then there was a vast quantity of valuable mining machinery in the nature of large and small excavators used for the raising of iron ore.

There was also Gretton tunnel on the L.M.S. railway, and finally an important L.M.S. railway viaduct.

Later in 1940 (November) it was decided that the Islip sub-unit could be more efficiently administered by the 3rd (Oundle) Battalion, and thus all personnel, arms, and equipment were transferred.

Thereafter the 6th Battalion operated throughout in the Corby area. In the early stages of the unit, a permanent guard was on duty within the works and in the mines and quarries area throughout the whole twenty-four hours.

The men volunteered to do an eight-hour shift immediately following their working shift in order to provide adequate protection.

### THE HEAVIEST-ARMED BATTALION

At the Battalion Headquarters in the Works a switchboard was installed, telephone cables were laid to all company headquarters, and by September 1940 permanent defence posts had been built around the perimeter of the Works, guards patrolling the whole of the perimeter of the wire during a twenty-four-hour period.

As previously noted, the 6th Battalion, on its formation, was able to enrol no fewer than 924 ex-Servicemen with war-time experience, and of that total, approximately 600 were still on the strength at "stand down".

The Battalion was the heaviest-armed Home Guard unit in the country. In addition to ordinary arms, it had various types of mortars and also Smith guns.

The Battalion gained the following proficiency badges:

| | | |
|---|---|---|
| Infantry | - | 534 |
| Artillery | - | 120 |
| Bomb Disposal | - | 52 |

making a grand total of 706, a figure believed to be a record for any battalion in the country.

The Battalion also had a very fine Pipe Band—surely a unique claim for a Home Guard Battalion attached to an English regiment.

In February 1943 Capt. J. Ferris joined the Battalion as Quartermaster and on 4 June 1944 the Battalion took over the A.A. defence of the Works and the "Y" Light A.A. Troop was formed.

C.S.M. A. E. Atkins (K.R.R.C.) joined as Permanent Staff Instructor in December 1941 and C.S.M. J. T. Fairley (West Yorkshire Regiment) joined as additional Permanent Staff Instructor in March 1943.

On two occasions men of the 6th acted as a royal guard of honour in Corby. Once was on 1 May 1942 when the Duchess of Gloucester visited the town, and the second occasion was 4 March 1943 when the King and Queen went to Corby.

### WHEN THEY LAUGHED

*After an exercise in the 4th (Kettering Town) Battalion an employer of a large number of men went sick and asked to be excused parades. He was a private and gave as his reason that he had been detailed by an N.C.O. (who in private life was his caretaker) to collect all the litter in and around the operation H.Q. "Orders being orders" he did the job—but the caretaker decided soon after to seek a new post.*

## Chapter VIII

# THE BATTALIONS REVIEWED (2)

WITH Capt. H. L. Allsopp as its commander, the Wellingborough Town Group (later the 7th Battalion) immediately underwent a comprehensive re-disposition. In addition to the companies and independent sections referred to in Chapter II, new sub-units had been authorized at the Gas Works, Almarco Ltd., United Steels Companies, the United Counties Bus Depot, and the Post Office, while the Co-operative Society, Wagon Repairs Ltd., and others were applying for permission to have their own platoons and a liberal share of weapons to mount their own guards.

To simplify organization and obtain better co-operation, Capt. Allsopp was already attaching these works units to companies when instructions were received that Groups should henceforward be known at Battalions and that these should consist of four companies, each divided into platoons and sections, as in the Regular Army. As a result of this, A and D Companies were amalgamated under Mr. H. J. Crane, B and C under Mr. A. H. Bull. To Headquarters Company, hitherto the mobile platoon, were added the signallers, bandsmen-stretcher-bearers, and, when Lewis guns first arrived, the town Lewis gunners.

During the autumn it became apparent that, although some of the factory units were first class, in general they did not fit into the normal company. Those in the south-east of Wellingborough were therefore separated from their original affiliations and formed into a new F Company, together with the Little Irchester platoon, transferred from the 8th Battalion.

Further minor adjustments were made, and in the New Year Messrs. Crane and Bull resigned.

Thus in February 1941, when the first commissions were granted, the organization which was to continue till mid-1942 had been fixed as under:

H.Q. Company. As above, Capt. T. Smillie in command.

A Company. North and West Wellingborough, with Wilby and Hardwick, and men of the United Counties Bus Company, commanded by Major W. S. Solley.

B Company. Centre and East Wellingborough, with the School O.T.C. detachment and the Post Office Section, under Capt. W. Fishwick.

C Company. Finedon and the Harrowden, Orlingbury and Isham men with personnel of the Wellingborough Iron Company's Mines, under Major J. Bennie.

D Company. Irthlingborough, with platoons incorporated from the Eastern Coach Works, Richard Thomas Ltd., and Great and Little Addington, under Major T. R. Curtis.

E Company. The L.M.S. Railway men, with Wellingborough Iron Company (Works) platoon, under Major A. E. S. Bayley, M.C.

F Company. Men of the Almarco, Ultra Electric, United Steel Companies, Whitworth's Mill and the Gas Works, plus Little Irchester, under Major E. Young, M.C.

The Intelligence personnel, and, for a time, the dispatch riders, pigeons, and pioneers all worked direct from Battalion H.Q.

The Rev. H. Bettenson acted as Chaplain to the Battalion.

Major A. H. Higgins, M.B.E., was released in August 1940 by the A.R.P. Wardens Service to act as second-in-command of the Battalion, and did good work in this capacity until the Stand Down.

The duties of intelligence officer and signals officer received early attention, but whereas Lt. A. J. Linnell, whose reputation was known far and wide in the first few months, and who did outstanding work throughout, was Battalion Signals Officer from 1940 until the end, there were no fewer than four intelligence officers: Mr. (later Capt.) E. E. Jones (who was also the first Chief Guide), in 1940; Lt. (later Capt.) H. G. Crawford-Jones, who, from 1941, did first-class work until he went to No. 3 Sector at the end of 1942; Capt. P. Freeman (who succeeded Capt. E. E. Jones as Chief Guide) in 1943, and Lt. J. Hand during 1944.

Major J. Arthur, M.D., was Chief Medical Officer, later with Capt. J. H. McGibbon (Irthlingborough) and Capt. P. Bell (Finedon) to assist him. Weapon Training Officers were Lt. T. Stout (O.T.C.) till 1943 and then Lt. E. Perkins (Wellingborough). Gas and P.A.D. Officers were, first, Lt. E. H. L. Way (Irthlingborough), then Lt. D. F. Burton (Wellingborough), who had previously done exceptional work as Camouflage Officer, in which appointment he was succeeded by 2nd Lt. A. F. Spencer.

Transport Officers were Lt. Alan Brown, then Lt. H. J. Harrison, and finally Lt. K. L. Arber, all of Wellingborough; Capts. E. Deighton and O. Mayers, Ammunition and Sub-Artillery Officers respectively, both came from the near side of Great Doddington. Lt. W. O. Gibson, who followed Capt. T. Smillie in command of

the mobile platoon in 1941, later became Contact Officer and subsequently graduated to No. 3 Sector. Pioneer officers were Lt. J. R. Partridge and then Lt. D. J. Evans. Lt. L. W. Eadon (Wilby) was responsible for petrol immobilization and disruption, while Capt. E. M. Ambler, second-in-command of E Company in 1940, became Railway Liaison Officer in 1942.

Capt. C. J. Chouler joined the Battalion as Adjutant in May 1941, when Capt. Barron resigned his post as Administrative Assistant. Capt. Chouler had previously raised a company at Wollaston and had also been Administrative Assistant to Lt.-Col. H. G. Sotheby, M.V.O., D.S.O., in 1940. To his hard work and efficiency the Battalion was greatly indebted. Capt. F. D. Forge came later as Quartermaster, and both these officers remained with the Battalion until the Stand Down.

### DEFENCE OF RIVER CROSSINGS

The 7th's operational area was defined to embrace Wellingborough, Irthlingborough, Finedon, and neighbouring villages.

The boundary swept south of Burton Latimer from Isham to the road junction west of Woodford House, thence north of Great Addington to the Nene and up the line of the river to Irthlingborough railway station, where there was a bridgehead on the south side; on to Ditchford Mill and Chester House. From Chester House there was a larger bridgehead of from 1- to 1½-mile radius round Little Irchester. Crossing the river, the line ran almost due West, excluding Great Doddington but including Wilby, then half-way to Mears Ashby and north-west to Sywell Wood. From here it followed the Northampton-Kettering Road to Badsaddle Wood and back between Orlingbury and Pytchley to Isham.

In 1942, the Ditchford bridgehead became the responsibility of the 8th Battalion and in 1943 the 7th took in Mears Ashby. In 1944, when railway communications became one of the special cares of the Home Guard, the viaduct across the Nene at Chester House was also taken over by the 7th from the 8th Battalion.

The strategic role of the Battalion in the early stages was mainly concerned with the defence of the river crossings at Wellingborough and Irthlingborough, the former on the military route from Northampton to Cambridge and the latter carrying "A.6" the London-Leicester road across the Nene.

The railwaymen had their own special job, which was to guard their traffic control centre. This was the chief of a number of "vulnerable points" for which the Battalion was responsible, controlling, as it did, all the rail traffic from Luton to just south of Leicester. There were also the Ultra Electric Works and the Inland Petrol Distribution Centre. At the former, where radio-location apparatus was assembled, many of the Home Guard were full-time and paid! The latter was considered sufficiently important for Command to issue special immobilization and disruption plans, and exercises were organized to test these.

In 1941 Wellingborough and Irthlingborough both became "Nodal Points", with the Battalion Commander and Major T. R. Curtis (O.C. D Company) as respective "Town Commanders". Incidentally, this title was superseded after a few months by that of "Senior Military Representative", in which capacity many Home Guard commanders up and down the country sat on invasion committees.

The Battalion also undertook, in 1941, and again in 1944, responsibility for reinforcing, if necessary, the defence of Sywell aerodrome.

## WELL OFF THE MARK!

Early in its career, the 7th earned the special commendation of the County Commander for the manner in which it turned out on an alarm raised about parachutists, which afterwards turned out to be false.

Again, early in August 1940, when the Battalion had scarcely "found its feet", inter-platoon competitions had already been started at Battalion Headquarters (in those days the School), in which such primary training items as drill, musketry, grenade throwing, landscape targets, stalking, and observation were included.

To one of these, Major-Gen. Sir Hereward Wake brought Brig.-Gen. Paynter of the North Central Sub-District staff. As a result, East Midland District asked for a similar demonstration for Sir Ronald Adam, the Army Commander, who came along on 5 January 1941 and witnessed the competition. He afterwards sent along a congratulatory note.

The visit was followed shortly afterwards by another from the then Director-General of the Home Guard (Lord Bridgeman), who also sent warm congratulations.

Finally, close on the heels of these "shows" came a request from East Central District to the Battalion to put on a demonstration of a village ambush for the Army Command in the neighbourhood. This was done early in 1941 and was attended by many officers.

## MINERS DEVISE ANTI-TANK WEAPONS

A word should here be said of the pioneers of the 7th Battalion. The Company raised in June 1940 by Mr. R. R. Partridge, an ex-Welsh rugger international, at the Wellingborough Iron Company's Thingdon Mines (near Finedon) consisted mainly of miners accustomed in their daily work to the use of explosives.

In magazines surrounding the mines

were large quantities of explosive, detonator, and fuse, much of which Mr. Partridge had been instructed to sink in flooded pits should the enemy come his way. Mr. Partridge did not like the idea at all.

His son, Mr. J. R. Partridge, an engineer, was also keen on putting the explosive to better use, and father and son soon interested their Group Commander, Capt. H. L. Allsopp, himself a scientist. Selected miners, therefore, and specialists from various parts of the Group, of whom Mr. F. Gardner, an automobile engineer, of Isham, and Mr. J. Shirley, of the Eastern Coach Works at Irthlingborough, together with electricians, draughtsmen, and other specialists, devised and constructed a number of anti-tank weapons, which attracted the attention first of Lt.-Col. Sotheby, then Sir Hereward Wake and Gen. Paynter of North Midland Area H.Q. As a result of this a War Office representative came down and watched some of the earlier demonstrations and made further suggestions.

From the first it was regarded as essential that the weapons and their users should be inconspicuous yet certain in action. In August 1940 the first completed weapons were demonstrated to Sir Hereward Wake and Col. Sotheby, and subsequently to zone and other group and battalion commanders.

During the next twelve months some twenty-four different methods of crippling tanks and destroying other motor vehicles were demonstrated. These varied from simple mines laid or drawn across the road, rather like white mice on fishing lines, to the flying mine and a push gun, which, hidden in batteries by the roadside, fired R.E. mines on trolleys or through the air at the wheels of passing vehicles.

Although intended as a short-range weapon, the guns were found capable of firing with reasonable accuracy for distances up to 180 yards. The main advantage was that they could be fired electrically from a distance limited only by the length of cable available and the horizon of the mobile squads which had prepared the traps. Several squads of pioneers were trained and in practice were known to set a trap and be in position for firing within a matter of thirty seconds.

In some cases the mines or guns were automatically detonated by the vehicles themselves, and the Eastern Coach Works squads made a large target which could be towed by a car for practice. The last general demonstrations of the weapons were attended by Col. P. Lester Reid, Zone Commander, and Col. Forrestier Walker, Sub-Area Commander (Bedford), in July and August 1941, when officers from surrounding counties as well as Northamptonshire were also present.

The representatives of the Corby Battalion may still remember one of their trucks, loaned in the absence of the lorry promised by the local regular troops, which was unintentionally damaged when the switch was set for a "near miss" which proved too near.

On Sunday morning exercises, with regular troops employing A.F.V.s, during the next two years, these devices were always judged to have been successful, and the enthusiasm and standard of training, both technical and tactical, attained by the pioneers was undoubtedly high. The pioneers subsequently took over the push guns, of which the Battalion at one time had fifty-seven, and the fougasses, and in 1942 marked out the mine-fields incorporated in the Battalion defence plans.

Unfortunately for the 7th, the work of Lt. Partridge came to the notice of a battalion commander in Worcestershire who offered him a post in his business of a nature which appealed and Lt. Partridge left to develop the Landmine Department in that Battalion. The 7th received *no*, repeat *no*, transfer fee. Fortunately, his deputy, Sgt. D. J. Evans, who was promoted to take charge of the pioneers, was an enthusiast and the good work went on. After 1941, unauthorized experiments were discouraged by higher commands, but the push-gun squads continued their work and, in 1944, when C.D. rescue and demolition parties were enrolled for work farther afield, Lt. Evans took parties to a C.D. course for training in what had originally been C.D. work and they were very highly commended on their performance. The pioneers also did good work in excavating among the ruined H.Q. and stores after the bomb incident in 1942.

The 7th Battalion signallers, under Lt. A. J. Linnell of Wilby, were early off the mark, and by September of 1940 many had already passed classification tests in Morse and procedure, a code being used which Lt. Linnell invented himself.

By mounting a large variety of signalling lamps, some borrowed from the O.T.C., others of a pattern which he originated, whereby a long tube narrowed down the beam, communications between Wellingborough, Orlingbury, Finedon, and Irthlingborough, as well as all the villages, were soon opened up. For internal working between Town H.Q. and O.P. on the outskirts, he procured literally miles of wire, and with home-made buzzer sets and telephones linked up the whole Battalion. Naturally, his services were in wide demand, both in his own and neighbouring battalions.

The dispatch riders, who originally worked direct under the Battalion Commander through R.S.M. Mason, and the pigeons, first procured by R.Q.M.S.

Boddington and fed and housed by him, were eventually also Lt. Linnell's responsibility, and were used on many occasions during the next four years.

Police permission had to be obtained to use the lamps in 1940, and to ensure that these could be rapidly aligned on the various terminals to which messages were to be sent, they were mounted on fixed tripods, permanent holes being made in concrete for the legs, in some cases two or three sets of holes at one station. Such a large organization made great demands on the man-power of the various companies, so by 1942 it had become the practice to use girls for indoor operational work and set free men for the outdoor and linesmen's duties.

The O.T.C. wireless was also used on schemes, sometimes by cadets but more often by the Battalion signallers. Lt. Linnell was also a keen member of the Sywell Aero Club and made efforts in the early months to obtain permission to fly in his own aircraft over the Battalion defence works to inspect the efficiency of their camouflage, but permission was not granted and the help of Service airmen had to be sought for the purpose.

### RE-FORMATION OF THE 8TH BATTALION

With the re-formation of the 8th (Wellingborough District) Battalion, Lt.-Col. Sotheby retired from the command in favour of Lt.-Col V. H. Sykes, M.A., Ll.B.

Capt. Sykes, as he was then, had previously commanded A Company, a post in which he was succeeded by Capt. Freer, who, in turn, following his keenly regretted sudden death, was succeeded by Major W. M. Horrell.

Lt.-Col. Sykes enlisted in the Middlesex Regiment as a private in 1908 on the formation of the Territorial Army and, following the outbreak of the 1914–18 war, went overseas on 3 September 1914, to serve in France and Belgium. He was commissioned in the field to a regular commission in the Sherwood Foresters and was severely wounded at Ypres. In the last year of the war he served with the Machine-Gun Corps and retired with the rank of Captain in 1919.

Lt.-Col. V. H. Sykes.

As president of Raunds Branch of the British Legion since its formation, he organized and led several ex-Servicemen's pilgrimages to France and Belgium.

Prior to recruiting for and transferring to the Home Guard on its foundation, Lt.-Col. Sykes served as Chief A.R.P. Warden of Raunds and district.

He also helped to recruit the 4th Battalion of the Northamptonshire Regiment prior to the 1939–45 war.

Major R. K. Green was Second-in-Command. Capt. Attley, Capt. J. H. Banks, Capt. Whyte, and Capt. Davis in turn served as Battalion Adjutants, with Capt. A. J. Pond as Quartermaster.

It is interesting to note here that the notice board used by A Company at Raunds formerly belonged to the local company of the 4th Northants Regiment, and was carried by them in Egypt, Gallipoli, and Palestine.

A Company also used the Drill Hall which was formerly used by a local company of "Terriers" prior to their proceeding overseas.

The Battalion area covered sixty-two square miles and extended from Ringstead in the north to Grendon and Bozeat in the south—a distance of sixteen miles and including eighteen parishes.

Headquarters were based on Rushden.

In addition to the usual Home Guard duties the 8th Battalion was charged with the special defence of Chelveston aerodrome.

The 8th Battalion company commanders were as follows:

A Company, Major W. M. Horrell, Headquarters at Raunds; B Company, Major A. D. Denton, Headquarters, Lovell's Factory, Rushden; C Company, Major J. C. Richardson, Headquarters, Fox and Hounds, Earls Barton; D Company, Major A. C. Pyrah, Headquarters, Botterill and Sons, London Road, Bozeat; E Company, Major A. Allebone, Headquarters at Swindalls, Station Road, Rushden; F Company, Major P. W. Bletsoe, Headquarters at the Town Hall, Higham Ferrers; and G Company, Major S. T. Reynolds, Headquarters at the Baptist School Room, Wollaston.

The specialist officers were: Medical Officer, Major R. W. Davis (Rushden); Chief Guide, Capt. S. R. Fox (Rushden) (Capt. Fox obtained a direct commission to the Regular Army in June 1943); Ammunition Officer, Lt. J. R. Biddle (Irchester);

Transport Officer, Capt. F. E. Brown (Rushden); Intelligence Officer, Lt. W. J. Wells (Higham Ferrers); Signals Officer, Lt. H. E. Allen (Rushden); Gas Officer, 2nd Lt. F. G. Beasley (Wollaston); Weapon Training Officer, Lt. A. G. Rogers (Wollaston); P.A.D. Officer, Lt. A. F. Weale (Rushden); Assistant Adjutant and Quartermaster, Lt. P. G. Whitney (Raunds); P.D.O. Officer, Lt. A. Warren; Camouflage Officer, 2nd Lt. J. A. Stokes.

## 9TH BATTALION'S DIFFICULT COUNTRY

The 9th (Brixworth District) Battalion Officer, Lt.-Col. G. S. Watson (Moulton), re-formed under its original Commanding Officer with Major R. Dickens (Billing Arbours) as Second-in-Command.

Headquarters were now located at the Drill Hall, Clare Street, Northampton, and Action Headquarters at the Rural District offices, Brixworth.

It was on 14 March 1941 that Capt. C. C. Oakey, M.C., was appointed Adjutant, and he remained with the Battalion until the final Stand Down.

Capt. G. D. Spriddell was Adjutant and Quartermaster.

The Battalion records also note that Miss P. Roberts came as the sole typist on 3 March 1941 and remained in this post until June 1945.

The 9th's company commanders were as follows:

A Company, Lt.-Col. G. Middleton (Boughton), Headquarters at Ward Arms, Guilsborough; B Company, Major J. D. Houison-Crauford (Chapel Brampton), Headquarters at R.D.C. offices, Brixworth; C. Company, Capt. Guy Lankester (Harlestone), Headquarters at Old Chapel, Harlestone; D Company, Capt. J. T. H. Pettitt (Overstone), Headquarters, Spendlove's Cottage, Moulton; and E Company (formed later), Major C. M. Newton (Overstone), with Headquarters at Sywell aerodrome.

Specialist officers were: Medical Officer, Major J. P. Traylen, M.C. (Northampton); Intelligence Officer, Lt. H. C. Palmer (Church Brampton); Transport Officer, Lt. F. W. Lang (Pitsford); Ammunition Officer, 2nd Lt. E. H. Smith (Moulton); and Signals Officer, Lt. P. G. Griffiths (Brixworth).

The terrain covered by the 9th Battalion was rich in parks and grassland, with many undulations, and threaded by many streams and rivers. These otherwise idyllic features had their potential dangers, however, for there were many places within the Battalion boundaries which could have provided concentration areas for parachute troops, or for the landing of gliders. The streams were barely sufficient to deter enemy light armoured vehicles, still less tanks.

The Battalion area was almost in the centre of England, and its most vulnerable flank was its eastern boundary, which was within seventy-five miles of the Wash.

It was intersected by main roads which fanned out from Northampton to Kettering, Market Harborough and Rugby, and by the Market Harborough-Northampton railway line which runs from north to south through the area. The Rugby-Northampton line cut through its south-west corner.

In addition to the ordinary defended localities, responsibility for guarding special danger points was distributed among the companies, e.g., Hollowell and Ravensthorpe reservoirs were the special care of A Company, and the river bridge at Brampton crossing was that of C Company. E Company would have had a particularly exacting task if the test had come, for they were due to co-operate with the Royal Air

Force station command in the defence of Sywell aerodrome.

The Battalions flanking the 9th were the 12th, the 8th, and the 11th.

Operations instructions issued by Battalion Headquarters were models of comprehension and foresight. Information and orders alike were as exhaustive as they were concise.

## LAMPORT'S LOCKED CHURCH

In connection with the instructions for the use of church bells for alarm purposes, the Battalion records contain an amusing cutting from a national newspaper regarding the locking up of Lamport Parish Church to prevent access to the bells by fifth columnists.

This simple and necessary precaution called forth a pontifical rebuke from the *Church Times*, which remarked that it was "like killing a pig for the sake of the ring in its nose"!

Here it may be remarked that cathedral towers were not included in the alarm scheme, Northern Command having issued the following letter in July 1940:

At the request of His Grace the Archbishop of Canterbury, the permission to use church towers for observation and inter-communication will NOT be applied to cathedrals. Towers or other portions of cathedrals will NOT be used for any military purpose.

Thus Peterborough Cathedral never went into war service in this respect beside its humble parish church neighbours.

## 10TH HAD BROADCASTING STATION AND ORDNANCE WORKS

In the Daventry area what was eventually to become the 10th (Daventry District) Battalion was originally commanded by Lt.-Col. G. R. D. Shaw of Whilton Lodge, Rugby.

Later he was succeeded by Lt.-Col.

G. W. M. Lees, Falcutt House, near Brackley, who had as his Second-in-Command Major P. L. Ransom, Winwick Warren, West Haddon, with Capt. P. H. Tye and Capt. P. Bradley as his Adjutant and Adjutant and Quartermaster respectively.

Lt.-Col. Lees joined the 17th Lancers in 1913 and served in France from 1914 to the end of the 1914–18 war and was in Germany from 1918 to 1920.

Leaving the Lancers, he joined the Northamptonshire Yeomanry Armoured Car Company as Captain in 1921 and served with them for seven years.

Lt.-Col. G. W. M. Lees.

There were five companies in the 10th Battalion and a British Broadcasting Corporation Company at the broadcasting station at Borough Hill, Daventry.

The companies, their commanders, and headquarters were as follows: A, Major E. B. Forwood (Rugby), George Hotel, Kilsby; B, Major T. C. Goodwin (Daventry,) Wheatsheaf Hotel, Daventry; C, Major T. C. Underwood (Long Buckby), Church School, Long Buckby; D, Major T. Coy (Hinton), Church Institute, Byfield; E, Major H. Draper (Flore), Romer Arms, Newnham; and the B.B.C. Company, Capt. F. J. Cooper (Daventry), Borough Hill, Daventry.

The specialist officers were as follows:

Medical Officer, Major W. A. Clements (Daventry); Chief Guide, Capt. P. H. Wykeham, M.C. (West Haddon); Intelligence Officer, Lt. A. Dommett (Daventry); Signals Officer, Lt. C. H. Parsons (Daventry); Transport Officer, 2nd Lt. A. P. Shepherd (Badby); Ammunition Officer, Lt. H. Field (West Haddon); and Gas Officer, Lt. G. W. Pardo (Flore).

Battalion Headquarters were at Badby House.

The operational area of the 10th Battalion was essentially rural, and was spread over a large part of the most "countrified" terrain in the county.

Rolling fields, dotted with woods and spinneys, filled the whole horizon.

Altogether the 10th carried responsibilities as heavy as they were exacting in point of the duty and training necessary to discharge them with credit. This the 10th certainly did as later events showed.

### 11TH BATTALION'S "HORSESHOE" AREA

The battalion organization of the 11th

Members of the 10th (Daventry) Battalion, provided a Guard of Honour at the opening of the Borough's Warship Week in February 1940.

It also included, however, such important places as the Borough of Daventry, the railway junction at Woodford, and the immense Ordnance Depot at Weedon—the latter enlarged beyond all previous recognition by the demands of war.

There were several extremely important vulnerable points which had to be guarded and defended, including the B.B.C. station on Borough Hill, Daventry, and the vitally essential tunnels on the L.M.S. main line at Kilsby and Catesby.

The whole area lay within a perimeter which, on the north-west and west, touched the counties of Leicestershire and Warwickshire, and on the south and east ran along a line from Woodford, through Weedon, Long Buckby, and West Haddon to Stanford.

(Hardingstone District) Battalion was carried out under its original district commander, Lt.-Col. A. J. Fraser (Hardingstone) who, assisted by the Marquess of Northampton, first recruited the district L.D.V. from twenty-five villages over a wide area forming a "horseshoe", enclosing a large portion of the eastern, and the whole of the southern and another large portion of the western boundaries of Northampton —quite one of the most difficult operational areas to plan strategically in the county.

Lt.-Col. Fraser paid high tribute to all who made both the original and battalion organization as readily possible as it was.

He recorded that both processes took many evenings' work attending meetings throughout the area, but he said:

Everywhere I went I met with nothing but

keenness to assist in every possible way. The companies were soon formed and I had no difficulty in selecting suitable company commanders in whom I had every confidence. My confidence was not misplaced, for a more conscientious, keen lot of men, performing duties voluntarily undertaken, you could not have found.

Having formed the companies, I then had to arrange for training, which, it must be remembered, could only be undertaken after work in the evenings, Saturday afternoons, and Sundays.

I have to thank the Infantry Training Centre, Northampton [added Col. Fraser] for very valuable assistance they gave me—assistance which evoked the keenest appreciation of many of my officers who were also indebted for the courteous treatment and useful instruction given them by Lt.-Col. A. St. G. Coldwell (Commanding Officer) and the Infantry Training Centre staff.

This appreciation, so well expressed by Col. Fraser, was shared by all battalions in the I.T.C. area. Whether it was a matter of combining in exercises, lending equipment, or laying on specialist and general courses for officers and N.C.O.s, Col. Coldwell and his staff, notably Capt. Arthur, were ever patiently ready, and cheerfully willing to oblige, and placed the whole available resources of the Centre at the Home Guard's disposal.

Lt.-Col.
W. J. Penn.

Later, with the introduction of the age limit, Lt.-Col. Fraser relinquished his command in favour of Lt.-Col. W. J. Penn of the Manor House, who served in the 1914–18 war as captain and adjutant in the South Wales Border Regiment. Lt.-Col. Penn had as his second-in-command Major H. Marland, then of Parkfield Avenue, Northampton.

The Adjutant was Capt. G. B. Godson, and administrative and quartermaster duties were carried out by Capt. J. T. Stone.

There were six companies, whose commanders and headquarters were as follows:

A, Major H. Hawkins (Weston Favell), Pearces Factory, Billing Park; B, Major J. R. Wilson (Preston Deanery), Yew Tree Cottage, Roade; C, Major P. E. Coles (Duston), The Church Schools, Duston; D, Major A. H. Butlin (Whiston), The Castle, Yardley Hastings; E, Headquarters Company at Hardingstone House, Northampton; and F, Major W. G. Smith (Kislingbury), The Schools, Kislingbury.

The specialist officers were:

Medical Officer, Major R. P. White (Bugbrooke); Intelligence Officer, Lt. W. C. Thomson (Northampton); Weapon Training Officer, Lt. C. Jones, M.C. (Castle Ashby); Transport Officer, Lt. J. T. Padbury (Great Billing); Bombing Officer, 2nd Lt. W. E. Revell (Duston); Ammunition Officer, Lt. C. F. Tilley (Northampton); Gas Officer, Lt. J. H. Spencer (Great Billing); and Camouflage Officer, Lt. H. H. Jones (Northampton).

### SECRET STORES IN FOREST

The primary vulnerable points in the 11th's area were No. 72 Maintenance Unit of the Royal Air Force in Salcey Forest (B Company's area), where were hidden and stored vast and priceless quantities of high-priority war materials; No. 21 V.R.D., Castle Ashby (D Company's area), a very large vehicle replacement and maintenance park; an essential landing ground at Denton (B Company's area) and, among communication responsibilities, the L.M.S. tunnel at Blisworth, and the Watling Street main road in F Company's area.

Indication of the far-flung area of the 11th is provided by its flanking battalions, which included the 12th and 15th (North-ampton), the 9th (Brixworth), the 7th (Wellingborough), the 8th (Wellingborough District), the 10th (Daventry), the 13th (Towcester), and even the 2nd Bucks!

## 12TH BATTALION REMOVES TO T.A.A. HEADQUARTERS

In the county town the re-formation into a battalion was rapidly effected with new and far more commodious headquarters at the Drill Hall, Clare Street, and with Major Manning remaining as officer commanding. The following officers were in the battalion command. (Note: Several of these appointments were made subsequently but are included here for readier reference.) Officers are of Northampton unless otherwise shown in parentheses. Company Headquarters are also shown in parentheses.

Second-in-Command, Major H. St. J. Browne, M.C., T.D.; Adjutant, Capt. H. D. Barton, M.C.; Administrative Officer and Quartermaster, Capt. A. W. Gardner.

A Company, Major P. Hutton (Horton) (21 Abington Grove); B, Major A. McFarlane (Warwick Arms, Bridge Street); C, Major A. G. R. Barton (Town and County School, Billing Road); F, Major A. S. Baxter (Drill Hall, Northampton); G, Major S. B. Patrick (The Barracks); H, Capt. R. B. Armitt (Drill Hall, Clare Street); 2001 (NN) M.T. Company, Major J. H. Mills (United Counties Omnibus Co., Houghton Road).

Specialist officers were: Medical Officer, Major G. H. Thompson; Intelligence Officer, Lt. A. C. Payne; Weapon Training Officer, Lt. V. J. H. Harris; Transport Officer, Lt. C. S. Catlow; Ammunition Officer, Lt. C. G. B. Allison; Signals Officer, Lt. G. A. White; Gas Officer, 2nd Lt. H. Allatt; and Camouflage Officer, 2nd Lt. F. Wood.

A vivid summary of the 12th's vulnerable points and the guarding and manning of them is recorded by Lt.-Col. L. E. Barnes in his *History of the 12th Battalion*. He writes:

It was clear that had invasion of this country taken place, some buildings, factories, and works of national importance would have been among the first objectives of the Germans.

In all their invasions of foreign countries, the Germans were not chiefly interested in the killing of soldiers, but their technique consisted mainly in destroying the nerves of the man or woman in the street. Among their efforts in this direction was the destruction of the means that affected the life of the inhabitants—water, light, railways, communications, etc. It was therefore essential that these should be denied to the enemy, and these were listed as vulnerable points.

Attacks on vulnerable points could take several different forms:

(1) Destructive raid carried out by enemy troops landed from the air.
(2) Smash-and-grab raid carried out by enemy troops landed from the air.
(3) Armed sabotage. Carried out by small organized parties who might already be in the country.
(4) Petty sabotage by individual agents already in the country, who would rely more on cunning and stealth rather than force, and which might take the form of stealing documents or obtaining secret information.

Against all these forms of attack we had to be prepared. On some of these vulnerable points it was necessary to have continuous guards, while on others they were only needed on "Action Stations".

Denial of petrol was of paramount importance, especially as there were personnel who were trained in the disruption and, at the last resort, demolition of these stores of petrol, which totalled some quarter of a million gallons. If the depots appeared likely to fall into the hands of the enemy they were to be blown up, and this entailed the training of men in the use of explosives, together with the arrangement of the various detonators. A special squad of men from E Company were detailed for this particular job. The Chief Constable (Mr. John Williamson, O.B.E.) and the Police Force undertook the destruction of the petrol pumps situated in the different parts of the town.

In 1940 we had guards on the following Vulnerable Points:

Northampton Electric Light Works.
Northampton Gas Works.
Post Office.
Express Lift Works.
Northampton Wireless Relay Station.
L.M.S. Railway Bridges, etc.
Northampton Transport Depot.
United Counties Omnibus Station.
Water Department—
    At Ravensthorpe.
    Main Pumping Station, Stimpson Avenue.
    Boughton Reservoir.
    Pumping Station, Billing Road.
B.B.C. Transmitter Station.
Various works on munitions in the town.

On a number of these it was not necessary to have a continuous night guard, for in some of the works men were working day and night shifts, and while work was being carried on there was no danger of sabotage; guards were only needed when the works and machinery were left unattended. On the railway the vulnerable points were not actually manned, but a nucleus of men were on duty at the Guard Room to proceed to any threatened point. In the case of the Wireless Relay, a guard of one N.C.O. and three men were to mount on "Action Stations", and the N.C.O. was empowered to give instructions to the staff to immobilize the station if it was in imminent danger of capture.

In addition a guard was mounted at the Drill Hall when the Regulars were not in residence there; while there was an armoury guard over Platoon Headquarters each night where more than thirty rifles were kept.

No one who was on duty at the Sub-Ordnance Depot at Martin's Yard will ever forget the experience. The old D Company began this guard on 25 November 1940, and on arrival found their quarters consisted of a hut with a cold concrete floor, very hard to attempt to sleep on, and with holes in the roof through which the wind whistled and the rain descended. Representations were made to the Ordnance authorities at Weedon that it was unfair to ask men who had to work the next day to spend their nights in such a "guard room", and after a short lapse the roof was repaired, a coke fire was provided, the concrete floor covered with boards, and "beds" fitted.

## FINE BODY OF D.R.s

No other battalion in the Zone will here begrudge a special mention of the 12th Battalion's H.Q. Dispatch Riders and a digression to relate their history in complete form.

The 12th's D.R.s were "born" in the battalion in May 1940.

About twenty riders who had machines of their own were selected from the Northampton Division and became the H.Q. D.R.s, and were put under the command of Mr. (later Lt.) A. C. Payne, an old motor cycle trials rider.

As these were the only D.R.s in the county in the early days, they came under the direct control of Major-Gen. Sir Hereward Wake, the Zone Commander, to whom they reported on "Actions Stations", and their area of operations was the whole county.

This entailed journeys to places as far apart as Peterborough in the north-east to Thorpe Mandeville in the south-west, and all the divisional and group H.Q.s were visited.

In September 1940 instructions were received to report to the I.T.C. at the Barracks, Northampton, on "Action Stations" and the area of activity was reduced to cover what were then the Wellingborough Town, Wellingborough District,

Harlestone, Brixworth, and Northampton battalions.

Later still the area was further reduced but the 12th Battalion D.R.s were always in demand by higher units and other battalions, and never was their assistance refused.

The closest co-operation was maintained with Zone E.C.D. at Dunstable, Sub-District at Bedford, and later Sub-Area and Sub-District Northampton and help was given to many other battalions. Training was also undertaken with the 9th Armoured Division D.R.s when this Regular division was stationed in the district.

To many the D.R.s were only known as the riders who led the 12th Battalion on their various parades and who rode whilst others marched, but this was only a very small part of their training, for the job they might have to do was often arduous and trying.

Lt. A. C. Payne, later 12th I.O., decided that the training should be divided into three categories:

(1)  To make them better riders.
(2)  To train riders to know the town and neighbouring country thoroughly.
(3)  To train the section to defend themselves efficiently.

All had their own machines, but many, like the average pre-war rider, were fair weather or main road motorists. They had to be trained to ride in all weathers and on all sorts of roads and tracks and to that end journeys were frequently made in rain or fog, rides were planned in muddy lanes, through watersplashes, and in the dark with only dimmed lights, and riders who could ride under these conditions could ride under any conditions.

In the early days the riding equipment was nil but, gradually, good waterproof riding suits were obtained together with crash helmets, goggles and gauntlet gloves. All the riders were supplied with 1 in. and $\frac{1}{4}$ in. Ordnance maps of all their districts besides having road maps of the town. They were all able to do ordinary running repairs while some were very experienced mechanics. Precautions were taken so that machines could be quickly immobilized.

Four W.D. motor cycles were issued in 1941. They were side valve 350 c.c. Royal Enfields, but were in extremely poor condition, and eventually were replaced by three O.H.V. 350 c.c. Royal Enfields, which were much better. When no petrol was available for civilian motor cyclists the riders were issued with "G" licences for their machines, and although never having too much petrol they always had enough for their training, and for this thanks were due to the Zone Commander, Col. Lester Reid, who always maintained a keen interest in the D.R.s.

### THE "PATHFINDERS"

Many communication tests were held and, in all, the D.R.s came through with flying colours. Whilst map reading was important it was always found that actual knowledge of route proved quicker and to that end riders had to know all the likely places they might have to visit and all H.Q., D.L.s, O.P.s, railway stations, important bridges and dumps in their area were frequently visited, and the D.R.s probably had a greater and more up-to-date knowledge of the disposition of troops in the district than any other body. The absence of road-signs, removed for war security, made route finding more difficult, but it had the advantage of making riders more self-reliant. No H.Q. were provided at first but later H.Q. were found at 127, Great Russell Street, just opposite to the Drill Hall, and later a move was made to larger premises at 10, Hunter Street.

DON R'S HAVE THEIR USES

Under Battalion arrangements all the personnel did gas training, went through the gas chamber and had bombing instruction and threw bombs, and throughout their training frequent use was made of the miniature and open ranges. All also fired the Sten gun. In fact the D.R.s as individuals had more firing practice than anyone in the Battalion.

The D.R.s took part in all the big exercises in which the 12th Battalion participated and in many others, besides being loaned to the Sub-Area at Bedford, the I.T.C. Sector, and Sub-District and other neighbouring battalions, without ever once failing to deliver their messages, and without having a serious accident, a record of which they were justly proud.

D.R.s were on duty and slept at Battalion H.Q. from Exercise "Megrim" on 6 April 1945 till long after all Company H.Q. had ceased to be manned.

They also took part in two Home Guard Pageants at Franklin's Gardens, organized by E. Company, led the Battalion to the Northampton County Ground for special occasions and on to the Northampton Market Square for the final parade.

Their massed and trick riding on the County Ground and their Victory "V" will long be remembered by those who saw it.

Forty-nine served in the D.R.s, eight obtained commissions, which was a much higher proportion than in the rest of the Battalion, and two later gave their lives in the Services, Flt./Sgt. I. T. Clarke and Sub/Lt. S. Yarde.

No report of the D.R.s' activity would be complete without mention of Sgt. J. F. Stevens, who always led the D.R.s on parade and was the intelligence sergeant. His efficiency, steadiness and help to all D.R.s at all times was outstanding. He was granted a Certificate of Merit by the G.O.C. Eastern Command.

The three lance-corporals, L/Cpl. Smith, L/Cpl. Goff, L/Cpl. Devonshire, and earlier Cpls. Coker and Hawtin did much good work to make the D.R.s one of the happiest and most efficient bodies of Home Guardsmen in the Battalion.

In the words of the Signal Officer of the I.T.C., after an exercise in 1940, the D.R.s were "A very keen section, showing the utmost interest in their job".

## WHEN THEY LAUGHED

*Conceited young Home Guard: "It's a fact. People often take me for a member of the Guards."*

*Bored Companion: "Really! Which?—fire or mud?"*

# Chapter IX

## THE BATTALIONS REVIEWED (3)

PREVIOUS mention has been made of Northampton's Post Office Home Guard unit.

On the formation of Post Office battalions of the Home Guard this company was transferred to the 24th Post Office Battalion, known as 47th Warwickshire (24th Post Office) Battalion, Home Guard.

The Regional Headquarters of the Northampton Post Office being at Birmingham, the Battalion Headquarters was in that city and the Northampton Company thus became E Company of the 13th Leicester Battalion.

Major W. R. Morton continued as Company Commander with Lt. J. S. Duke (also acting as Weapon Training Officer) as his second-in-command, and both continued to hold these posts up to the Stand Down.

The Post Office Home Guard had been formed in view of the many special problems associated with Post Office employees in L.D.V. units.

Training was on similar lines to that of non-Post Office battalions, but special attention was paid to the protection of Post Office buildings and of telephone systems and plant, etc.

Other duties included the arming of telephone repair workers when necessary, the provision of guards for Post Office vehicles on rural journeys when required, and the guarding of vital points in the main north-south telephone system passing through the district.

Certain essential workers were earmarked as men not to be released for Home Guard duties until the last moment. These men wore blue and white flashes on their battle-dress sleeves.

Officers of this company included: Intelligence Officer, Lt. W. J. Dean (also Platoon Commander); Quartermaster, Lt. S. C. C. Boyce (also Platoon Commander); Lts. F. D. Browett, J. T. Jeffery, O. E. Butcher, A. J. L. Knights, and H. Underwood.

The P.O.H.G. were also instructed to provide signals officers at Formation H.Q. where required; to be responsible for organizing *all* means of communication available in addition to the P.O. telephone system. Thus, Lt. W. J. Dean was appointed to Northants Sub-District. Lt. A. J. L. Knights to No. 2 Sector, Northants S/D (this officer was killed in a cycle accident on 29 September 1944), and Sgt. C. H. Parsons was transferred to 10th (Daventry) Battalion and commissioned as Signal Officer to that Battalion. A signal section was also trained by Lt. Dean to assist Northants S/D in emergency.

### 13TH BATTALION HAD SILVERSTONE AERODROME

Now separated from the Brackley District, Towcester's Home Guard became the 13th (Towcester District) Battalion, with Lt.-Col. P. Y. Atkinson (Cosgrove) as Battalion Commander, with Battalion Headquarters at the Territorial Club, High Street, Towcester, and Battle Headquarters at Paulerspury.

During the 1914–18 war, Lt.-Col. Atkinson served with the 5th Dragoon Guards, attaining Captain's rank and the award of the Military Cross for gallantry.

His battalion officers were as follows: Second-in-Command, Major R. Wyndham Lewis M.C. (Slapton); Adjutant, Capt. E. Lewin (Paulerspury); A. and Q., Capt. W. E. Wetherall (Northampton). A Company, Major J. C. Grant-Ives (Bradden), Company Headquarters at Blakesley; B, Major H. Pebody, M.M. (Milton), Headquarters at Blisworth; C, Major W. G. T. Griffin (Towcester), Headquarters at the Pomfret Hotel,

Lt.-Col. P. Y. Atkinson.

Manor); and Signals Officer, Lt. M. W. G. Chitty (Caswell).

The 13th's area totalled roughly 150 square miles. It was bounded on the north by Milton, the boundary running west to Pattershall, Lichborough, and south to Maidford, Canons Ashby, and Astwell Mill, then east through the Crown Lands at Silverstone and Luffield Abbey, leaving Silverstone and Whittlebury well within the battalion area.

South-east it ran to the River Ouse at Thornton, following the river north-east through Passenham, thence across Watling Street at Old Stratford (east of Cosgrove),

13th (Towcester) Battalion units marching past the Director-General, Viscount Bridgeman, in October 1941. The officer in centre is Lt. Sacheverell Sitwell.

Towcester; and D Company, Major J. N. Beasley, M.C. (Stony Stratford), with Headquarters at Wood's Farm, Potterspury.

The 13th's specialist officers were: Medical Officer, Major A. E. Reid (Paulerspury); Chief Guide, Capt. R. N. Beasley (Potterspury); Intelligence Officer, Lt. G. R. Roberts (Towcester); Ammunition Officer, Lt. S. P. Tyzack (Paulerspury); Gas Officer, Lt. N. C. Moore (Plumpton); Transport Officer, Lt. F. J. Snelson (Towcester); Contact Officer, Lt. The Lord Hillingdon (Grafton Regis

then north via Yardley Gobion to Bosenham Mill, and Stoke Bruerne, thence to Milton.

No battalion had more exacting responsibilities than the 13th, for it was *entirely* responsible for guarding the immense aerodrome at Silverstone.

The lines of communication it had to keep open and its V.P.s were also highly important, for the Watling Street ran north to south through the centre of the battalion area, together with a long and essential stretch of the L.M.S. railway with many bridges on the line.

## THE WIDELY DISPERSED 14TH BATTALION

Following the Brackley District's division from Towcester, Brackley became the 14th Battalion. For a few months, the Battalion was commanded by Brig. W. Allason, D.S.O., of Chacombe, who then relinquished his command in favour of Lt.-Col. Noel C. Furlong (Marston St. Lawrence), who had previously formed A Company and served as its company commander.

Headquarters were sited at 20 St. Peter's Road, Brackley, and the battalion officers were as follows:

Adjutants, Mr. Sitwell, succeeded by Capt. C. Rickett, succeeded by Major Dermot McCalmont, M.C., succeeded by Capt. G. F. Firmin of Charlton; A. and Q. Capt. A. Turner of Brackley. The companies were as follows: Major E. L. Donner (Sulgrave), Headquarters at Thenford House, Thenford; B, Major E. Lassen, succeeded in 1943 by Major R. T. I. Law (Brackley), with Headquarters at 7 High Street, Brackley; C, Major G. L. Guinness (Banbury), with Headquarters at Astrop Hill Farm, Banbury; D, Major J. F. Blakison, C.I.E. (Syresham), with Headquarters at The Grove, Syresham; and E Company, Major F. C. Kench (Eydon), with Headquarters at Wayside, Eydon.

Specialist officers were: Medical Officer, Major G. N. Stather (Brackley); Transport Officer, Lt. E. B. Langdon (Brackley); Signals Officer, Lt. E. Belcher (Overthorpe); Camouflage Officer, Lt. G. D. Draycott (Brackley); Gas Officer, Lt. G. E. F. Okell (Moreton Pinkney); and Ammunition Officer, Lt. V. H. V. Franklin (Evenley).

The 14th's first Administrative Assistant was the late Mr. Sidney Lassen. He put in wonderful self-sacrificing service in the early days. When the first regular adjutant was appointed, Mr. Lassen carried on in charge of the Battalion Headquarters office almost to the end. This, alas! he did not live to see for he died of heart failure while actually working in the office. Truly a case of a man who died doing his duty and at his post.

Like their fellow battalions, the 14th performed invaluable duty in 1940 when they manned observation posts throughout a district that was particularly ill provided in point of existing communications. Thus, one company was twelve miles from Battalion Headquarters.

Telephone contacts were often very difficult. In E Company's area there were two telephone districts and to speak to his nearest platoon the Company Commander had to place his call through Northampton and thence Banbury!

So widely dispersed were the Battalion's units that exercises on battalion scale were almost impossible. In case of emergency it would, in fact, have been a case of "Each sector for itself and the Lord help us all!"

The platoon commanders would have been the key men in such circumstances, and this was proved in the course of various exercises.

As might be expected in such a sparsely populated area, the 14th was the smallest battalion in the county, averaging a strength of nine hundred.

## MORE "PARACHUTISTS" AND "SABOTEURS"

Lt.-Col. Furlong recorded an exciting, if highly amusing, incident in the infancy of the 14th.

It began when on a summer afternoon in 1940 the police rang up to say that parachutists had been seen landing near Magpie Farm, Thorpe Mandeville, and requested the Battalion to turn out as soon as possible. After much excitement some forty men mustered and turned out on cycles, cars, lorries, etc., to search the whole country round the supposed landing. No Germans were found. The report had been started by a maid who, seeing some hay-cocks going up in a whirlwind, had rushed to the police with the news that the Germans had arrived!

Another lighter side story of the 14th concerns E Company, whose Commanding Officer, Major F. C. Kench, received one Saturday morning in 1940, prior to the issue of either uniforms or rifles, a message that two armed men had deserted from a troop train which had been stopped by a signal "out in the blue".

The men were said to be making for Eydon, and the local platoon commander and one or two others had set out in search.

Returning to the village later the patrol met the local constable, who informed them that the desperadoes had been found—and that while intensive search had been going on, the men were being regaled with eggs and bacon in a nearby cottage. They turned out to be men returned from Dunkirk, who were being sent out abroad again.

One of the 14th's best achievements was the building of its own rifle range on Lt. Chinner's farm at Chalcombe. It was a good 400-yard range and was the means of bringing the 14th's marksmanship to a high level.

## WHEN THEY LAUGHED

*They were taken to the range on the musketry course. They fired at 200 yards, but no one hit the target. They were tried next at 150 yards; still everyone missed. Then 50 yards was tried, and still all failed.*

*"Attention!" roared the W.T. Sergeant. "Fix bayonets! Now charge . . . it's your only chance!"*

## Chapter X

## THE ARMY WITHOUT A HOME

HAVING reviewed the battalion organization as it was conceived and set up in the summer of 1940, it is an essential duty of this history to place on record some details of the infinite ingenuity and resource which went to the discovery and adaptation of headquarters for all units, from battalion down to platoon and, in case of remote villages, to section level.

Paradoxically enough, in its earliest days, the Home Guard had no home at all of its own, not, at least, as a military force.

Even when it did eventually contrive to put roofs over its head it never achieved one hundred per cent comfort or convenience.

It is true that, in many cases, generous people placed at its disposal accommodation which, by comparison with others, might be termed palatial, but in the main the Northamptonshire Home Guard lived and had its being in places that ranged from loose boxes in hunting stables to empty (and derelict) houses in the back streets of towns.

It was not only a question of shelter for the headquarters of sections and platoons, companies or battalions. There was A. and Q. to be accommodated.

There were many orderly rooms which were quite unsuitable for coping with the "paper war" which, as the administrative staffs knew only too well, progressed on the snowball principle.

Many of these were in such places as the back kitchens of condemned cottages in the country, where mildew and mice vied for supremacy.

In environments such as these, and equipped with a few folding tables, some rickety chairs, a piece or two of dog-eared blotting-paper, and some pens and ink that were common property, orderly room staffs struggled with the insatiable demands for returns of this and that—and the quartermasters (who frequently shared the abode of the "back-room boys") interviewed those who had lost everything save their honour, and kept their meagre stores practically at their elbows.

Much accommodation was gained by requisitioning. Even so, the Home Guard had to have what was left over by the Regulars, who could hardly be blamed for taking their pick of the nice dry billets!

Nor was the Home Guard adequately catered for in the matter of Nissen and other huts, for in all the county only twenty-three huts were provided to serve as company and/or platoon offices and storerooms.

In the towns the personnel fared a little better. Such places as ex-Servicemen's clubs, schoolrooms, garages, drill halls, factory premises, and empty houses were requisitioned.

In the county areas the requisitioning included cellars, loose boxes, and saddle rooms for platoon and company stores.

At Badby House, for example, five rooms, four loose boxes, and a garage were requisitioned for the storage of small arms ammunition.

Chapel schoolrooms were put to secular use, while some units revelled in the luxuries of urban council premises.

A Company of the 2nd (Peterborough) Battalion used two rooms and a cellar for a company store in the Manor House at Ailsworth, while C Company had the billiards room at Dogsthorpe Manor as a platoon store. They certainly went in on the "cush" if not off it.

Meanwhile, B Company of the 2nd Battalion took possession of the gun room and a loose box at Uffington House, which afterwards was taken over by the 1st Polish Paratroop Brigade.

## DANCING ACADEMY AS COMPANY HEADQUARTERS

Some members of the 3rd (Oundle) Battalion appropriately occupied the Drill Hall at Thrapston, and were thus able to stretch themselves with comparative ease, while the 4th (Kettering) Battalion had the whole of Avenue House, Rockingham Road, Kettering, as Battalion headquarters and stores.

The 4th also took over Millers Dancing Academy in Trafalgar Road, Kettering, as a company headquarters—a resort which probably explained the grace which, certain facetious fellow units suggested, characterized their marching thereafter.

The 5th (Kettering District) Battalion requisitioned a warehouse in Goodby's Yard, Kettering, as well as a small factory at Rothwell and a large club-room at Cottingham, while the 6th (Corby) Battalion, being more fortunate in the matter of accommodation, were content with taking over a school at Gretton and one or two huts at Corby.

The 7th (Wellingborough Town) Battalion, among other places, took over the old Salvation Army Hall at Irthlingborough, and Evington House in Castle Street, Wellingborough, as Battalion headquarters—while the 8th (Wellingborough District) Battalion had such diverse homes as a room in the old skating rink at Raunds, a factory at Rushden, stables, a garage

at Grendon Hall, and a bakehouse at Bozeat!—also a disused chapel at Higham Ferrers.

In the area of the 9th (Brixworth) Battalion the troops were just as versatile. They adapted the Kennels Cottage at Brixworth, a room at the Artichoke Inn at Moulton, a spare kitchen and a saddleroom at Spratton Manor House, and three loose boxes and a loft at the Ward Arms at Guilsborough.

The 10th (Daventry) Battalion Headquarters went into residence at Badby House, occupying five rooms and four loose boxes as well as a garage. They also took over the Boys' Club at Daventry and the club-room of the Admiral Rodney at Long Buckby.

The 11th (Hardingstone) Battalion Headquarters staff made themselves comfortable in seven rooms at Milton Chambers, Derngate, Northampton, while one of the companies took over the old Rectory at Quinton.

The 12th (Northampton) Battalion were comfortably quartered at the Drill Hall, Clare Street, Northampton, while some of the companies were no less content in requisitioned private houses.

D Company, after its formation later in the war, lived in a dilapidated house at Kingsthorpe, which sadly belied its name of "The Rosary". Time and the Canadian Army had reduced the place to anything but a military bed of roses.

The reporters' box on the county ground was the first headquarters of No. 8 Platoon 12th Battalion, and to this "hut" the first rifles and "denims" were taken and issued to the platoon.

The headquarters of the 13th (Towcester) Battalion was at Dunkley's House, Towcester, and this battalion, too, had a varied assortment of accommodation, ranging from a squash court at Wappenham and the caretaker's house at the Bacon Factory at Blisworth, to three rooms and a landing at Stoke Bruene Rectory!

The 15th (Northampton) Battalion, whose late formation is dealt with in subsequent pages, did little requisitioning. They were quite happy at the Brewery House, Black Lion Hill, Northampton, with platoons at requisitioned premises such as the bowls and croquet pavilions at Franklins Gardens, Northampton. Altogether, they lived in pleasantly inspiring surroundings.

There were, it is good to note, scores of public-spirited people who, with that ready generosity which is one of the best characteristics of the British people, offered rooms and quarters freely—or at very nominal rents.

Many of these benefactors did not mention rent at all—and were content with a small grant made to them to cover the cost of renovations.

### COMPLETE HUT "WON" BY NIGHT

By accident or design—inquiries now would be indiscreet—a large percentage of the platoon and section headquarters were to be found in various hostelries, where they waged their defensive war under picturesquely assorted signs, ranging from Foxes, Gates, Locomotives, and Lambs, to Bells, Crowns, Cocks, and Lions of all the primary colours.

Some went so far as to build their own headquarters, with what material they could beg or "win", and at least one company "scrounged" a complete headquarters in the form of a commodious hut which, under cover of darkness, they removed bodily on a large lorry, from a temporarily empty Army camp. One or two of the "scroungers" engaged a lone sentry in conversation about the "exercise" in which they were engaged while the main raiding party detoured, and silently, stealthily, and swiftly "collared" their prisoner.

The hut is still in use—as a boys' club—at a site which must remain as nameless as the Home Guard unit concerned.

In spite of all these difficulties, or perhaps because of them, the Home Guard carried on, and it may be that these "divers places" where so much was done in such unprepossessing surroundings, are still peopled with genial ghosts, who once in the flesh cracked the old jokes that are a traditional, if unprintable, part of the language of the British Army.

Under all these circumstances it was only natural that, at times, the Home Guard cast envious eyes upon the relatively palatial buildings that seemed to spring up, at the taxpayers' expense, for the sole use of the Civil Defence Forces. It was not that they begrudged their fellow service this comfort, but they were left wondering why they could not have been spared even a modicum of similar consideration.

None of these discouragements seemed to abate the keenness either of the Home Guards already serving or of thousands of would-be recruits who continued to flow into battalion headquarters. So great was the influx, in fact, that, in view of the lack of training facilities and equipment, enrolments had temporarily to be suspended at the end of July. Names continued to be taken but they were filed for enrolment later.

### RAILWAY GUARDS REGULARIZED

It was on 30 July 1940 that Railway Home Guards were first regularized. Extracts from a relative letter stated:

Railway Home Guards will be enrolled to form integral parts of existing battalions, companies, etc.

They can be given duties in direct static

defence of railway V.P.s as agreed with the railway liaison officers.

A railway Home Guard cannot be used to guard a non-military V.P. or be taken to arm the outskirt defence of towns, unless agreement is reached with the railway authorities concerned.

Railway Home Guards should not be left at the bottom of the priority list for arms and equipment, as the static defence of railway V.P.s is at least as important as that of villages.

In towns, the first essential is to arm the Home Guards in the perimeter defence, and railway Home Guards within this perimeter and who do not join the perimeter defence cannot expect to be armed until the perimeter defence Home Guards are equipped to a reasonable scale.

Railway units were formed throughout Northamptonshire on these lines and performed some of the most arduous and valuable service in the county.

## MILITARY SECTOR COMMANDERS APPOINTED

Coincident with the raised military status of the Home Guard following the regularization of battalions, Military Sector Commanders were appointed "in charge of all troops of Home Guard in their sectors in emergency and . . . to work directly under the Area Commander of the East Midlands Area".

The sectors were thus commanded as follows:

*Market Harborough Sector*—(Kettering, Corby, and Oundle District), Lt.-Col. L. A. Lynden Bell, Someby.

*Weedon Sector*—(Daventry and Towcester districts), Major M. Borwick, D.S.O., Weedon.

*Peterborough Sector*—(Soke and City District), under 1st Corps.

*Northampton Sector*—(Brixworth, Wellingborough, Northampton Borough, and

Hardingstone districts), Lt.-Col. A. St. G. Coldwell, The Barracks, Northampton.

Shortly afterwards the War Office authorized the appointment of the first Home Guard permanent staff instructors, a measure which was hailed with infinite relief. This relief was a little premature, however, for at the outset only six were allocated to East Midlands Area, three to Northampton and three to Leicester, with the suggestion that they should spend a week in turn in each group or battalion area!

Nevertheless, the Home Guard was grateful even for the smallest mercies in gaining proficiency.

Not only this need of tuition seemed at last to have become apparent to the "powers", but also the heavy demands that were made upon the Guard.

## UNDUE AMOUNT OF DUTY

Thus, on 23 August 1940 we find the following letter circulated:

The Army Council have had under consideration representations that an undue amount of duty is in some cases required of members of the Home Guard.

Men who are employed for long hours on heavy work during the day have been required to undertake as many as two night watches a week as well as to attend parades and musketry practice, the result being that they lose time from employment to obtain adequate sleep. Insistence on such duties impairs efficiency and may lead to numerous resignations from the Home Guard. . . . Save in grave emergency it ought not to be necessary to ask a man to give up more than his leisure time or to trespass on the rest which is required to maintain his efficiency.

From that letter it might appear that the Home Guards themselves had complained or that some officers were, individually, making "undue" demands. Save in a few inevitable cases that was not so. It was a fact that the Guards were voluntarily impairing their health in an endeavour to live Jekyll and Hyde existence as soldier-civilians.

The same concern was reflected in a letter from the County Commander to East Midlands Home Guard Area Command, asking what the wishes of the Commander were in the matter of the continuance of manning observation posts at certain hours of the night and morning.

I do not know [wrote Sir Hereward] whether observation by Home Guard, i.e., looking out for enemy is still regarded as an essential part of the scheme for Home Defence.

Observation duties come very hard on Home Guards in rural districts, where the civil work continues from daylight to dusk, and if no instructions are received I propose to cease manning observation posts.

Eventually, except in the case of highly vulnerable points, this duty ceased, though it continued until 15 October 1940.

What observation entailed can be assessed from the following instruction of duty hours issued from County Headquarters on 20 September 1940:

Hours for manning Observation Posts after the morning of 22 September:

| | |
|---|---|
| 22 September | 10 p.m. to 6 a.m. |
| 23 September | 11 p.m. to 6 a.m. |
| 24 September | 12 midnight to 6 a.m. |
| 26 September | 12.30 a.m. to 6 a.m. |
| 27 September | 1 a.m. to 6 a.m. |
| 28–30 September | 5 a.m. to 6 a.m. |

## PERSISTENT WEAPON SHORTAGE

Of all the Home Guards' early trials, none caused them more irritation and impatient anxiety than the shortage and intermittent supply of weapons.

At this time all units were feverishly engaged in manufacturing Molotov Cocktails, i.e. bottles filled with petrol or other inflammable material mixed with tar or resin and with an inflammable "fuse" attached. The idea was to light the fuse, usually consisting of tarred rag, and then to fling the bomb at an enemy tank upon which the glass would break thus releasing the petrol and enveloping the target in flame.

For the making of these bombs bottles were "scrounged" from everywhere and, in practice, usually carried out with an old chassis hauled by a car, they seemed to be quite effective.

An amusing "aside" concerning early bombs is recorded by Lt.-Col. L. E. Barnes in his *History of the 12th (Northampton) Battalion* as follows:

In the early days of improvisation many of us returned from courses at the first Home Guard training schools at Osterley Park and Denbies with various recipes for home-made bombs in our note-books. Inspired with enthusiasm, some of us set to work, first by procuring the necessary ingredients by sundry ways and means, and then in our sculleries endeavouring to mix and mould these into the familiar jam-tin bomb, reminiscent of 1914 days.

Sgt. E. Martin, of D Company, who had also been to Osterley, and myself experimented at the Cedos Works, Northampton, of which he was the proprietor, and evolved several weird-looking objects that we hoped would achieve their purpose.

If the town authorities ever found some unaccountable holes in the roadway at the rear of Mill Lane, we now plead guilty that they were made by our experiments with our 1940 improvised grenades.

Although these improvisations would, no doubt, have been better than nothing, the manufacture of any quantity was far beyond our capabilities, and it was not until some time later that we had an issue of grenades capable of dealing with enemy tanks.

The best unofficial products it will be seen were still primitive, and when the first official self-igniting phosphorus bombs arrived (bottles of handy size whose contents ignited and burned furiously on breaking) they were treated with profound respect, not only in point of their future, but also of their present, potentialities. Thus, in the absence of proper storage facilities, these S.I.P.s were secreted in all manner of caches—in one case, a hole in a group commander's garden, and in another, sunk in the lake of a sports ground.

Few adjacent civilian residents can have imagined just what this, that, or the other small dump or mound contained at that time. It was just as well that they didn't!

Returning, more seriously, to the weapon shortage at this critical time, our space will not be wasted if we digress to bring out the situation with such emphasis as may, it is earnestly hoped, contribute to avoid any risk of its arising again.

### THE NAKED BLUFF OF 1940

The position was such as to constitute, in 1940, a veritable nightmare from which, for months, there was no awakening.

In 1940, in fact, all that the Home Guard could have put up was the nakedest kind of bluff, and even when that had been backed up by the traditional dogged courage of the British race, it would have proved pathetically ineffective against the enemy's ultra up-to-date armament.

Most Home Guards went on patrol with ash plants, while others, as we have previously noted, begged, borrowed, or "scrounged" air pistols, revolvers, shotguns, and sporting rifles, and their temporary owners were envied as are men who hold priceless things.

Thus, little by little, these old soldiers accumulated what, in retrospect, was a pitiful show of arms. Only the grim need hid the farcical side, for some of these weapons were worse than useless.

Indeed, in some units, local museums were ransacked for muskets which could, indeed, have been described as lethal but far more so to the musketeer than to the enemy.

Yet, this position was far from new in British history.

There had been two relatively recent occasions when the stark facts confronting the British people were deadly serious in their implications.

The imminence of the Napoleonic invasion was one, and the German breakthrough in 1918 was another.

Nevertheless, in all records, nothing so awe-inspiring had ever arisen as the position immediately after the fall of France.

Posterity will find it almost impossible to believe that there were then only some 70,000 rifles in the country and a mere sixty tanks.

These, with the tiny but incomparable Army and Air Force, and the immense asset of the Royal Navy, were all that stood between us and the apparently invincible might of the German divisions.

There were, therefore, no weapons to spare for the Home Guard.

It is true that the original idea was to equip each volunteer with a rifle, bayonet, and steel helmet, but it was an utter impossibility to issue even this meagre outfit.

It is, perhaps, the finest tribute which can be paid to the Home Guard and a fact that should never be forgotten, that these men faced the appalling menace of invasion with no other weapons than their walking-sticks, their incurable optimism, and their courage.

### THE FIRST RIFLES

It was a happy day, indeed, for the Home Guard when the first issue of real rifles, mainly of the Ross type, took place—although this delight was tempered by the fact that the rifles had, for the time being, to be shared.

However, the Guards were glad to have a few rather than none at all, especially since the first issue included a number of Short Magazine Lee Enfields, a fact which gave the "old sweats" a special thrill of pleasure.

To feel their fingers closing round the satiny woodwork of this beautifully balanced and proportioned weapon was a joy.

To tuck the butts into their shoulders, squint along the sights again, and to feel that they and their rifles were one again was a dream come true.

The joy of possession, however, was short-lived, and the Ross and S.M.L.E. rifles were withdrawn shortly afterwards for reissue to the Regulars.

In fact, during the winter of 1940 and up to the summer of 1941 all output of arms was reserved for the Regulars. So, with keen regret (often embroidered with unprintable qualifications) the Home Guard reluctantly handed over its first real weapons to its Regular brothers-in-arms.

### THE AMERICAN RIFLES

After the end of 1941 the Home Guard was equipped almost entirely with weapons forged in British workshops. There was, however, one notable exception—the American Springfield rifles—which arrived in the late summer of 1940. Their calibre was .300 and they were marked on the stock with a red band to prevent confusion with .303 calibre.

It was a gesture by the United States which the Home Guard will always remember. They arrived, these long and somewhat heavy rifles, in wooden cases, accompanied by a generous amount of ammunition.

There were 800,000 of them altogether, and for the first time the Home Guard felt itself armed, though even this generous loan meant only one rifle to approximately every three men.

But it gave the Home Guard a fresh heart as they unpacked these treasures from the glutinous grease which enveloped them.

These, with a few grenades of the period, really represented the turning-point in the Home Guards' progress to the status of a really formidable force.

It was later suggested that this arming of the Home Guard influenced Hitler to postpone his invasion.

Certainly the screeches which came over the Nazi radio at the time evidenced the insane anger which possessed the enemy at this arming of a nation's civilian manhood.

The Home Guard were quite unperturbed, and went on with their musketry training.

There were several minor, but well-meant, criticisms of the American rifles, due, almost entirely, to comparison with the Short Magazine Lee Enfield. It was heavier for one thing, and the soldier notices things like that very quickly!

It was also longer and seemed at first to be clumsier. But, concentrated arms drill soon altered this opinion, and when it came to work on the ranges, men whose eyes had lost the keener vision of youth found the aperture sights more suitable.

## Chapter XI

# FIRST CAPTURE OF ENEMY SPY

THROUGHOUT Northamptonshire, in common with the rest of Great Britain, arms drill and musketry instruction now took on a new lease of life. In wooden huts, on village greens, in drill halls, and in improvised headquarters, the old soldiers renewed their acquaintance with "the slope" and "the order"—and memories a quarter of a century old became realities once more.

They were soldiers again, and it was good to feel fingers gripping wood and steel, to feel a bayonet against their thighs, and to hear bolts click home as the breeches were closed.

Better still was it, on the range, to see the white discs marking the "bulls" and signalling that, in spite of almost forgotten youth, age had not "told" quite so harshly after all.

### ARRIVAL OF SEVENTY LEWIS GUNS

Little less joy than that aroused among the riflemen was that experienced by ex-machine gunners when, on 2 September 1940, the County Commander informed battalion commanders that seventy Lewis guns were coming and that efforts were to be made to train crews.

Enthusiastically, old Lewis gunners stepped forward and so "warmed up" their knowledge and experience as to be ready when the guns arrived, only four days later, to act as instructors to selected crews who soon grew to share their tutors' regard for what, rightly, ranked as one of the finest weapons of the early twentieth century.

### ALARM AT LAMPORT

It must not be overlooked that during this period the Home Guard, in common

with the rest of the country, were continuously in an "electric" state of vigilance amid which alarms were continually raised.

Genuine or otherwise, these calls nevertheless provided numerous tests of the Home Guard's alertness despite all of its manifold preoccupations with training for field warfare.

A Lewis machine gun "nest" trained on the Buttocks Booth (Northampton) cross-roads road block.

Typical of this alertness was that displayed by members of the 9th (Brixworth) Battalion when at 6.45 p.m. on 20 August 1940, a report was received that a parachute had been seen over Lamport.

Local keenness reached such a pitch that not only were the local Home Guard able to commandeer all the cars available to rush off to Short Wood—towards which the alleged parachute was making—but the whole population of Lamport, women and children, also joined in the chase.

PARENTAL DISCIPLINE?

ON THE RANGE

[*Photo: J. Wright*]

A 12th (Northampton) Battalion Lewis gun in action during an exercise near Bushland Road School, Northampton.

The alarm was sent out to Maidwell and Old, and for the space of about an hour this normally quiet countryside was teeming with excitement.

Anti-climax followed as the "parachute" turned out to be a barrage balloon which had broken from its moorings and which eventually came to rest at Thorpe Malsor!

Such keenness was creditable, but it had it's tactical demerits as an instruction issued a week later by the County (now designated Zone) Commander indicated. Ran an extract:

Cases have occurred where, on report that one or two parachutes have been seen, the whole of a village section of the Home Guard have gone off to the scene. On receiving such a report the section commander should send an armed patrol to investigate.

The remainder should assemble at Headquarters to deal with landing if serious.

The finding and collecting of empty parachutes is not the business of the Home Guard.

The same sound idea of detachable mobile units was extended to embrace battalions by the Zone Commander when he issued a letter to group and battalion commanders that such units should be formed "where possible without delay".

Each Mobile Unit [ran the letter] is to consist of not more than one platoon of two officers and thirty-six other ranks exclusive of drivers. (School O.T.C. units excepted.)

Personnel to be active, intelligent men, living within easy reach of their headquarters.

Each man to be armed with a rifle and forty rounds. Lewis guns and grenades to be provided where issued.

Small lorries, vans, and buses to be earmarked for transport, two drivers per vehicle.

One day's ration to be carried on emergency.

OBJECT. To reinforce local units if attacked. To act only on orders of local Military Sector Commander or Home Guard Battalion Commander acting under his orders. Limit of action generally ten miles from their stations except in exceptional circumstances.

Needless to add there was a rush to be enrolled in these specialist units and, in several cases, quite amazing ingenuity was shown in fitting up improvised transport with all that such a unit might need on detachment.

## GUARDING UNEXPLODED BOMBS

Although, by comparison with some other counties, Northamptonshire had but a mild share of the intense enemy bombing at this time, it was repeatedly attacked by lone nuisance raiders and many bombs were dropped by enemy bombers which, being harassed by the Royal Air Force, were content to unload their balances of ammunition anywhere in order to "hare" for home.

Fortunately, thanks to the inferior workmanship of many German armament manufacturers, quite a large proportion of these bombs failed to explode, but they presented "unhealthy" possibilities while they lay around.

In this connection many county units put in good, and not a little dangerous, work mounting guard over these unwelcome deposits until experts came to render them innocuous.

Thus on 16 August 1940 Mr. A. K. D. Bishop, of the Kilsby L.D.V., was at the village guard-post with a Mr. Storr and four other volunteers when at 12.15 a.m. they heard what they thought was an enemy aircraft. It passed over the village going in a westerly direction. Searchlights at once ranged round for the aircraft but though it was a light night there were low clouds and they were unable to pick up their quarry.

Mr. Bishop reported that having passed over the village it turned in an easterly direction.

At this stage [he wrote] I warned the remaining four men on duty to stand to in the roadway, and at that moment bombs were dropped. One I estimated at 150 yards from the post in a field on the right side of Kilsby turn.

I sent a man to call out the A.R.P. and then went with Mr. Storr to examine any damage, while one man with a motor-cycle patrolled the roads to make sure they had not been damaged, after which we allowed traffic to continue.

Then at Mr. Storr's request, I placed sentries over two unexploded bombs and continued the usual patrol. My men were relieved this morning by Regulars.

At daylight I searched for craters and any damage that might have been invisible in the poor light, and found that fourteen unexploded bombs had been dropped. These were then reported to R.E.H.Q. for examination and removal.

The merit of this report and the calm decision it reflected must be judged in the light of the slender experience the L.D.V. had then gained, by which standards it deserved the commendation it received from Sir Hereward Wake.

## CAPTURE OF GERMAN SPY

Now came one of the most notable events in the war story of the Northamptonshire Home Guard—a parachute landing by, and the capture of, a German spy. It enabled the Guard to perform one of its most valuable pieces of work, in point of the potential menace to Britain that the central figure presented.

The landing occurred in the area of A Company (Capt. W. J. Penn) of the 11th (Hardingstone District) Battalion (Lt.-Col. A. J. Fraser, D.S.O.).

(Capt., later Lt.-Col., Penn succeeded Lt.-Col. Fraser in command of the 11th.)

It was at about five o'clock in the evening of 2 September 1940 that a Mr. Patrick Daly, in the employ of Mr. G. C. Beechener, farmer and racehorse trainer, of The Elms, Denton, and a member of the Home Guard, reported to his employer that he had seen a strange-looking man lying under a bush in a ditch in one of the farm fields, apparently asleep or disabled.

Mr. Beechener, taking up his Home Guard rifle, at once proceeded to the ditch, and called upon the man to come out.

the number—and in addition the date was wrong.

Further, Mr. Beechener noted the huge knot in his tie which would have "given him away anywhere".

Mr. Beechener was now convinced that this was no ordinary stranger and demanded to search the man who meanwhile

Home Guard security duty included the checking of civilians' identity cards. A scene during the "Scorch" exercise of December 1941.

Eventually there emerged a youngish man, wearing a green sports coat with grey flannel trousers, fawn raincoat, grey felt hat, very light brown brogue shoes of a Continental type, and wearing horn-rimmed spectacles. Finally, his tie was tied in a huge, un-English knot.

Since he also had a suit-case, Mr. Beechener's suspicions were at once aroused, and challenging the man, he asked for his identification card.

"Certainly," said the stranger, and produced a card with an address at Yardley, Birmingham.

There was a suspicious error, however, in the card, for the address was in Continental style—street-name first and then

tried, in perfect English, to carry on a nonchalant conversation.

It was then found that the stranger carried an automatic pistol, and when this was extracted, he smiled and said, "I give up".

"You wouldn't have got me," he added, "if I hadn't got a crack on the head from this as I landed," and he pointed to his suit-case which, being opened, proved to be a portable radio transmitter.

Subsequent search revealed that the man had landed by a fine-quality silk parachute and was well equipped with a ground sheet, small clock, compass, maps, torch, tablet of soap, chocolate, and flasks of whisky and rum.

He had a wallet containing approximately £300 in English notes.

At an interrogation by Capt. Penn, Section Leader E. E. Smart, and the local policeman, who had been summoned, the latter tried, unsuccessfully, to "break" and unload the prisoner's pistol.

"Can I help you?" said the German, and being permitted to do so, while care was taken to see that he did not "try any funny stuff", calmly pressed a catch and scattered the cartridges on the table.

He told his captors that he had come from Hamburg and had been dropped at about 3 a.m. He believed that he was somewhere between Stratford-on-Avon and Banbury.

Since the man was in civilian clothes, he was finally handed over to the County Police.

**MASSING OF ENEMY SHIPPING**

This capture lent particular significance to the broadcast delivered by the Prime Minister nine days later.

Said Mr. Churchill:

There are now considerable gatherings of shipping in the German, Dutch, Belgian, and French harbours—all the way from Hamburg to Brest, finally there are some preparations made of ships to carry an invading force from the Norwegian harbours.

Therefore we must regard the next week or so as a very important period in our history.

Every man or woman will therefore prepare himself to do his or her duty whatever it may be with special pride and care.

Our fleets and flotillas are very powerful and numerous. Our Air Force is at the highest strength it has ever reached and is conscious of its proved superiority, not indeed in numbers, but in men and machines. Our shores are well fortified and strongly manned, and behind them, ready to attack the invaders, we have a far larger and better equipped mobile army than we have ever had before. . . .

Besides this, we have more than a million and a half men of the Home Guard, who are just as much soldiers of the Regular Army as the Grenadier Guards, and who are determined to fight for every inch of the ground in every village and in every street.

It is with devout but with sure confidence that I say—Let God defend the right. . . .

The Home Guard were so ready, and this unreserved acknowledgment of the fact lent redoubled energy to their now rapidly advancing progress towards efficiency.

*WHEN THEY LAUGHED*

*Sergeant: "Good heavens, man! I never saw such shooting in all my life. Twenty shots and you haven't even once hit the target. What the deuce is the matter with you?"*

*Recruit (looking down at the barrel): "I really don't know, Sergeant. They're leaving* THIS *end all right."*

## Chapter XII

## ENEMY AIRCRAFT ENGAGED

IT was at this period that it was decided to integrate Post Office units with Post Office battalions, a measure which was keenly regretted alike by the local commands and the men concerned.

At the time there were four separate Post Office units in the county:

Wellingborough with a strength of 15, Kettering with a strength of 82, Northampton with a strength of 251, and Peterborough with a strength of 150.

The County Commander did his best to prevent the detachment of these units, whose members, quite apart from the benefit they had derived from training with adjacent battalions, had also built up strong links of comradeship with their battalion officers and men.

Thus Sir Hereward wrote to the Home Guard Commander of East Midlands area:

I understand it is proposed to transfer General Post Office units from their local Home Guard battalions to a Post Office battalion with Headquarters at Leicester, as also the Post Office personnel in rural areas.

The War Office letter of 29.7.40, however, states that where it is more convenient, Post Office employees may remain in their local Home Guard units by mutual arrangement. . . . a Post Office battalion at Leicester is very far from convenient, and against the interests of the men, nor do they desire it. They would be cut off from training facilities and supervision by Home Guard officers.

. . . I trust the mutual arrangement suggested by the War Office may be made in the interests of the men.

The Post Office, however, declined to make the "mutual arrangement" suggested, and the personnel concerned, with the exception of the fifteen men at Wellingborough, who were unable alone to defend their premises, were transferred to the Leicester and Peterborough Post Office battalions with their arms and equipment, although, happily, all of the units continued to liaise with their old battalions and regularly joined them in exercises.

### INVASION PRACTICE

A clarification of the order in the event of invasion was now issued by the County Commander. It ran as follows and will recall to every Home Guard in Northamptonshire the details of its practice which were rehearsed on every possible occasion until "clockwork" precision had been reached:

MAN POSTS. . . . If invasion takes place Home Guards concerned will receive the message Man Posts from the Military Sector Commander.

This will mean that enemy forces are, or soon will be, in the neighbourhood.

On receipt of this message Home Guards will assemble at their headquarters at once; man O.P.s and V.P.s; man road blocks; send out patrols; render all asistance to police re traffic control if asked.

The order involves cessation of work from factories, farms, etc., but will not be sent to places where the situation allows work to go on.

The order will not be passed on to neighbouring Home Guards unless ordered.

Church bells will not be rung.

It was recognized that in the event of invasion, whether as a large-scale operation or a supplementary to coastal assault, Northamptonshire, as the virtual centre of

England, would be among the most likely initial enemy objectives whereon to establish and consolidate mid-country strong points from which an ever-widening perimeter of occupation, dislocating British internal communications, could be developed.

In this connection it is significant to note that never once did the enemy subject Northampton town to intensive bombing, although several lesser county towns were visited repeatedly.

These assaults and other emergencies provided the Home Guards in the area concerned with opportunities to prove that their capabilities were not confined to their military duties.

Whether it was a case of getting a direct "crack" at the enemy; of filling a breach when necessity demanded; of effecting a rescue with promptitude and decision or of "jumping in" beside the police, Civil Defence, and Fire Service in dealing with the effects of air bombing, the Northamptonshire men always acquitted themselves with credit.

Many instances in this history illustrate the prevailing spirit.

Two of them occurring at this period are here recalled.

### WELLINGBOROUGH ATTACKED

On a Sunday morning in late September 1940 just as the men of Wellingborough Ironworks Platoon (Lt. W. D. Holton) were dismissing after a parade at the works, where their H.Q. overlooked the L.M.S. London-Leicester main line, a low-flying aeroplane suddenly zoomed past on a course following the track of the railway and dropped bombs which narrowly missed the sidings.

At once Lt. Holton led his men at the double to the platoon armoury and drew and loaded rifles in time to see the aircraft returning, apparently to renew its attack.

The newly learned "Aircraft action" was ordered and, as the plane approached, it was given hot bursts of fire from thirty rifles.

At once it went into a steep evading turn and made off rapidly without taking further hostile action.

Lt. Holton subsequently received a certificate for gallantry and good service in recognition of his prompt action.

The 8th (Wellingborough District) Battalion (Lt.-Col. V. H. Sykes) were next concerned when at 10.15 a.m. on the 3 October 1940, and with no warning, enemy aircraft suddenly dropped eighteen high explosive bombs and twelve incendiaries in twenty-five seconds in the area of the then 12th Company (Major A. D. Denton) at Rushden.

The first bomb fell within fifty yards of the Company Headquarters.

Within three minutes of the first explosion, men of the A, B, C, and D platoons of the Company were in action at the bomb craters.

One unexploded bomb dropped in a busy thoroughfare, and the Home Guard formed a cordon round the spot from midnight to dawn until relieved by the police. Home Guards were also on traffic duty at all parts of the bombed area until dawn.

One factory received two direct hits and at the request of the manager, No. 12 Company mounted a guard from 7 p.m. to 7 a.m. each night from 4 October to 13 October.

The police expressed great appreciation of the services thus rendered by the Rushden Company.

### A SECOND SPY CAPTURED

On the following day the Northamptonshire Home Guard gained some measure of revenge for these assaults by capturing a second enemy parachutist.

Strangely enough, this second visitor "out

of the blue" also landed in the 11th Battalion area—apparently a popular one for this class of Nazi enterprise!—his contact point, between Bozeat and Yardley Hastings, being only two and a half miles distant from that of his predecessor.

He had been noticed as a stranger when passing through Bozeat but no one had any suspicions.

His dress and kit were practically identical with those of the first arrival even to his £300 in notes, which seems to have been the "regulation allowance".

Mr. Len. Smith, a smallholder on the Grendon Road, claims to have first discovered the spy.

Mr. Smith was visiting his cowshed when he saw the German coming out. He cross-examined him and asked for his identity card, and then, becoming suspicious, he stopped the first car coming along the road. The driver was a Home Guard, Private P. Keggan, who detained the man and sent for fellow Home Guards and also sent a report to the County Police, who later took the intruder in charge.

Home Guards concerned in the case, apart from Private Keggan, were the Company Commander (Captain W. J. Penn), the Section Leader (Sergeant E. E. Smart) and Volunteer R. Ingram.

His parachute was later found in some farm outbuildings and his wireless set in Hollowell Planting, Easton Maudit.

**A NIGHT ORDEAL**

Wellingborough District now returns again to the record with some fine work in the No. 11 Company area on 9 October 1940.

At 4.30 a.m. Capt. V. H. Sykes received a report from the surveyor to the Raunds Urban District Council that unexploded enemy bombs were lying east of the Reservoir and between Raunds Grange and the village of Hargrave, thus rendering the road from Hargrave to Raunds unsafe until the bombs had been located. Accordingly, sentries were at once placed at the north-west end of Hargrave village and at the south-west end of Mere Road and a message was sent to Keyston to stop traffic via Raunds stations.

At 5 a.m. it was dark and raining heavily but Capt. Sykes rightly decided that it was necessary to evacuate the danger area and adjacent farmers were also informed that their stock should be removed.

A thorough investigation was then made, with the aid of Sgt. Bywaters of the Raunds platoon, in the area from Mere road in a north-west direction towards the reservoir and two craters made by unexploded bombs were found.

Other members of the platoon then arrived, and a comb-over was made of the ground flanking the Raunds-Hargrave road.

After five hours' arduous and hazardous work, five other craters were located. They measured eighteen inches across and deep and were obviously difficult to find and easily passed by even at a few yards distance in ploughland.

The authorities were informed of the bombs' locations and at 12.30 p.m. sentries of the Essex Regiment relieved the Home Guard.

At 1.30 p.m. Capt. Sykes, accompanied by Platoon Commander J. E. Lee and Section Leaders Percival and Freeman, visited each bomb crater again and marked each with a red flag Both 11th and 12th Companies were commended by Sir Hereward Wake.

**COMPLETION OF BATTALION REORGANIZATION**

Most of the Home Guard's observation and guard duties having been suspended by this time, to enable the men to concentrate on training, and seeing that recruiting had also been temporarily suspended, the Commander-in-Chief Home Forces now directed the completion of the Guards' battalion reorganization.

Said an East Midlands area letter:

Battalions will be organized in four companies lettered A, B, C, and D.

Each company to consist of four platoons numbered 1 to 16 throughout the company.

Major-Gen. Sir Hereward Wake replied to the above:

The Area Commander's orders involve careful consideration.

As you are aware the organization of the Home Guard in this County is based on local circumstances which vary everywhere, and the existing grouping of companies and platoons has been necessitated by the difficulty of finding suitable commanders.

However, the reorganization took place a month later and was retained with slight local variations until the end.

At the same time the Northamptonshire Home Guard was affiliated to Regular Units as follows:

Peterborough Town and Soke to the 14th Royal Fusiliers at Peterborough; Kettering Town and District and Corby Works battalion to the Leicestershire Regiment at Kettering; Northampton Borough, Brixworth and Hardingstone battalions to the Infantry Training Centre at Northampton, and the Daventry, Towcester and Brackley battalions to the 6th Leicestershire Regiment at Ashby St. Ledgers.

This final confirmation of the Guards' military status gave widespread satisfaction and marked the end of such elements of public levity as the force had previously suffered.

The Home Guard was to be taken in unqualified seriousness and now the people so took it.

## POWER STATION INTRUDER

Late in the month of October 1940 a disturbing result of the removal of guards occurred at the Northampton Electric Company's huge power station serving power over a thirty-mile radius including the vital district of Corby.

One night it was discovered that an intruder had penetrated the barbed wire surrounding the station and he would almost certainly have been captured had there been any sentries.

As it was, he was able to escape when disturbed, fortunately without having caused any of the incalculable damage he might have wrought.

## A CATASTROPHE AVERTED

Many of the actions performed by the Home Guard were quite unspectacular, and were done under cover of darkness with no encouraging crowds at hand to appraise or applaud them.

Into such a category fell the probably unique Home Guard exploit performed by men of the 28th Company (Major F. L. Nickalls) of the 10th (Daventry District) Battalion on 30 October 1940.

On that night an enemy pilot scored a lucky hit on the canal bank at Wolfhamcote in the Daventry area, causing a wide breach through which the liberated water began to surge in an ever-increasing torrent.

It became clear that something had to be done and very quickly if miles of adjacent countryside were not to be disastrously flooded.

There were numerous occasions when the Home Guard could have claimed "UBIQUE" as their motto, and this was a monumental instance.

For, even at that deserted spot, a member of the Home Guard was on duty, and he at once called out Lt.

W. C. Berry, commanding the Braunston platoon.

A gale of wind was blowing and rain was pouring but Lt. Berry promptly collected nine of his men and rushed to the scene. Arrived, Lt. Berry made a swift appreciation of the situation and then procured—goodness knows how—a number of heavy baulks of timber which he and his men hauled to the breach. With these, helped in the later stages by Lt. W. S. Mitchison, who had also hurried to the scene, after incredible labours in the darkness they managed to stem the torrent.

Danger remained, however, unless the water was stopped about a mile and a half away. Accordingly, Barby, the nearest post to the spot, was notified, and men rushed to the canal to place more baulks in position and dam the water.

But for their prompt combined action, fourteen miles of canal water would have been lost with incalculable effects.

As it was, the level of the water dropped only fifteen inches.

The Platoon Commander and all concerned were highly commended by the General Officer Commanding Northern Command, the East Midlands Area Commander (Brigadier R. S. Abbott), the Zone Commander (Major-Gen. Sir Hereward Wake) and the Northampton County A.R.P. Controller (Mr. J. Alan Turner).

**BATTALION GUIDES APPOINTED**

The same intimate knowledge of their district as enabled the Braunston men to lay their hands on timber baulks just when they were needed was typical of all units and of rural platoons in particular.

This invaluable specialized knowledge was fully appreciated by the General Staff and a letter received on 6 November 1940 underlined that appreciation.

It ran:

One of the most important roles of the Home Guard in country districts is to act as guides to the Field Army in the event of their being called out to operate in an area which is not familiar to them.

The best method is for the Battalion Commander to appoint a Chief Guide per Battalion and get him to be responsible to the Battalion Commander for the training of guides in the Battalion area. The Chief Guide will be selected for his intimate knowledge of the whole area. He might be a master of hounds or a huntsman but he must be physically and mentally active and, if possible, possess some military knowledge.

The Chief Guide will have attached to him, say, three men from each section of Home Guard to be trained during the winter so that, in the spring, they are able to give fullest information and assistance to Regular units and formations, particularly those newly arrived in the vicinity.

The training of Guides is to be extensive and is to include map reading, keeping direction by the sun and stars, minor tactics and timing of various routes on foot or otherwise.

The men will be relieved of all other training.

Battalion guide officers and men were the result of this letter and many of them were called upon to an effect which won warm appreciation from Regular units they were able to assist, though not, as it happened, under action conditions.

One part of the instruction was, however, disobeyed. It was that which stated that the men would be relieved of all other training. They were not so relieved because they declined to be.

The Guides also acted as "water diviners". Pumps, wells and springs were located in all towns and villages and, had the normal water supply failed, each platoon would have known where it could obtain a supply of water pure and fit for drinking.

In 1942 when the defence of road

junctions in towns led to the development of "Defended Localities" the question of water supply became one of first priority. At Wellingborough and Finedon alone, men of the 7th Battalion located over 100 old wells from which samples were sent to Battalion Headquarters for testing, and, at the request of the Invasion Committee, very many of these were put into working order by the Urban District Council. Sterilizing powder and detasting tablets, guaranteed to make emergency water supply fit for use on operations, were issued, but the detasting tablets were not popular.

## WHEN THEY LAUGHED

*Sympathize with the disappointment of the American officer who, being invited to participate in a local H.G. "T.E.W.T.", due to begin at 1000 hours, asked if he might attend one in the evening, as he "couldn't get to a booze-up in duty hours"!*

*Only when the roar of laughter had subsided could he explain that in the U.S.A. the word "toot" describes a "binge", "night out" or general "soak".*

# Chapter XIII

## GLOWING PARLIAMENTARY PRAISE

ON 20 November 1940 came another of those national tributes to the Home Guard which served, in some measure, to compensate the force for its many setbacks and discouragements.

It consisted of a glowing debate in Parliament from which some extracts are here recalled.

The debate was opened by Sir Edward Grigg, Parliamentary Secretary, War Office, who made a statement on the Home Guard which he described as "the product of the force of events and the British character and tradition which usually rose superior to events".

It was untrue that the Regular Army had adopted a stepmotherly attitude towards the new force. The Army had realized its value from the start and done everything to promote its efficiency and growth.

Equally far from the truth was the idea that the Regular Army now wanted to regiment or dragoon the Home Guard. He had seen it stated that old soldiers wanted to make it a playground for "dugouts" and "brasshats". [Laughter.] That idea was absurd.

It would be a catastrophe if the force, or any part of it, lost heart owing to the lack of sympathetic attention to its needs or difficulties. Some measure of organization was manifestly required. He described the system of command and administration it was proposed to introduce.

The Higher Command would remain vested in the Commander-in-Chief Home Forces, Sir Alan Brooke.

Lord Gort, who had been appointed Inspector-General of Training, was a master of military training in all its aspects, and above all was a practical soldier with great fighting experience.

He had seen the German Army in action—the kind of thing the Home Guard might have to resist—and his assistance as Inspector-General would be of great practical value to the force.

A Home Guard School, based on the admirable school started at Osterley had been established.

There would be a permanent staff instructor to each battalion but the Home Guard must produce its own staff—and it was full of talent available as instructors.

The force would be manned by its own commissioned officers and recommendations would be made by selection boards consisting almost entirely of members of the Home Guard.

The selection boards would be required to satisfy themselves that any commander they recommended had been efficient in command and trusted by his subordinates from battalion commanders downwards. Officers must be physically fit under active service conditions and the age limit of sixty-five would therefore be adhered to so far as those categories were concerned.

The administrative system of the Home Guard would continue to be operated through the Territorial Associations which would, where necessary, be strengthened. The Director-General of the Home Guard would be Major-Gen. Eastwood, who had been commandant at Sandhurst and who had lately held command of a Regular division.

The Director-General of the Territorial Army, Sir John Brown, would continue in that post.

Full armament had been provided for 1,000,000 men, which was twice the number anticipated when the Home Guard was first raised. On behalf of the Home Guard he would like to raise his hat to the President, Congress, and people of the United States.

The Home Guard must have made a special appeal to them, because they certainly owed a great deal to their sympathetic understanding and help.

### HOME GUARD BRITAIN "INCARNATE"

The Home Guard was a national asset not only of military but of moral value. It was Britain incarnate, an epitome of the character enabled all sorts and conditions of patriotic men to express themselves in service, with tonic effect, and it was well that it should be so.

Welded as it was into the defence system of the country, the Home Guard was a national asset of priceless worth, and it proved that this nation, for all its years, had the gift of eternal youth. [Cheers.]

THE NEW PIP

of the race in its gift for comradeship in trouble, its deep love of its own land and its surging anger at the thought that any invader should set foot on our soil. [Hear, hear.] St. George, St. Andrew, St. David and St. Crispin were alive and marching in its democratic ranks. [Hear, hear.]

As an example of this spirit he need only quote the help the Home Guard had given the Civil Defence Service in recent air attacks, when whole companies had been out helping night after night, despite the fact that these men had their own work to do during the day.

The Home Guard was no slave to routine but would turn its hand to anything. It had

To the subsequent debate *The Times* devoted a leading article no less earnestly complimentary.

Said the writer:

Yesterday's debate on the Home Guard showed that all parties in the House of Commons are equally proud of this formidable body of citizen soldiers, which has sprung spontaneously into existence since the threat to our shores became dangerous last May; and all are equally anxious that its members should be given the fullest facilities for training, equipment adequate to their vital responsibilities, and the public honour they deserve.

Mr. Eden, who wound up the debate, reminded the House yet again, as Sir Edward Grigg had done, that the enemy's massed battalions are still ranged opposite our shores, They may launch their attack at any moment.

Whether that is their intention, or whether they merely seek, by maintaining the threat, to compel us to retain within our coasts large bodies of troops that otherwise might be applied in offence, the reply depends very largely on the vigilance and strength of the Home Guard.

## WHEN THEY LAUGHED

*"Now, you men," said the Irish sergeant as he dismissed the section, "you will parade again at 2 o'clock precisely. And, begorra! when I say 2 o'clock precisely I don't mean five past. I mean five to."*

# Chapter XIV

# THE GREAT BLITZ

THUS, in little over six months, had the Home Guard consolidated itself in national esteem, an esteem rendered the more remarkable by the fact that Britain was now being subjected to the fiercest aerial bombing ever suffered by any country, though bearing no comparison with what was soon to descend upon the enemy.

The effect of that blitz might have been expected to undermine the confidence of the nation even in its Regular forces. As it was the effect was the extreme reverse and this applied no less to the Home Guard than to any other force.

From their inception the Home Guard had endeavoured to co-operate to the utmost with the Civil Defence Services while carefully avoiding any suggestion of encroachment or overlapping.

With the beginning of the first major blitz the opportunity came to turn that co-operation to account and a special order was issued to all battalions in the following terms:

Recent technique of German night attack on towns has been to begin by dropping a very large number of incendiary bombs. Subsequent H.E. bombs frequently break water mains. Fires are then difficult to extinguish and, in addition to damage caused, the lighting up of the target area facilitates later attack. It is consequently of the greatest importance that incendiary bombs should be extinguished at the earliest possible moment after falling.

The A.R.P. Services have, in certain places, found difficulty in coping with large numbers of incendiary bombs sufficiently quickly, and the Ministry of Home Security has asked for assistance from the Home Guard where local conditions make it desirable and practicable.

The Commander-in-Chief, Home Forces, has decided that the Home Guard may be used for this purpose. The intention is that such employment would be temporary, to meet any emergency lasting for a matter of hours only. In the event of invasion they must assume their proper duties, which take priority over all others.

## DESBOROUGH STATION BOMBED

In connection with the blitz we may here note an incident in the 5th (Kettering District) Battalion area when on 20 November 1940, bombs were suddenly rained on the railway track near Desborough station about 9.10 p.m., only a few yards away from a Home Guard railway patrol. A truck was immediately set on fire and this was tackled by Civil Defence personnel, but a Home Guard detachment patrolled the railway track for some miles to make sure that no further damage had been done that might have threatened oncoming trains. Since this patrol set out before the raider could be assumed to have concluded his operation it can be described as having been completed under the constant threat of fire.

## AMENDED ORDERS

Orders for this type of work as well as for the Home Guard's main role continued to be amended or extended as the situation developed.

Thus on 27 November 1940 the County Commander issued an instruction confirming the Home Guard's self-assumed undertaking to render assistance if requested by civil authorities in putting out fires, forming cordons, etc.

As steel helmets are not yet part of equipment of the Home Guard [added the order] they will not be expected to operate during the worst of an aerial bombardment—but when it slackens will assemble in battledress . . . at platoon headquarters, draw rifles and be prepared to assist. . . .

Works platoons will confine their activities to their own works.

Company commanders to use discretion as to dismissing platoons from this duty and battalion and company commanders are to get into touch with police and A.R.P. and draw up plans.

Air raid warnings [the order concluded] should not interrupt classes of instruction until the air raid actually takes place.

Coincidentally, Northern Command issued the following invasion instruction:

The role of the Home Guard if the enemy lands by air is to sally out and attack him, engage him by fire, harass and delay him, and if possible destroy him before he has time to organize and assemble his units.

The other duty of the Home Guard is to stop and destroy the enemy in cars and tanks by means of village ambushes and surprise at road blocks.

The close of November saw several alterations in designation and commands.

Thus "Stewarts and Lloyds" Battalion was renamed "Corby Works" Battalion; Capt. P. Y. Atkinson was appointed to command the 13th (Towcester) Battalion vice Lt.-Col. F. Douglas Pennant resigned, and Major G. S. Watson was appointed Commander of the 9th (Brixworth) Battalion vice Major B. Faulkner resigned.

**WELCOME ARRIVALS**

Finally, late in the month, and as welcome as honoured guests, came 390 .3 rifles from York. These were distributed among the battalions—fifty to each except Northampton Borough, which had forty, and Corby Battalion 100.

In this connection the care the Northamptonshire men were lavishing on their precious arms was reflected in a special letter issued by Sir Hereward Wake.

It ran:

The County Commander commends the Home Guard on the care they have taken over their rifles. Examination has shown that they have been kept in very good order and the recent Ordnance examination tells the same story. In view of the shortage of cleaning materials this reflects great credit on all units.

The "shortage of cleaning materials" was also noticed in the domestic store cupboards of thousands of households. They had gone on National Service in the Home Front army!

**THE FIRST CHRISTMAS**

And now came the Home Guard's first Christmas. Goodness knows there was little enough of "peace on earth" but there was, at least, plenty of "goodwill to men" among members of the force.

Thus they celebrated the festival to the full extent that circumstances permitted and in the consciousness of a right to do so established by downright hard labour and "sweat and tears" of the genuine Churchillian order.

The County Commander generously acknowledged the fact with the following order issued on 19 December 1940:

I send you Christmas Greetings.

I congratulate you on your efforts to attain efficiency, your perseverance under difficulties, and your loyalty to your Commanders and the Cause.

A severe test may be in front of us. If or when it comes the result must not be in doubt. We must know how to meet the enemy, how to use the weapons we have, how to act—promptly, skilfully, with firm resolve, without waiting for orders.

The country depends on you. Do not relax your efforts. Be prepared.

May the New Year bring us all Victory and Peace.

Two days before Christmas the battalions' designations were finally confirmed as previously recorded and regimental adjutants were also authorized.

Whether under the influence of Christmas or no, the War Office also waxed suddenly beneficent under two headings.

Home Guards were informed that they would "be allowed travelling expenses (normally third-class fare) for *journeys to and from hospital* in connection with free medical treatment of disabilities attributable to Home Guard service" and that permission had been granted "for Home Guard Commanders *to purchase cap badges from local retailers* if not otherwise available for issue". (The italics are ours!)

Two appointments took effect at this period, that of Lt.-Col. T. A. Thornton, C.V.O., to command Northamptonshire Central Group, which included Daventry, Brixworth, Hardingstone and Northampton Borough battalions, and that of Major N. Furlong to command the 14th (Brackley) Battalion vice Brig.-Gen. W. Allison resigned.

The year closed, notably enough, with an address given by Field Marshal The Earl of Cavan, K.P., to over 2,000 Guards, drawn from battalions throughout the county, at the Exchange Cinema, Northampton, on 29 December 1940. For no apparent reason every man was required to bring his rifle and twenty rounds of ammunition to this event, yet when on 4 January 1941 the Guard was again honoured by an address given at the Drill Hall, Northampton, by the Army Commander Gen. Sir Robert Adam, K.C.B., the orders were uniform only. No one ever knew the "answers" to these odd inconsistencies.

## MORE WEAPONS ISSUED

Before proceeding to the story of 1941 we may take another look at the Home Guard armament which was now gradually building up to appreciable proportions.

But before dealing with more effective weapons, passing—and only passing!—reference should be made to the Harvey Flame Thrower of which most battalions had—and hid—a few.

[*Photo: G. Turnill*

Flame Thrower. Demonstration given at Denbies Home Guard Training School, February 1942.

## A "ONE SHOT" WEAPON

A typical commentary on the Harvey is made by Lt.-Col. Barnes, who writes:

In the early days, in the absence of a really effective weapon to stop the enemy tanks, many and varied were the suggestions offered, and many the contrivances to be used. One of these Heath Robinson contraptions was the Harvey flame-thrower, and in 1941 we were given twelve of these weapons, one per road block. Various of our officers attended demonstrations of this weapon and all came away with the same conclusion, that they were better than nothing.

They were difficult to move and to conceal, their range was limited, the area of their effectiveness small, and the period of the flame was only some 25 seconds. In addition they were certainly a "one shot" weapon, and the manipulators would most decidedly have been a suicide squad.

So altogether we were not enamoured with the Harvey. Our twelve were stored in the goods yard of the L.M.S. Station, and here they peacefully reposed until their withdrawal in 1943. Whatever may have been their value in the early days, with the advent of the Spigot they became completely out of date.

## A FLOOD OF GRENADES

From 1940 onwards the grenades began to trickle in, beginning with the old 36 and ending in a positive flood, which included the 68, the 73, the "Sticky", the 69 or Bakelite and the 75 anti-tank.

This was travelling a long way from Molotov cocktails and the Guard began to feel in greater heart proportionately.

It was reassuring indeed to envisage the effect of the "sticky" or the "75" on an enemy tank.

What, however, most Home Guards thought of one grenade is well expressed by Lt.-Col. Barnes.

With all the types of grenades [he writes] with the exception of one, we felt perfectly safe. This exception was the 68, fired from the cup-discharger. Throughout the country there were many fatal accidents with these, not always, I am sure, due to the official explanation that the firer had placed the grenade in the discharger the wrong way round. In any case, many prematures occurred, and as the firer was not alive to tell the tale the reason for them was never found. Although White and I fired some hundreds of these 68's we

always sighed a sigh of relief when the grenade left the discharger successfully.

I must relate one amusing incident that occurred in those days of 1941 soon after the issue of the E.Y. rifle and the cup-discharger. I was on the County Ground with C Company to demonstrate the new weapon, using dummy grenades for the purpose. We took up our position near the Ladies' Stand and fired first with the gas-regulator fully open. The grenade travelled some 80 yards; then with the regulator half closed we reached a distance of some 150 yards. At this point some inquisitive member of the Company inquired how far the grenade would go if the regulator was fully closed. Always willing to oblige, we proceeded to demonstrate. The bomb was placed in the discharger, and a ballistite cartridge in the chamber, and the trigger pressed. To our surprise the grenade sailed through the air at a tremendous height, clearing the Football Stand at the other end of the ground and finally came to rest in a garden of a house in Abington Avenue; the biggest hit ever made on the County Ground. Fortunately no damage was done, and the efficiency of the weapon was certainly proved to all the onlookers. Incidentally to settle all arguments as to the meaning of E.Y., it stands for the initials of Edgar Yule, the inventor of the cup-discharger in the last war.

## "DRAIN PIPE" ARTILLERY

The Guard had now become fully familiar with their rifles and the Lewis Gun, and there were also companies "glorying" in the possession of a Vickers' machine gun.

So far, however, the Home Guard had no artillery support. This position was now to be slightly rectified.

There appeared in various platoon and company headquarters sundry lengths of metal tubing, which, when assembled, resolved themselves into tripods supporting what appeared to be a length of drain pipe.

This apparently primitive "set up" turned out to be the famous Northover Projector —referred to in its manual by the alternative title of "sub-artillery".

It was, in all conscience, far from a "pretty" piece of work, and forever remained the "ugly duckling" of the family. Indeed its début in the Home Guard was received with some consternation and not a little derision.

Nothing like it had ever been seen before. It had a breech block and a simple firing mechanism. There was nothing complicated about it and, as these facts came home at their true worth to the Home Guard, opinions gradually altered.

Its simplicity, in fact, was soon hailed as an invaluable feature and its popularity was confirmed when it proved to be reasonably portable, easy to master, and extremely accurate when properly used.

[*Photo: G. Turnill*

Demonstration—Northover Projector, Denbies Home Guard Training School, February 1942.

First hailed as "drainpipe artillery", the Northover Projector later gained general respect. A public demonstration by B Company 12th (Northampton) Battalion at Northampton.

### WHEN THEY LAUGHED

*Wrote a rural Guard: At Saturday's social the major claimed to have made us what we are. But now we are wondering whether he was boasting or apologizing!*

## Chapter XV

# EMERGENCY FEEDING PLANS

By late January 1941 air raids had ceased somewhat after the terrific autumn blitz, but bombs continued to be dropped intermittently in the Northamptonshire area. One such raid brought the 2nd (Soke of Peterborough) Battalion into the picture when a stick of bombs was dropped on railway property north of the city.

Corporal Methven and a squad of members of D Company of the 2nd (Major T. G. Avery) on guard duty in the area affected, at once proceeded to the spot, and called out the police and Civil Defence.

They were able to give the exact locations of the bomb bursts and the authorities were thus able to take immediate action with a saving of much valuable time.

The squad then stood by and rendered assistance until the situation was clear.

Otherwise January 1941 passed with little of importance with the exception of inquiries from County Headquarters asking for numbers and sizes of battledress to complete establishment.

With delightful *naïveté* the inquiry added that "any man over forty inches or under twenty-seven inches round the waist will require a special size".

Formal application forms for commissions in the Guard had now also to be completed by all company and platoon commanders.

**STRANGE FOOD CONFERENCE**

February opened with a report of a strange conference held at an equally strange place by unnamed people who apparently met to decide under what conditions, if any, the Home Guard should be fed in the event of operations.

The conclusions of the conference make curious reading beside the regardful concern expressed at higher levels for the welfare of the Home Guard. Here is a summary which speaks for itself:

1. Home Guards are responsible for feeding themselves from their homes in the normal way for as long as possible. Individuals should be encouraged to collect their own emergency rations, which they should not consume until other supplies have failed.

2. The Civil Authorities' responsibility ends with supplying retailers in bulk. They cannot undertake to supply tinned foods other than those which may be available in retail shops.

3. Reponsibility of Military Authorities to feed the Home Guard does not arise merely because Home Guards have been mustered —but will only arise in the following cases:

   (a) When detachments of the Home Guard are called upon for duty in isolated posts or beach defences, or where it is not possible for them to feed from their homes.

   (b) When the Home Guard is fighting shoulder to shoulder with the military and can properly be said to have become attached to a military unit.

   (c) When all sources of civil supply have failed—or when owing to being in contact with the enemy it is no longer possible for the Home Guard to feed from home.

Pretty obviously the road to the army cookhouse door if "the Day" had come would have been a long one for the Home Guard, so long, in fact, that he would never have reached it at all. As it was, once more, the emergency never arose, but it had to be provided for and what happened in the 12th Battalion affords a striking example of the general situation.

## RATIONS FOR 24 HOURS

Writes Lt.-Col. Barnes:

In the Regular Army, with its various branches, the R.A.S.C. act as the supply column for the Infantry. With the Home Guard this was quite impossible; we had in case of necessity both to fight and feed ourselves. It was clear that however perfect the plans made, it would take some little time after "Action Stations" for things to get into working order. Hence the instruction that each man when called up should bring with him sufficient rations for twenty-four hours, by which time it was hoped that food would have been drawn and platoons be self-supporting. Each Platoon had been registered as a Catering Establishment with the Food Office and were entitled to draw food from the various grocers, butchers and bakers in their vicinity, who were required to keep stocks on hand for this emergency.

As cooking would have to be done in the Defended Localities by the platoons themselves, it was essential that each had at least one man who could cook. To this end, on 1 November 1941 a course in cooking was arranged by the I.T.C. at the Talavera Barracks, and twenty-five members of the Battalion attended the week-end instruction. As time went on, and camps were arranged, the cooks got plenty of practice, and so well did they do their job that I had no misgivings on the score of feeding had we been called out. In some parts, particularly in the country districts where the strength of the Home Guard was low and where, consequently, men could not be spared for cooking, the W.V.S. took this upon their shoulders and on various exercises functioned very efficiently. D Company, I am sure, will never forget that night at

Spratton on the Buzz Exercise when the ladies of the local W.V.S. toiled all through the night so that there was always a hot cup of tea or soup for those coming off or going on duty.

## EMERGENCY PACKS

I am certain that had we called upon them, the W.V.S. of Northampton, despite their other commitments, would have responded in a like manner. However, we took the view, rightly or wrongly, that, as the cooking for the Home Guard would have had to be done in the Defended Localities, which would probably have been in the centre of the fighting, it would have been unfair to ask the ladies to work in them. And so, if enemy action had taken place, the Battalion would have been fed by its own personnel.

In June 1942 Emergency Packs arrived at Headquarters. These contained rations for ten men for twenty-four hours and were only to be used if no other food was available. We received sufficient to cover all the members of the Battalion. They were stored at the Drill Hall, and as they were never required, there they remained until after Stand Down. Did I say all? I regret to have to state that some were missing, but with Regular units in residence for most of the war, the wonder was that so many remained.

The supply of cooking utensils was never satisfactory, and there is no doubt that the Home Guard would have been left to "improvise" as usual. With the evacuation of the civilian population from the Defended Localities, this would have presented little difficulty to those ingenious persons, the cooks.

The 7th Battalion was lucky in having an ex-Army W.O. cook who ran first-class courses for company cooks, but eventually the catering manager of the local Co-operative Society, Lt. H. J. Allen, was made Battalion Catering Officer and was responsible for providing hot meals in each of the Defended Localities. His organization was well tested in various exercises and seemed likely to have been as adequate as any garrison would require.

**DEPARTURE OF SIR HEREWARD WAKE**

February 1941 also brought a widely regretted event—that of the departure of the County Commander (Sir Hereward Wake), for Sir Hereward had reached the age of 65 and the War Office had decided that the duties of Zone Commander must be entrusted to younger men. He remained a member of the Home Guard in the 11th Battalion till the end of the war.

Before he left he met and confided in his senior officers and the final words of his address to them can well be recorded.

I think [he said] that we have worked together these nine months very well and very happily. I hope you think so, too. We have all done our best to meet the difficulties and keep smiling all the time. We have achieved a great deal.

I am most grateful to you and to all ranks of the Northamptonshire Home Guard for the way you and they have helped in the show.

I am dreadfully sorry to leave you but in my successor, my friend Col. Lester Reid, you will have a leader with very desirable qualifications as you all know.

**FAREWELL ORDER**

Sir Hereward also issued a special order to the Zone in the following terms:

On giving up my appointment as Zone Commander I desire to thank all officers and men of the County Home Guard for their loyal assistance and co-operation, and to place on record my high appreciation of their patriotic efforts during the nine months I have had the honour to command them.

Much has been achieved, and I feel confident that under my successor the Home Guard of Northamptonshire will maintain their efforts towards efficiency, so that, if the enemy dares to set foot in our country, they will be prepared to meet him and to deal with him with resolution and success.

Following is the concluding paragraph of a letter addressed to the County Commander just before his departure, by General Sir Robert Adam, Army Commander, Northern Command, York:

I should like to say how grateful I am for all the work you have done in initial organization and making the Northamptonshire Home Guard into the efficient show it is.

That gratitude was, surely, shared by every member of every battalion throughout the shire for it is certain that at no period of the Home Guard's existence was any command charged with heavier cares and labours than obtained in Northamptonshire during these first exacting and anxious nine months.

**COL. LESTER REID TAKES OVER**

To succeed Sir Hereward in the post was to undertake no light responsibility and it says much for the high sense of duty and readiness for self-sacrifice of Col. P. Lester Reid, C.B.E., then commanding the Brackley Battalion, that he accepted the appointment which was confirmed on 21 February 1941.

Like his predecessor, Col. Reid brought to the office, not only the essential wide measure of personal popularity the post demanded, but also the right type of high military experience, both in administration and in the field, that was essential to the discharge of the command.

Col. P. Lester Reid.

He was well known in Northamptonshire, particularly among ex-Servicemen, and members of the British Legion, and, up to a few months previously, had been president of the Northamptonshire County Council of the Legion.

Col. Reid's military career began in 1902 when, on leaving Sandhurst, he joined the Irish Guards.

He became a brigade-major to a Territorial brigade, and at the outbreak of the 1914–18 war he rejoined the Guards and went to France with them in 1914, being wounded in the following year.

On attaining his majority he was given command of the 2nd Battalion Irish Guards and, later promoted, served on the staff of General Headquarters. He was

response, either in co-operation or encouragement.

Coincidentally, Lt.-Col. H. Burditt, M.C., T.D., became second-in-command at Zone H.Q., and the commands of battalions, as previously detailed, were confirmed by commissions as lieutenant-colonels of the fourteen battalion commanders. Lt.-Col. Sir V. L. Robinson, Bt.,

Winners of the 1942 Manning Shooting Cup of the 12th (Northampton) Battalion. No. 4 Platoon of B Co. *Left to right back row:* Pte. J. Church, Pte. S. E. Redwood, Pte. L. S. Luff. *Front row:* Pte. E. H. Beckwith, Sgt. S. Haynes, Lt. L. W. Lucas, Cpl. A. Chambers and Pte. C. Potter.

four times mentioned in dispatches and was awarded the O.B.E.

Settling at Thorpe Mandeville after the war, Col. Reid took up farming, and in 1926 became a member of the Northamptonshire County Council, where he sat for eleven years. In 1931, he served the County as High Sheriff, and in 1936 was made a magistrate.

The news of Col. Reid's appointment was received with unanimous approval throughout the Zone, and all ranks determined to afford him all the loyalty and support they could offer. They did so and never found their new leader wanting in

M.C., and Lt.-Col. V. W. Sykes succeeding Col. Burditt and Lt.-Col. H. G. Sotheby, M.V.O., D.S.O., in the 5th (Kettering District) and 8th (Wellingborough District) commands respectively.

Two notable instructions circulated at this time were those authorizing warrant rank for those Home Guards who, although eligible, were not desirous of taking commissions, and the abolition of group commands with effect from 9 March 1941.

Sector commands were to follow but that was a later development.

On the arms side the period was also memorable for the arrival of the first

Thompson sub-machine guns in any quantity. The first distribution totalled twenty-two, but this was stepped up to 338.

## FIRST EFFECTIVE FIELD EXERCISES

With the coming of spring in 1941 the Guard was sufficiently trained and equipped to engage in its first really effective field exercises.

Northamptonshire saw now—instead of poorly armed civilians with slung gas-masks in cardboard boxes and ash-plants in their hands, slinking almost furtively into the darkness—ranks of khaki-clad men on parade, and heard the staccato commands that locked and unlocked the formations.

Squad, platoon, and company drill began

Oundle's air raid wardens set a lead to the area by taking weapon training under Home Guard Instructors. Picture shows a sergeant of the 3rd (Oundle) Battalion, demonstrating to a wardens' class.

Those which had been staged previously had so sadly lacked the necessary means as to have had little more than theoretic value.

Now the battalions got down to it in earnest, often in combination with Regular troops and the incidental physical demands threw strange, unwonted stresses on men who, in the majority, had, for a quarter of a century, been resting on laurels won in an earlier war.

Few of them were of an age when muscles respond easily to sudden calls, or minds answer with the resilience of youth.

Drill also kept in step with this expanding activity and the patrols, which had covered the whole countryside with an almost invisible network, were withdrawn, and were succeeded by evening and Sunday parades.

to have its wholesome disciplinary effect, and mercifully calculated periods of physical training served to limber up men who, in most cases, were well past the forty mark, with arms drill adding a burnished finish to the whole.

Imperceptibly, almost, the Home Guard had grown from untrained or half-trained civilians, into real soldiers, learning to walk before they could run, and when they had done that, turning their energies to mastering new weapons and to the real tactics of fighting.

Wider fields now opened, in which they could "spread themselves" and win some sort of reward for the earlier monotony.

Theory, painfully absorbed in section huts and platoon headquarters, developed into practice. Suburban streets and village environs saw skirmishes without number by troops who had garnished themselves with weird and wonderful camouflage.

Quiet spinneys, normally the exclusive haunts of lovers and nightingales, bristled over the week-ends with weapons and re-sounded with the simulated din of battle.

Village school classrooms and old barns became the nerve centres of attacking or

thing as it was possible to devise. In fact, it was impossible, except for the most jaded minds, to take part in them without a stirring of the blood and a welcome and unwonted excitement.

To have a share in some attack which swept on through some blistering forenoon, or to creep relentlessly through the pitch blackness of an English winter night, was

The Shooting Team of No. 6 Platoon B Company of the 12th (Northampton) Battalion photographed after winning their Company Cup presented by P. C. Williams. Left to right standing are Privates H. Richardson, H. C. Fisher, A. C. Lewis, W. Underwood, L. E. Payne, A. H. Sturgess and D. L. Sharman. Seated: Sub-Section-Leader A. C. Woolnough, Section-Leader J. W. Wigfall, Platoon Officer W. A. W. Evans, Section-Leader H. W. Revell and Sub-Section-Leader E. Boswell. (March 1941.)

defending units, and dark and lonely lanes echoed softly to the sinister footsteps of reconnoitring patrols.

From small beginnings, this training widened in its scope and included, long be-fore the end, schemes which embraced huge tracts of countryside and thousands of troops.

Though, by now, these night operations and week-end exercises are dimmed by the passage of time, few who took part in them will ever forget them. They held a species of thrill which was as near to the actual

to be a participant in something which was more than "make believe"—something that some day might be the real thing.

Nor did the defence lose anything by their often passive roles. It was worth while, perhaps, stubbornly to defend some "keep", or to fight some desperate rear-guard action against long odds.

It was not actuality, of course—there was no death abroad and no pitiful wounded to succour—but imagination, let loose as it so often was, untrammelled and unchecked, lent conviction to dry plans and ordered schemes until they really "lived".

A Northover Projector of the 12th (Northampton) Battalion covering the Harborough Road, Northampton, during a big Home Defence Exercise in August 1941.

The readers of this history will no doubt recall many such times, and to keep their memories green there are recorded in these pages the stories of TYPICAL operations, in which "old warriors" may haply again "smell powder" and catch once more the thrill of battle.

## DIFFERENCES OVER DRESS

Several interesting developments emerged at this period in Zone Command orders, notably those regularizing the numbering of battalions, the appointment of medical officers, the issue of a limited number of medical haversacks, the appointment of honorary chaplains, uncommissioned, and permission to mark steel helmets with the badge of the County Regiment.

This "decorative" concession serves to recall several "incidentals" of Home Guard "make-up". There were, for instance, the few who insisted on wearing their old regimental badges instead of that of the "Steelbacks". These were kindly, but firmly, dealt with in due course, and they fell into line with the majority, who were only too proud to "sport" a badge symbolizing so much honour and glory.

"Stop!" A military staff umpire intervened just in time to prevent a "spot of bother" when hand-to-hand fighting developed in Kettering Cattle Market during an exercise in September 1942, in which the 3rd, 4th, 5th and 6th Battalions, plus the 13th Leicesters, participated. As it was (*inset*) there was at least one genuine casualty.

Then there was the slight controversy over the action of the ultra-smart in stiffening their haversacks and gas-mask containers with cardboard. While any such attempts to emulate the Brigade of Guards had not to be discouraged, it was pointed out that the cardboard was needed for salvage anyhow, and that any stiffening process could better be applied to the jaw.

The new Marching Order for the Home Guard demonstrated by R.S.M. R. Collier Permanent Staff Instructor of the 12th (Northampton) Battalion.

Finally, there were the few "rebels" who, having no buttons on their battledresses to polish, insisted, against orders, in appearing on parade with the brasswork on their respirators burnished until its twinkling points could be seen a mile off. It was difficult to deal with this sort of enthusiast, and generally speaking, he was left until his surplus energy tired and his brilliance tarnished.

Simultaneous with the numbering of battalions just recorded, works platoons were also absorbed into battalions with new nomenclature. Thus in the 12th

Northampton) Battalion the Electric Light became No. 1 Headquarters Platoon, the Gas Company Platoon No. 2, Headquarters Platoon. A Company Mobile Platoon became No. 3, the Borough Water Platoon No. 4, the Express Lift Platoon No. 5, and the United Omnibus Co. Platoon became Headquarters Platoon No. 6.

### BOMBS AT BILLING

Although, as we have noted previously, air raids had now slackened considerably, lone raiders were frequent visitors, and in the small hours of Good Friday (11 April) 1941, one of these brought Great Billing platoon (A Company, 11th Battalion) into rapid action by planting four bombs on the Northampton Sewage Disposal Works at the south of the village adjacent to the large Billing Flax Mills which, being then engaged in producing war material, were probably the raider's objective.

One bomb caused a temporary blockage of the lower road to Ecton, a second hit a flax storage barn without igniting its contents, a third opened a crater in the Sewage Works' main road, and a fourth was a time-bomb which fell in nearby ploughland.

As soon as the explosions occurred, Lt. J. H. Spencer (Platoon Commander) turned out with all available members of the platoon, who then mounted a cordon of guards around the delayed action bomb to prevent public approach.

The bomb did not explode until thirty-six hours later, during which time the guards waited, watched, and listened!

In the same raid, though whether by the same aircraft was never determined, an approximation to a "Brock's Benefit" of flares and incendiary bombs was released over the north-west of Billing.

None of these, fortunately, found a target, but the platoon's then second-in-command, 2nd Lt. B. G. Holloway, was engaged for some four hours from dawn scouring the district in a car to pick up a load of "dud" bombs and other "souvenirs" including the remains of a "Molotov bread basket", as multiple incendiary containers were termed.

## FIRST BIRTHDAY BOUQUETS

Now came the first anniversary (14 May 1941) and with it a shower of public

I thank them for the service which they freely give at considerable sacrifice of leisure and convenience, and I am confident that, in co-operation with their comrades-in-arms of the Field Army, they will fit themselves to meet and overcome every emergency and so make their contribution to the victory which will reward our united efforts.

GEORGE R.I.

To Northamptonshire came also the following letter to Col. Lester Reid from

Part of the Harlestone Platoon which included some 30 per cent of ex-Service-men. The Commander was Lt. G. St. J. Rands. (April 1941.)

bouquets for the Home Front Army, including the following message from the King, issued as a Special Army Order:

I heartily congratulate the Home Guard on the progress made by all ranks since it was established a year ago to-day. On many occasions I have seen for myself the keenness with which they are fitting themselves for the discharge of vital duties in the defence of our homes. They have already earned the gratitude of their fellow citizens for the prompt and unstinted assistance which they are constantly giving to the Civil Defence services.

The Home Guard stands in the direct line of the various bodies of militia, trained bands, fencibles, and volunteers, the records of whose fine spirit and military aptitude adorn many a page of our history.

Brig. R. S. Abbott, C.I.E., M.C., of the East Central Area Command:

Headquarters East Central Area,
Stanley Road,
Leicester.
15 *May* 1941

DEAR LESTER REID,

May I add my congratulations to all ranks of the Home Guard to those you have already received, on the wonderful progress made in the first year of its existence.

The keenness displayed in their training has brought all units in this Sub-Area to a remarkably high standard of efficiency, which inspires confidence in the reception they will give to the enemy if the occasion arises.

Yours sincerely,
R. S. ABBOTT

The anniversary was marked by special church and other parades and a notable feature of the former was the earnest interest and attendance of the general public whose members had now come to appreciate the Home Guard at its true worth.

A Home Guard Parade was a feature of a fête at Harpole in August 1941. Lt.-Gen. Sir John Brown who was actively identified with the foundation of the force, was present and is here seen making an inspection.

### THE TRIANGLE SCHEME

Almost coincident with the first anniversary came the first announcement of what was generally hailed as a brilliant and ingenious scheme for dealing with sudden isolated landings of one or more parachute spies, saboteurs, or advanced patrols of larger forces to follow.

It was the inspiration and work of Col. H. Burditt, of Desborough, who had spent much spare time in its perfection.

The isolated type of landing was, of course, the Guards' special responsibility and this scheme enabled such a landing to be contained with the promptitude which was vitally essential.

The scheme which was revealed at an officers' night at Northampton on 29 May 1941 was known as the Triangle Scheme because it provided for the division of areas into triangles, each of which was identified by a number. For a given number of triangles there was a previously determined post identified as "Report Centre", designed to serve as a rapid clearing-house for information within its area.

In operation, the triangle in which an enemy landing occurred became identified as the "Action Triangle" and all Home

On the way to a National Day of Prayer, four of the platoons of B Company of the 11th Battalion Northamptonshire Home Guard are here seen led by Company Commander Maj. F. A. Thompson (immediately behind the band). (March 1941.)

Guard units within "Action" area immediately went into action. Coincidently they informed "Report Centre" which, in turn, informed all Home Guard units in triangles adjacent to "Action Triangle", which triangles were termed "Stand To" triangles whose Home Guard units at once sent out patrols and stood ready to cordon the area or support "Action Triangle".

Report Centre also warned, in turn, the senior military commander of the area, the Home Guard company commander concerned, and the Police.

It was also laid down that each village should have a card for each triangle which abutted on its own showing (a) number of triangle, (b) the names of the villages and the forces available for the triangle, i.e. strength of men and arms including automatics available, (c) name of report centre, and (d) all important telephone numbers.

Each village was at all times to maintain touch with adjacent military units in the triangles all round and keep up-to-date records of essential information.

Periodical tests of communications were also to be made.

The scheme impressed the majority of rural Home Guard leaders as an excellent one and in operational tests it worked with remarkable smoothness and celerity.

But, for an unexplained reason, it was allowed to lapse, and no more was heard of it after a few months.

## WHEN THEY LAUGHED

*"What is a teetotaller?" asked the young intake of the Q.M.S.*

*"A teetotaller," said the Q.M.S. gravely, "is a man who suffers from thirst instead of enjoying it."*

## Chapter XVI

# THE ART OF CAMOUFLAGE

CASUAL previous reference has been made to the use of camouflage by the Home Guard. Until the spring of 1941, however, it had been mainly of an improvised "home-made" character with little relation to the highly advanced technique which had been developed in the Regular Army.

This technique was now to be absorbed by, and applied to, the Home Guard, and the story of the process cannot better be told than by Capt. F. S. Courtney, 12th (Northampton) Battalion, then Principal of the Northampton School of Art, who was subsequently appointed Camouflage Officer on the staff of the Zone Commander.

Here is that story as he relates it:

Camouflage came to the Home Guard after we had been established about a year and it was some time before it became part of every-day training.

My first introduction to it was an invitation from my Company Commander, Major (later Lt.-Col.) N. P. Andrews, to take a course at Denbies, the No. 1 Home Guard Training School.

I went with Major (later Lt.-Col.) L. E. Barnes, who appeared to spend all his spare time there, and although the course was mixed I was there especially for camouflage.

Here I watched demonstrations and attended lectures by Rowland Penrose, a

[Photo: J. Wright

A not so innocent log pile. Camouflage artfully conceals the sniper whose rifle muzzle is visible on left.

painter with surrealist leanings. We were shown sniper suits—large cumbersome hessian hoods and cloaks painted in disruptive shapes —and the use of nets over a "spider" which folded easily for carrying, but the most impressive demonstrations came from the legendary

All ranks obliged each other
in facial camouflage.

Yank levy, who taught us various crawls (and how to use the knife in dramatic and effective ways) and showed us the value of fine and careful craftsmanship in the siting and clean digging of slit trenches.

Within a week or two of my return, a programme of company visits was arranged for me, and I gave evening lectures on (1) General Camouflage, and (2) Personal Concealment.

At this time, as a corporal, I was the only one in the battalion concerned (officially) with camouflage training, and I doubled this with company guide duties.

## A TOUGH AND DRAMATIC COURSE

In other battalions some officers went to another school, a semi-official one run by Capt. Langdon-Davies on very severe and realistic lines, where Fieldcraft was the principal subject.

It was a tough, dramatic, and very convincing course, designed by officers with experience in the Spanish Civil War, especially for the Home Guard.

The course created great enthusiasm, and in at least one battalion, the 7th, the enthusiasm was infectious.

There Lt. Burton began to train his own and other platoons in Langdon-Davies methods. Lt. (later Major) Newton, of the 11th Battalion, also became interested and tried out his ideas.

Still another school was heard of, Welwyn, and Lt. Newton and I went for a concentrated week-end course to the Camouflage School there.

A Capt. (later Major) Bull had converted his private gymnasium into a lecture room, museum, and workshop for the creation of aids to camouflage. This was an intensely interesting course, full of new ideas and an infectious enthusiasm from Capt. Bull and his assistant (later Capt.) Money-Coutts.

Female disguise adopted by a
Yardley Gobion Home Guard
to get right inside an enemy
H.Q. in a 1942 exercise. The
bouquet concealed a bomb!

The four chief features were:

(1) A hood or headdress made from a sandbag and garnished with small knots of camouflage scrim;

(2) "Scrim string"—knots of scrim tied every seven inches in lengths of thickish string;

(3) Small net screens of rabbit wire garnished with bows of scrim;

(4) Dark face cream.

The demonstrations in the neighbouring park were carried out by soldiers using Capt. Bull's methods. Here we began to see for the first time that camouflage need not be static, but with the light, comfortable, and extremely effective new disguises individuals and even numbers of us could move to new positions

weapon in static positions. We learned new ways of using rubber bands (on the arms, legs, and helmet) into which we tucked grass and small leaves.

## WEEK-END CAMOUFLAGE SCHOOL

About this time Major Bull was given the job of making the whole of Eastern Command camouflage-conscious. He spent several days each week at Command Headquarters and the

A good example of siting and camouflage by No. 3 Platoon of D Co. of the 9th (Brixworth) Battalion in the July 1942 invasion of Northampton exercise. The weapon pit which held this Northover Projector was an adapted heap of sand on the roadside.

unseen though within range of enemy vision. We were taught how to move so that sudden jerks would not give our position away; how to kill all shine; how to make use of the background; how to defeat observations from the air. All this was brought back to our battalions, and in evening lectures to platoons we demonstrated these new ideas and showed how the equipment could be made.

At a later visit to Welwyn we were introduced to two new materials and some more ideas. Rolls of rabbit wire were produced already prepared with attached stained feathers (cullacorts) or steel wool, both painted a quiet green-grey. We were shown several ways of using these two materials and learned the technique of handling them. Major Bull also showed us how to garnish strawberry and fish nets with small bows of scrim and how effective these could be in concealing man and

rest visiting battalions throughout the command. With his inspiration and persuasion camouflage officers with the rank of captain were appointed to each Sub-District. I was appointed to Northamptonshire and was asked to start a week-end school.

Accommodation and feeding was a great difficulty; but in the end we compromised on a one-day (Sunday) course held in the Art School. I was assisted by Major Newton, Cadet Lt. Smart, a few enthusiastic Home Guards, and a variety of Army Cadets from the Art School and Technical College.

We collected and made lecture and demonstration equipment and trained helpers to carry out the demonstrations effectively on some neighbouring waste land. We began with battalion and company commanders, timidly and fearfully following Major Bull's advice of beginning at the top and working downwards so that camouflage could come to each battalion from its colonel who would, we hoped, be converted, if need be, by our work at the school. The first course was well received and we continued the school to the end of the Home Guard activity, our full total of students being several hundreds of officers and N.C.O.s of all ranks.

A novel idea for fixed fire points. The "lid"—camouflaged wire netting on a wooden frame—could be dropped instantaneously, rendering the trench practically invisible.

A typical school course contained an introductory lecture, one on personal camouflage, one on the camouflage of weapons, a lantern lecture on the air view, and a field demonstration in which men and weapons were involved and including every kind of Home Guard and sub-artillery weapons. Although this was the general limit of our responsibility, we talked also of the camouflage of such buildings as Home Guards were likely to use and of the lorries which, later, were our official transport. In evening lectures we gave demonstrations to transport units and illustrated our talks with drawings, pictures, photographs, and actual materials. The school, too, became a central store from which cullacorts, steel-wool, paint, nets, etc., were distributed.

To what effect Capt. Courtney and his staff translated their instruction the accompanying pictures bear more eloquent testimony than any written word.

## AN "INVISIBLE" CAMP

How camouflage training was taken up in the battalions was well exemplified by an innovation created by Lt. Burton, Camouflage Officer of the 7th (Wellingborough Town) Battalion (Lt.-Col. H. L. Allsopp), who practised what he preached at the Battalion Camouflage School.

Sited in the centre of a spinney, it had to be "pin-pointed" to be located, and then it was quite unrecognizable as anything but a perfectly innocent spinney!

A "rabbit-hole" in the hedge was the entrance, and so well restored were the tracks, etc., that it remained for small inconspicuous notice-boards to provide the guiding clues.

One of these was a broader guide. Its epigrammatic inscription ran "Dirty hands? — Sometimes. Dirty arms? — NEVER!"

Each Saturday afternoon parties of Home Guard marched out from Wellingborough to Harrowden and were self-supporting at this school until Sunday evening. Capt. (later Major) W. G. Gilbey was the unconscious, but willing, provider of many a rabbit for the cook's pot.

## GALLANT RESCUE IN 2ND BATTALION AREA

Home Guard exploits throughout the country continued to be reported from time to time, but two at this period need special record.

The first concerned the 2nd (Soke of Peterborough) Battalion and occurred on the afternoon of Saturday, 17 May 1941, when a British Hampden bomber crashed near Manor Farm, Uffington, and immediately burst into flames.

Lt. J. E. Conington, a platoon commander of B Company of the 2nd, happened to be about eighty yards from the spot and, despite the fact that live ammunition was exploding in all directions and that there was every possibility of a major explosion at any moment, he rushed without hesitation towards the plane.

Through an inferno of blazing petrol and exploding ammunition, he saw a man desperately endeavouring to extricate himself from the plane cockpit, and at once went to his aid. Lt. Conington managed to get a grip on the still conscious pilot to drag him from the wreckage and to carry him forty-five yards from the wreck. Hardly had he done so than there was a violent explosion from the plane, probably due to bursting oxygen cylinders.

Lt. Conington lay with the rescued airman, now unconscious, until the flying bullets decreased, by which time his second-in-command, 2nd Lt. A. G. Teesdale, had arrived on the scene with Pte. E. E. Cooke.

2nd. Lt. Teesdale and Private Cooke, seeing another airman lying near the plane, apparently blown out by the explosion, went to his rescue and got him away, but he was dead.

The action of Lt. Conington and his assistants earned the special commendation of the Area Commander and the Zone Commander (Col. P. Lester Reid), and but for the fact that all were off duty and not in uniform at the time it would almost certainly have won for them military awards.

## BOMBER CRASH IN TOWN CENTRE

The second episode was also concerned with the Royal Air Force, but it also concerned a whole town, including its police and Civil Defence forces.

Suddenly at 5.15 a.m. on 15 July 1941 sleeping Northampton was awakened by a terrific crash in its town centre immediately followed by clouds of smoke arising from what appeared to be a serious fire.

A Stirling bomber had crashed in the centre of one of the main thoroughfares, having just missed the tower of the town's principal church of All Saints before "pancaking" and breaking into a thousand fragments, smashing windows, breaking stonework, and setting fire to several adjacent business premises.

The then Officer Commanding the 12th (Northampton) Battalion (Lt.-Col. T. E. Manning) happened to be visiting O.P.s in the district at the time and was, in fact, at a post only a short distance from the spot. He was, thus, one of the first people to arrive at the scene of the crash and at once turned out all available members of the 12th Battalion, who arrived in uniform, and set to work with the police and Civil Defence forces, controlling traffic and keeping crowds away from any possible danger, for a number of unexploded bombs had crashed with the plane.

Those who were present will never forget the scene. The upper part of Gold Street, part of George Row and the area in front of All Saints was almost knee-deep in shattered debris. There was also a stench of gas from fractured mains, and houses and shops round about had to be evacuated. Yet, amazingly enough, there was only one casualty, that of an errand boy, and his injury was not fatal.

The most significant feature of the occurrence, however, as it related to the Home Guard, was the fact that when the Stirling's crew baled out, north of the town, they were sighted at once by Home Guards at O.P.s, who did not know whether they were enemy or otherwise, and each airman landed straight "into the arms" of Home Guards of three different platoons.

This proof of the alertness and prompt action of the Home Guards in the area was highly acclaimed as affording striking evidence of what would have happened to enemy parachute troops.

Finally, the Northampton Chief Constable and A.R.P. Controller (Mr. John Williamson) sent a special letter of thanks to Lt.-Col. Manning for the valuable assistance the Battalion had rendered.

The 12th (Northampton) Battalion Home Guard were participants in Northampton's 1941 Warship Week. They are seen arriving for the "quarterdeck" service on the Market Square, Northampton.

## WHEN THEY LAUGHED

*The youth was about to take his proficiency badge. His father, a senior Home Guard, sought to give him some advice.*

*"Now, my boy," he said, "I hope you understand perfectly what I mean."*

*"Yes," replied the youth. "What it boils down to is this: If I do well it's because of heredity, and if I fail it's my own fault."*

## Chapter XVII

## INTELLIGENCE THE "CINDERELLA"

WE have shown that in 1941 camouflage first came into the serious picture. Now also emerged "Intelligence" in the military sense, to supplement the Home Guard's specialist sections. As it had been for decades in the Regular Army, Intelligence in the Home Guard began as a "Cinderella", for even many enlightened and experienced commanders were loath to regard with unqualified respect any units which were not primarily combatant.

However, Home Guard Intelligence triumphantly justified itself as the intelligence records of all the Northamptonshire battalions testify. Space precludes the reproduction of all those records, and summaries of those of two battalions, both of advanced merit, must suffice to illustrate the whole.

The first is the Intelligence Section at battalion headquarters of the 12th (Northampton) Battalion, which was one of which its intelligence officer (Lt. A. F. Payne) was justifiably proud.

The personnel of this live section were "handpicked" from all parts of the borough, and to some extent this had its disadvantages at first, because, although individual men knew their own area "like the back of their hands", they, like many townsmen, had only the sketchiest idea of many other districts, into which, normally, they only penetrated at intervals, and, usually, then only along the main bus routes.

This, however, was soon obviated, and, eventually, members of the Intelligence Section of the 12th became fully cognizant of all places of military and strategic

importance by making *actual visits* to all of them, large and small.

This meticulous method made it possible for extremely detailed lists of water supplies, police boxes, telephones, and other items to be compiled, all of which would have been priceless had emergency arisen.

The resultant information was also marked on the various maps of the defended localities, so that, in the end, the nerve centre of the 12th knew practically everything about Northampton that was of even the slightest strategical or tactical importance.

The section did not use pigeons, but they had what was well described as the finest crowd of dispatch riders inside the county boundaries. Tribute to these D.R.s is paid on an earlier page.

### MESSAGES TO BE SWALLOWED

Ciphers and codes were never actually used, but a cipher issued by the East Central Command and changed at fairly frequent intervals was one of the Battalion's intelligence officer's "headaches". Other ciphers of a much simpler character were taught at various courses, but, again, were never brought into actual use.

The D.R.s were warned to destroy all messages entrusted to them if necessary, either by swallowing them or dropping them into the petrol tank.

The work of the Intelligence Section was hard—and sometimes humdrum—but it had its compensations, for, intermingled with the dull matter, there was a whole lot of fascinating material.

THE INTELLIGENCE SECTION

MAP READING

There is a reminiscence about an exercise at battalion level without troops, during which two keen and apparently energetic umpires, in relays, fired questions at the battalion I.O. from 7 p.m. one evening to noon the next day. This, while coming under the category of hard work, could never be described as "humdrum".

The usual method of sending messages

Battalion area where Capt. Langham officiated as Battalion Intelligence Officer.

The I. Section of the 4th was, in effect, the original Guides Section, composed of two men from each company under a Chief Guide, i.e., eighteen men and one officer.

The extended training programme for guides as set forth in Home Guard Instructions took effect round about June 1941,

Model H.Q. demonstrated in No. 3 Sector in May 1943 as part of an Intelligence Course organized by Lt. P. Perry (Sub-Area I.O.) and Lt. H. G. C. Jones (Sector I.O.). The Commander, played by Lt. Jones, is putting the Invasion Committee chairman "wise" to the situation. Note the message board at rear.

was by D.R., but there were other means— for example, via the searchlight stations, the Observer Corps, and the Police. There was also the telephone.

Everyone who has been "in the know" at any Home Guard exercises will remember the famous "Battle Boards" which were used for incoming and outgoing messages.

The 12th Battalion Intelligence Section evolved a drill for this useful piece of "secret" furniture, and were consequently never at a loss when the occasion arose to use it.

### INTELLIGENCE IN THE 4TH

For our second example of "I" efficiency we move into the 4th (Kettering Town)

and this programme was in fact practically identical with that which was later issued for "Intelligence".

The Guides Section, therefore, also provided the I. personnel and became known as the G. and I. Section. The arrangement was ideal for a concentrated battalion such as the 4th, as when the need for guides, as such, became no longer necessary, the previous training which had extended over eighteen months made the old guides section particularly useful as Intelligence personnel.

When the first large-scale exercises, such as "Terrier" and "Scorch" were made, this personnel performed excellent work in manning the "Ops." room which, even at an early date, was complete with maps, battle board, messages, etc.

In those early days, however, there was no signals section as a separate entity, and this meant that the I. Section had this work as well, which nearly doubled their labours.

Early difficulties, which were fairly numerous, consisted among other things of a dearth of maps, message pads, summaries

(This work took about two months of hard slogging.)

(*b*) *Bridges and Culverts.* With dimensions, approaches, and carrying strengths.

(*c*) *Police.* Showing central points for traffic diversion, evacuation, etc., as required by the military situation.

(*d*) *Civil Defence.* Showing headquarters of all services, food stores, V.P.s, rest centres, first aid posts, etc.

The Model H.Q. attacked. The German intruder was "liquidated" by a ruse following a mock surrender.

and intelligence logs, but, with a praiseworthy resource, these were privately printed, and were ready for use by the time "Terrier" exercise started in 1941.

In 1941 the I. Section was able to borrow from the Borough Surveyor of Kettering (and other sources) enough 6-in. maps to cover a twenty-mile area, including, and around, the Battalion's boundary, and the G. and I. Section, in their spare time, made tracings of these from which prints were taken. These were of great value, both from an operational and training angle.

Maps were also made for the purpose of locating:

(*a*) *Water Supply Auxiliaries*, showing wells, tanks, pumps, etc., in full detail.

(*e*) *Military Route Signs.* These signs, which have since disappeared, were kept in repair with wood, paint, etc., by the guides.

Changes due to quarrying, aerodrome building, the cutting down of woods and spinneys, and the closing of roads and routes due to War Department activities, etc., were also recorded on the 6-in. maps, and copies sent to Command (via sector) on maps 1/25000 scale.

## WOMEN "I" AUXILIARIES AND PIGEONS

A voluntary section of women auxiliaries was formed in August 1942 and trained to take the place of intelligence other ranks in the operations room. It is believed that this was the first party of women formed for such work in the Sub-Area. They were marvellously efficient and too much praise cannot be given to them for the enthusiasm and energy displayed.

The pigeon method of sending messages was encouraged by the Bedfordshire Sub-Area and a section was formed in the 4th about June 1941, which, under the expert direction of the Pigeon Officer, Lt. Brockhurst, became very proficient.

The birds were used successfully in most of the large-scale exercises, and in exercise "Hector" (1942) the sceptics were nonplussed when a pigeon arrived at an outpost in Stanton Pits (which had been cut off by the enemy) with a message that the time of receipt was three minutes earlier than the time of origin!

In a later Battalion exercise, these birds fully proved their worth, when over fifty messages were transmitted from all points of the compass without a single loss—a quite remarkable achievement.

The only unorthodox code used by the 4th Battalion was for night "recce", when ordinary field signals were transmitted by the use of shielded torches (which each guide carried) and a simple system of flashes. For "recce" patrol work the recognized Army "Recce Code" was used.

Well deserving of recognition in this history are the members of Northampton units of a body formed quite early in the war and titled Women's Home Defence. These pictures were taken at their camp at Overstone Park in July 1942. They show (1) Off for physical training. (2) Target practice. (3) A genuine casualty for the First Aid Section. Victim had a dislocated shoulder. (4) Learning the fine art of unarmed combat. (5) Cookhouse call. On right is Mrs. Birdie who was one of the prime organizers with Miss Koop, a mistress at Overstone School.

Capt. Langham relates that the miscellany of lethal "weapons" carried by his men in the early days, such as throttling cords, daggers, etc., would have amazed the hardiest **Commando!**

He adds that the intelligence training was a great and never-to-be-forgotten training for all of them. The work encompassed such a varied and interesting ground, from knowing the enemy, his guns, equipment, and O.B., to knowing and touring and sketching their own countryside, that the Section never once got "browned off". There was always something new to learn and to instruct.

The liaison work was always enjoyable, and enlarged the circle of friends.

On the debit side may perhaps be recorded the cost of expensive binoculars, prismatic compasses, and slide rules, tracing and printing materials, epidioscope, and, last but not least, the depreciation suffered by members' cars during desperate endeavours to get from "here to there" across impossible ploughed fields and ditches in search of alternative routes.

Assuredly "I" in the Home Guard justified itself, and in the closing stages there was no section of which the commands at all levels were more appreciative. They had learned as the Regular Army had learned before them, that "I" was the "eyes and ears" of any force.

### ANOTHER SPY HUNT

B Company of the 5th (Kettering District) Battalion again entered the central picture in June 1941, when at 0300 hours on the 27th of that month a message was received from the police asking for help in rounding up a suspected spy who had fired at a policeman near Cransley Reservoir.

The call-up worked admirably and by 0320 hours the first patrol was out.

Patrols then combed the company area towards Cransley for hours without success and they were dismissed at 0630 hours, regular troops and police having taken up the search.

### FIRST RUMOURS OF COMPULSION

The early summer of 1941 brought such large demands for men for the Regular Army that the Home Guard was now heavily drained of its younger members and recruiting drives began again in many battalion areas.

Few of these gained the success anticipated and for the first time there was "talk" of plans for the roping in of the "slackers" by compulsory measures.

The whole body of the existing Home Guard deeply resented even the suggestion of the idea, for the voluntary spirit was of the very essence of their being, and its abandonment, it seemed then, could hardly fail to bring about the collapse of the force.

No more was heard of compulsion—for a time.

Coincidentally came the first official instructional films which, being shown in the local cinemas, were keenly enjoyed by the men as a change from text-books and field training.

Week-end camps were also now being organized in increasing numbers and were not only greatly appreciated from a social angle but were also invaluable in enabling commanders to "lay on" training in a sequence unbroken by the return of the men to their homes as was unavoidably the case after evening and Sunday parades. Thus concentration was increased a hundredfold.

Meanwhile all battalion areas were scoured for disused quarries and sandpits which could be converted into bombing ranges, and residents adjacent to all such places had thereafter many "lively" evenings and week-ends while their local Home Guard "let themselves go" against

The Abington Mill Platoon, 12th (Northampton) Battalion. In the centre are Platoon Commander S. B. Patrick and Platoon Officer A. L. Bason. (March 1941.)

BOMB
THROWING
No. 36

imaginary enemy formations and armoured vehicles.

Any suitable spot for a rifle range was also promptly commandeered by the local Home Guard unit, sometimes with effects which needed tact to dispel and repair.

Thus in the 14th (Brackley) Battalion area, E Company did much of their firing practice on unofficial ranges.

As the officer commanding asked, "What makes a better butt than a high railway embankment?"

But, on one occasion, the men forgot the wire fence at the bottom of the embankment and, after the firing was over, the local station-master complained that all the fence wires had been cut by bullets.

With a "home-made" turreted background platoons of the 12th (Northampton) Battalion H.Q. and E Coy. of the 12th combined in a tournament titled "From Reveille to Lights Out" at Franklin's Gardens, Northampton, on August 17, 1941. Above are seen a drill demonstration and some of the participants waiting to make their contribution.

This matter was smoothed over by humble and contrite promises that it wouldn't happen again, and the station-master reported the "collapse of faulty wiring" in so-and-so section of the line.

## HOME GUARD IN SOLE CHARGE

Although the people of Northampton were quite unaware of the situation at the shock of any preliminary airborne landing, in or around the town, would have had to be taken by the 12th and its adjacent battalions.

It need hardly be added that all ranks in the area concerned, far from waxing anxious at the prospect, were highly gratified by such unmistakable, if indirect, recognition of their work.

In September 1941 the 12th Battalion "Reveille to Lights Out" Tournament was repeated. Here watching the show are left to right, Major R. Manning, Capt. A. W. Gardner, Major A. MacFarlane, Major L. E. Barnes, Capt. O. J. Hargraves, Major N. P. Andrews, and Lt.-Col. T. E. Manning.

time, the fact remained that, as from August 1941, the military defence of the town devolved entirely upon the Borough Home Guard Battalion, for in that month the Northampton Infantry Training Centre, whose troops had hitherto formed the core of the defence strength, was moved, and the 12th Battalion was left with the support of only a few scattered detachments of Regulars, and most of these were administrative personnel.

Obviously, had Northampton proved an enemy objective in any large-scale attack, this position would have been relieved by substantial reinforcements, but the initial

## ENTER THE CONCRETE CYLINDERS

It was in the summer of 1941 also that a weighty proposition rolled into the Home Guard scene.

This was the concrete cylinder road block.

Writes Lt.-Col. L. E. Barnes, commenting upon the innovation:

The concrete cylinders were deposited at each road block to supplement the steel rails and to prevent the tanks from having a clear rush at these obstacles. On Sunday, 31 August, a practice closing of all the road blocks was held. Much difficulty was experienced in moving these heavy and unwieldy cylinders, which were not easy to get quickly in position, but by experience we found that the provision of long iron bars which fitted through the centre rendered the work less laborious and speeded up the closing. The time to effect the closing caused concern; we should not be allowed anything like the average time taken, and although with practice this time was reduced, yet it was plain that a quicker method of closing must be found. The

This necessitated the construction of Defended Localities within the town itself. No fewer than fourteen of the original blocks had to be given up and only three were retained.

New blocks had to be reconstructed in the Defended Localities, all cylinders moved to the new positions, while some hundreds more were needed. Altogether, when the work was complete, we had 750 of these around the town. As time went on and the threat of a

A detachment of Far Cotton (Northampton Town) Home Guard participated in the borough's Anzac Day parade in 1941. Here the Guards are seen entering the Towcester Road Cemetery.

difficulty was overcome by closing most of the road with the steel rails and cylinders, leaving a sufficient gap for our own vehicles, which gap could be speedily closed on necessity.

## A TANK-PROOF TOWN

When all these road blocks were complete and their closing had been practised on various occasions, a bombshell was dropped in our midst in September 1941, by the decision that Northampton was to be made into a "Nodal" point and that the existing road blocks were, in the majority of cases, too widely dispersed and presented plenty of opportunity for tanks to jink round them and so enter the town. A new plan, therefore, had to be drawn up, making Northampton into a tank-proof town.

full-scale invasion receded, the road blocks lost their early importance, and although the cylinders were kept near to their positions they only served as a reminder to the population of what might have happened in those days of 1940–1.

## AWARD OF PROFICIENCY BADGES

On 4 September 1941 came the introduction of a system of recognition of merit which did more than anything to raise even higher the standard of training in the Home Guard.

This was the award of proficiency badges consisting of a small square of scarlet worn on the sleeve to all men who had reached a degree of proficiency enabling them to pass an appropriate examination.

The system was announced in an East Central Area letter as follows:

Each company will establish a Board for the purpose of examining members of another company. The Board to be composed of the company commander, or his second-in-command, and two other suitable officers selected by the company commander.

Proficiency tests—drill, weapon training, map reading, anti-gas, and general knowledge.

Full marks—100.

Each candidate must attain 50 per cent to be awarded badge.

Volunteers must have a 75 per cent attendance over four months immediately preceding the test to enter.

Almost immediately after came another innovation with a Zone letter to battalions in which officers commanding were asked to forward names of officers and other ranks selected to attend qualifying courses prior to appointment as battalion ammunition officers.

There was quite a rush for these appointments, although there might not have been had the candidates realized at the time that theirs would be one of the most anxious responsibilities, nothing less than the storage and safety of "enough powder to blow up the parish" with no adequate means of ensuring either good storage or reasonable safety. The ingenuity of some unfortunate A.O.s in finding and guarding ammunition stores was, in fact, classic.

## VISIT OF DIRECTOR-GENERAL

Visits of inspection by "brass hats" do not normally gratify the rank and file of any force, but when it became known that the, then, Director-General of the Home Guard, Major-Gen. the Viscount Bridgeman, D.S.O., M.C., was to visit Northamptonshire on 18 and 19 October 1941, all

**PROFICIENCY TEST**

battalions were hoping that they would see something of him, for Lord Bridgeman had

A snap at a 1941 tattoo staged by the Earls Barton Home Guard. On the left is Colonel H. G. Sotheby, D.S.O., in centre, Sergeant-Major J. Welch and, behind, 2nd Lt. J. Walpole.

proved that he was not only a capable soldier but that he had the interests of the Home Guard close at heart—interests

he had never shown any hesitation in championing.

On arrival at Northampton H.Q., accompanied by Capt. L. A. Impey, the Director-General was welcomed by the Zone Commander, Col. P. Lester Reid, with whom, and the Zone Staff Officer (Major T. C. Shillito), he spent an hour or so in close conference before proceeding to meet Lt.-Col. T. E. Manning and the officers of the town battalion, whose stores and some of whose defence works he also inspected with critical appreciation.

Later he had conferences with a number of other local battalion commanders and their seconds, also an assembly of company commanders, and then proceeded to Corby and Wellingborough, at both of which places he held further conferences with the commanders and made several inspections.

Then, on the Sunday, he visited the Zone camouflage school, took a look at the 11th (Hardingstone) Battalion at their range, and also passed through the Towcester and Brackley areas, reviewing the former battalion and witnessing a bombing display by the latter.

Major-Gen. Viscount Bridgeman, D.S.O., M.C. (Director-General of the Home Guard) pictured during an inspection in the 13th (Towcester) Battalion area in October 1941. With him is Capt. W. G. T. Griffin and following are Col. P. Lester Reid, Lt.-Col. P. Y. Atkinson, C.O., and, on left, Capt. Enos Lewin (Adjutant).

Unaffected and unostentatious throughout, the "D.-G" impressed all with his knowledge of the Home Guard's job and of its difficulties and was obviously genuinely impressed by all he saw. "I shall have no anxieties about Northamptonshire," he said as he bade farewell.

## W.V.S. RECOGNIZED

Working quite unofficially, many members of the Women's Voluntary Service had assisted the Home Guard in many ways up to this time and their help was now recognized in a letter from Col. Lester Reid to the battalions in which War Office sanction was revealed for Home Guard co-operation with the Women's Voluntary Service. It was suggested that in cases of emergency the W.V.S. could assist with cooking for the Home Guard and the letter added that W.V.S. organizers had been asked to contact the Home Guard commander in their locality to find out how best they could help, it being pointed out that while the Home Guard could provide the rations, they could not provide cooking utensils.

The idea was widely taken up and many Home Guards on night operations or at the conclusion of a particularly exacting day exercise ending in an area remote from "civilization", were gratified to see a W.V.S. van with hot tea, coffee or cocoa, and etceteras.

## ZONE STAFF APPOINTMENTS

The increasing responsibilities of the Zone Command now called for an extension of its staff. Thus, in the autumn of 1941, Col. Reid's staff was increased by the appointment of a Zone Medical Adviser (Lt.-Col. L. D. B. Cogan, D.S.O.), an assistant to the Zone Commander (Capt.

J. W. Care), and a Zone Intelligence and Public Relations Officer (Lt. B. G. Holloway.

In accepting the post of Zone Medical Adviser, Lt.-Col. Cogan assumed a task of a peculiarly, if unavoidably, involved character.

Just how involved, the following summary of Army Council Instructions and War Office letters relative to a medical adviser's duties will illustrate.

It was the responsibility of these officers in collaboration with their battalion medical officers to co-ordinate the available local medical facilities

Lt.-Col.
L. D. B. Cogan.

with the possible needs of units and sub-units and see that both sides made the appropriate contact.

Equipment was authorized for regimental aid posts and medical officers were to be reimbursed for any private medical equipment expended in connection with their Home Guard duties during active operations.

But, and what a big "but" it was, Civil Defence facilities were to be used wherever possible, and since the Home Guard had no wheeled transport, its responsibility for many casualties had to end at a point beyond which they could not be carried by hand.

The Home Guard, it was laid down, were responsible for field dressing facilities only, but Home Guard regimental aid posts could be set up where there were no Civil Defence facilities.

Once Home Guard casualties were brought to a Civil Defence casualty organization, however, the responsibility for their care devolved on the Civil Defence, and evacuation of casualties from Home Guard regimental aid posts was the responsibility of the Regional Commissioner, and was to be co-ordinated between Civil Defence services and the military commanders by the regional hospital officers of the Ministry of Health, and the military liaison officers at Regional Headquarters.

It will thus be seen that Lt.-Col. Cogan and his subordinates had to contrive to establish and carry on their organization and duty with "one foot" in their own "camp" and the other spread over a multiplicity of others over which they had no direct control.

It was, indeed, just as well that Lt.-Col. Cogan brought to his task considerably more than the average military experience.

What that experience was can be judged from his service record.

Having previously served in two expeditionary forces in West Africa and received the Ashanti medal, Lt.-Col. Cogan was in camp with the Northamptonshire Yeomanry, whose medical officer he was, on the outbreak of the 1914–18 war. He at once volunteered and went overseas with the East Anglian First Field Ambulance, the first Northampton doctor to see active service. Later he had charge of the 88th Field Ambulance attached to the 29th Division at Gallipoli, where he showed conspicuous gallantry in attending wounded under heavy fire.

Later he had charge of the 88th Field Ambulance in France and was wounded in the arm by machine-gun fire.

Afterwards he went to Germany with the Army of Occupation.

Before leaving England he was gazetted Captain and in January 1917 was made Lieutenant-Colonel.

He was awarded the D.S.O. in April 1916 for his services in France.

11

A Home Guard flag was suggested in the spring of 1942 but it did not materialize. Here Mr. Louis Loynes, heraldic artist, is designing the flag comprising the Union Jack, crown, church bell and a castle, cottage and oak tree.

**TELLING THE PEOPLE**

We have lately referred to the appointment of an intelligence officer to the Zone Commander's staff.

Part of this officer's duties were to establish and conduct a Northamptonshire Home Guard Public Relations service which was instituted by Col. Lester Reid to ensure that all newspapers in the Zone were supplied with accurate weekly reports and photographs of principal Home Guard activities throughout the county. Copies of these reports were also circulated to all battalion commanders with the object of keeping all areas in the Zone fully acquainted with the doings of their fellow battalions and of ensuring that

Stripping and reassembling the Lewis gun at the E Company's (12th Battalion) 1941 Tournament.

A section of the grandstand. Seated in front, left to right, are 2nd Lt. C. H. Brown, Capt. A. W. Gardner (Adjutant 12th Battalion), Capt. A. N. Other, Lt.-Col. T. E. Manning (O.C. 12th Battalion), Capt. Garrard (I.O. Northampton I.T.C.) and Major E. W. Powell (E Co. Commander).

all new and sound ideas, either in training or administration, could be generally known.

This service, apart from its military purpose, assisted local editors to avoid publication in the Northamptonshire papers of the many wild rumours and erroneous statements concerning the Home Guard which appeared in newspapers in other parts of the country, not excluding some of the responsible national organs— statements which not only irritated and discouraged the Home Guard, but often proved seriously damaging.

A tug-of-war event in the Northampton (E Co. 12th Battalion) Railway Home Guard tournament staged in July 1941 at Franklin's Gardens, Northampton.

## WHEN THEY LAUGHED

*Home Guard (relieving sleeping colleague on night post)*: "*Wake up, old chap, it's time for you to go off duty.*"

# Chapter XVIII

## EXERCISES, PARADES, TRAINING FILMS

### EXERCISE "TERRIER"

PREVIOUS mention has been made of memorable exercises carried out in the area and in the battalions, and one of these now enters the record under the sprightly name of "Terrier". It was designed to test communications and administration, and many of the participants have held ever since that it could more appropriately have been titled "Terror".

·It was a "paper" exercise carried out over the whole of the Beds, Hunts, and Northants Sub-Area during the week-end of 1–3 November 1941, and the "I" log of the 9th (Brixworth) Battalion permits of the writing up of a précis which incidentally serves also as an illustration of the excellent administrative work of this battalion.

The log has only one brief entry about the climatic conditions, but it is quite sufficient. It says "Dark night—rain" and thus epitomizes what the dispatch riders described in far more lurid terms.

It is clear that from the onset Battalion Headquarters were alive to the danger of fifth columnists, and were not going to be "led up the garden path" by any old-fashioned ruses—or by any new-fangled ones either.

Thus at 2248 hours a gentleman who described himself as "Funf" reported on the telephone that the Germans had captured Wellingborough. There was no panic. The voice was immediately recognized as one very well known in Home Guard circles, and the "I" log reports "no action".

Two minutes later, a message signed by a "Major Morris" of the 12th Battalion was received. It contained the news that a private car, driven by civilians, had fired on Home Guards at the Boughton road-block. As there was known to be no such person in the 12th Battalion as "Major Morris" the 9th also ignored this obvious attempt to start a war of nerves.

At 2255 hours a further message was received from "Mr. Jones" of the Telegraph Inn, reporting that the Home Guard at Brixworth had been overpowered by paratroops. Unfortunately, the sender of this spurious message had, somewhat strangely, overlooked the fact that to have tried to mislead members of the Home Guard over the names of local innkeepers, was a far more difficult job than to have passed a very large camel through the eye of a very small needle.

No action was taken, and so three deliberate attempts to upset the morale of the 9th Battalion failed ignominiously.

Nothing very much occurred after this until at 0629 hours on 2 November 1941 paratroops were reported as being dropped one and a half miles south-west of Sywell. The 8th and 11th Battalions were informed. At 0640 hours a runner brought information that further paratroops had been dropped one mile south-east of Holcot. This was serious enough, but worse was to follow. One of the umpires reported that there had been an enemy landing on the south and east coasts.

Things were now livening up. At 0855 the Bedfordshire Sub-Area reported paratroops active near Bedford, St. Neots, and Peterborough, and that spray gas was being used by the enemy. Following this, at 0859 came the alarming news that a full-scale invasion was imminent. This message, and the one about spray gas, was sent immediately to all companies, and the gas officer warned. At 0925 hours the situation became slightly better. Sub-Area was informed that paratroops in the 9th area were destroyed, and that forty-five enemy had been killed and one prisoner handed over to the police. The log adds that this message was not accepted by the umpires, who presumably thought it was too early yet to win the battle.

## A BUSY MORNING

At 0956 hours the umpire put the Headquarter telephone out of action until 1030 hours, and a D.R. was at once sent to the Post Office Home Guard at Northampton asking for priority repairs. At 0956 a runner brought the news that seventy Italian prisoners had escaped from Boughton Park camp, and D Company was given the job of rounding them up.

At 1031 the telephone was tested and found to be in order.

At 1330 hours the umpire sent a message that D Company had had heavy casualties. It was reported that the Company had lost fifty killed and thirty-three wounded, and ambulances were detached from White Hills to collect the latter. But D Company, although heavily depleted, had shown their teeth to some purpose, as at 1345 hours they reported that they had accounted for all enemy paratroops—killing forty and taking prisoner another twenty.

At 1410 hours Battalion Headquarters guards were doubled as a precaution against fifth columnists.

At 1445 hours a runner from C and D Companies reported all Italian prisoners accounted for. Ever mindful of good work, the Commanding Officer sent a message to the Officer Commanding D Company congratulating all ranks on their gallant conduct.

Matters then became comparatively quiescent until 2020 hours on 2 November, when an umpire from Sub-Area reported that one enemy Panzer division was advancing in the Kettering-Stamford area, and added the disquieting news that the British 9th Armoured Division was retreating before them. Two enemy Panzer divisions were also reported advancing north to east and their advanced elements were only twenty miles south of Oxford. Parachute descents were widespread. The 11th British Corps and the 54th Division were said to be retiring from Braintree.

## "PANZER DIVISIONS" AT YARMOUTH

Piling Pelion on Ossa the message added that a further Panzer division had landed at Yarmouth and had penetrated ten miles inland. This was at 1730 hours—three hours beforehand. The situation appeared to be critical—nay, was critical. Battalion Headquarters awoke to electrified action. At 2030 hours D.R.s were sent forth ordering special troop dispositions. Grenades were issued. Preparations were made to immobilize all petrol supplies.

At 2052 the 6th Battalion telephoned to say that enemy columns were advancing from Stamford and approaching Great Weldon. The 4th and 5th Battalions were informed of the ominous news. At 2145 a message was received from Sub-Area that the enemy were operating east of the Sub-Area. This message was three hours late— and it was charitably assumed that Sub-Area had been annihilated before the 9th received the message.

At 2130 and 2145 respectively the 4th and 5th Battalions reported enemy tanks approaching Great Welford and Walgrave. D Company was thereupon warned by

D.R.s as were troops on duty at No. 1 road block. At 2200 hours the Officer Commanding D Company reported enemy tanks approaching Sywell, and added that they could not be held. Apparently heavy casualties had again been sustained by this gallant company, who had now expended all their ammunition.

Would it stop for a "Soup Plate" lying in the road. Early Home Guard hoped so! A picture during an October 1942 exercise in the 9th (Brixworth) Battalion area.

At this point a note was sent from Officer Commanding 9th Battalion to Officer Commanding 12th Battalion stating that two enemy tanks with crews had been captured and that he was willing to exchange the lot for 2,000 rounds of S.A.A.

Lt.-Col. Barnes replied: "Have no ammunition to spare. You will know what to do with the tanks!"

It was here that the pikes, newly issued to the Home Guard and of which more anon, came into their own. The 12th Battalion were advised that all ammunition had been expended along the line of the enemy's advance, and that the defence had been forced to take to their pikes.

In the face of this desperate position maps and secret documents were dropped down a well at Stone Walls, Moulton, in a waterproof box.

2240 hours saw Battalion Headquarters about to move to Brampton Golf Club, and officers commanding companies were so informed. The message added that in the event of Battalion Headquarters being "scuppered", Major Pettitt, Officer Commanding D Company, was to assume command of what was left of the 9th.

### AERODROME "IN FLAMES"

By 2224 hours Sywell aerodrome and works were in flames and enemy tanks had been moving towards Mears Ashby. This news was telephoned to the Officer Commanding 12th Battalion with the additional information that the 9th Battalion Headquarters would remain at Moulton. At 2250 hours Headquarters of the 12th were bombed out.

The stubborn defence of the 9th Battalion, however, had its reward, for at 2246 hours the Bedfordshire Sub-Area was informed that enemy tanks on the Kettering-Northampton road had been held—and, what was better, diverted east. Casualties were reported as "heavy", and all ammunition had been expended. Zone Headquarters were asked for replenishments.

The tumult and the shouting were now dying down, for when at 2311 hours the Town Commander of Northampton asked for further information regarding the conflagration at Sywell, he was informed that no further information was forthcoming, and that Moulton was no longer threatened.

The area was described as "clear". It was presumed (thankfully no doubt) that the enemy tanks proceeding to Bedford via Rushden had rejoined their main column.

At 0030 hours the operation came to a close, and the 9th Battalion, in common with all the other toiling and sweating Home Guards engaged were able to direct their thoughts and their steps towards

"Home Sweet Home" and a rest from their labours.

## 8TH BATTALION'S SPECIAL PARADE

In December 1941, Lt.-Gen. Sir John Brown took the salute at a march past by the 8th Battalion—and expressed himself delighted with the turn-out and parade.

He was accompanied by Col. P. Lester Reid (Zone Commander), Lt.-Col. W. E. Lyon of the Hussars, and Major T. C. Shillito (Zone Staff Officer).

The band of the King's Royal Hussars played for the march—which was a very spirited affair.

Afterwards visiting officers were entertained to tea at the Battalion Headquarters where Lt.-Col. Sykes and Capt. H. W. Attley (Adjutant) received many congratulations on the parade.

The Rushden W.V.S., including Mrs. Sykes, Mrs. Attley, and others, "waited" at tea-time.

Incidentally, the 8th Battalion included in its ranks one of the oldest soldiers serving in the Zone. He was George Jolley—then aged seventy-six—who had served in Ireland, India, Burma, South Africa, etc. He was too old to serve in the 1914–18 war!

## TRAINING FILMS

How to continue training in the winter months was a problem which was greatly lightened from 1941 onwards by the loan of films by the War Office.

Many of the earlier films were of pre-war vintage and out of date. Such films as *Fighting Patrols, Concealment from the Air,"* etc., often showed the horse-drawn company limber, with company commanders dashing about on horseback!

As time went on, however, there was a great improvement and the films issued were right up to date. In 1942 a Security

film, *Next of Kin,* was much in demand and was shown to practically all platoons.

By 1943 and 1944 there was a wide range of films from which choice could be made, dealing with Battle Drill, Gas, Camouflage, Street Fighting, Locating the Enemy, etc.

The films created much interest and there was always a full attendance in all units on the evenings when these were shown.

In this connection, credit is due to the proprietors of many cinemas in all county areas which were made available for the showing to the Guard of full-size training and other military films whenever these were available.

All of these cinemas and their managements and staffs gave generously of their facilities and services but none will deny special mention of the Exchange Cinema, Northampton, and its manager (Mr. M. Crowley), for this large hall was repeatedly used, not only for film shows, but also for lectures by distinguished visiting commanders, etc.

## EARLY INVASION COMMITTEES

A notable development at this time in anti-invasion precautions was the formation of Local Invasion Committees under which all forces in each area were co-ordinated. The question of which centre was really the first to "get going" in this important respect has often been debated but the honour is claimed by Wellingborough, whose first meeting was held on 14 November 1941, appropriately at the 7th Battalion Headquarters.

To Wellingborough also may here be handed the further credit of instituting at this date a regular series of "quiz" questions from its Home Guard battalion headquarters, that of the 7th Battalion (Lt.-Col. H. L. Allsopp).

Under the pertinent heading of "What

would you do, chums?" the questions went out with weekly battalion orders and covered almost every conceivable Home Guard subject.

The solutions were issued a fortnight later.

Here are three typical questions:

You are leading a patrol when you suddenly detect the presence of gas, but are unable to identify it. What would you do?

You and your pal are instructed to make a

1941. It must indeed have been a humorist who named this, for the night was as unlike "scorch" as it was possible to be—wet and cold and everything that good exercise weather should be.

It was the first large-scale operation held in these parts by the Command, and portrayed as close a picture to invasion conditions as it was possible to get. Regular troops, R.A.F. personnel, Home Guard and Civil Defence all took part, while 50,000 troops were used as the enemy with armoured columns, etc.

The Zone Commander (Col. P. Lester Reid) on right, and other officers viewing and umpiring at a combined manœuvre between Regulars, Home Guard and Air Training Corps (under F./Lt. S. P. Tyzack).

slit trench at a certain spot for two men. What would you do to carry out this instruction effectively?

You are N.C.O. in charge of a guard in your guard room. You have two sentries on duty outside. A 36 grenade is thrown at the guard room and one of your men is cut by broken glass. What would you do?

## EXERCISE "SCORCH"

Just before Christmas 1941 came another important exercise, that titled "Scorch", for which "Terrier" had been the "paper" preliminary.

We can do no better than to quote Lt.-Col. Barnes in reproducing a typical record of the event.

Scorch [he writes] will never be forgotten by the Home Guard serving on 5–7 December

I am not going to enlarge on the results of the exercise and the many lessons it taught, for the battle never reached Northampton and so we were denied any chance of really functioning as a fighting unit. But the exercise did enable us to get our administration going. Sleeping accommodation for reliefs and feeding arrangements had to be made, and both these were successfully accomplished.

As Dr. Thompson and I made a round of the platoons, never in war-time did I see so much food. One platoon had a dish of rabbit stew; where the rabbits came from I could have guessed, but discretion being the better part of valour I maintained a discreet silence. "Them that asks no questions isn't told a lie." Anyway the stew was very good.

The Home Guard, true to soldierly tradition, had improvised very well and all platoons had comfortable quarters more or less. The amount of money that changed hands that night in games of "skill" must have been enormous. Not that feeding and pontoon were the only things that happened on the historic night, observation was well kept and sentries did their job nobly in the wet, while added interest was given by a police message that a certain car was wanted.

This gave the Home Guard the opportunity

difficulty of providing sufficient men to maintain a reasonable defence of their area.

Christmas-time was, however, an untimely occasion on which to call for such a return, and the responsible authorities can hardly have imagined that, at least, one company commander (B Company of the 5th Battalion) received the request by D.R.

"One plain, one purl." Capt. S. B. Patrick, 12th (Northampton) Battalion, gives No. 7 Platoon, C Co. "the wire" as to the "woof and weave" of Dannert "embroidery". A Sunday morning scene at Abington. Spectators in the left-hand picture are Lt. C. H. Brown (Platoon Commander) and Lt.-Col. T. E. Manning (Battalion Commander).

to stop all cars and examine identification cards. However, despite the good that we derived, there was an intense feeling of disappointment that we had not had a chance to show the efficiency of our training.

## THE PROBLEM OF STRENGTH

Christmas 1941 was marked by two important occurrences, one the arrival of the first Northover projectors—earlier reference to the Northover has been made in a section devoted to weapons—and a call for reports from all companies as to the quantity of extra men they needed to bring up their numbers to adequate strength.

In the latter call, commanders saw an intensification of the compulsion possibility—a possibility they now regarded with less hostility born of the ever-increasing

while he was actually sitting down to his Christmas dinner.

The festive season of 1941 was charged with little less underlying grimness than that of 1940 for the invasion threat remained undiminished.

What few people knew at that time, however, was that even a Channel tunnel invasion was being seriously prepared for, and that a group of Admiralty experts were spending long anxious hours in a fifty years old disused railway drainage tunnel near Dover listening with special equipment, for any sounds of enemy drilling!

The possibility was not fantastic. The Government had been told by their advisers that modern equipment made the project feasible within a reasonably short time. Four months had been mentioned.

The Germans, it was held, would probably plan for a "master" tunnel to within a short distance off-shore with tributaries from it fanning out to behind the cliffs. There German paratroops might establish a bridgehead to allow the tunnel troops to emerge.

Subsidiary "listening posts" were therefore set up over a wide stretch of the channel coast as a precaution against the fact that the subsidiary fanning-out tunnels might be some considerable distance apart and to guard against the possibility of more than one master-tunnel being bored.

In 1944, German prisoners taken in Normandy said they had heard that an invasion tunnel had been talked about in Germany. They did not know that, whether Hitler intended the tunnel or not, Britain was prepared for it!

## Chapter XIX

## COMPULSION INTRODUCED

THE opening of 1942 marked a major turning-point in the history of the Home Guard.

The long rumoured and much debated possibility of compulsion became a reality. It was announced on 1 January that the Guard would be placed on a compulsory basis in the following month and that new defence regulations to effect the change would be drafted and would be issued approximately a fortnight later.

Members were allowed one month after the publication of the regulations in which to exercise a right to resign.

All men between eighteen and fifty-one it was stated were liable for enrolment in the Home Guard, but it was intended to conscript men only in areas where units were below strength. Parades and drills were to be compulsory up to a maximum of forty-eight hours per month, at the discretion of local commanders.

After the publication of these advanced details the War Office anxiously awaited the effect in point of the number of resignations which might follow. Actually there were relatively few and these consisted, in the main, of men whose jobs rendered it impossible for them to continue on any fixed basis.

As for the idea of compulsion itself, this was now generally conceded as dictated by circumstances and little of the original bitter hostility was now apparent.

Nevertheless, it could not be denied then, and cannot now, that "something went out" of the Home Guard from the moment that compulsion came in. The sense of duty remained and the progress to efficiency never faltered but the underlying warmth of spirit animating the force was dampened and was never wholly rekindled.

With the actual introduction of compulsion, in February 1942, Mr. Sandys, Financial Secretary to the War Office, paid a convincing tribute to the Home Guard.

I trust [he said] that this measure will not only meet the operational needs of the military situation, but will also have the effect of impressing on the country at large the importance of the part in our defence system assigned to the Home Guard and the urgent necessity of bringing it up to the highest level of efficiency and preparedness.

**AGE LIMIT FOLLOWS**

In the same month a further major change was made in the commands of the force with an order which laid it down that all Home Guard operational officers above the age of sixty-five were to be replaced by younger men and that only in exceptional cases would this rule be waived and then only with the approval of the Army Council.

It was a drastic decision and caused much inevitable heartburning in "borderline" cases but, taken on the whole, it was a wise one.

For, while many perfectly efficient, popular and still active officers were unfortunately superseded, many others went with them who were little more than useless figureheads and whose obvious incapacity, though probably due to no other reason than that of advanced years, was extremely bad for the morale, and even worse for the discipline of the units they commanded.

Among the "unfortunates" *not* in the latter category was Lt.-Col. A. J. Fraser of the 11th (Hardingstone) Battalion.

In 1942 [he recorded], having reached the age of sixty-five, I was obliged by War Office regulations to retire, and on my recommendation, Major W. J. Penn was appointed to take over command. To him I handed over a very

feet over the Home Guard positions, while "bombs" were exploding in all directions.

The Commanding Officer and all ranks were warmly commended by the Sub-Area Commander (Col. E. A. Stokes Roberts, O.B.E., M.C.), who witnessed the event, on a splendidly realistic piece of training.

After the "show" the Sub-Area Commander took the opportunity of presenting

Three scenes at the 11th (Hardingstone District) Battalion's demonstration at Castle Ashby in February 1942. They show left to right, (1) Stretcher bearers in action after an attack by dive bombers of the R.A.F. which participated as "enemy". (2) Lt.-Col. A. J. Fraser, Battalion Commander, then retiring under the age limit in favour of Lt.-Col. W. J. Penn, presenting his shooting cup to Lt. A. Merritt (No. 5 Great Houghton and Brafield Platoon of A Co.), the current winners. (3) The Sub-Area Commander (Colonel A. E. Stokes Roberts), congratulating Sgt. A. Bell (4 Platoon A Co.) after presenting him with a Certificate of Merit for gallantry. With Cpl. F. W. O. Linaker, of the same platoon, who also received a certificate, he made a courageous though unsuccessful attempt to rescue the occupants of a crashed and blazing R.A.F. bomber which fell in their area.

efficient and smart battalion, the result of hard work, devotion to duty and loyalty of all officers and men.

### FINE ANTI-AIRCRAFT DISPLAY

Soon after, the 11th (Lt.-Col. W. J. Penn) and the 7th (Lt.-Col. H. L. Allsopp) Battalions entered the "headlines".

The 11th's event was a parade on Sunday, 22 February 1942, of more than 60 per cent of the Battalion at Castle Ashby to put up a splendid display of anti-aircraft and anti-gas defence action with the special co-operation of Royal Air Force fighters which roared down to within fifty

Certificates of Merit to Sgt. A. Bell and Cpl. F. W. Linaker, both of No. 4 Platoon A Company, in recognition of a gallant but unsuccessful attempt to rescue the occupants of a blazing bomber which had crashed in the neighbourhood.

The 7th's credit came for a particularly impressive parade on 8 March 1942 as part of the inauguration of Wellingborough's Warship Week. Together with the local Civil Defence units they laid on a march past of an almost faultless order of bearing and order and Col. the Marquess of Exeter, who took the salute, stated that the more he saw of the Home Guard the more impressed he became with its soldierly bearing and efficiency.

## REPEATED COMMAND CHANGES

Few aspects of Home Guard administration at the higher levels were quite as baffling as the seemingly endless changes which occurred in the superior commands and commanders.

officers it involved, before yet another change was made.

This time Northamptonshire moved into the Command it should always have occupied—the Eastern Command which, at first, operated through two subsidiary commands, i.e., East Central Area and the Bedfordshire, Huntingdonshire, and Northamptonshire Sub-Area.

At Earls Barton Warship Week Parade in March 1942. A full turnout of the local company of the 8th (Wellingborough District) Battalion was inspected by the Zone Commander (Col. P. Lester Reid), who is seen (*inset*) passing down the ranks, accompanied by Capt. J. Richardson (Co. Commander) and Lt.-Col. H. G. Sotheby.

At the outset, what was then the Northamptonshire Zone of the Home Guard was in the Southern Command operating through two Midland Area Commands—the Central and South Midland.

Later a complete transfer was made to the Northern Command, with Headquarters at York, which operated through an East Midland Area Command, and a North Midland Area Command.

Hardly had the Guards "mastered" and become familiar with this change, and all the changes of names of command staff

Even that, however, was not the end, for, while remaining in the Eastern Command, further changes were soon made under which subsidiary commands were recast and retitled the East Central District and the Northamptonshire Sub-District respectively.

Almost simultaneously with this latter change, the previously gradual process of regularizing the control of the Guard was suddenly speeded up and consolidated to an effect under which the office of Zone Commander lapsed and its operational authority with it.

Thus, the former Northamptonshire Zone was now directly controlled by the Northamptonshire Sub-District from Headquarters at the old Northamptonshire Regimental Depot on Barrack Road, Northampton.

The Sub-District Commander, a regular officer with the rank of Colonel, directly commanded the Northamptonshire Home Guard and, while no prejudice or personal animosity entered into the matter, the Northamptonshire Home Guards felt very deeply what they regarded as an unwarranted supersession of their own senior leader, who knew them intimately and whom they knew; who knew also, far better than any stranger could ever hope to learn, the "lie" of the local country and, above all, who knew the "soul and spirit" of the Home Guard and all it demanded of a leader.

Resentment, however, is of little avail in such circumstances. This thing had, apparently, been decided upon as the best thing and it was not for members of a disciplined military force to question it. Least of all did the officer it most affected question it. Together with all ranks down to the lowest level, he loyally fell into line with the new system and became Home Guard Adviser to the new Sub-District Command, thus filling a post of that unenviable type which demands responsibility while withholding power.

All ranks felt then, and still feel, that the proper course to have taken would have been one whereby the existing Zone Commander would have had a Regular Sub-District commander as *his* operational adviser and not the reverse.

### CHANGES, AND STILL MORE CHANGES

However, the new Sub-District "took over" and in common with the "quick change" acts of the higher commands soon began to "swap" its commanders and staff officers about in the style of a sort of military musical chairs.

It may be set down as an historical fact that the Northamptonshire Home Guard, in the relatively short period of its existence, had no fewer than seven Army commanders, nine Area or District commanders, and seven Sub-Area or Sub-District commanders with accompanying innumerable changes in all of these commanders' staffs!

Little wonder that in their dealings with all of these people Home Guard commanders and administrative staffs hardly knew from one minute to another with whom they were dealing, while the effect upon correspondence files and references can be better imagined than described.

At the same time came an almost equally continuous change in orders and directions which literally "plastered" Home Guard offices with amendment or cancellation slips.

For the purpose of this history, only the Sub-Area (later Sub-District) commanders need be identified and recalled, for they alone came into direct and regular personal contact with the Northamptonshire Guards.

The first commander came in March 1942 in the person of Col. A. E. Stokes Roberts, O.B.E., M.C., and, despite the rather strained atmosphere in which, inevitably, he arrived, he soon gained widespread respect and popularity. The son of a Brigadier-General, he bore a fine record of service. In the 1914–18 war he served at Gallipoli and later in France, and in the 1939–45 war in France and Norway.

Col. A. E. Stokes Roberts.

He then served as G.S.O. of a command and of a corps before coming to Northampton.

Col. Stokes Roberts at once threw himself into the task of getting acquainted alike with his Regular and Home Guard subordinates and with his command area.

He also initiated administrative improvements, and a number of highly profitable exercises recorded in subsequent pages were of his devising.

Meanwhile, exercising infinite tact and combining with it a genial personality, he rapidly gained the full co-operation of the Home Guard battalions.

### "MOBILE" TO "STATIC"

Swift on the heels of compulsion, the age-limit regulations and the new Command came a further sweeping change in the Home Guard field role which aroused more hotly debated controversy than any other single measure introduced in the force's history.

This was a definite change from a "mobile" to a "static" system of defence.

Ever since its inception individual battalions had hovered between the two and had sought to effect a compromise, but always it had been felt that the primary function of the Home Guard was, and should always remain, that of harassing and delaying the enemy rather than resisting him on a solid front or fronts.

This view was dictated not merely by the conditions that the Guard was, in any case, quite unequipped to maintain static defences and that a highly mobile enemy would certainly by-pass all static strong-points—this method of avoiding "hedge-hogs" was, indeed, later regularly adopted by both the German and the Russian armies in the eastern campaigns—but by recognition of the fact that the Guard's rank and file, with all their invaluable and intimate knowledge of their own territories, could have been relied upon to outwit even the most formidable enemy and to have given him a really uncomfortable time if left to exploit that special knowledge to the full.

### DEFENDED LOCALITIES

However, it was not to be, and many months of hard work, spent in devising ingenious and intricate schemes of guerrilla warfare, particularly in rural districts, now went by the board.

Home Guard units were now to man a central "keep" surrounded by "defended localities". They were to *stand* and fight for as long as they could *in* these places, the only exceptions being special mobile units which were retained at the keep for use at the discretion of the commander as the situation demanded.

The facetious criticism that the change evoked was well expressed in a string of verses composed by a battalion commander for "private circulation" and not for battalion records.

Here they are:

The brigadier we had last spring
Said "Static roles are not the thing,
As mobile as the blanket's flea
Is what the Home Guard ought to be".

Accordingly our schemes were set
To make the Home Guard thirstier yet,
And all agreed that brigadier
Had interests in Phipps's beer.

He went; another came instead
Who deemed mobility quite dead,
And thought the Home Guard on the whole
Much better in a static role.

We did not mind; our partialities
Were then transferred to Home localities,
And one can usually sleep
Just as well inside the keep.

Besides, some fresh and fertile brain
Is bound to change it all again
And perch us possibly up trees
Like monkeys and the Japanese.

No doubt some high strategic plan
Beyond the ken of common man
Dictates these changes in our job
From "Mob" to "Stat" and "Stat" to "Mob".

Still, it would help us all to know
More positively where to go
In case when Bosches do appear
We cannot find a brigadier.

Static defence had to be accepted and accordingly exercises on the lines it demanded were organized by the score.

The sweeps of the Northamptonshire landscape now seemed to be brimming over with hundreds of Home Guards, who were either attacking a heavily defended place or defending one heavily attacked.

In a miraculously short period of time the whole county was covered by a network of defended localities, manned by eager men, every one of whom knew his role, his battle position, his particular job, and exactly what he had to do in any given situation.

Peaceful farms were "invaded", suburban streets were enfiladed by teams of Lewis gunners and Blacker bombardiers, back gardens were turned into ambushes, barbed wire was thrown up in profusion, and strong points erected everywhere at the cost of much muscular strain and copious sweat.

Often, in the winter months, partaking in these exercises spelt age-long hours in a bitter wind, or heavy going over greasy ploughland, while in the summer, battle-dress and steel helmets turned many a scheme into a foretaste of purgatory with smoke bombs and thunder flashes lending the final touch of realism.

Apropos of this ever-increasing call for intensfiied versatility an anonymous humorist member of one battalion penned and sent to his H.Q. the following richly facetious summary of the Home Guard "picture" at that time:

A Flash after "cookhouse call" in C Company of the 12th (Northampton) Battalion. Major St. John Browne (Company Commander), is standing fifth from right. On left is Cpl. H. M. Lawrence, who was M.C. Taken at a Supper and Social at the Cock Hotel, Kingsthorpe, in January 1941.

THE GREAT UNPAID

The Home Guard is the unpaid, part-time, part-worn, couponless, sockless, shirtless, and breathless Army.

Its members are supposed to put bullets in the bull of a target (which they can't see); to be ferocious bayonet fighters (this entails making extraordinary faces, grunting, and grinding the teeth); to be also all-in wrestlers and long-distance runners.

They are supposed to know the weight, killing power, mechanism, and working parts of the rifle, several machine guns, countless grenades, and a number of strange sub-artillery weapons, to say nothing of truncheons, toggle-ropes, shot-guns, and pikes.

When they become proficient in any particular weapon it is immediately declared obsolete and a new one is substituted. The idea of this is to ensure perpetual training and to prevent them "digging for victory", going to the pictures, or nursing the baby in their spare time.

They are supposed to be able to change themselves into nigger minstrels, Zulu medicine men, or mythological gods with vine leaves in their hair in a few seconds. To make it sound easy, this is called camouflage.

They must know all about extermination, decontamination, consolidation, and abomination, to say nothing of salvation.

They have to know all about and recognize and describe aeroplanes and tanks of all nations at sight, and know how to deal with them. They must also support the Regulars, which sometimes happens after closing time.

Incidentally, they are supposed to earn their own living . . . if time permits.

## ENTRUSTED WITH THE DEFENCE OF BRITAIN

Out of all this travail, however—imperceptibly at first but with clearness later that was undeniable—grew that advanced proficiency in attack and defence which completely justified, at a later date, the decision of the Army Council to entrust the Home

Guard with practically the whole of the defence of Great Britain.

Literally, hundreds of exercises and schemes paved the way for this onerous responsibility.

Arm-in-arm across a street. An incident in the "show" put up by the 12th Battalion for the Director-General (Major-Gen. Viscount Bridgeman) in May 1943.

Some of these, such as "Scorch" and "Buzz", were on an immense scale, involving thousands of troops. Some were merely local affairs. No layman, indeed few Home Guards, ever guessed at the amount of staff work required for even a modest show, and of the work that commanding officers, adjutants, quartermasters, company and platoon officers, N.C.O.s and the staffs of orderly rooms put in to make these practices the successes they were, no praise can be too high.

## BATTLE DRILL

It was early in 1942 that what became known as "Battle Drill" superseded many of the old and now out-of-date notions of battle craft. The old technique was by no means completely abandoned, but what was now about to take place was an adaptation and a co-ordination of the older technique to present-day standards.

12

The new battle drill "caught on". At least it represented a change from what was sometimes monotonous repetition, and at its best it soon became clear that the new drill was going to prove its full worth whenever, and if ever, it was called into active use.

An incident during a demonstration of street fighting in blitzed and derelict houses by the 12th (Northampton) Battalion.

But is was still performed under imaginary conditions and continued thus until, at last, it was deemed both practicable and proper to put various battle squads through what became known as "Battle Inoculations". It was a thrill which those who experienced it will never forget. You can do a lot with the aid of thunder flashes to make things realistic, but it is impossible to simulate the "real thing" with any degree of conviction.

Several battalions reached a stage at which live ammunition became a frequent and regular item in their training, and the records of the 9th Battalion provide a notable example.

The 9th created a Battle Squad consisting of members of all ranks drawn from all units of the Battalion. This demonstration squad, as a preliminary measure, was trained "to a hair", until it was as near perfection as possible. The course extended over a period of five weeks in a sand-pit kindly loaned by Major Frank Jordan, and at the end of it every man of the squad returned to his own unit with a vivid sense of realism.

On Sunday, 28 December 1942, the demonstration squad of the 9th gave an almost perfect display of the application of battle drill and the meticulous use of battle craft.

They did this in accordance with tactical schemes plotted by Capt. C. C. Oakey, M.C. (Adjutant) and Capt. A. H. Jackson, and were watched with intense interest by members of the 9th Battalion who were shortly to come under fire in their turn.

The squad, passing by carefully devised stages to their objective (an enemy post) came under overhead fire from Capt. Oakey, whose role was that of an "enemy" sniper, and bursts of machine-gun fire put over by selected gunners loaned by the Air Force Regiment.

It was a thrilling performance. All the rules of all-round observation and defence —of planned covering fire—and of final consolidation in good position—were splendidly observed. The Battalion Commander (Lt.-Col. G. S. Watson), it was good to note, personally led each squad under its baptism of fire, a gesture that all ranks warmly appreciated.

The "enemy" afterwards explained that one of the difficulties *they* encountered was that of deliberately *missing* their obvious targets. Reminders that this was absolutely necessary were supplied by rough targets placed at exact points upon which the overhead fire was to be concentrated.

arriving, and practice with them was a ticklish job and the task of looking for "duds", often buried in snow, was even more ticklish. Practice with this and other new weapons now available, together with ever-increasing theoretical training was also necessitating considerable evening overtime all round.

The demonstration squad of the 9th (Brixworth) Battalion going into action in December 1942 during a display of the battle inoculation course carried out in a sand-pit. Real fire was provided by Capt. Charles Oakey (Adjutant) and machine gunners of the R.A.F. Regiment, seen in inset firing overhead.

## "HOME-MADE" FIELD RADIO

About this time the 11th (Hardingstone) Battalion amazed many fellow battalions by appearing in the field with their own home-made field radio sets! Behind this really brilliant achievement in signals lay the tutelage of Pte. (later Lt.) W. T. C. Smeathers who also devised and made, in conjunction with the Battalion's signals units, a number of field telephone sets which were the envy of the less fortunate units called upon to engage the 11th in exercises.

The No. 68 A.T. bombs were now

To alleviate this position the 5th (Kettering District) Battalion set a fine lead by establishing a completely equipped weekend school at Desborough. It was splendidly organized by Col. H. C. Burditt, who also placed his factory canteen at the disposal of students and himself worked untiringly to make the school a success.

We have just referred to new courses of training. Among these now came unarmed combat, which being first demonstrated to the Home Guard by experts from the Regular Army—any one of them would readily strip to the waist and, totally unarmed, tackle an opponent with a rifle and unprotected fixed bayonet!—soon aroused the younger, if not the older, Home Guards' enthusiasm.

And, after a little training, many of these younger men became so proficient that when, later, they joined the Regular forces from the Home Guard, they soon became

Said Lord Mansfield in the House of Lords:

The invasion season might be said to be almost upon us. All through these last months practically nothing has been done, but something has happened which is of great importance.

The Home Guard have been issued with

Hardingstone Machine Gunners with an ingenious and "home-made" Lewis machine-gun carrier. In the picture are seen, left to right, standing: Cpl. F. Downie, Pte. S. Wreford, Pte. T. Holt, Lt. W. H. Clay (Platoon Commander), Major F. A. Thompson (Co. Commander), Sgt. H. B. S. Bland, L.-Cpl. F. Brown and Pte. P. Westley. Kneeling: Cpl. H. Burbidge, L.-Cpl. F. Smart and L. Botterill.

instructors themselves in this subtle and amazingly effective method of self-defence.

## BACK TO "BEEFEATERS"

No historian of the Home Guard can refrain from reference to pikes—much as he would prefer to forget them.

We have already made passing reference to them. Now their sorry story must be set down.

Officially pikes had been issued as far back as October 1941, but most commanders had sought to hide and ignore them. The secret "would out", however, and when in March 1942 the issue became public knowledge a howl of derision went up from Parliament and Press alike.

substantial consignments of pikes. The Home Guard throughout the country are anxiously waiting to see whether they are going to be supplied with any more medieval knick-knacks of a similar sort, because, frankly, they regard these pikes as little more than an insult.

If they had been supplied in the same proportion throughout the country as they have been to the battalion in which I serve, I estimate that already not less than 1,000 tons of valuable iron and steel have been wasted in this way, and that is little short of deplorable!

Lord Croft, Joint Under-Secretary, War Office, thought that most members of the Home Guard would agree that where they had not the full complement of modern arms any weapon was better than none.

A bayonet is a useful weapon [he said]. If that bayonet is prolonged by a stave it is a still more useful weapon, and I think it is a mistake to allow the idea to go forward that you cannot resist the enemy under conditions of night or street fighting without the most modern weapons.

It is imperative [he concluded] to impress every man and woman in the country that this land stands in greater peril than ever before in its history.

But neither Parliament, people, Press, nor Home Guard were moved by this affirmation. Pikes were "laughed out of court", as they deserved to be, and after clumbering up battalion armouries for some months they were silently withdrawn.

The weapon that was gently "lost" by the Home Guard as soon as it was issued. A corporal demonstrating the much-derided pike.

## Chapter XX

# SNAPSHOTS OF TRAINING

THE Oundle area now gained prominence as the result of an exercise held on Sunday, 22 March 1942, when the Home Guard and Civil Defence units combined in a full-scale test of the town's newest defence scheme.

The attack, made by troops under the command of Capt. E. St. C. Gainer, opened at surprise points round the perimeter of the town. This attack had been preceded by a heavy "blitz", which was so realistic that the A.R.P. and N.F.S., together with the police, had their fill of "incidents" throughout the day.

Inside Oundle, the beleaguered garrison under Capt. H. Hewitt, fought desperately. They were under orders to fight to the last man, and never to withdraw, and this "last ditch" order gave rise to many grim struggles.

This exercise was noteworthy because the Royal Air Force co-operated with the Home Guard, and dropped messages concerning the movements of the enemy to those besieged in the inner "keep".

It was a fine show—although it is regrettable to have to record that the Drill Hall, being inadvertently left minus a guard, was taken by an enemy patrol almost before the show began!

Incidentally, it may here be recalled that the 3rd (Oundle) Battalion (Lt.-Col. F. R. Berridge) set a good lead by arranging a special O.C.T.U. course for members desirous of obtaining commissions in the Home Guard. The course was devised by the Battalion Adjutant (Capt. H. Naylor) and No. 1 Sector Training Officer (Major W. H. Metcalfe). It was designed to determine individual suitability and capacity of the candidates who, later on, demonstrated so well what they had learned at a one-day camp parade, that they earned the congratulations of the Sub-Area Commander, Col. J. L. Short.

## A COMPANY DAY BY DAY

Behind all these special events, what was the day-to-day programme of the Northamptonshire Home Guard?

A glance through a typical company diary provides terse but telling answers.

Consider these random extracts from the diary of B Company of the 5th (Kettering District) Battalion for the sundry dates in 1942.

March 1.—Big TEWT at Oundle to introduce us to the new idea of defended localities. Many hours' work preparing defence scheme for Desborough in twenty-five sub-divisions with appendices and maps. Each village to become a defended locality. Plans of defence to be prepared, men familiarized with the idea, and then tested out in numerous inter-platoon schemes. Storm sections getting plenty of practice.

Training in first aid started. Stretcher-bearers detailed for each platoon.

Night operations being taken in earnest. Sensation in Desborough when section turned out with blackened faces.

April 14.—Meeting at Northampton to herald formation of Invasion Committees in the county. Very lively time for deputy regional commissioner.

April 26.—Trip to Mildenhall for

demonstration of dive bombing para-chutists, air co-operation.

April 30.—Battery of flame fougasses fixed up in the garden of a house facing strategic cross-road. Owner of house un-enthusiastic but resigned.

May 17.—Big combined exercise at Wellingborough. C Company lost their way and drove their transport straight into the middle of Finedon defended locality. Crossing of the open drains in Welling-borough sewage farm a ticklish business and not always successful.

May 23.—Second Battalion camp at Boughton Park. Capt. Lane again gave his celebrated imitation of a Regular officer mounting guard. Local publicans unable to provide refreshment so forays had to be made at a distance. Capt. Lane very successful as mess president and thanks of all officers due to him.

Church parade service taken by a private in uniform.

June 24.—Training of signallers ordered. So many specialists of one sort and another that no one left to use the rifles.

June 28.—Combined Home Guard and Civil Defence exercise at Desborough to test working of invasion committee. Ameri-can officers present as observers.

July 12.—Exercise at Wilbarston. Men took things so seriously that a squad lining a dry wall used the stones as bombs, and stretcher-bearers had real work to do—also the ladies of the Village First Aid Post.

July 15.—First introduction to battle drill.

July 21.—Training started of men directed to the Home Guard. Numbers in Desborough made up to 180. These men soon became at home with the old L.D.V. and worked well. Most of them became very keen on the job.

July 24.—A.R.P. asked for assistance in crop watching in view of danger from in-cendiaries. Patrols organized to turn out whenever an alert sounded. These con-tinued until harvest had been gathered in, being discontinued on 20 September. On 25 July numerous flares were dropped in the neighbourhood of the new 'drome and the parachute attached to one of the canisters was salvaged by a patrol.

## U.S. TROOPS ARRIVE

August 1–3.—Third camp at Boughton Park. Attendance not so numerous. Ger-man plane brought down close by.

September 1.—Weapon training officer appointed to sector. Came from a Regular battalion and for some time expected Home Guard training to approximate to that of the Regulars. Soon recognized the limita-tions of part-time training and was most helpful and popular.

September 15.—Arrival of American troops in Desborough in connection with big bomb dump. Officers most helpful and fully co-operative in connection with local defence, troops being put at disposal of the military commander of Desborough.

October 28.—Night exercise. Capt. Ginns in charge told me that conditions were ideal, not too light to be seen easily and not too dark to see—and then he promptly walked into the edge of an iron gate standing open, collecting a beautiful black eye.

November 8.—Range practice with Spigot mortar. Col. Burditt offered prize to anyone hitting framework of canvas target and bringing it down. Prize won with last round of shoot—probably by accident.

November 22.—Whole of 5th Battalion area involved in combined scheme with Civil Defence. American troops joined in with a number of heavy weapons.

Combined headquarters crammed with observers of all kinds.

December 27.—American officer shot dead by a negro private who took to the woods with a rifle. Home Guard asked to turn out to help round him up. Fortunately he surrendered without trouble.

December 28.—Desborough men turned out to help capture escaped Italian prisoner. Scores of half-finished buildings on aerodrome to search in pitch dark and pouring rain. Many open trenches half-full of water as traps for the unwary. Prisoner taken near Pipewell.

Just how much time, labour, anxiety, *and* good fun lay behind all those terse but eloquent entries only ex-Home Guards may fully appreciate.

### APPEAL FOR A BOAT

And, to the good fun, we may add here the story identified with an all-night exercise in the 14th (Brackley) Battalion (Lt.-Col. N. C. Furlong) when the Officer Commanding E Company received a message that an imaginary enemy general was in the neighbourhood. The message contained a full description of this nebulous warrior.

After several more "fool" communications of a similar nature had been received, the O.C. Company sent a message to Battalion headquarters saying that the "general" had been located at a certain map reference. This, when worked out, proved to be the centre of a large reservoir.

The message from Company implored Battalion headquarters to send a boat to assist in his capture.

### VISIT OF NATIONAL HERO

To revert to our chronological story we must return to 12 April 1942 which date will ever be memorable in the 10th (Daventry) Battalion (Lt.-Col. G. W. M. Lees) by reason of the fact that it marked an address from, and parade before, that grand old British sea hero, Admiral of the Fleet Sir Roger Keyes.

Sir Roger gave a graphic lecture on Commando training—the story of his gallant hero son's exploits in that branch of warfare are part of national history—and he was received with roars of cheers from a packed audience when he was introduced by the Battalion Commander.

Sir Roger said that the Home Guard must learn to operate with deadly accuracy and effectiveness by night, and suggested that at least 75 per cent of their training should be carried out in the dark, or in a mock darkness simulated by the use of smoked goggles.

(This latter suggestion was adopted by at least one section of a platoon of the 12th Battalion who, inspired by their forceful section sergeant, spent several hours on a sunny summer night in the semi-obscurity caused by daubing their anti-gas goggles with dark blue paint.)

Officers present included Col. P. Lester Reid (Zone Commander), Col. J. G. Lowther (Group Commander), Lt.-Col. W. J. Penn (Commanding Officer 11th Battalion), Major T. C. Shillito (Zone Staff Officer), Major L. E. Barnes, second-in-command 12th Battalion, and others.

### NEW MEDICAL ORDERS

13 April 1942 was a "red-letter" day in Home Guard medical organization since it marked the issue of an A.C.I. which thereafter became the "standard work" for the "Red Cross Brigade".

It formulated in fine detail a scheme of casualty collecting posts on a platoon basis through which casualties were to be evacuated to the Civil Defence casualty organization.

The duties of medical officers were also

Admiral of the Fleet Sir Roger Keyes takes the salute at a march past of the 10th (Daventry) Battalion, Northamptonshire Home Guard, after addressing the members on Commando Training at Daventry in April 1942. In the larger picture are (*left to right*) Lt.-Col. W. J. Penn (Commander 11th), Col. J. G. Lowther (Group Commander), the Mayor of Daventry (Councillor A. E. Hall), Col. P. Lester Reid (Zone H.G. Adviser), Major T. C. Shillito (Zone Staff Officer), Lt.-Col. Geoffrey Lees (Commander 10th), Major F. A. Thompson (11th,) Capt. J. R. Wilson (Guide Officer 11th), and the Admiral. (*Inset*) the Admiral chats with Lt. B. G. Holloway (Zone Intelligence and P.R.O.). In centre is Sgt.-Major R. D. J. Bean, the 10th Battalion P.S.I. Below is seen a section of the Battalion during the march past with the Admiral on right.

Some members of Billing's Home Guard in February 1941. In centre are Platoon Commander J. H. Spencer and Platoon Officer Bernard Holloway. Sgt. Frank Leatherland, 1914–18 veteran who was a platoon sergeant, was absent when this picture was taken.

detailed, as were the circumstances under which they could be mustered for civil or military duty.

This provision caused some resentment among the medical officers, who naturally wished to be mustered with their units.

The Government held, however, that medical man-power did not allow for whole-time service with the Home Guard on invasion as the civilian population must have adequate medical facilities and could not be left without doctors as it was in France.

Other medical developments included establishment details for medical orderlies and stretcher-bearers, courses for H.G. medical officers at Cambridge, regular conferences between the M.O.s and the publication of two valuable manuals, *Medical Memoranda for the Home Guard* and *First Aid for Fighting Men*.

The efficiency of the Northamptonshire Home Guard medical organization was strikingly demonstrated by the stretcher-bearers in the battalions in inter-battalion and sector competitions, and subsequently scores of bearers went on to take their St. John Ambulance Association certificates.

## 13TH'S TOUGH ASSAULT COURSE

In a preceding page we have referred appreciatively to the 9th Battalion's Battle Squad course. Little less "tough" was the assault course of the 13th (Towcester) Battalion (Lt.-Col. P. Y. Atkinson).

It began when B Company of this battalion, determined to keep themselves fit and in readiness for any "rough stuff", constructed the assault course in an old brickyard at Milton.

It was a communal affair, each platoon in the company being made responsible for the construction of a part of the course.

Although not approaching the demands of a Regular Commando assault course, it was quite tough enough to make a trying ordeal even for the younger elements.

To take this Home Guard "Grand National" the troops were lined up in sections in full battle order under their N.C.O.s and sent off at intervals.

First they had to climb a sandbag barricade, and lingering about on top of this was strictly *"Verboten"*. Under cover of some rough ground, bayonets were fixed, and in open order a specially shaped trench was attacked.

Home-made smoke bombs plus a dash of "stinker", 12-bore blanks, some fireworks and a dozen imaginative "etceteras" lent robust realism to the assault course of B Co. of the 13th (Towcester) Battalion in August 1942.

To get to this trench it was necessary to cross a ditch by means of sleepers laid on edge, and then get through, or round, or over, a whole lot of nasty barbed wire entanglements.

The crossing of the sleepers was a delicate sort of affair, as treading on a loose board was apt to cause a sandbag to rise up and hit one in the face.

Other surprises were supplied *ad lib* by enthusiastic cadets, who seemed to revel in making things as awkward as possible. There was no rest for the candidates who, by now hot and dusty, had to attack an imaginary machine-gun post at the other end of a small valley, through a smoke bomb screen.

Those smoke bombs were home-made ones, but they were all the more effective for that. They were produced by Cpl. Mudd of No. 1 Platoon who, together with members of the Milton platoon, was also usually responsible for the accompanying sound effects on this course.

Respirators were always worn, and to make things still more awkward 12-bore blanks were let off either just overhead or at the feet of the participants at irregular intervals. This was not all, either, as real bombs were exploded—far enough away to be safe, but still near enough literally to make things hum.

Emerging from the smoke-screen, the troops then fired five rounds rapid at moving targets, and, probably, thanked their gods that that was over at last.

The Royal Armoured Corps laid on a fine demonstration of anti-tank warfare for the 13th (Towcester) Battalion at Tiffield in April 1942. Here is the final destruction of an immobilized raider.

# Chapter XXI

## HIS MAJESTY BECOMES COLONEL-IN-CHIEF

CAME another month of May and with it the second anniversary of the Home Guard bringing with it a royal commander-in-chief.

Again His Majesty honoured the Guard with a message issued on the 14th of the month, but with it a final paragraph which handed to the Guard the highest honour it had so far received. Ran the message:

The second year in the life of the Home Guard, which ends to-day, has been one of marked and continued progress. I have watched with satisfaction the growing efficiency of the Force in training, equipment, and co-operation with the Regular Army, as well as the Civil Defence services. Many of the original volunteers have by now unavoidably left the Home Guard, and many have joined the Regular Forces. They leave behind them a great tradition of service and comradeship, which will inspire the new recruits now enrolling for the defence of their country. Whatever the coming year may bring, I know that the Home Guard will offer the fiercest resistance to any enemy who may set foot on these shores, and that its members will spare no efforts to make themselves more ready for battle.

In order to mark my appreciation of the services given by the Home Guard with such devotion and perseverance, I have to-day assumed the appointment of Colonel-in-Chief of the Force, and send my best wishes to all its members.

GEORGE R.I.

To this royal message Mr. Winston Churchill added another, cast in typical phraseology.

Said Mr. Churchill:

When France fell out of the war two years ago and we were left alone we were in imminent danger of invasion, and at that time we were not only destitute of an army but we were an unarmed people.

But at the same time that we reorganized our Army the Home Guard sprang into existence, and now we have the best part of 1,750,000 men trained to the use of arms, conscious of their military characteristic, accustomed readily and rapidly to come together at any point, fixing their minds upon the possibilities of contact with the enemy, which are never to be excluded.

This body, engaged in work of national importance during all hours of the day, and often of the night, is nevertheless an invaluable addition to our armed forces and an essential part of the effective defence of the island.

More especially is this true in view of the fact that airborne invasion becomes more and more a possibility and a feature of modern war. If in 1940 the enemy had descended suddenly in large numbers from the sky in different parts of the country, he would have found only little clusters of men, mostly armed with shot-guns, gathered round our searchlight positions.

But now, whenever he comes—if ever he comes—he will find wherever he should place his foot, that he will immediately be attacked by resolute, determined men who have a perfectly clear intention and resolve—namely, to put him to death or compel his immediate surrender.

Therefore, to invade this island by air, apart from the difficulties of facing the Royal Air Force by daylight, is to descend into a hornets' nest.

A glowing message was also issued by

Lt.-Gen. Sir Bernard Paget, Commander-in-Chief Home Forces, in a special Order of the Day.

You know your task [said the Commander-in-Chief] and your means for carrying it out are being steadily strengthened. Yours is a great responsibility, having in mind the vital part you will have to take in the security of the United Kingdom.

The test has yet to come, and when it does the strain on our endurance and on our faith will be great. It will call for the best that is in us of courage and self-confidence.

**CADET FORCE "FEEDS" HOME GUARD**

Finally, a searching and stimulating message was issued by the Home Guards' own Commander-in-Chief, Major-Gen. Viscount Bridgeman, D.S.O., M.C., the Director-General, as follows:

On an anniversary, one can look forward, and look back. On this second birthday (14 May) of the Home Guard, it is well to do both.

However much there is still to do (and there is a lot) much has been achieved. Co-ordinated defence schemes exist in place of haphazard plans. All, except the newly joined, have anti-gas equipment, steel helmets and battledress. Though the full issue of weapons is still not complete they have been coming in steadily during the last twelve months. Grenades of all types are far more plentiful than a year ago; the sub-machine gun and the anti-tank weapons are in the hands of every Home Guard detachment.

Strength is being maintained, not merely by compulsory enrolment, which has received general approval throughout the country, but by volunteer recruits. In particular, the Government plan for registration of youths has stimulated the flow of young men of seventeen into the Home Guard ranks, and this flow will henceforth be assured by the expansion of the Cadet Force which is training boys of fourteen to seventeen and passing them into the Home Guard.

During the past winter, the Home Guard have put in a lot of solid, unspectacular work. Training has been going on in the evenings, hidden by the blackout, but the Home Guard has emerged from the winter better trained in its weapons and subjects such as fieldcraft and unarmed combat necessary for dealing with the invader.

Its ranks have been largely purged of those members who were inefficient, whether through old age or failure to put in the requisite training time. The resignations which took place in February last on the application of compulsion are proving a source of strength rather than weakness and those who remain are keen to improve their efficiency and bring on the new recruits in the right way. Much still remains to be done to strengthen the leaders, and this is in great measure a matter for local commanders. Many who have borne the burden for so long must now give place to the younger men whom they themselves have trained.

To this result the assistance from the Regular Army has contributed much. Everywhere, with a few exceptions, regular instructors have helped the Home Guard to improve their training, and it is now possible to allot more Regular officers and N.C.O.s for permanent duty with the Home Guard.

So much for the past. As to the future, the destiny of the Home Guard, like that of the whole of the armed forces of the country, depends on the course of the war as a whole, for on that depends the likelihood of invasion. Now that the spring is here, there are better opportunities for each unit to train in its own battle role. Since the Home Guard is a local force, each company and platoon, whether from city or hamlet, has its own task to perform.

Some must improve their skill in street fighting; some in patrols and anti-parachute tasks, by day and night. The training of junior leaders is specially important. So is the training in co-operation with the Civil Defence services and in mutual assistance so that the duties of everyone, in emergency, may be properly integrated.

There is a wide variety of specialist

training to be carried out: signalling, dispatch riding, first aid, and special weapons. The use of Home Guards in anti-aircraft and coast defence duties began during the winter and must be largely extended, so that Regular troops may be released from static duties to join the Field Army.

The Home Guard is a local force, and cannot assume any other character, since the men who comprise it are the local citizens, nearly all of whom perform civilian duties of

by this time becoming really advanced in all such exercises. Thus in this large exercise devised by Col. A. E. Stokes Roberts, to test the town's defence system, real "stinker" gas was used, to the acute discomfort of many civilians who, with a fine disregard for orders and suggestions, venture into the streets without their gas masks.

Afterwards the Sub-Area Commander

No. 2 Platoon of A Company of the 12th Battalion participating in the Civic procession of Northampton's "Russia Week" Church Parade in March 1942.

national importance, alongside their Home Guard duties till the emergency arises. Even then, most of them must needs serve within reach of their homes and civil employment. Thus the Home Guard will be a local one, for the Home Guards are the original Local Defence Volunteers. To train for the Home Guard battle will, therefore, be the task of the local leader, with all the help and support which the War Office and the higher command can give. It is on local leadership that the Home Guard depends for success on its tasks.

## REAL GAS STARTLES A TOWN

Mr. Churchill in his message had used the term "hornets' nest".

It was a description which the people of Wellingborough might well have applied to their own town on 17 May 1942 during a special exercise by the 7th Battalion.

Realism in both attack and defence was

addressed the participants and expressed his warm appreciation of the work done by all ranks. His address was followed by a combined march past, at which he took the salute.

## FINE EMPIRE DAY PARADE

Among the many church parades organized by the Northamptonshire Home Guard throughout the war, one of the most impressive was credited to the 11th (Hardingstone) Battalion—an Empire Day Service of Witness held at Duston on 24 May 1942.

It was conducted by the Rev. L. J. Thompson, Vicar of Duston, assisted by Mr. C. H. Battle (Lay Pastor, Duston), the Rev. W. F. Need (Yardley Hastings), the Rev. L. E. Browne (Castle Ashby), and the Rev. C. J. Barker (Curate of Duston); anthems were sung by a combined choir and the 12th Battalion band played for the hymns, and also for a smart march past, at which the salute was taken by the Zone Commander, Col. P. Lester Reid, accompanied by the Zone Staff Officer, Major T. C. Shillito.

The admirable organization reflected great credit on all ranks responsible.

Col. P. Lester Reid, in the course of an address, voiced an earnest call for more consistent co-operation between the Home Guard and the Civil Defence services. "There are many," he said, "particularly in the smaller villages, who do not know what to do if an extreme emergency should arise."

The service concluded with warm expressions of thanks to Col. W. J. Penn and to all his officers and men for a very fine turnout and parade.

**SPLENDID NEW WEAPON**

During the summer of 1941 a persistent rumour had begun to circulate around the Home Guard.

It was being whispered that a new and secret weapon was being manufactured in enormous quantities, and that it was going to be issued to the Home Guard practically *ad libitum*. Further, those in the know stated that its production cost only a few shillings.

At a May 1942 Church Parade of the 11th Battalion at Duston. The Zone-Commander (Col. P. Lester Reid) takes the salute at the march past. With him is Lt.-Col. W. J. Penn, Battalion Commander. In the larger picture is shown a particularly smart turnout by No. 14 Platoon of C Co. Bottom right—an amusing diversion when a Duston cow with the Home Guard spirit sought to bar the intruders from their parade ground.

[*Photo: B. Bernstein*

Sten gun practice by the 12th (Northampton) Battalion marksmen on the R.E.M.E. range at Far Cotton, Northampton.

For once the rumour was not lying.

The *"ad libitum"* suggestion proved to be a slight exaggeration, but the rest was founded on fact.

In June 1942 the Sten Carbine, as it was known, was released to the Home Guard, and the Northamptonshire battalions had their fair share of this remarkable weapon. Like the Northover, it was not prepossessing. There was a crudity in its design and finish which somewhat shocked the more fastidious tastes of people used to the more elegant and polished weapons.

At first it was issued with a wooden stock, but later issues were complete with a skeleton metal stock which did not improve its appearance.

It fully bore out the suggestion that it could be made cheaply, and its reception was an extremely dubious one. At once these weapons were nicknamed "Gas Lighters".

Appearances, however, are proverbially deceptive, and the Sten Carbine, after the initial shock caused by its strange appearance, proved an immense success.

## PRODUCT OF BRITISH BRAINS

No gun was ever designed, the prototype made, tested, and tried out and then ordered as quickly as the Sten. It was a 100 per cent production of British brains and was as accurate as any gun in its class. It fired almost as fast as the Thompson, and the Schmeisser, the German gun.

The men who designed the gun worked in the Ministry of Supply Armaments Design Department. "S" and "T" were their surname initials and "EN" stands for England. They were part of a team which achieved this revolution in arms manufacture, but theirs is the chief credit.

"S" and "T" got down to their drawing boards in December 1940, and in one month they had completed a design and also made a prototype gun. By the end of

January the new gun had been demon-strated to the War Office, passed, and the first order for 100,000 units placed with ordnance firms. The Sten had fifty-nine parts, counting washers and pins, the Thompson had ninety parts and the Schmeisser had a hundred and four.

A home-made Sten gun mounting for a motor cycle designed and made by D. R. R. J. Humphrey of 1 Platoon, D Company of the 10th (Daventry) Battalion. On left is Sgt.-Major R. D. J. Bean (10th Permanent Staff Instructor).

## A CLEVER DEVICE

Apropos of the Sten, a bright instance of Home Guard ingenuity was provided by the 11th Battalion with the production of a clever arrangement intended to develop a keen sense of target location in the dark or in a dull light.

A Sten carbine was fitted with a small electric bulb in the breech which lit up when the trigger was pressed.

In a darkened room the gunner was then given a succession of fire orders on a land-scape target with which he was familiar and his sense of direction was proved by the spotlight which appeared on the target as he fired.

## A DEVASTATING WEAPON

It was in May 1942 also that the Guard received its first issues of another notable weapon, the Spigot mortar. This was quite a devastating piece of sub-artillery in-vented by Major Northover which while it shared, in the opinion of many, the "one-shot weapon" disadvantage of the Harvey Flame Thrower, would, nevertheless, have made a pretty mess of any tank receiving one of its direct hits.

Lt.-Col. L. E. Barnes tells an amusing story of the weapon which might easily have been attended by serious results.

He writes:

The Spigot mortar was the sub-artillery weapon that found most favour with the Home Guard. They were first issued to us in May 1942, and at once became a popular weapon.

[*Photo: G. Turnill*

Spigot mortar practice by a section of E Company 2nd Northants Home Guard, 1943.

In connection with the Spigot there was one incident that might have led to a serious acci-dent, but fortunately the luck of the 12th held and no serious result occurred. On 10 June 1943, a Spigot team were practising on the grounds of the Town and County School when, by some mischance, an inert bomb found its way into the dummies. When the gun was fired, to the dismay of the firer, and probably more to the corporal in charge, the inert sped on its way in the direction of Cranmere Avenue. The Battalion I.O., who resides in this select neighbourhood, had the shock of his life when he saw the bomb pass by his front bedroom. Missing houses, it crashed into a fence and came to rest farther down the avenue, which, luckily, was deserted at the time so that the only casualty was the fence, which was considerably damaged.

By a whip-round among the members of the platoon this was repaired, and nothing more was heard of an incident which might have had serious consequences had it occurred some time earlier when several children were at play in the avenue.

In June 1944, with the Home Guard assuming a more mobile role, Spigots were trooped to render assistance to infantry with enemy brought to bay.

It was not easy to arrange for live ammunition to be fired from this gun as the danger area of the burst was 400 yards, and there were no places round Northampton that gave this margin of safety. However, one firing practice was arranged, and this took place on 27 August 1944 at the Harlington range, near Dunstable. At the same time the opportunity was taken to practise the Smith gun teams of D, G, and H Companies, both in direct and indirect fire. Altogether twenty-eight Spigot and twenty-two Smith gun teams had their first and only firing with live ammunition.

It should not be supposed, however, that the Spigot mortar and Smith gun were not fired with live. There was firing in the 11th Battalion and the 7th, also, were using, from July 1944 onwards, a really first-class range near the "Roundhouse" on the Finedon-Thrapston road. The Battalion had been among the first to provide itself with a range for battle inoculation and had also reconstructed the old T.A. range on the road from Wellingborough to Doddington, so that, having found the ground with sufficient danger area near Finedon, the

The Spigot mortar demonstrated by a 12th (Northampton) Battalion team.

C.O. had no lack of experienced officers and men to construct a "field firing range" for his sub-artillery. Thanks to the persistence of Col. Fulton of No. 3 Sector H.Q., the site was approved by higher authority after some delay, and he and Capt. Chouler (7th Battalion adjutant) assisted by Capt. O. Mayers, who measured the range and made blinds for indirect firing, and Capt. E. Deighton, who made the targets and range indicators and produced flag-poles, found no difficulty in getting voluntary labour from the Battalion—or, ultimately, fatigue parties when firing commenced. It is said that the quantity of mushrooms to be found had something to do with the eagerness shown by the latter. The farmer kindly turned a blind eye. Some really good shoots with the Smith gun resulted, and H.E. with the Spigot was found to be really accurate and such as would have caused a lot of damage.

## Chapter XXII

# FULL-SCALE CAMPS

ALTHOUGH camps of varying degrees of size and importance had been unofficially organized by many Northamptonshire Home Guard units previous to 1942, it was not until that year that they were officially sanctioned and emerged on a grand scale.

Major Hereward Wake, K.R.R.C., son of Major-Gen. Sir Hereward Wake, on left, lecturing at an officers' camp of the 12th Battalion held in Overstone Park in August 1943. On right are Lt.-Col. L. E. Barnes, M.B.E. (C.O.), and Lt.-Col. J. A. Brawn, O.B.E.

No man, unless he be dead to all feeling, can ever lose his boyish delight in the novelty of sleeping under canvas. To do this he will cheerfully march a dozen miles, and take a chance with sciatica.

Having arrived, the years slip off old shoulders and he becomes a boy again, thrilling at the sight of bell tents and marquees, of the smoke-blackened cookhouse, and the long lines of washing troughs.

Most of all does he thrill at the idea of spending so many hours in the open, in the best company in the world, his own comrades, and of eating and drinking and sleeping with the blue sky above him and a natural carpet beneath his feet.

So it was that week-end camps caught on and brought rejuvenation to many Home Guards who were forced to spend long war-time hours compassed about with brick and stone.

Many pages could be devoted to a description of these camps, most of them standing camps held from May to October annually by all battalions in the Zone and particularly of the many novel camp events devised by commanders to impart variety.

Thus, E Company (Mobile) of the 4th (Kettering Town) Battalion invariably went to camp at Boughton Park, Weekly, and on one occasion during a camp exercise which was "laid on" unknown to rank and file the camp was "attacked" by a party commanded by the C.O.

The Demolition Officer had laid charges underground in and around the camp to simulate mortar fire.

Unfortunately, these were a trifle too large—and when they were detonated the result can be imagined.

On some camp sessions live ammunition was also used to give an atmosphere of realism and there was a curious result on one occasion when a corporal was struck in the eyebrow by a piece of 36 grenade at a range of *170 yards*! Ironically enough, this N.C.O. had spent four and a half years in the 1914-18 war without a "scratch". He received his only wound while serving in the Home Guard.

AT CAMP

Whitsun Week 1941. Members of a company of the 13th (Towcester) Battalian perfecting their machine-gun training. The officer on right is Lt. Green.

On the bayonet drill ground at the 13th Battalion's training camp at Whitsun 1941.

"Prepare to throw—THROW" and over go the grenades. Another training
scene in the 13th (Towcester) Battalion area in 1941.

Inspecting a demonstration by a signal section of the 13th (Towcester) Battalion are left to
right, Lt. N. A. Cooke, Capt. J. W. Millar, Major H. Pebody, M.M. (Commanding B Co.),
C.S.M. H. A. Yates, Lt.-Col. P. Y. Atkinson, M.C. (Battalion Commander), Major J. N.
Beasley, M.C., Lt. W. F. Woolacott, Capt. E. Lewin (Adjutant and later Captain and Q.M.
to Battalion), and P.S.I. W. E. Wetherill.

**FINE WORK BY W.V.S.**

Another fine camp at this period was that held by the 3rd Battalion (Lt.-Col. F. R. Berridge, D.S.O., M.C.)

Ideally located in Lilford Park, it ran throughout the summer months, and each week-end members of the Oundle, Thrapston, Barnwell, and Brigstock W.V.S., of

and march past, and also viewed all sections of the Battalion's camp training programme in progress.

In a telling address to the parade, the District Commander complimented the Battalion upon looking him straight in the eye. "It is what an inspecting officer always likes to see," he said.

Major N. P. Andrews (Company Commander), inspecting kit at A Co.'s August 1942 Camp (12th Battalion) at Overstone Park.

which Mrs. G. E. Belville was Centre Organizer, "covered themselves with glory" by serving a hot lunch to the whole of the participating members of the Battalion.

When it is appreciated that these never numbered less than half of the Battalion and that the whole of the cooking was by field kitchen, the achievement can be assessed for the really fine job it was.

On Sunday, 31 July 1942, guests at the al fresco officers mess included the District Commander, the Home Guard Zone Commander, Col. P. Lester Reid, a colonel of the American Air Corps, and Major T. C. Shillito. Afterwards the District Commander witnessed a smart Battalion parade

**"WITHOUT DISCIPLINE, NO VICTORY"**

"We have come to a critical stage in this war," he warned them, "and all must be prepared for anything that may come along.

"Cohesion and battle discipline were the essentials," the Commander added, and concluded by quoting his regimental motto: 'Without discipline, no Victory'."

Just what standard the 3rd Battalion camp training attained can, perhaps, best be judged from the fact that a unit of the Regular Army took several of the camp courses.

Incidentally, a special compliment should be recorded to the C.O., and his worthy adjutant, Capt. H. Nailer, upon the planning and, especially, the canvas and equipment of the camp. Whence and how they obtained such "pukka" tents—new and roomy rectangulars of the finest quality—was a mystery.

The 7th Battalion held their camps mainly at Castle Ashby on the estate of the Marquess of Northampton, although some were at Harrowden Hall, where Major W. G. Gilbey, who succeeded Major Bannie as Company Commander, had his H.Q. These camps were usually on a company basis, well patronized, and a regular feature of the Battalion programme from 1941 onwards.

## A BUOYANT BATTALION

The buoyancy of the sundry records of these camps was typical of the high spirits and gay cameraderie which always characterized them—the spirits which expressed themselves in a hundred "masterpieces" of Home Guard humour.

Here is one of them from the 9th (Brixworth) Battalion, the menu of a supper apparently consumed at Holcot:

Compote mystérieuse Holcote
"Soixante Huit"

Bandeau rouge—très dangereuse
Poulet Poche et Volaille Volée
Bruxelles Scroungées

"Your job now is to take back all you have learnt this week-end to your platoons and sections." (1) The final address by the C.O. (Lt.-Col. G. S. Watson) to a 9th Battalion N.C.O.s' camp. On extreme left is the Battalion Adjutant, Capt. C. C. Oakey, M.C., and in centre of this group the 9th's instructor, P.S.I. H. Billingham. (2) R.S.M. J. R. Bird is in centre of this "conversation piece", which includes the C.O. on right, and, on left, Major R. Dickens (second-in-command), and Major T. C. Shillito. (3) C.S.M. N. Girdlestone (*on left*), discusses "amendments" in an informal conference.

Pommes de terre trouvées

Toutes Eminces varieuses

S. I. P.

(Sans intérieur peut-être.)

*Vins*

Coupe Dischargeur

Sten Supérieur—action rapide

Grand bouteille—'73

Eau de pompe—très sec

Torpille bangalore

Battalion at Franklins Gardens on 28 June. In the competitive events, No. 1 Headquarters Platoon carried off all the "pots" apparently in accordance with their established tradition.

Features of the tournament were the use of an amplifier presented by the Baltimore and Ohio Railway to the Northampton Railway Company, and selections by the Railway Guard band during the event.

Inter-platoon competitions of E Co. of the 12th (Northampton) Battalion in September 1942, were accompanied by an inspection of the Company by Earl Spencer (Hon. Col. of the Northamptonshire Regt.). Our photo shows the inspection in progress. Left to right, the officers behind are Capt. H. D. Barton (Adjutant), Major L. E. Barnes (Acting C.O. 12th Battalion), 2nd Lt. K. G. Bayes, Capt. R. J. Marfleet and Major E. W. H. Powell (Company Commander).

## A FINE TOURNAMENT

Amid all its training preoccupations, both grave and gay, the Home Guard did not lose sight of the value of a little judicious "showmanship", usually devoting the proceeds to Service charities.

In this respect a number of successful tournaments and other displays were regularly staged by the battalions.

1942 was marked by a particularly fine show put up by E Company (Major E. W. Powell) of the 12th (Northampton)

## DESBOROUGH'S DEFENCE TESTED

June and July 1942 brought several exercises which so convincingly exemplified the Home Guard's progress as to merit more than passing reference.

One was staged in the 5th (Kettering District) Battalion area at Desborough. Devised by Col. H. C. Burditt (Group Commander), it kept the local Home Guard and Civil Defence services fully extended for some three and a half hours on 28 June.

After the show the County A.R.P. Controller (Mr. J. Alan Turner) thanked Col. Burditt for the opportunity thus given to the Civil Defence units to co-operate with the Home Guard forces engaged.

### BIG "SHOW" IN NORTHAMPTON AREA

The second exercise took place on Sunday, 5 July—a most ambitious invasion operation known as "Eleanor", which was staged in Northampton and the area around it.

An invasion army, which had landed in East Anglia, had detached a portion of its force to attack Northampton, supported by bombing formations, which, according to plan, spread considerable havoc in the county town. Paratroops had also been dropped in many parts.

The enemy was represented by the 10th and 14th Battalions together with detachments of the 9th, 11th, and 13th Battalions. The defenders were the 9th, 11th, and 13th, holding respectively the north, east and west, and south sectors of the borough's forward lines. The 12th Battalion had the honour of holding the town's inner defences.

There was a lot of confused and desperate fighting, and the enemy, although grim and determined, did not escape without heavy losses. Meanwhile, the borough police, N.F.S., and A.R.P. were coping magnificently with a blitz that had destroyed half the main buildings of the town, blocked main roads, smashed the gas, water, and electric light mains, and inflicted hundreds of casualties.

The exercise was devised and directed by Col. A. E. Stokes Roberts (Sub-Area Commander), the Civil Defence controllers, the Chief Constable of the Borough (Mr. John Williamson), the Clerk to the County Council (Mr. J. Alan Turner), and the Town Clerk (Mr. W. Kew).

### A CLEVER RUSE

There were several highlights during this intensive exercise, among such being the exploit of C.S.M. Briam of the 14th

One of the most formidable and toughest of "enemy" units which attacked Northampton in a great civil and military combined invasion exercise in July 1942 was the East Haddon Platoon of the Northamptonshire Home Guard here seen advancing in cover.

Battalion, who was operating with the enemy forces.

C.S.M. Briam, *en route* to Northampton, "burgled" a rural police station, "borrowed" a complete policeman's outfit, and made his way, thus attired, into the heart of the defended area and actually carried on a conversation with a real policeman—managing, by this *tour de force*, to extract the exact information his comrades needed.

Probably the most humorous incident of the day was that which occurred to the Walgrave and Holcot platoons, who were operating as "Jerries", and got well into the inner defence perimeter by skilful use of cover, and by availing themselves of back alleys and the like.

At one stage they had to pass right through a house from back to front, and the lady of the house remarked—"I hope you're not the enemy." "No, madam," they assured her, "we're Huns." "In that case," replied the unsuspecting housewife, "I'll get you a cup of tea."

While they were drinking it, the good lady remarked that it was a pity her husband was not at home to meet them, but he was also on duty—and with a gesture, she pointed out a house. "That's his company headquarters," she added.

Three minutes later, *that* company headquarters was well and truly bombed and captured.

# Chapter XXIII

## SUB-AREA COMMAND CHANGES

JULY 1942 brought the first of the several changes in the Sub-Area Command previously referred to.

After holding the office for four months, Col. Stokes Roberts left to take up the appointment of Military Commander of Trinidad and carried with him the warmest good wishes of the Northamptonshire Home Guard.

Before leaving, Col. Stokes Roberts issued the following Special Order:

On relinquishing command of the North-amptonshire Sub-Area, I should like to place on record my very high appreciation of the loyal support and co-operation I have received on all sides.

In wishing all ranks God speed, I can with confidence say that the general standard of efficiency has improved on all sides.

If put to the test, I know you will acquit yourselves well.

I wish you all the best of luck, an early victory, and a safe and speedy return to your families.

Col. Stokes Roberts's tenure of office seemed short enough, but all records in "commandobatics" were broken by his successor, Col. J. W. L. S. Hobart, D.S.O., M.C., who hardly had time to identify his own staff, much less his Home Guard commanders, before he was moved to a Scottish Command exactly three weeks after his arrival!

Col. Hobart also issued a Special Order before his departure, in the course of which he said:

. . . From what I have seen in the last three weeks I am convinced that the spirit of enthusiasm and endeavour shown by all ranks

both in the Regular units and the Home Guard . . . coupled with the close co-operation with the Civil Authorities, will combine in a resolute determination to defeat the enemy should he ever dare to invade this country.

After Col. Hobart came the third commander of what had now changed its title to the Northants Sub-District, and this time the post was to be occupied for a reasonably lengthy period.

Col. J. L. Short, C.B.E.

The new commander was a New Zealander in the person of Col. J. L. Short, C.B.E.

Col. Short originally studied for the law but at the same time served as a member of the New Zealand Territorial Army.

Thus, on the outbreak of the 1914–18 war, he was included in the first New Zealand Expeditionary Force and served with them in Egypt, Gallipoli, and France.

At the conclusion of the war he was given a regular commission in the North Staffordshire Regiment and, in 1926, received accelerated promotion into the King's Regiment, of whose second battalion he was subsequently given command. Command of the Staffordshire Territorial Brigade followed.

Probably born of his early legal training, Col. Short soon proved himself a stickler for detail in every respect of Home Guard administration and training.

Very early in his tenure of the command he made it his business to make a thorough inspection of all battalion headquarters and of battalion records and office systems and also organized major exercises in all battalion areas embracing also all departments of the Civil Defence services.

He never called upon others to perform what he was not prepared to do himself, and during arduous exercises in difficult country he was invariably to be seen forging across ploughland, stubble, or through woodlands and undergrowth while keeping right up with the van of the operations in progress.

He also took an active and close interest in local affairs and associated himself with a number of town and county bodies directly or indirectly identified with the Northamptonshire war effort.

## A ROCKET A.A. BATTERY

It was on 20 July 1942 that there was formed a Northamptonshire Home Guard A.A. Battery. They were the only such unit in the county and they were honoured as much as they were envied by their fellow Home Guards of the shire.

The Battery was designated the 101 Northants Home Guard "Z" A.A. Battery and came into being after a meeting at 2nd A.A. Division between Home Forces, A.A. Command, T.A.A., and G.S. Home Guard.

The command of the Battery was invested in Major E. W. Bromige of the 1st (Peterborough City) Battalion, who was given the task of raising a battery comprising some 1,500 men who had just been released from local factories to join the G.S. Home Guard; but owing to the extreme necessity of A.A. defence it was agreed to divert these men into the Battery.

The problem thus presented to old L.D.V. stalwarts reminded them of the early days of 1940, as, without staff or organized headquarters, enrolments were due to begin on 20 July at the rate of thirty men per day for seven days a week.

Let us leave them here working with a T.A.A. Administration clerk and Home Guard clerks kindly lent by Capt. Pilley, Adjutant of the 1st Northampton Battalion, to examine the composition of a Home Guard "Z" A.A. Battery.

The Battery was directly under A.A. Command for operations. To achieve this a nucleus of Regular R.A. personnel, consisting of a battery commander (Major), a second-in-command (Captain), four subalterns, one A.T.S. officer, fifty other ranks, and fifty A.T.S. was encamped on the selected gun site.

These regular troops trained the Home Guard for their operational role. The training consisted of basic infantry work, projector drill, plotting and instrument drill, aircraft recognition, operational schemes, and anti-gas.

The Home Guard battery was in reality eight complete batteries, each self-contained under the command of a captain, the whole unit being under the command of a Home Guard Major. A Regular Captain was posted for administration duties.

Each sub-battery, or relief, performed one whole night's duty one night a week, parading at seven o'clock when the duties for the night were allocated.

A manning drill was performed and then dinner was served—a hot meal equal to the regular units' midday dinner.

After a "break" in the NAAFI, more instructions and drill were undertaken, and "lights out" ended the somewhat strenuous evening. Provided no alerts were sounded, the Home Guard retired for the night on Army beds. Breakfast was provided, and the men were released from the site in time to return to work at the usual starting times. For the Home Guard it was a night of real "Army life".

## BATTERY'S FIRST HOME

To return to Unity Hall—the first home of the Battery. Within a week an office had been formed and the services of Mr. J. Woodward, a well-known retired post office clerk, enlisted as chief T.A.A. clerk, a typist, and a storeman were engaged, and the task of enrolling began to take some definite form.

On 25 July 1942 the first Regular contingent arrived. It was usual for the Home Guard to be formed before the Regular unit. In most batteries it was the practice to form the Home Guard on an already operational Regular site and, as the Home Guard became proficient, to replace the Regular personnel by Home Guard. Peterborough was faced with the reverse, a new site, *"sans* guns"*, an untrained Home Guard battery of 1,500 men, and a partly formed Regular battery.

However, before many weeks passed, Major C. R. Elwis, T.D., R.A., arrived to take charge, and born of his untiring enthusiasm and complete understanding, training progressed and the site began to improve.

The late summer evenings gave ample opportunity for training, and anything up to two hundred men were on the site each night training in the new "Z" rocket weapon—then on the secret list. This job was tackled by the Regular Sergeant-Major, B.S.M. S. Royal, with enthusiasm and gusto, much to the amusement of the files on parade.

Meanwhile, at Unity Hall, men were being fitted out with uniform. Here the transfer of Battery Q.M.S. Jones from the 1st Northamptonshire Battalion Home Guard was a "godsend".

## A SUBALTERN'S ORDEAL

Memorable in the early months of the Battery was the first lecture attended by eight raw recruits, all of whom became relief commanders, when Gen. "Ben" Crossman arrived and stayed for the lecture, much to the embarrassment of the Regular subaltern lecturer.

Then there were the tents forming the first camp, not forgetting the officers' mess, complete with hurricane lamps, and the trooping parades on 10 and 11 October, when the mass of half-trained recruits paraded and were divided into Reliefs and Troops. Here the biggest problem presented itself.

In Peterborough the percentage of shift workers were very large and the scheme of one night in eight was not practicable, for when men were on night work they could not man the guns; so far, in other batteries, these men had been refused admission into the A.A., but in Peterborough it was the shift worker or NO BATTERY!

A complicated arrangement of "one night in seven" with alternative reliefs taking week-end manning when on night work was devised. Only one person knew how it was done—but it worked!

The general principle of no officer or N.C.O. being appointed until passing a suitable course was rigidly adhered to, and by the end of the year officers and N.C.O.s were rapidly made. At the close of 1942 the officers were—Battery Commander, Major E. W. Bromige; relief commanders: Capts. W. A. Heighton and F. H. Martin, Lts. T. A. Irvine, W. T. Dryland, V. S. Hammersley, F. Biggin, H. G. Merchant, and X. A. Halliday.

Christmas 1942 showed how the Regular component had been accepted as good pals and had chummed up with members of the Home Guard, for on Christmas night, apart from two or three duty men—the Battery not being operational—every man was entertained at some Home Guard fireside.

Only a month after the A.A. Battery, i.e., in August, there was formed another of the Northamptonshire Home Guards' crack units.

**THE "GREEN LANYARDS"**

This was what was known as the Northants Sub-District Mobile Company, though for administrative purposes it was attached as G Company to the 12th (Northampton) Battalion.

This company was built up from carefully selected personnel who combined physical fitness with alertness, resource and initiative and they were raised to form the Special Mobile Reserve of the Sub-District Commander, Col. J. L. Short.

Their training was directed to the end that they might be capable of applying a determined offensive spirit in all circumstances and they were essentially designed to embody a hard-hitting force capable of being dispatched, at short notice, to deal with any difficult situation.

The Company was distinguished by the wearing of green lanyards.

It was, obviously, the younger men of the Northampton Home Guard who were selected for this company, and this had

its disadvantages as well as its advantages, as the Company was subject to constant depletion of its numbers through the calling up of its personnel for military and other service.

This, however, had its compensations, as the Company were proud of the fact that it was consistently and valuably contributing to the Regular forces.

At a complete parade in full battle order on Sunday, 10 January 1943, the Company was inspected by Col. Short, and later staged a series of well-executed drills with their sub-artillery and other weapons.

The colonel emphasized that they must always keep fit and active in order to be a hard-hitting unit, and hinted that later on they would be equipped with powerful additions to their present offensive weapons.

The principle officers of "The Green Lanyards", the only mobile reserve company in the Northamptonshire Home Guard, were as follows:

Company Commander, Major S. B. Patrick; Second-in-Command, Capt. F. C. Whiting; Intelligence Officer, Lt. V. H. Purdy; Transport Officer, Lt. V. B. Allinson; Signals Officer, Lt. F. W. Barker; Company Q.M.S., C.Q.M.S. T. I. Pepper.

No. 22 Platoon: Platoon Commander, Capt. A. E. Cleaver, M.M.; Platoon officers, Lt. H. L. Simon and Lt. R. L. Wheeler.

No. 23 Platoon: Platoon Commander, Lt. P. H. Rowe.

No. 24 Platoon: Platoon Commander, Lt. J. Watts.

No. 25 Platoon: Platoon Commander, Lt. C. M. Edwards.

**HOW SMITH GUN WAS "BORN"**

When the Sub-District mobile company was first formed there was much speculation as to the new and special weapons with which it was said they would be equipped.

THE MOBILE SECTION !

There was talk of light artillery, and when this was known to have "arrived"—*very "hush-hush" and concealed behind "locked doors"*—there was even more speculation as to its type and capabilities.

Later, the Smith gun became well known, not only to every Home Guard, but also, by virtue of its effective participation in Home Guard displays and demonstrations, to many thousands of members of the general public as well.

But, its history was not so well known, even to those who regularly manipulated the weapon.

Actually, though quite fortuitously, the idea of the gun came almost simultaneously with the formation of the Home Guard, and just before Dunkirk, to its inventor, Major William H. Smith, M.I.Mech.E., M.I.Struct.E., managing director of a well-known engineering firm with works at East Molesey, Surrey.

Said Major Smith, describing his invention:

It appeared obvious to me at that time that the bulk of our army comprised infantry, who were unable, equipped with rifles, either to attack or defend themselves adequately against the mechanized appliances of the enemy, particularly light armoured vehicles and small tanks.

There was also the difficulty of turning out the enemy from behind obstacles which could not be penetrated, and I naturally felt that something in the nature of a shell or bomb which could be fired from a weapon easily handled by infantry would be more effective.

I appreciated that in the last war the Stokes mortar had been used to great advantage, but that this was restricted to high-angle fire, and was totally unsuitable for firing point-blank when the occasion demanded.

Nevertheless, I bore in mind the fact that circumstances can arise in modern warfare

[*Photo: B. Bernstein*

The wheels formed also base and protection. The ingenuity of the Smith gun well illustrated in a demonstration by G Company 12th (Northampton) Battalion.

when high-angle fire has to be adopted at a moment's notice.

I realized also that with terrific speed of movement to-day, it was essential to be able to change the direction of fire rapidly through a minimum of 90 degrees, but for preference through the full circle.

Again, it seemed evident, due to rapidity of movement, that the weapon should be capable of being brought into action in the least possible time, and I knew that, even with the Stokes mortar, more time was taken in setting this up, and in altering it from one bearing to another, than circumstances usually permitted.

### WHEEL SERVED AS GUN BASE

My intention, therefore, throughout the whole of the work involved in the design was to keep the equipment absolutely simple, both from the point of view of handling, maintenance, and manufacture, and I think you Home Guards appreciate that, although this gun can hurl a 10-lb. projectile over 1,000 yards with reasonable accuracy, it is built on the simplest lines possible, and has a breech mechanism which can be adjusted by any ordinary mechanic.

The present weapon embodying the principle of the two wheels on which the gun can be towed, but which, when thrown on to its side with one wheel serving as the gun base, permits of full traverse, while the top wheel gives protection from splinters to the gunners, was not conceived in the early stages, but was actually the result of development running over a period of five months, during which time five distinct models were designed and built.

Naturally [added Major Smith] the design of this weapon which is on very revolutionary and unorthodox lines, involved a considerable amount of thought and energy, but, quite frankly, I suppose the hardest part of the work undertaken was in getting "authority" to make a decision as to its acceptance.

The Prime Minister, personally, in the early days, saw this weapon and was present at certain trials, and no doubt his energy went a long way to assist in getting it taken up for the benefit of the Home Guard and other Services to-day who appear to appreciate its merits.

The Northampton Home Guard G Company certainly *did* appreciate its merits despite the fact that they were left to devise—and supply—their own methods of towing (usually by private cars) and had they been called upon to take the Smith into action it is certain that the enemy would have appreciated its merits also.

### PETERBOROUGH MOVES OUT

It was in the month of August 1942 that the Northamptonshire Home Guard regretfully bade farewell to Nos. 1 (City of Peterborough) and 2 (Soke of Peterborough) battalions who, in accordance with a dispositional plan which had been discussed for some time, now moved over into the Huntingdonshire Zone.

Although by reason of their "remoteness" at the northern tip of the county, the 1st and 2nd had but rarely figured in the general scene of the Zone, they had, nevertheless, attained a very high standard of efficiency and had always "played up" well in all combined activities.

In spirit they were still part of the Northamptonshire force and thus they figure as fully as possible in this history.

## Chapter XXIV

## MORE ENEMY BOMBING

THE scene now moves into drama in the 7th (Wellingborough Town) Battalion district—drama with a no less undramatic setting than a Bank Holiday charity fête being held in Wellingborough itself.

It was a warm sunny evening, and the fête was thronged with happy people endeavouring to forget for a while the anxieties of a war.

About 6 p.m. the peace of evening was shattered by the wail of the air raid siren, and almost immediately a low-flying enemy plane zoomed out of the sky and planted a stick of bombs on the town.

The raider then circled Wellingborough School fields where the fête was in progress and appeared to be threatening it when a British fighter sped out of the clouds and got on to the enemy's tail.

The chase which followed was short for the enemy was brought down in flames just beyond Finedon, the news being passed to Northants Sub-District through the Irthlingborough H.G. headquarters and Battalion headquarters at Wellingborough literally within a matter of minutes.

But in Wellingborough he had left houses, flats, and other buildings reduced to piles of debris, under which lay the dead, dying, and injured residents.

The 7th Battalion rapidly proved their mettle on that fateful evening.

Placing themselves at the disposal of the Police and Civil Defence authorities, they performed splendid work.

This included the plugging of gas mains shattered by the explosions, the extrication from the reeking ruins of the trapped victims, and the removal of live ammunition from one of the Battalion's magazines.

This had been damaged by a bomb, and was a potentially serious danger spot in itself.

The removal of this menace was undertaken by the Battalion Adjutant, Capt. C. J. Chouler, who, with his men, hazarded their lives in a most "unhealthy" operation.

Others taking prominent parts in the operations after the raid were the Commanding Officer, Lt.-Col. H. L. Allsopp, Major A. E. S. Bayley, M.C., C.S.M. Orton, and Sgts. T. E. Allen, F. E. Mitchell, and Lloyd, railwaymen Home Guards of E Company, Major E. Young, M.C., of F Company, and Capt. H. C. Pearson of H.Q. Company. Home Guard cordons and sentries were on duty following this incident for three days.

### HOME GUARD H.Q. BOMBED

Less than three weeks later the 7th Battalion were again literally on active service, when, at 11 p.m. on a Saturday night, the town was again straddled by bombs.

On this occasion, the D.R.s, the Adjutant, and the Duty Officer very soon reported to the Commanding Officer, and all companies except two rang up to report men standing to in case of need.

The two companies which did not ring up had been deprived of their headquarters by a bomb which, passing directly through the guardroom of Headquarters Company, exploded in the main battalion store, also destroying the company offices and store of both Headquarters Company and F Company, and starting a fire which caused trouble in a magazine containing grenades and small arms ammunition.

Unhappily, the same bomb killed Pte. D. Lyman, aged seventeen, and seriously injured Pte. A. A. Sherwood, who was on guard with him in the headquarters.

An impressive military funeral was held for Pte. Lyman, at which Col. R. P. A. Helps (Sector Commander), Lt.-Col. H. L. Allsopp (Battalion Commander), and other officers were present. A guard was formed of men of his company, who fired a volley in tribute over the grave.

A third bomb destroyed another guard-room in another part of the town, and finally demolished the ammunition shelter which had been damaged three weeks before. Fortunately, here there were no casualties.

From this disaster Headquarters Company, under Capt. H. C. Pearson, were able to recover all their rifles and records without serious damage, and to establish themselves in a new headquarters within fourteen hours of the raid.

F Company were not so fortunate, and the loss of the battalion stores was a handicap from which the Battalion suffered serious inconvenience for some time. The battalion supply of pikes did not escape destruction.

The pioneers and some of the railwaymen who had done so well three weeks before again did good work in excavating under the ruins to retrieve stores and ammunition.

Special commendation was received by the 7th from the Sub-District Commander for its work in these two assaults, and some of those concerned were awarded certificates for gallantry.

## END OF "PRIVATE ARMIES"

"Works" units were the subject of a special announcement on 2 September 1942 in the following terms:

Many factory Home Guard units operating practically as private armies are to be called on to play a wider part in the defence of their districts and come under the more direct control of area commanders.

The process will be gradual and in some places has already begun.

Drastic changes, however, both in training and in personnel, must inevitably follow.

Many executives, for example, who are Home Guard officers more by virtue of their positions in the factory than by their soldiering ability will have to go.

That reorganization came to pass shortly after, not without some heart-burning in some cases, but with undoubted enhancement of the Home Guards' cohesion and co-operative capacity.

## FULL PARADE OF THE 12TH

We now pass on to September 1942 to record a number of varied but equally important events in that month.

The first was a full parade of the 12th (Northampton) Battalion which took place on Sunday, 6 September, and which was aptly described as one of the most impressive and heartening spectacles seen in Northampton during the war. Seventy-five per cent of the Battalion's personnel turned up on parade.

The march discipline gained the warm commendation of the Northants Sub-District Commander (Col. J. L. Short) and of the Home Guard Adviser (Col. P. Lester Reid) who inspected the parade and afterwards took the salute at a march past led by the band of E (Railway) Company of the 12th.

Afterwards the Battalion marched from the racecourse to the Guildhall, where a second salute was taken by the Mayor of Northampton, Alderman J. E. Bugby, who was accompanied at the saluting base by Lt.-Col. T. E. Manning (Commanding Officer of the Battalion), Major T. C. Shillito, the Town Clerk (Mr. W. Kew), and the Chief Constable (Mr. John Williamson).

By invitation of Canon Trevor J. Lewis, the parade then attended divine service at All Saints' Church.

The Mayor was amazed at the smartness displayed by the Battalion and said he had no idea the Home Guard were so well clothed and shod, nor that they had attained such a high state of efficiency.

Further compliments were added by the Chief Constable who, among other things,

said, "If these are a sample of the Northampton men who are ready to greet the Huns, it is safe to say that the visitors are in for a hot time."

The Mayor expressed his thanks to the Commanding Officer, to Major L. E. Barnes (Second-in-Command), and to Capt. H. D. Barton (Battalion Adjutant), who was largely responsible for the parade and the organization connected with it.

## SOME VIVID REALISM

A fortnight later the 10th (Daventry) Battalion staged a combined military and civil defence scheme at Daventry which was declared to be the most realistic, in point of battle effects, that had been staged in the district. The Civil Defence

At a 12th (Northampton) Battalion Church Parade and March Past in September 1942. In the larger picture the Mayor (Alderman J. E. Bugby) is taking the salute in front of the Guildhall. *Inset:* The Sub-Area Commander (Col. J. L. Short) chatting with an old soldier during a review on the Racecourse. Also seen, left to right, are the Home Guard Adviser (Col. P. Lester Reid), Major H. St. J. Browne, Capt. H. D. Barton (Adjutant), and Lt.-Col. T. E. Manning (C.O.).

played up well and civilians for once obeyed the rule of keeping out of the field of operations.

A feature of this well-planned exercise was the diversion or holding up of all traffic, during which the police, assisted by the Home Guard, took the opportunity of a thorough check-up of identity cards.

### "FIFTH COLUMN" ACTIVITIES BANNED

Then came another fine show by the 4th (Kettering Borough) Battalion held on Sunday, 20 September, when Kettering was subjected to a two-pronged attack from the east, preceded by air bombardment and supported by a parachute attack from the north-west.

The defenders of the home town were the 4th Kettering Battalion of the Home Guard and 5th (Kettering District) Battalion, and one platoon of the 13th Leicestershire Home Guard.

The attack was strenuously made by the 3rd (Oundle) Battalion and a detachment of the 6th (Corby Works) Battalion.

All the Civil Defence forces, including the invasion committee and the police, were in operation, and the general concensus of opinion was that this exercise was the most successful yet held in that area.

One result of the exercise was the banning (except under special control) of all fifth column activities in future invasion exercises.

This ruling arose when a Kettering fire service tender and team unknowingly passed through the advancing enemy lines. Here it was captured, and the enemy, with great *élan*, commandeered the uniforms of the N.F.S. team, turned the engine round, and drove it back into the town.

Such dash and initiative deserved all the rewards they could win, and in this case the prize was the police station, which the disguised enemy captured and used, resulting in a partial paralysis of the defence administration for over three hours.

Included in Brington's War Weapons Week in May 1941 was a march past of the local Home Guard, under Lt. R. N. Day (*on left*), and an inspection by Major-Gen. B. Burrows (*inset on right*). On left (*inset*) is Earl Spencer.

Finally, it was decided that if the exercise was to continue, the police station *must* be released. Nevertheless, this dashing exploit received "full marks" from the Sub-District commander.

## 11TH'S TOURNAMENT AT HARDINGSTONE

Now followed on 27 September 1942 a really impressive military tournament staged by the 11th (Hardingstone) Battalion at Hardingstone cricket ground.

This fine display was typical of the organization of the 11th Battalion and of its efficiency and fitness. It included displays of drill, weapon exercises, and sports. Music was supplied by the band of E Company of the 12th Battalion, and amplified commentaries were made via loudspeakers and a field telephone system installed by the Hardingstone Platoon signals section.

Teas were supplied by local voluntary

The Deterding Shooting Cup Winners. Members of the Newnham Platoon of the 10th (Daventry) Battalion in May 1941. *Left to right in back row*—B. Howard, F. D. Wright, F. Warren and D. Wright. *In front*—J. Tysoe and Platoon Commander R. D. J. Bean, D.C.M., M.M.

women workers, and there was a good attendance of spectators, who thronged the gaily decorated ground.

Colonel R. P. A. Helps (No. 3 Group Commander) on left, attended a demonstration of landscape target firing, with harmonized sights, at the 11th Battalion range. Also seen, left to right, are Lt.-Col. W. J. Penn (O.C. 11th), Capt. G. B. Godson (Adjutant), Major H. Marland (second-in-command), and Major H. Hawkins (O.C. A Company).

The Sub-District Commander (Col. J. L. Short) addressed a battalion parade prior to taking the salute at a march past. He said, "I offer my congratulations to Col. Penn and his officers and men who have put up this first-class show and made such a splendid turnout."

In a special appeal to the ladies he added: "I ask all wives, mothers, and sweethearts to believe that when their menfolk have to go on Home Guard parade they are off to do a first-class job of work, and are *not* making for the nearest public house."

Other visitors were Col. P. Lester Reid, Col. R. M. Raynsford, and Lt.-Col. G. S. Watson (Officer Commanding the 9th Battalion).

## WHEN THEY LAUGHED

*The Medical Squad were doing squad drill just after a medical lecture. The N.C.O. rapped out the order "Pick up your dressing". Said one man apologetically, "Sorry, Sarge, but I left it in the lecture room."*

## Chapter XXV

## MEMORABLE DAY FOR H.G. MARKSMEN

SEPTEMBER 1942 closed with a loss to the 12th Battalion when its Commanding Officer (Lt.-Col. T. E. Manning) announced his resignation owing to failing eyesight.

Lt.-Col. Manning had held the command of his force since the L.D.V. days and was

In a Special Order announcing his resignation he said:

I have been very proud of the Battalion, and I trust each one of you feels proud of it too ... so that if the supreme test comes it will be found worthy of the high traditions of the

A tribute to comrades killed in the 1914–18 war. Two contingents of the 12th (Northampton) Battalion Home Guard march past the Northampton and County War Memorial after attending the Remembrance Day service at All Saints' Church on Sunday November 14, 1941.

responsible for piloting the Borough Battalion through the manifold initial difficulties of early 1940.

He carried this out with a high degree of self-sacrifice, which resulted in the 12th Battalion ranking among the most efficient borough battalions in the county.

Northamptonshire Regiment, whose badge we are privileged to wear.

He was followed in the command by an eminently worthy successor in the person of Lt.-Col. L. E. Barnes, the former second-in-command, who has thus written of Lt.-Col. Manning's departure:

The Battalion suffered a severe and unexpected blow by the retirement of Lt.-Col. T. E. Manning. Always cheery and with an abundance of tact, he had carried the Battalion through those very difficult early days. As the one who was in closest touch with him in those times, and was aware of the many obstacles that had to be overcome, I know that we owe him a deep debt of gratitude for all his

he should have continued as intelligence officer of F Company and have been with us on all our parades.

The officers of the Battalion spontaneously desired to show their deep appreciation of his work, and at a little gathering at the Peacock Hotel, Northampton, on 9 October 1942 they were able to express their feelings by a presentation of a silver salver as a memento to

No. 8 Platoon of C Company of the 12th (Northampton) Battalion Northamptonshire Home Guard, 1941, winners of the Nelco Shooting Cup in a hard-fought contest. *Front row:* Sgt. J. Spiers, Vol. D. G. Farndon, Sgt T. Cameron, and Vol. F. Sharpe. *Second row:* L.-Cpl. H. G. Clarke, Vols. F. N. Coles, J. E. Knighton, S. R. Doolan, Lt. A. G. R. Barton, Sgt. W. Noble, 2nd Lt. E. G. Turner, Vols. K. A. Evans, D. H. Wilson and A. T. Downing. *Third row:* Platoon Sgt. A. V. Williams, Vol. H. A. H. Holt, L.-Cpl. S. D. Kennell, Vols. A. E. Wheatcroft, A. Bean, R. H. Dunn, S. Simons, N. S. Jacklin, Cpl. J. Hambleton. *Back row:* Cpl. W. L. Covington, Cpl. C. Hiam, L.-Cpl. H. H. E. Barrett, L.-Cpl. F. T. Parker, Cpl. F. W. Jeyes, Vol. R. Smart, L.-Cpl. A. W. Goodman, Vols. T. Ringrose and T. W. Bradshaw.

unsparing efforts to get the show going and to make it a success.

We all regretted his decision, taken on the advice of his medical adviser, and I pleaded with him to take six months' leave, during which time I would carry on, and then with his health improved he could resume where he had left off.

But my efforts were unavailing. It is typical of the man that, although feeling incapable of carrying the burden of commanding officer,

him of the happy times we had spent under his leadership.

The 12th's new commanding officer first joined the Army as a private in the East Lancashire when the 1914–18 war broke out. He was soon transferred as a cadet and after training took his commission with the 3/4th Northamptons. Later he was posted to the 7th Northamptons, with whom he went to France and served through most of the Battalion's heavy fighting.

In 1918 he was so severely wounded as to suffer the loss of his left eye.

Upon demobilization he continued to serve with the 4th (T) Battalion and was made Battalion Sports Officer. As Captain he commanded A Company and was subsequently promoted Major.

In July 1926 he was awarded the M.B.E. (Military Division) in recognition of his services with the Territorial Army.

## THE E.C.D. RIFLE MEETING

In October 1942 came a memorable date for Home Guard marksmen—the East Central District Home Guard Rifle Meeting, open to all battalions in the five counties of the district.

Ranges used were, for numbers 1 to 9 battalions—Sywell, and for numbers 10 to 14 battalions—the range at Yelden.

The competitions were: Queen Mary (based on T.A.R.A. Competition), the Hamilton Leigh (similarly based), a Sten Carbine competition (based on T.S.M.C. Course).

There was a Championship Shield to be awarded to the battalion making the highest score in all the competitions aggregated.

The results were as follows:

The 2nd (Soke of Peterborough) Battalion (Lt.-Col. A. H. Mellows, O.C.) "went home" with the Challenge Shield and were runners-up in the Queen Mary event, the 10th (Daventry) Battalion (Lt.-Col. G. W. M. Lees, O.C.) were runners-up in the Challenge Shield, and the 12th (Northampton) Battalion (Major L. E. Barnes, Acting O.C.) were runners-up in both the Hamilton Leigh Falling Plate competition and the Sten event. The final placings were:

Challenge Shield: Winners, 2nd (Peterborough) Battalion; runners-up, 10th (Daventry) Battalion.

Queen Mary Competition: 4th Bedfordshire Battalion; 2nd (Peterborough) Battalion.

Hamilton Leigh Competition: 4th Herts Battalion; 12th (Northampton) Battalion.

Sten Carbine Competition: 3rd Herts Battalion; 12th (Northampton) Battalion.

There was sympathy with Bucks, who were unlucky not to gain a showing among the leaders in any of the four contests.

## T.A. SECRETARIAL CHANGE

Previous reference has been made to the Home Guard's indebtedness to its Territorial Army Association. Now in November 1942 came the retirement of a devoted and popular secretary, by whose work much of this indebtedness was occasioned.

The secretary was Lt.-Col. Richard Montague Raynsford, D.S.O., who had discharged the duties with characteristic courtesy and thoroughness ever since he was appointed sixteen years previously to succeed Major J. C. Wetherell, O.B.E.

His retirement also severed a long ancestral link with local military forces.

This was the third war in which Col. Raynsford had served, for he began his long and distinguished military career with the Prince of Wales' Leinster Regiment (the Royal Canadians) as far back as 1897.

Col. Raynsford's successor was Lt.-Col. O. K. Parker, M.C., an appointment which was hailed with widespread pleasure, for he was already well known locally through his service at the depot at Northampton and through his long association with the Northamptonshire Regiment.

Col. Parker was one of the very few officers who survived the early stages of the 1914–18 war.

He was in the front line and in the retreat from Mons until he was wounded.

For his gallantry he was mentioned in dispatches and awarded the Military Cross.

Col. Parker was first commissioned to the Northamptonshire Regiment in 1911.

### REAL TANKS IN 9TH'S EXERCISE

The closing months of 1942 brought a still greater intensification of exercises.

Wellington bombers, thanks to the Royal Air Force.

This exercise was also particularly noteworthy because, at the height of the battle, when a determined enemy was practically "at the gates", the Civil Defence personnel were pressed into service by the defending garrison, and were armed with every

Pictorial records of a public tournament staged by the 9th (Brixworth) Battalion, at Overstone. (1) Seated left to right, Col. P. Lester Reid, Lt.-Col. G. S. Watson, (O.C. 9th Battalion), Major R. Dickens (second-in-command 9th Battalion) and Major T. C. Shillito (Zone Staff Officer). (2) Lt. C. M. Newton (*left*) and Capt. P. R. Patrick. (3) Lt. T. Norton Merry (*on left*) and Regular officers and Home Guards who participated (August 1941).

Thus the 9th (Brixworth) Battalion staged a particularly ambitious exercise on Sunday, 25 October, when a combined civil and military scheme was held in the Brixworth area. Real tanks, kindly supplied by the Royal Armoured Corps, were used by the attacking force, as were

weapon which could be procured—including pikes!

All the Home Guard troops were drawn from the 9th Battalion.

### SUGGESTION FOR LEAVE

Incidentally, it was about this time that

the Commanding Officer of the 9th (Lt.-Col. G. S. Watson) voiced the suggestion of leave for the Home Guard as follows:

(1) Members of the Home Guard joining before May 1941—one month.

(2) Members joining after May 1941 and before 16 February 1942—fourteen days.

(3) Fourteen days to all ranks on completion of one year's service.

The Home Guards who knew the suggestion had been made waited hopefully, but the idea, like the "old soldiers", merely "faded away" and nothing more was heard of it.

## AMERICAN TROOPS COMBINE

Desborough and Rothwell were the scenes of the next big show put up by the 4th and 5th (Kettering) Battalions on Sunday, 22 November 1942.

The enemy was represented by the 4th Battalion and the 6th (Corby Works) Battalion, supported by detachments of Regulars—and their attacks were directed against the villages of Cottingham, Stoke Albany, Rushton, Thorpe Malsor, and the towns of Desborough and Rothwell.

The defence was entrusted to the 5th Battalion, under Lt.-Col. Sir F. V. L. Robinson, Bt., plus a unit of the Regular forces and a large detachment of American troops, mainly detailed for ambulance and anti-aircraft duties. The Americans were under the command of 1st Lt. G. A. Fulgham. Their presence was welcomed later by the Sub-District Commander, who also thanked them for their assistance.

## SPLENDID COMMUNICATIONS

Then, on 29 November 1942, Oundle had another disturbed Sunday when it was the scene of another invasion exercise.

The 3rd (Oundle) Battalion was responsible for the defence of the town against a splendid yet grim attack carried out by Regular troops, who used troop carriers and other light armoured vehicles.

Once again the town was rocked out of its usual Sunday calm by continuous explosions, which gave realism to what would have been a heavy blitz, and which kept the Civil Defence services fully extended.

A notable feature of this exercise was the remarkably good liaison, which caused the Sub-District Commander (Col. J. L. Short) to remark that he had never seen an exercise in which the communication

Taken at an Invasion Exercise of the 4th, 5th and 6th Battalions at Desborough and Rothwell in November 1942. On left U.S. troops combined in the operation mainly in anti-aircraft and anti-tank actions. *Centre:* There was a 25-feet "crater" under the window. This was how a Desborough rescue squad bridged it. On right, an anti-infiltration post ready for delaying action.

was so good. This was due to the layout of the telephone system by the Town Commander, Capt. H. P. Hewitt. The system enabled all forces, at all times, and in all key places, to be fully informed of all phases of the situation.

Scarcely an exercise passed without being accompanied by a humorous incident, and at Oundle the comic relief was furnished by the Sub-District Intelligence Officer (Lt. Peter Perry), who penetrated the town in civil attire as a spy, carrying on his person complete plans for the destruction of Oundle.

When challenged, after gaining admittance to the Rectory, he produced a *German* identity card. A sentry questioned it, but, being assured it was a "special" pass, let the "spy" through. He was not caught until he practically forced his own arrest!

### "WOUNDED" REFUSE TO RETIRE

Finally, on Sunday, 13 December 1942, the 7th (Wellingborough Town) Battalion (under Major A. H. Higgins, M.B.E., second-in-command), assisted by tanks and armoured fighting vehicles, made a determined and relentless attack on Rushden, which was defended no less determinedly by the Home Guard garrison, consisting of B and E Companies of the 8th Battalion under Majors A. D. Denton and A. Allebone respectively.

In this exercise it appeared that the Rushden Home Guard were more interested in carrying on the fight than in getting wounded—for it is on record that although the umpires labelled at least twenty-five men as "wounded", only four arrived at the first aid posts. The other twenty-one had calmly pocketed their "wounded" labels and gone on with the good work. Fortunately, for the content of the medical services, the civilians were more punctilious, and poured into the dressing stations.

The exercise was directed by Col. R. P. A. Helps (No. 3 Group Commander) with Col. F. D. Fulton, D.S.O., as his staff officer.

U.S. troops took part in a December 1942 exercise in the 7th and 8th Wellingborough area. Shown here are Capt. M. J. Derouen and Capt. N. G. Cameron learning some of the points of a Spigot Mortar from the 8th (Wellingboro') Battalion's P.S.I., Sgt.-Major H. S. T. Bassett (Northamptonshire Regiment) at Rushden, the central scene of the action.

Scenes during an October 1942 Wellingborough exercise. (1) Mobile reserve mop up the side streets after enemy infiltration. (2) Who left this Northover projector unattended outside battle H.Q., plus a cycle to transport it if necessary? (3) Col. R. P. A. Helps (No. 3 Group Commander and Chief Umpire) on left, congratulated on the exercise by the Sub-Area Commander (Col. J. L. Short), in centre. On right is Capt. S. J. N. Bartley (Sub-Area Staff) and, with back to camera, Major E. R. Buckley (Senior Umpire, attacking troops). (4) How many feet of sacked potatoes afford cover from fire?

# Chapter XXVI

## SCENES IN EARLY 1943

THE "behind the scenes" situation at the opening of 1943 is well illustrated by the following extract from the company diary of B Company of the 5th:

Training now tightened up under the Sector Training Officer. Office work multiplying. Detailed programme of work to be submitted monthly. Hours of work every month in office. Proper Company office started in Desborough. Typewriters supplied by Lawrence & Co. Squad of ladies enrolled to run office, ably led by Miss Coleman.

New ideas were continually coming along, and one was evolved by the 11th (Hardingstone) Battalion, who conceived the notion of teaching battle craft by demonstrations at varying speeds.

On Sunday, 3 January 1943, No. 19 Platoon (Lt. W. H. Clay) of E Company of the 11th gave a demonstration of battle platoon right flanking attack, first in slow motion, and then "at the double".

The demonstration reflected the sense of confidence and determination which the drill was intended to impart, and Col. R. P. A. Helps (No. 3 Group Commander), who witnessed the demonstration, congratulated all ranks on their effective work.

One of the most notable 1943 church parades was that held by the 8th Battalion (Lt.-Col. V. H. Sykes).

Eight hundred members of this Battalion united with four hundred members of the United States forces stationed in the vicinity, in a combined church parade at Rushden on Sunday, 10 January. Led by the band of the Northamptonshire Regiment (Bandmaster Marriott), the parade marched to the Ritz Cinema where the service was conducted by the Rev. E. A. Green, Rector of St. Mary's, Rushden.

The lesson was read by the commanding officer of the 8th, and a spirited address was given by a United States padre.

Later, at a march past, the salute was taken by Col. Shiells, of the American forces.

### A CLUB DINNER

Four days later there was another memorable Home Guard event with a gathering of officers of the 9th Battalion at the George Row Club, Northampton.

Fifty-seven officers of the Battalion attended (practically 100 per cent), and Lt.-Col. G. S. Watson (Officer Commanding) was host, with Major R. Dickens (Battalion second-in-command) as president.

The guests were Col. J. L. Short, C.B.E., (Sub-District Commander), and Col. P. Lester Reid, C.B.E. (Home Guard Adviser), and the visitors included Col. O. K. Parker (Secretary of the Territorial Army Association), Brigade-Major S. J. N. Bartley (A.D.C. Sub-Area), and Major H. St. John Browne, M.C. (second-in-command of the 12th Battalion).

The toast of the Northants Sub-District was proposed by Major J. T. H. Pettitt and the response was given by Col. Short.

The toast of the 9th Battalion was proposed by Col. Reid and the response was by Lt.-Col. G. S. Watson.

The toast of the visitors was by Major R. Dickens and the response was by Major H. St. John Browne.

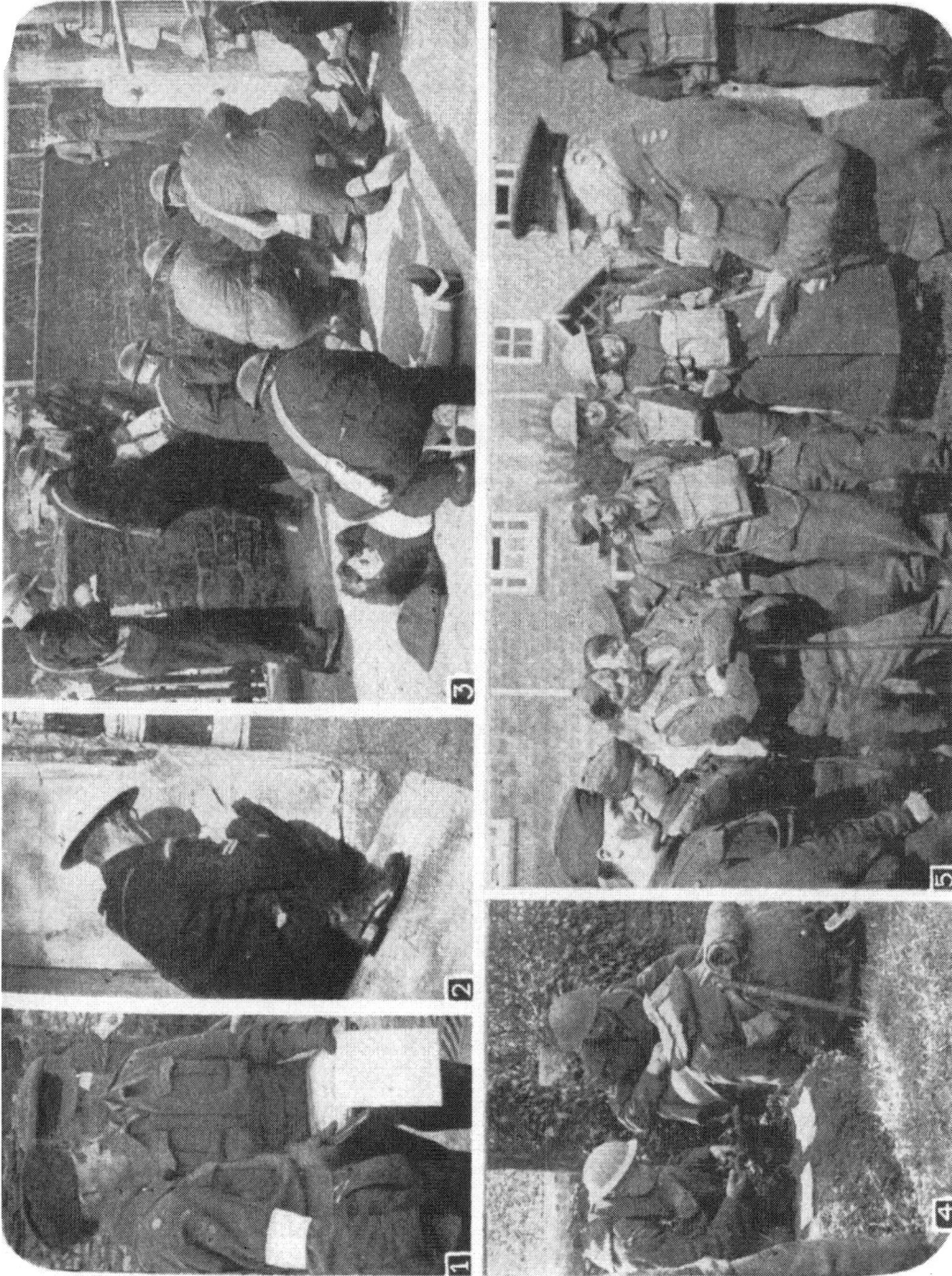

During an April 1943 invasion exercise in the Duston area Home Guards and Civil Defence forces collaborated. Pictures show: (1) Lt.-Col. W. J. Penn (O.C. 11th Battalion and Military Director of the Exercise) on right, discussing plans with his second-in-command, Major H. Marland (Chief Military Umpire). (2) This warden took good cover when he sent back a valuable message concerning the enemy's position to the Duston Home Guard Commander. (3) Duston's First Aid Post dealt coolly and efficiently with blitz casualties. (4) Such was the completeness of the Duston Home Guard communications system that when a move from garrison H.Q. was ordered a well-sited emergency field telephone exchange, connected to all posts, was in full working order within four minutes of the move. (5) Officers, many still in their camouflage, listening to a review of the exercise by the Sub-Area Commander (Col. J. L. Short).

## A.A. BATTERY'S RED-LETTER DATE

Every unit at "stand down" was able to look back to one date as the red-letter day of their service.

For the 101 Northamptonshire Home Guard "Z" A.A. Battery *the* date was 25 January 1943.

It was the occasion of their first night of operational duty with one troop housed in a temporary Nissen camp.

All felt that they were pioneers, and they did their duty in good heart, feeling at last that the weeks of training had been worth while.

The construction of their permanent camp, however, had been started and the occupation took place in June.

This was another great day—for the Home Guard were admitted as members to NAAFI, Sergeants' and Officers' messes.

Each night on duty they were regular soldiers, for here let it be said the Regular personnel co-operated in and encouraged the unity of the Battery, accepting the "once a week soldiers" as equals.

In April 1943 the Battery lost its commander. A new appointment of Home Guard A.A. Adviser had been made and the Brigade Commander selected Major E. W. Bromige to be his adviser for the area covering Peterborough, Leicester, and Cambridge, with the promotion of Major Bromige to Lieutenant-Colonel.

Captain W. A. Heighton was promoted Major and given command of the Battery.

The occupation of the permanent camp brought the Battery to its first birthday and life continued much the same with the usual Home Guard worries of absenteeism, members leaving to join the forces, etc.

Much anticipated and enjoyed were the frequent firing camps on the coast when some 150 were taken by special trains for a day's firing. Never to be forgotten was the first time the rocket projector was fired!

Christmas 1943 will also live for ever in the memory of all who "manned the guns" during that week.

The Regulars had to be on the site; but each Home Guard came on duty nightly prepared to do his bit. All agreed that joint festivities as far as operational duty would allow should be enjoyed, and dances, concerts, etc., were arranged. The Home Guard were all out to give the Regular boys and girls a good time, and on their part the Regular troops built a stage and decorated the NAAFI.

The Regular unit remembered, and repaid, the previous Christmas!

## KISLINGBURY AS OBJECTIVE

The spate of field exercises continued unabated in the early part of 1943, but the first of prime importance was that concerning the 11th (Hardingstone) Battalion held at Kislingbury on Sunday, 24 January 1943, with the village of Kislingbury the objective.

It was assumed that the A.F.V.s of an invading force, seeking to establish communications through the village, had been repulsed, but had afterwards renewed their attack with air and infantry reinforcements.

The simulated blitz was extremely well handled by the police and Civil Defence personnel—particularly as to the removal of casualties.

An enemy infantry attack followed the blitz, in which assault the enemy was well represented by C (Duston) Company of the 11th Battalion.

The military director was Lt.-Col. W. J. Penn, and the chief umpire Major M. Marland. Other participating officers included Brig.-Gen. M. F. Gage (County

Two memories of the visit by the Director-General of the Home Guard, Major-Gen. Viscount Bridgeman on May 26 and 27, 1943. In picture on left Lord Bridgeman (left) is discussing Sten gun ammunition with Lt.-Col. W. J. Penn (C.O. 11th Battalion), in centre, on the 11th Battalion's range near Whiston. On right is Lt.-Col. W. H. Tatham. In picture below Lord Bridgeman (fifth from left) watching Capt. F. E. Courtney (in foreground) demonstrating Spigot mortar camouflage to a class at the Zone Camouflage School at Northampton.

A picture taken during a January 1943 attack on Kislingbury, which formed part of an exercise staged by the 11th Battalion.

Liaison Officer), Lt.-Col. R. M. Raynsford, Lt.-Col. R. D. B. Cogan, Major R. P. White, and Capt. G. B. Godson (11th Battalion Adjutant).

## PARADE AS TRIBUTE TO COMPANY

Came then, on 7 February 1943, a triumphant full parade of the 2nd (Soke of Peterborough) Battalion at Stamford.

A final assault on an enemy post (represented by the pylon) during a January 1943 demonstration of Battle Platoon drill by members of the 11th Battalion.

The 2nd Northamptonshire (Soke of Peterborough) Battalion's Home Guard Rifle Team (October 11, 1942), winners of the East Central District Shooting Competition. *Standing*, Lt. R. Northcott, M.M., 2nd Lt. J. Teesdale, Capt. R. P. Carter, Lt.-Col. A. H. Mellows, T.D., Capt. —. Jervis, C.S.M. Stone, Lt. C. E. Wiseman. *Kneeling*, Sgt. F. Bentley, M.M., C.S.M. J. Earl, Sgt. C. J. Saunders, Sgt. W. E. Day, Sgt. — Dolby. Members of the team were Northcott (H.Q. Co.), Teesdale and Dolby (B) Co., Bentley, Earl, Saunders, Day and Wiseman (E Co.).

On the Civil Defence side were Mr. T. E. G. Francis (A.R.P. Officer Central Division), Mr. M. B. Dickens of Kislingbury (Chief Umpire), and the incident officers, Messrs. F. Yorke, H. Todd, H. Facer, and F. Fennimore.

The parade was primarily a tribute to E Company of the Battalion, under Major L. G. Turhell, who had provided five out of the eight members of the team which had carried off the Challenge Shield in the East Central District shooting competition—open to battalions of five counties.

The General Officer Commanding Eastern Command was present to hand this magnificently shot-for trophy to the Battalion Commander.

This prize might have been sufficient for any shooting team, but the 2nd Battalion never did rest on their laurels, and the same team also gained the runners-up

harmonized sights was the 11th Battalion (Lt.-Col. W. J. Penn).

The 11th's landscape target depicted a wide variety of country in nice perspective and well sprinkled with good reference points, and was quite a "work of art".

In this respect credit was due to Major H. Hawkins (A Company Commander), a seasoned mapping expert, who designed the target, and fourteen-years-old

An example of Home Guard resource pictured in November 1943. The improvised raft which carried the "casualty" over the water was made of nothing more than odd pieces of timber, oil drums and motor tyre inner tubes, supported by floats.

places in the Queen Mary and Hamilton Leigh events in the same competition.

The presentation was made on the playing fields of Stamford School. The G.O.C. heartily congratulated the team on winning the trophy from among fifty-three battalions. He also expressed his pleasure at seeing so many on parade as, although the district is a very scattered one, no fewer than four hundred members of the Battalion had paraded for the occasion.

The G.O.C. then inspected the Battalion and took the salute at a subsequent march past.

**BOY ARTIST PAINTS TARGET**

One of the first battalions to set up its own outdoor landscape target for use with

Master Christopher Webster, son of Mr. and Mrs. C. D. Webster, 62 High Street, Weston Favell, who carried out the painting of the miniature, in water colour, and also of the actual target, measuring 10 ft. by 3 ft., in oils.

**D-DAY ANTICIPATED**

A novel twist was given to an exercise carried out by the 13th (Towcester) and 14th (Brackley) Battalions at Towcester on Sunday, 14 February 1943, for it anticipated D-Day by assuming that Britain had already invaded Europe, and now had to deal with a counter-invasion by the enemy. Therefore it had become necessary to keep the main roads open for reserves.

One of England's most vital arteries, the

old Roman Watling Street, was now threatened by an enemy airborne force represented by the 14th (Brackley) Battalion (Lt.-Col. Furlong), and the 13th Battalion (Lt.-Col. P. Y. Atkinson) had the onerous job of preventing the enemy from occupying Towcester itself.

The attackers, under Major E. J. Lasson, made good use of these labyrinthine advantages, and before long a ding-dong battle was going on in the town.

### ENORMOUS CASUALTIES

As a result, although the attackers could

"Enemy" crossing the Tow at Towcester and (*on right*) crossing a wall. Two ticklish operations during an exercise attack on Towcester in a 13th/14th Battalions' exercise at Towcester in February 1943.

The 13th acquitted themselves well, for although they were actually under strength at the time, they defended their home town from one of the most determined attacks ever seen in any local exercise.

Three diversionary and flank-protecting attacks were thrown against the little market town from the north-west, south-south-west, and south-south-east.

Shortly afterwards, the main attack crashed in from the south-east through a congested sector of the town, which was definitely a "headache" for the defenders.

legitimately have claimed to have penetrated into Towcester, their casualties were so enormous that only "mopping-up" operations would have been necessary to clear the town altogether.

It was a grand show, and the director (Col. J. G. Lowther) congratulated the 14th on a skilfully handled attack. His praise, however, did not hide the fact that he estimated that 75 per cent of them would have been casualties—an estimate that in itself conveyed a subtle and well-deserved compliment to the gallant 13th.

We now pass to the 10th (Daventry) Battalion to appraise a scheme at Braunston on Sunday, 10 February 1943.

On this Sunday the Home Guard of Braunston adequately demonstrated their capacity to dominate command of their village, and of the two important bridges below it. They did this, although their abilities to do so were keenly tested.

The enemy holding their gains at Braunston Bridge in a 10th (Daventry) Battalion invasion exercise in February 1943.

The defenders were No. 5 (Braunston) Platoon (Lt. W. C. Berry), of C Company of the 10th Battalion, and the attacking force, under Capt. T. Davis, was made up from Company Headquarters and three battle platoons of B Company.

Preceding the engagement, Braunston was well and truly blitzed and all the police and Civil Defence forces were in operation.

The defenders came through their fiery ordeal with success. An enemy advance force, supported by two armoured cars, and detailed to clear the way at Braunston for a mobile force driving towards Coventry and Birmingham, was halted—and defeated.

Flushed with success, the defenders then awaited the main attack, which was expected from the north and north-east, following an outflanking movement. Instead of this the enemy, doubtless embittered by the wiping out of his advance force, made a suicidal attack up a steep hill, entirely in the open! Not a man could have hoped to reach the summit! It was magnificent—but it was not war!

Apart from this, the attack was skilfully handled, and in the words of the Sub-District Commander (Col. J. L. Short) was put in with great dash. The defence, however, would have held the road and denied it to the enemy.

The military director was Col. J. G. Lowther, the chief umpire, Major R. C. G. Foster, and the senior umpire, Major W. V. Marshall (Adjutant of the 10th).

### SUNDAY BATTLE AT GEDDINGTON

The historic Eleanor Cross at Geddington saw a realistic modern battle on Sunday, 28 February 1943, when No. 3 (Geddington) Platoon of the 5th (Kettering District) Battalion, under Lt. F. Wycherley, defended the village against an attack by numbers 1, 2, and 4 Platoons plus the Mobile Platoon of D Company of the 3rd (Oundle) Battalion. The platoons were commanded respectively by Lts. Smith, Blackmore, Ward, and Cooper.

The enemy planned a cunning and distracting show from the north to hold the attention of the defence while he detoured his main body to get in from the east. Simultaneously another enemy force was due to come in from the west and south-west—thus fastening Geddington between the jaws of a pair of pincers.

The defence, by sheer hard fighting, managed to hold the northern sector, but as the enemy infiltrations grew in volume from the east and west, the garrison commander found himself in an awkward dilemma. He had no wish to split his mobile reserve, but nevertheless he was threatened with "sandwiching" by two strong bodies in his defended locality.

What he did proved to be the wisest thing—and as it turned out, the right thing.

He dispatched his mobile reserve to clean up the most vulnerable sector, and it so happened that the two enemy attacks had failed to synchronize, and there was thus time for the reserve to do its job and return to base to tackle the other one.

Unfortunately, before they could achieve this double-barrelled victory, the exercise was called off.

It was the opinion of the umpire that the defence, although put to an extreme test, had withstood the attack.

The military director was Col. H. Burditt (No. 1 Group Commander), and the chief umpire, Capt. C. E. Pierson. The Civil Defence controller was Lt. T. J. Francis, R.N. (ret.).

The exercise was viewed by the Sub-District Commander (Col. J. L. Short), Lt.-Col. Sir F. V. L. Robinson, Bt. (commanding the 5th Battalion), and Major S. J. N. Bartley (Sub-District Brigade Major).

### AT ARMY EXHIBITION

On 20 March 1943 a nice compliment was paid to the 12th (Northampton) Battalion when they were afforded the honour of supplying a contingent of members to represent the Home Guard at the opening parade of the Northampton Army Exhibition.

It was a splendid turnout and a credit to the Zone, not only in smartness of bearing but in march discipline.

The contingent, which would have done

The famous Eleanor Cross looks down on a scene of war during a February 1943 exercise at Geddington. The pictures show (1) the Cross. (2) Enemy troops behind the wall lobbing bombs on to a defence post manned by machine gunners. (3) A well-concealed and elevated machine-gun post in the "keep". (4) Good use made of a series of concrete "bridges" for enemy approach. (5) Post-exercise conference. On left is Col. H. Burditt (Director of the exercise) and, leaning on car, Col. J. L. Short (Sub-District Commander).

credit to the Guards' Brigade, paraded the town together with units of the Regular forces and the A.T.S., the whole swinging

training schools. Right from the L.D.V. days there was always the greatest keenness to improve military knowledge by attending

One of Daventry's main cross-road defence posts under heavy fire from the enemy 400 yards beyond the road in a March 1943 exercise engaging the 10th (Daventry) Battalion. The N.C.O. is dictating a reply to a signal for which the D.R. is waiting.

A credit to the Zone. The contingent of the 12th (Northampton) Battalion which represented the Home Guard at the opening parade of the Northampton Army Exhibition in March 1943. Note the accurate sizing.

proudly along behind the band of the Northamptonshire Regiment.

### TRAINING COURSES

All of this time selected members of battalions periodically attended specialist courses at Regular and Home Guard

courses whenever and wherever they might be held.

In the first few months many Volunteers at their own expense attended the course at Osterley Park, which was the forerunner of all Home Guard courses. Others, unable to get away, availed themselves of instruction at the Infantry Training Centre, Northampton.

Among the many courses attended by members of the Northamptonshire Home Guard were the following:

Osterley Park, I.T.C. Northampton; Denbies H.G. School; Army School of Chemical Warfare; H.G. Gas School, Chorley Wood; E.C.D. School, Welwyn; W.T. School, Dorking; Bomb Disposal School, Ripon; Sub-District Camouflage School; Sub-District Signal School; A.O., Saffron Walden; Fieldcraft School, Burwash; W.T. School, Amwell; School of Signals, Catterick; E.C.D. Intelligence School; Unarmed Combat Courses, Dunstable; Bombing Course, Kempston; Travelling Wings from Denbies; G.H.Q. Town Fighting Wings at West Ham and Birmingham; Combined Civil and Military Senior Officers' Course, Nottingham; and Senior H.G. Officers' Courses at Frinton, Bedford, Ampthill and Harpenden.

### LOSS TO 8TH BATTALION

Frequently and inevitably the Northamptonshire Home Guard suffered the loss of capable and popular members, and such a loss came to the 8th (Wellingborough District) Battalion in March 1943 by the sudden death of Major A. H. Freer, Commanding Officer of A Company.

Major Freer, in civil life, was manager of Messrs. Bignells boot factory at Raunds, and he left the works at 5.45 p.m. on his motor-cycle and on reaching home sat in a chair and almost immediately passed away. All ranks of the Battalion felt his loss most keenly.

Major Freer was accorded a military funeral—all company commanders acted as pall bearers. The Raunds Temperance Band led a large parade to the church, and later to the cemetery, where the Last Salute was fired.

Major H. Hawkins, Commander A Company of the 11th (Hardingstone) Battalion, inspecting a parade prior to a Company route march in March 1943. Behind is Capt. H. A. Skinner (second-in-command).

# Chapter XXVII

## PREPARATIONS TO INVADE EUROPE

COMING events were now casting their shadows before, and nowhere was this more graphically reflected than in an introduction to Battalion Training Instructions for the period April to June 1943 issued by the 12th (Northampton) Battalion, Commanding Officer Lt.-Col. L. E. Barnes.

Ran this introduction:

The time is coming when the Field Army will turn from its defensive role to an offensive overseas. When this happens the Home Guard will assume greater responsibilities in protecting the country against seaborne or airborne raids.

In raising their efficiency to the highest possible standard, the Home Guard will contribute to the strength of the general offensive by releasing further Regular troops, and to this extent the scale of the offensive will depend on the fighting efficiency of the Home Guard.

All ranks must be made to realize that the opening of a Continental offensive necessitates efficient protection at the base, which will be the British Isles, and that the Commander-in-Chief, Home Forces, will rely largely on the Home Guard for this protection. The necessity for training of every man in the Home Guard in his operational role is thus an urgent necessity.

### "BEST PLATOON ATTACK YET SEEN"

The 11th (Hardingstone) Battalion in general and the Kislingbury Platoon in particular, must have glowed with pleasure on Sunday, 11 April 1943, when they heard the words of the Sub-District Commander (Col. J. L. Short), who said:

Particularly, I want to congratulate Kislingbury Platoon. Quite honestly I can say they put up the best Home Guard platoon attack I have yet seen.

This, coming from such a source, was praise indeed, and was bestowed after an invasion exercise in the Duston area in which C Company of the 11th (Major P. E. Coles) were the defenders and F Company (Major W. G. Smith) the attackers.

The military director was Lt.-Col. W. J. Penn, chief military umpire Major H. Marland, senior defence umpire Major H. Hawkins, and senior attack umpire Major A. H. Butlin.

The Civil Defence director was Mr. F. E. J. Francis (Divisional A.R.P. Officer, Central Division).

### DETAILED "A" EXERCISE

A smaller, but no less important, exercise was held by the 9th (Brixworth) Battalion during the week-end 24-5 April 1943. It was an administration exercise, taken from the booklet by Capt. R. J. Pizzey, which had been issued down to platoons.

As a preliminary "canter", this exercise was confined to No. 1 Platoon (Moulton) of D Company (Lt. A. Chappel).

As all telephonic communication was ruled out, an especially stern test was put on communications.

On the Saturday, at a secret hour, the platoon was mustered and remained so mustered for the remainder of that day and the first half of the succeeding day (Sunday) under full active service conditions.

All ranks had to be fed and slept, and

the scheme was carried out down to the smallest details. Ammunition issues were properly noted, as was ammunition expenditure. Returns were sent punctually to headquarters and "token" payments to the men were made. This included the necessary arrangements with the bank and the transport of the "funds".

Sleeping arrangements worked excellently, as did reliefs and liaison with the local authorities—the latter feature being one of the main tests of the exercise. Water supply and civil evacuation tests went off without a hitch. It can be said, in conclusion, that whatever else was revealed by this well-drawn-up and excellently carried-out scheme, one fact emerged upon which there could be no doubt— that was that the Home Guard were extremely popular in Moulton.

A scene from a battle platoon competition final in the 9th (Brixworth) Battalion area in July 1943. The bridge is swept by enemy fire from the far side. The platoon attacking have to cross the line above. Should he not have waded under the bridge?

Scenes during an April 1943 exercise carried out by the 9th (Brixworth) Battalion. (1) Moulton Church tower O.P. commanded a panoramic field of view. (2) Sentry posting was well plotted. This man was the guard of the gate leading to headquarters. (3) Cookhouse took full account of Napoleon's immortal "A" dictum.

### CIVILIANS TO DIG TRENCHES RUMOUR

We have previously shown that the Home Guard was peculiarly assailed with rumours.

These rumours, on the principle of the "bush telegraph", spread from end to end of the various commands.

One rumour which raised hopes that were doomed to be shattered was that of an issue of socks to the Home Guard. This caused a flutter in many a feminine breast, and wives who had so often been "browned off" through repairing the ravages of their men's civilian socks felt a thrill of relief.

This issue was raised in Parliament when the Secretary of State for War was asked if he would contemplate the issue of socks to the Home Guard. The reply was in the negative—and up to the "stand down" the Home Guard paraded, marched, and doubtless would have fought, in their own hosiery.

The enrolment of women in the Home Guard was another intriguing subject which went the rounds and disappeared, generally speaking, into the limbo of forgotten things.

It was suggested that a sort of "Cooks Brigade" would be invaluable to assist in feeding the Home Guard, if and when they were mustered. This roused pleasurable anticipation in many a gallant heart. Men cooks, and even male mess waiters, while proving the truth of Milton's dictum that "they also serve who only stand and wait", do not always give piquancy to a meal!

The matter actually came under review, and the Secretary of State for War announced in October 1942 that arrangements for enrolling women auxiliaries in the Home Guard was then under discussion. Their duties, it was stated, were to include cooking, telephony, clerical work, and taking messages.

However, in April 1943 came the news that the Home Guard was to have its own "A.T.S."—and there were some cynical enough to raise the point as to what husbands would say when they found that their wives had been detailed for a week-end exercise.

Northamptonshire had a Women's Home Defence body headquartered at Overstone, whose members had carried on gamely, even in the face of lack of encouragement, and they would have formed an invaluable nucleus for the local Women's Home Guard had it matured in full.

As it was, only a few battalions actually enrolled women members, but the record of the 7th (Wellingborough Town) Battalion in this respect was remarkable.

Here some sixty women auxiliaries were officially enrolled, and were chiefly trained by Lt. A. J. Linnell, the Battalion Signals Officer. The girls, who operated mainly in company intelligence sections, and as telephonists, were equipped with uniform, partly at their own expense, and looked very smart in their khaki skirts and cream blouses.

Their marching in ceremonial parades did full credit to C.S.M. Golbourn, from whom they learned their drill.

They also formed a miniature rifle club among themselves, and on one occasion defeated a team of men on the range.

Special reference should also be made to the women who carried out excellent clerical, administrative, signalling, and guide work duty in the 4th (Kettering Borough) Battalion, which battalion was a pioneer in this respect, for it was in November 1941 that their women were first enrolled.

In the 4th Battalion they were attached to the I. section under Capt. H. C. Langham as telephonists and operation room clerks.

Some companies of the 4th also had

women enrolled as cooks in the event of hostilities and, although they were never called upon, they were always ready. The 4th Battalion had twenty-five of these women on their books.

The 12th (Northampton) Battalion also claimed two devoted women auxiliaries in Mrs. S. B. Patrick (wife of Major S. B. Patrick), who served at G Company's headquarters from its inception until the stand down, and Miss Tench, who served similarly at F Company headquarters, while at Zone H.Q. at Northampton, Miss Greig put in invaluable and highly efficient service.

No uniform was provided for these auxiliaries and their only reward—their only material reward—was a Home Guard badge made of plastic material.

## THE THIRD BIRTHDAY

As the war progressed the years seemed to grow longer and longer in point of the general public's yearning for the decisive action which would herald the beginning of the end.

But in the Home Guard the weekly round was so crammed with activity that it seemed hardly a "month or so" after the second birthday of the force that the third birthday was attained on 14 May 1943.

This was, naturally, an occasion for unprecedented honouring.

As before, the King, but this time as Colonel-in-Chief, issued a special message. Here is its text:

On this, the third anniversary of the formation of the Home Guard, I, as your Colonel-in-Chief, would like you to know how greatly I appreciate the regularity with which, in spite of many difficulties, you keep up your attendance at parades, and how gratified I am by the high standard of proficiency to which you have attained. It must, I am sure, be encouraging to you to know that the value of your

training has been so clearly felt by those who have left to join the Regular Army.

Many of you now take your place side by side with my Regular Army in the anti-aircraft and coastal defence, and as that Army passes more and more to the offensive, so will your responsibility for the defence of this country grow heavier.

The importance of your role will, therefore, inevitably continue to increase.

The Home Guard has built up a tradition of service and devotion to duty. I am confident that the coming year will add to that tradition, and to the debt that my people owe to you.

GEORGE R.I.

## P.M. BROADCASTS FROM U.S.A.

On the evening of the 14th the Prime Minister also made another masterly broadcast from Washington, U.S.A., where he had gone to confer with the President.

Said Mr. Churchill:

I have felt for some time a great desire that a tribute should be paid throughout Great Britain and in Ulster to the faithful, unwearying, and absolutely indispensable work done by the Home Guard month after month and year after year. Accordingly, next Sunday, military parades and religious services will be held throughout the land, to associate the nation and Home Guard in the celebration of its first three years of life.

. . . All British war energies depend upon the unfailing defence and adequate nourishment of our small island home, which lies only twenty-one miles from the German batteries and only a few minutes' flight from their airfields. . . . In this zone there burns the light of freedom—guard it well, Home Guard!

. . . Anthony Eden, as Secretary of State for War, called upon the Local Defence Volunteers to rally round the searchlight positions; shot-guns, sporting rifles, clubs, and staves were all they could find for weapons. It was not until July that we ferried safely across the Atlantic the 1,000,000 rifles and 1,000 field-guns, with ammunition proportionable, which were given us by the Government and people of the United States as an act of precious and timely succour.

You remember how we had special trains waiting to carry the rifles to all the Home Guard areas, and how you worked night and day to clean them, from the grease in which they had been stored for a generation; and you will remember how we hardly dared to fire a round for practice, so dire was the stringency, but this was the great turning-point in your story, and I asked that your name should be changed and that you should assume the proud title of Home Guard.

. . . Since 1940 many of the Home Guard have joined the Regular forces, some older men have retired, having done their duty in the hour of need. Younger men owe to them the experience and leadership they have inherited.

Nearly a year ago compulsory enrolment was introduced, and directed men, as they were called, have proved as good and willing as the original volunteers. With them come the lads of seventeen, many of them already trained in the Army Cadet Forces. New units have been formed for special duties, many hundreds of A.A. guns are manned by the Home Guard, scores of batteries have been in action, and have acquitted themselves worthily. Women have played an even larger part with the guns. The coast defence and motor transport units which have been formed will grow in efficiency throughout the year.

### 2,000,000 TRAINED MEN

Credit is due not only to the Home Guard men themselves [continued Mr. Churchill] but to all who have helped them—to the employers and managements, to the wives and mothers, and to the voluntary women helpers. . . .

We have now nearly 2,000,000 resolute, trained, and equipped men, all of whom do their daily work in field or factory and add to it, free gratis and for nothing but honour, the last and proudest duty of a citizen of the Empire and a soldier of the King.

Let me assure you of this, that until Hitler and Hitlerism are beaten into unconditional surrender, the danger of invasion will never pass away.

The degree of invasion danger depends entirely upon the strength or weakness of the forces and preparations gathered to meet it. . . .

You Home Guardsmen are a vital part of those forces; you are specially adapted to meet the most modern form of oversea attack—the mass descent of parachute troops.

And if the Nazi villains drop upon us from the skies . . . you will make it clear to them that they have not alighted in the poultry run, or in the rabbit farm, or even in the sheep fold, but that they have come down in the lion's den at the Zoo. Here is the reality of your work—here is that sense of imminent emergency which cheers and inspires the long routine of drills and musters after the hard day's work is done.

But I have more to say to you than this. I am speaking to you now from the White House at Washington, where I am staying with my honoured friend, the President of the United States. These are great days; they are like the days in Lord Chatham's time, of which it was said you had got to get up early in the morning not to miss some news of victory. Ah! but victory is no conclusion; even final victory will only open a new and happier field of valiant endeavour, the victories gained by the way must be a spur.

### FREEING TROOPS FOR ASSAULT ON EUROPE

We must prepare for the time that is approaching [concluded the Prime Minister]. The time that will surely come, when the bulk of the armies will have advanced across the seas into deadly battle on the Continent.

Just in the same way as the Home Guard render the Regular Forces mobile against an invader, so the Home Guard must now become capable of taking a great deal of the burden of home defence on to themselves, and thus set free the bulk of our trained troops for the assault on the stronghold of the enemy's power.

It is this reason which, above all others, has prompted me to make you and all Britain realize afresh, by this Home Guard celebration and demonstration, the magnitude and lively importance of your duties, and the part you have to play in the supreme cause now gathering momentum as it rolls forwards to its goal.

## THIRD BIRTHDAY PARADES

Needless to add, special events and parades to mark the third birthday were held by every unit and these were crowned by a mass parade in London, at which the salute was taken by the King—a parade viewed with sharpened interest by the 6th (Corby) Battalion, inasmuch as only in the preceding March (4 March 1943) they had formed a special guard of honour when the King and Queen visited Corby Steel Works.

Although the bulk of the Home Guard personnel for the national celebration were drawn from the London area, all parts of the country were represented by one or more participants.

Representing Northamptonshire Sub-District was C.S.M. George Quartermain, of E Company, 12th (Northampton) Battalion, a choice well justified alike by the C.S.M.'s record, efficiency, and popularity.

C.S.M. Quartermain, 78 Delapre Road, Northampton, held the D.C.M. and M.M. from the 1914–18 war, when he performed gallant service, as a C.S.M. with the Northampton Regiment, on the Somme.

He was wounded three times, being discharged at the end of the war.

He held two parchment certificates for meritorious service—one signed by Major-Gen F. I. Maxse, in November 1916, and the other by Major-Gen. R. P. Lee, in February 1917.

He joined the original L.D.V. immediately upon its formation and soon gained promotion to C.S.M. of E Company of the 12th Battalion Home Guard.

C.S.M. Quartermain, as a railwayman, was known in the L.M.S. as Driver Quartermain, and was selected to drive the Northamptonshire engine when it was christened.

Typical of Northamptonshire events was the 10th (Daventry) Battalion's athletic meeting on the sports ground at Daventry, where an enjoyable afternoon was spent by a large crowd of relations of the Guards from over a very wide area. There were the usual entertainments and, as a result, a fine sum was raised, which was divided among local military charities.

At Wellingborough, led by the Battalion band and motor-cycle dispatch riders, each company armed to the maximum and with Smith guns in rear of the column, 1,000 officers and men of the 7th Battalion marched to Eastfield Park, where the Sub-District Commander, Col. J. L. Short, took the salute. There followed demonstrations of training, leading up to a final platoon attack in which smoke was used and stretcher-bearers were in action. The Sub-District Commander and other notable spectators spoke in very complimentary terms of this impressive display, which was watched by literally thousands of spectators.

The 9th (Brixworth) Battalion celebrated with marches past and demonstrations in various parts of the area. In all cases large crowds attended and they were entertained with exhibitions of battle training, first aid, camouflage, signalling, and other Home Guard activities, as well as demonstrations of the firing of the Guards' different arms, including the Northover projector, Spigot mortars, the E.Y. rifle, and grenade throwing.

A Company's demonstration was at Guilsborough, B Company's at Brixworth, C Company's at Brington, and D Company's at Overstone Park.

Photographs taken at the 3rd Birthday Celebrations of the 12th (Northampton) Battalion held at the County Ground, Northampton, in May 1943. Pictures show (1) The 12th's display of clearing and occupying a house. The fly walk with the toggle rope delighted the crowds. (2) At the saluting base are seen on right—Col. P. Lester Reid (Zone Adviser) and Major T. C. Shillito (Zone Staff Officer). (3) Lt.-Col. O. K. Parker (Northamptonshire Regt.) taking the salute at the March Past of the 11th Battalion at Hardingstone. Also at the base are, left to right, Squadron-Leader J. E. R. Avery, R.A.F., Major A. J. Frazer (former Colonel of the 11th Battalion), in mufti, Lt.-Col. H. N. C. Wyburd and Col. H. J. Johnson.

The latter was the most ambitious demonstration, being preceded by a march past at Moulton, at which the salute was taken by Lt.-Col. H. G. Sotheby (High Sheriff of Northamptonshire). He was accompanied at the saluting base by Col. J. L. Short (Sub-District Commander), Lt.-Col. G. S. Watson, Major S. J. N. Bartley (Brigade Major, Northants Sub-District), and Capt. C. C. Oakey, M.C. (Adjutant of the 9th).

Another and remarkably ambitious birthday show was that produced by the 11th Battalion at Hardingstone, where no fewer than 2,000 members of the public attended to witness a grand display of Home Guard training and weapons.

## HOME GUARD TESTED BY R.A.F.
### DEFENCE

How would members of the Home Guard fare against R.A.F. men?

The question was asked in the 10th (Daventry) Battalion area, and local detachments of the Royal Air Force sportingly undertook to provide the defence in an exercise carried out by the 10th on Sunday, 30 May 1943.

A certain area was assumed to be of vital importance, and the Royal Air Force plus two small units of the Home Guard were detailed to hold it against attack by selected battle platoons of the 10th, under Major T. Coy, who eventually attacked at several points on a wide arc.

To afford the defence as much advantage as possible, they were equipped with radio telephones (the Home Guard did not receive radio telephones until the following July) and a full complement of signals.

But, in spite of this advantage the Air Force had undertaken a job against long odds. Their lack of infantry training decided the battle, for the attackers rapidly paralysed all communications and attained their objective with comparative ease.

They did so largely as the result of a "fifty-to-one chance", taken by a Home Guard platoon commander (Lt. G. A. Inwood) of the enemy force that turned the scales to an amazing and amusing effect.

Without breaking any of the dress or other rules of the exercise, Lt. Inwood marched his platoon (No. 1 Battle Platoon, B Company), almost in ceremonial order, straight up to the outer defence perimeter.

## PARALYSED BATTLE H.Q.

There, with the aid of a forged order, he represented that his platoon was detailed to reinforce the defences, and his whole force was not only passed straight through the lines of defence, but was actually *escorted* by defence guides to the garrison commander's battle headquarters!

"We're relieving this post now." Lt. Inwood (*right*), foxing an R.A.F. M.G. Defence Post commander with a "forged" order in a May 1943 exercise in which the 10th (Daventry) Battalion attacked and took an R.A.F. aerodrome.

With "poker face" solemnity, Lt. Inwood "reported for duty" to the garrison commander and then—his men meanwhile having "relieved" the guards and adjacent weapon posts—suddenly, by a pre-arranged signal, gave the "hands up" to the whole H.Q. in one stroke before an S O S could be got out.

It is possible that the defence headquarters, which was captured, would have been retaken later, but the cost would have

As usual, it was successful, for the 7th knew how to "put these things over".

The items included an amusing memory of the old L.D.V. days with a parade by a platoon, bearing a weird assortment of weapons, including shot-guns, whose members were then inspected by "Col. Thunderbolt". There were roars of laughter

One of the most diverting items in a 7th (Wellingborough Town) Battalion tattoo in July 1943, in which the early L.D.V. days of 1940 were vividly recalled. Here is "Colonel Thunderbolt" inspecting a platoon.

been heavy, and the intruders would have had ample opportunity and time in which to play "merry hell" in the defence area.

The Royal Air Force "boys", who thoroughly enjoyed their new role, generously and sportingly admitted that the exercise had given them an illuminating insight into ground warfare which they would not lightly forget.

**SEVENTH'S THIRD TATTOO**

The 7th (Wellingborough Town) Battalion built up quite a tradition for its tattoos.

It held its third annual one on Saturday, 12 July 1943, on the Dog and Duck ground at Wellingborough.

when one of these antique weapons went off during the inspection. There was also a comic march past which delighted the spectators. D Company made themselves responsible for this piece of well-practised fun.

Then a new and secret weapon was solemnly announced, and proved to be "mechanized", as it was hauled on to the field at the rear of a bicycle. It was manned by a crew in red and yellow, and when it was fired it appeared to cause more casualties among the crew than anywhere. Anyhow, the crew flung themselves flat at each explosion!

There were, of course, many serious items as well, for the Home Guard had a serious message to convey at that time. Several splendid demonstrations were staged, including a very fine drill display under C.S.M. P. Salter (A Co.).

A large crowd included Col. J. L. Short, Col. P. Lester Reid, Col. O. K. Parker, Col. H. M. Roberts, Col. H. Burditt, and other officers.

One of the two judges—the other was Lt.-Col. L. D. B. Cogan (Sub-District H.G. Medical Adviser)—was Capt. L. Couper, just back from two and a half years' active service in North Africa.

Marks were awarded under seven heads: dress, equipment, reconnaissance,

At the Northamptonshire Zone First Aid and Stretcher-Bearing Finals held at Harlestone in June 1943. Left to right are Col. L. D. B. Cogan (Zone Medical Adviser), Capt. L. Couper, Major T. C. Shillito and Col. P. Lester Reid (Home Guard Adviser). The team was assumed to be under fire.

## SUB-DISTRICT FIRST AID FINALS

Bearing in mind those early days when first aid in the H.G. lagged inefficiently in the rear of training, it was good to see on 27 June 1943 the Northamptonshire Sub-District finals in the East Central District First Aid and Stretcher-bearing Competition, held at Harlestone, Northampton.

From being the "Cinderella" of Home Guard activities, regarded as the "soft" duty to which anybody was welcome, these contests proved that the vital importance of field rescue was now fully recognized and its organization and discharge expertly mastered.

approach, treatment, first aid, general competence, and time.

The results and scores were as follows:

1st: 2 Platoon, B Company, (4th Kettering Borough) Battalion (Lt.-Col. G. Holborow).

2nd: 2 Platoon, E Company, 7th (Wellingborough) Battalion (Lt.-Col. H. L. Allsopp, T.D.).

3rd: 3 Platoon, C Company, 6th (Corby) Battalion (Lt.-Col. J. R. Menzies-Wilson).

The battalion M.O. of the winning team was Major W. Shirkey.

The competitions were witnessed by Col. P. Lester Reid (Home Guard Adviser) and Col. J. G. Lowther (Sector Commander), who were thanked for their attendance by the Sub-District M.O. in an address in which Lt.-Col. Cogan also commended the contestants for the hard and keen work their displays reflected.

## "TOO LITTLE SYMPATHY"

Captain Couper added a summary of his impressions:

I can sincerely congratulate Northamptonshire upon a fine display of knowledge and technique [he said], but there has been too much regard for technique and too little sympathy for the patient.

First aid parties must remember that their patient is in pain—probably agonies of pain. Their first duty is to get him back to expert attention quickly.

In this case the doctor was only a couple of hundred yards away, yet many teams wasted valuable time in tying fancy knots and fancy bandages, tucking in the ends, etc.

Always remember [he added] that speed is essential—get to your patient, treat him for shock and bleeding, get him out of pain and as comfortable as you can, and then get him back.

The duties of marshal, starter, and recorder were carried out by Major T. C. Shillito (Zone Staff Officer).

## AN EXERCISE FOR WHOLE BATTALION

We have just previously detailed a company administrative exercise in the 9th (Brixworth) Battalion. On 20 June 1943 the 9th followed this up with a similar exercise embracing the whole of the Battalion.

This exercise was enlivened by secret and sudden attacks by G Company of the 12th Battalion, under their Commanding Officer, Major S. B. Patrick, who were armed with Smith guns.

Their job — a difficult one — was to deliver secret and surprise attacks while the 9th Battalion was preoccupied in its administrative plans.

In spite of the elements of surprise which G Company staged so well and so realistically, the 9th Battalion were not caught napping. They were too much on the alert. Several grim "scraps" took place during the exercise, and in at least one case, that of an isolated headquarters, the "softening" propensities of the Smith gun was adequately and impressively demonstrated.

## A WEIGHTY ARGUMENT

On the same date B Company of the 11th Battalion also had a busy Sunday.

Numbers 7, 8, and 9 platoons of this Company, under Major J. R. Wilson, had the duty of defending Roade to the last—which the rest of the Company, under Major A. Butlin, attacked with great *élan*.

It was during this exercise that a weighty argument arose, viz.: When should garrison headquarters leave its keep? The textbook answer, of course, was "Never!" But what if the commander considered that by so evacuating he stood a better chance of defeating the enemy and of subsequently regaining his lost headquarters?

That, anyhow, was what Major Wilson contended, and he had some nice arguments in favour of it.

The situation arose because his operation headquarters was bombed out as soon as the operation began, and he then removed to an alternative headquarters still inside the keep area, and connected by a very fine telephone system, wired in parallel to all defence posts.

For a time the enemy were held, but a *"schwerpunkt"* attack later pierced the defences, and the enemy rushed in to invest the keep and bomb the second head-quarters out of existence.

What was the defending commander to do?

He had still substantial forces in other defended localities not yet attacked, so he decided to conserve his mobile reserve and make a fighting retirement to his nearest gun post—just *outside* his keep—where he could regain his telephonic communications.

This was done—and he was able to summon adequate reinforcements who, plus the mobile reserve, made a vigorous counter-attack, which not only cleared the keep, but was pressed onward to catch and annihilate the enemy.

His justification for cutting across one hitherto inviolable Home Guard ruling was that, by doing so, he had been enabled to maintain his communications—which fact proved a decisive factor in the end.

The exercise was fought out with re-markable zest and keenness, and earned the warm praise of the Commanding Officer and the Zone Staff Officer—Major T. C. Shillito.

## COMPETITION SUCCESSES

Some notable successes were announced at this period, among them that of No. 3 Platoon of A Company of the 3rd (Oundle) Battalion, who won the No. 1 Sector final in the E.C.D. Battle Platoon Contest. The Platoon gave a brilliant, finished exposition of a platoon in attack, the platoon commander made a good and deliberate "reccy", his plan was sound, and all orders were lucidly given and well translated.

Secondly, No. 15 Platoon of D Company of the 11th (Hardingstone) Battalion won the Battalion Fraser Cup for good shooting with aggregate marks of 295. The runners-up were No. 19 Platoon of E Company with 270 marks, and No. 11 Platoon of C Company with 265 marks.

In an accompanying Battalion Land-scape Target Contest the winners were No. 16 Platoon of D Company with 94 marks, closely followed by No. 13 Platoon with 73, and No. 3 Platoon with 68 marks re-spectively.

# Chapter XXVIII

# FINE SHOW BY STRETCHER-BEARERS

The Northants Sub-District failed by seven marks to gain the championship and silver cup in the finals of the East Central District First Aid and Stretcher-Bearing Competition, which were decided in July 1943. (The Northants Sub-District Final is recorded on a preceding page.)

A brigadier and two colonels of the Regular Army were the judges of contests in which marks were awarded for tactics and fieldcraft as well as for the primary tests of first aid and rescue.

So uniformly high was the all round standard that the judges confessed that they had found considerable difficulty in arriving at their final decisions.

The 5th Herts were first with seventy-six points out of a hundred, and the 4th Northants second with seventy.

The competition was at platoon level and Northampton's representatives were 2 Platoon B Company, 4th (Kettering Borough) Battalion (Lt.-Col. G. Holborow), who had previously won the Sub-District Platoon Championship.

The winning team each received memento pocket knives in addition to the trophy, but so impressed was the Northamptonshire Medical Adviser (Lt.-Col. L. D. B. Cogan) by the Kettering Platoon's show that he, personally, presented them with souvenir knives.

One of the tests was that of a casualty whose head had been blown off.

His weapons, ammunition, identity card and other important papers on him were brought in.

The judges also looked carefully to see that all wounded were relieved of any ammunition clips or grenades, etc., they might have slipped into their pockets, and also noted particularly the choice of routes to and from the casualty taken by the contestants, and their methods of approach.

At the conclusion the E.C.D. commander said he was more than pleased with all he had seen. He warmly congratulated all units upon the really remarkable advances they had made in their first aid and stretcher-bearing, and thanked them for the amount of time they must have given up to their training to have reached such a high standard.

## 3RD BATTALION'S SHOOTING ACHIEVEMENT

The other important East Central District event for 1943, the annual shooting competition, saw a splendid exhibition put up by the 3rd (Oundle) Battalion (Lt.-Col. F. R. Berridge).

The winners were the 2nd Bucks with a score of 462, but the 3rd tied for second place with the 4th Herts, with 456.

The final results in the events were as follows:

Queen Mary Competition: 1, 6th Beds, 356; equal 2, 3rd (Oundle) Northants and 4th Herts, 345.

Hamilton Leigh (Falling Plate) Competition: 1, 3rd (Oundle) Northants, 48; 2, 12th Bucks, 49; 3, 2nd Bucks, 55.

Sten Gun Competition: 1, 4th Herts, 71; 2, 2nd Bucks, 70; 3, 10th (Daventry) Northants, 68.

The 3rd (Oundle) Battalion, although unlucky in the Shield, were warmly commended upon their runner-up success and also upon gaining the championship of Northamptonshire and Huntingdonshire. Team and scores were:

Queen Mary Competition (H.P.S. 56): Lt. Tompkins (A Co.), 50; R.S.M. Cottingham (H.Q.), 47; Lt. Thorne (A Co.), 45; Sgt. Brigge (C Co.), 44; Pte. Jeffs (D Co.), 43; Lt. Billinghurst (D Co.), 36; C.S.M. Loveday (D Co.), 46; Cpl. Hamilton (B Co.), 34. Total, 345.

Hamilton Leigh (Falling Plate) Competition Team: Lt. Tompkins, Lt. Thorne, R.S.M. Cottingham, Pte. Jeffs.

Sten Gun Competition (H.P.S. 20): C.S.M. Loveday, 17; Sgt. Reeves (D Co.), 19; R.S.M. Cottingham, 10; Lt. Tompkins, 15. Total, 61.

The team was coached and captained by Capt. E. A. Barnes (Battalion W.T.O.)

## UNWIELDY BATTALION DIVIDED

For some months up to this time it had become increasingly apparent that the 12th (Northampton) Battalion was waxing far more unwieldy than was commensurate with efficiency in point of the capacity of its command to maintain the requisite cohesion.

It was, indeed, a marvel that Lt.-Col. L. E. Barnes and his subordinates had for so long contrived to administer and train a battalion of more than twice the normal size.

Accordingly in July 1943 there came into being the 15th (Northampton) Battalion with Major N. P. Andrews promoted from the command of A Company of the 12th to be its battalion commander.

The choice of the new battalion commander was as sound as it was unanimously approved.

Lt.-Col. Andrews was educated at Westminster School, where he was football and cricket captain and company sergeant-major of the O.T.C.

During the First War he served in the 1st Grenadier Guards, of which Lord Gort was for some time C.O. He was gazetted out 1st Lieutenant and remained in the special reserve of officers until 1923.

One of the founders of the Northamptonshire Branch of the Grenadier Guards Comrades' Association, he had been vice-president since formation.

Lt.-Col. Andrews.

In the Home Guard he had commanded A Company of the 12th since its formation and had brought his company to a pitch of efficiency at which it was regarded as one of the best in Northamptonshire Sub-District.

Its company camps were models of organization and reflected the splendid cameraderie which Lt.-Col. Andrews' leadership had largely inspired.

A good sportsman in every sense of the word, Lt.-Col. Andrews was also a crack cricketer, who had turned out for the County in several seasons.

The 15th was built from D and E Companies of the 12th together with the Northampton Electric Light Company's unit which had been, in turn, a headquarters platoon and then a platoon of B Company of the 12th. The strength of the Battalion throughout was always about 1,000.

Six companies were formed, the old E Company of the 12th Battalion being divided into two companies. It was expected that, after the formation of the Battalion, the strength of these companies would be materially increased but such was not the case.

The fact that so many of its members were doing work of vital importance made it difficult to keep its operational role within its capacity. A tremendous task was performed by the railway companies under the most difficult conditions, and it would not have been strange had more of the workers been "excused" Home Guard duties.

Nevertheless the original volunteer railwaymen gave most diligent service throughout the period of their duties.

The need of maintaining services vital to the life of the community made parades and training often a matter of difficulty to many more of the Battalion.

It was inevitable that a great deal of work would have to be done by a permanent staff and in this respect the Battalion was very well served.

The Adjutant, Capt. J. C. Hubbard, of the Royal Norfolk Regiment, was posted to the Battalion on 12 July and quickly became the friend of everyone, and remained so until he left at "stand down".

A Regular soldier of many years' standing he quickly adapted himself to Home Guard limitations and conditions.

The courses of instruction for officers and N.C.O.s were models of their kind, and were of great assistance to many of those appointed to commissioned and non-commissioned rank.

The 15th's operational area was detailed as follows:

All that part of the Borough of Northampton west of the main road running north and south. (The 12th Battalion retained the responsibility for the defence of South Bridge); the area covered by the Northampton Electric Light and Power Company, Ltd., together with its environs; the railway tracks to Peterborough and Bedford, with considerable sidings and material depots attached thereto; the L.M.S. main line to London as far as the south end of Hunsbury Hill tunnel, and the branch line to Blisworth as far as the furnaces; the L.M.S. railway line running

north to a point where the Rugby and Market Harborough lines divide; in the west to Upton, and in the north to Hopping Hill.

The second-in-command of the 15th Battalion was Major R. Manning, M.C.

The company commanders of the 15th Battalion were as follows:

H.Q. Company, Major O. H. C. Amberg; A Company, Major F. M. Molden; B Company, Major P. G. Jones; C Company, Major S. Bennett; D Company, Major J. Nightingale; E Company, Major S. Hasler.

Battalion Headquarters (Administrative and Operational) were located at the Brewery House, Black Lion Hill, Northampton, and Headquarters Company (Administrative and Operational) at the Express Lift Company, Ltd., Abbey Works, Northampton.

The following were the other company headquarters:

A Company at St. John's Street, Northampton (Administrative) and the Generating Station at Hardingstone (Operational); B Company at 74 Harlestone Road, Northampton (Administrative and Operational); C Company at St. Andrew's Street, Northampton (Administrative) and the Roadmender Club, Broad Street, Northampton (Administrative and Operational); and E Company at the Castle Station, Northampton (Administrative and Operational).

### FIRM'S VALUABLE ASSISTANCE

The Battalion Commander was greatly assisted in the matter of company headquarters, etc., by the splendid co-operation of the directors of the various undertakings within the Battalion area.

Thus accommodation was provided for both administration and operational purposes for Headquarter Company by the Express Lift Company, for A Company by the Northampton Electric Light and Power Company, for C Company by the Northampton Gaslight Company, and for D and E Companies by the London Midland and Scottish Railway Company.

C Company also had administrative quarters at the Semilong Working Men's Club and received from the officials of that club whole-hearted assistance and co-operation throughout its existence.

### DETAILS OF THE 15TH'S COMPANIES

Here are some of the details of the companies, whose commanders are detailed with other battalion specialist officers on a preceding page:

*Headquarters Company.*—The personnel of this unit was drawn entirely from the employees of the Express Lift Company. Formerly a platoon in the 12th Battalion it was organized on a company basis on its formation, and in addition to two platoons, a bomb disposal squad was formed. This squad attained a high degree of efficiency, and on a special trip to Ely for the purpose passed the Eastern Command test with flying colours. In competitive shooting events, this company gave a very good account of itself, and one of its members gained the highest marks in the marksman's qualification test. For this he was presented with a silver cup, given by an officer of the Battalion. This company also trained a team for the two-pounder gun, which had been allotted to it.

*A Company.*—Formed as a headquarters platoon of Battalion Headquarters of the 12th and subsequently transferred to B Company of the same battalion, this unit became a company on the formation of the 15th. Its strength was made up of employees of the Northampton Electric Light and Power Company, and its task, the protection of the highly important generating plant supplying, as it did, power to a very

large area through the "grid", was under constant guard throughout the whole war, and this arduous task was undertaken and most effectively maintained, particularly during the invasion of Europe, until the allied forces had obtained a sure hold in France. This company also trained a team for the two-pounder gun.

*B Company.*—As has already been stated, this company was the only completely general service company, and as such its training was of necessity most varied. A large part of the unit had originally been designated D Company of the 12th Battalion. A great number of men passed through this unit into the forces, and this added to the difficulties of training. The Company maintained a good reputation for its shooting, both on the miniature and open ranges. The "Fork" competition was eagerly competed for by platoons of this company during its time as D Company and the final competition took place in September 1943, when drill, battle drill, Lewis-gun bombing, Northover projector, and Spigot mortar teams showed great enthusiasm in competing.

*C Company.*—This company was composed of two "G.S." platoons, the third being the unit formed out of the employees of the Northampton Gaslight Company. This platoon had the task of protecting the gas-producing plant and the approaches thereto, and a system of defence works had been constructed. Of the other two platoons, one had a comparatively static role, whereas the other was constituted as a battle platoon. This platoon was selected to act as the enemy in the attack on Hertford in the memorable exercise Buzz 3 in March 1945.

### AN ALL-NIGHT OPERATION

Leaving Northampton at 4.30 p.m. on Saturday afternoon, it was conveyed to the rendezvous by motor-coach, and the zero hour for the exercise was 2030 hours. From that time until 0900 hours the next morning, the unit was on the move over difficult and strange country, being given three separate objectives.

The first of these, a railway viaduct, was successfully demolished at 0300 hours, and the act of demolition was so realistic that the inhabitants must have thought that a genuine raid was in progress.

It was then put in for an attack on the railway station, which was also successfully accomplished at 0625 hours, and it is not surprising that the final attack on the enemy's headquarters was declared to have been unsuccessful at 0900 hours when the "battle" ended!

During the night, the troops had travelled many miles, and were justly proud of their achievement and ready for the excellent breakfast provided.

At the end of the engagement the question of whether the weather had been "sufficiently inclement" to warrant a rum issue was settled by an officer on the spot without reference to higher authority, and to the complete satisfaction of the troops.

The issue was to be one dessertspoonful, but the final amount was settled by the capacity of the jar.

Breakfast, accompanied by a sing-song, terminated a memorable Home Guard experience, and the platoon arrived back at Battalion headquarters at 1315 hours on Sunday.

*D and E Companies.*—The combined strength of these two companies was more than four hundred, all of whom were employees of the London Midland and Scottish Railway Company. There were very special difficulties, as will be understood, in arranging parades and training, since a very large number of the men were "shift" workers.

These shifts worked by the operating staff precluded many of the men attending as often as they would have wished, and, moreover, Sunday was a day on which traffic was often at its heaviest. During each of the summers of the Home Guard's existence, however, camps were held each week-end, and for that purpose Long Buckby Station was made available.

On Saturday afternoon or early evening parties numbering from thirty to fifty proceeded by train or lorry to the station, there to set up complete camps, the arrangements including cooking, etc.

It afforded those who went opportunities for training which would otherwise not have been available, and battles were fought against platoons from the neighbouring villages. Firm friendships were established with the enemies after the fight, and it is pleasing to record that they exist to this day. The evenings spent at Brington will long remain a pleasant memory.

### DEFENCE AGAINST SURPRISE AIR ATTACK

The strategic role of the 15th was governed very largely by its composition.

With the changing fortunes of the war there were, quite naturally, changes in the general role of the Home Guard, but to the end the role of a large part of the 15th Battalion remained the defence of the vital communications and installations within its area against a surprise attack from the air, but a few more of the G.S. units were available for a more mobile role and for local reinforcement.

In the days before the invasion of the European continent the guarding of the intricate system of railway lines with its many bridges, including the Hunsbury Hill tunnel, placed upon the available manpower of the Battalion a heavy load which was at all times discharged with great goodwill. The Battalion in its turn provided the mobile platoon, which was in readiness every night under the direct operational command of No. 4 Sector.

Unarmed Combat was a feature of the 12th (Northampton) Battalion's display in May 1943.

The general nature of the operational area consisted, in large part, of the built-up area of the Borough of Northampton, but in addition to the network of railways, there was the flat, open country between the Weedon Road and Hunsbury Hill, said, by those best able to judge, to be an ideal "dropping zone", from its flat nature and prominent landmarks. The distinctive topographical feature of the area was Hunsbury Hill, which dominated the whole of the south-west aspect of the town, and the river line.

## SOME ONEROUS V.P.s

The Battalion's V.P.s were very onerous ones, including as they did the railway system with its many bridges, etc.; the Northampton Electric Light and Power Company's generating station (an elaborate system of pill-boxes, wire, and other defence works had been constructed, all points in this system being linked by an internal telephone system. An observation post was constructed on the roof of the station, with a commanding view over a large part of the Nene Valley near the town); the Northampton Gas Works; the Express Lift Works where vital war material was being produced; bulk petroleum storage tanks situated on railway property (certain personnel of the Battalion were trained for the destruction of the supplies. Demolition sets were in position and the whole of the supply of this petrol could have been destroyed at very short notice); Hunsbury Hill tunnel and the central material depot of the London Midland and Scottish Railway. (Great stores of railway material were kept at this depot, including equipment ready for restoring destroyed bridges, etc.)

## Chapter XXIX

# THE DEVELOPMENT OF CAMOUFLAGE

In July 1943 Lt.-Col. G. S. Watson relinquished the command of the 9th (Brixworth) Battalion to the great regret of all ranks. This regret was tempered by the knowledge that their popular commanding officer had received and had accepted an invitation to command one of four new sector commands then in process of establishment and whose history is related in subsequent pages.

Col. Watson, with characteristic generosity, sent an invitation to all officers of the Battalion to meet him at the White Lion, Moulton, on 12 July 1943.

Forty-two officers responded, and at this farewell gathering, a silver salver, inscribed with the exact replicas of the signatures of the donors, was presented to Col. Watson as a token of the great esteem in which he was held by his fellow officers.

The presentation was made by the Battalion second-in-command, Major R. Dickens, who said that Col. Watson's leadership had been an inspiration and an example to all ranks.

Lt.-Col. Watson's Special Order of the Day to the 9th Battalion, dated 5 July 1943, stressed his great pride in the steady progress of the Battalion, and the real pleasure he had had through the devotion to duty and the loyalty displayed by all ranks.

Lt.-Col. Watson was succeeded in the command of the 9th Battalion by Major J. T. H. Pettitt, promoted from the command of a company.

Major Pettitt was another ideally qualified commander with a particularly gallant record. In the 1914–18 war he enlisted in August 1914 in D (E. R. Mobbs') Company of the 7th Battalion Northamptonshire Regiment, was promoted corporal a month later, and platoon sergeant in October. Going to France with the 7th in August 1915, he was wounded at Loos. Subsequently he was commissioned to the Somerset Light Infantry, with which he again went to France and was again wounded in 1917. After recovery in hospital in England he returned to France for the third time and was for a third time wounded.

Lt.-Col. J. T. H. Pettitt.

Now graded B.2, he was then posted to a reserve battalion of the S.L.I. until promoted Captain and again sent to France to another battalion of his regiment, with which he continued to serve until demobilized in 1919.

### CAMOUFLAGE FOR ALL

In preceding pages are recorded some details of the progress of camouflage in the Home Guard.

It is timely at this point to return to this important aspect of Home Guard training and to note how rapidly it had progressed in the interim.

Capt. F. E. Courtney, therefore, here resumes his story.

As the war progressed we read reports of new camouflage ideas from the various fighting fronts and modified our instruction to suit the new intelligence.

255

Often, too, one or more issues of material were withdrawn and substitutes had to be found, e.g., before the invasion of North Africa all face nets were withdrawn and so we improvised with a piece of garden or fish net, to which rows of scrim were attached.

We learned more, too, of actual fighting conditions, and realized that good camouflage lay in providing the minimum of material and teaching the men to make skilful use of "found" material—anything that lay to hand —and that the best camouflage was correct and sensitive behaviour, where and how to walk and move, a consciousness that the enemy might be above or at any position around us, how to use ground and other cover, and how to work without noise.

At this stage one was conscious of the very real and sound way in which camouflage was being used. It was no longer treated as a specialist subject but as an integral part of training, and was constantly practised.

Organization, too, became more complete. The plan was to appoint an officer in each battalion who would see that this training and integration would be complete and constant, and almost every battalion did appoint such officers, who became my simplest contact with each battalion, and with whom I arranged battalion and company demonstrations.

The organization was not too rigid and instruction proceeded in places and on lines differing slightly from the "official" ones. A notable case was the week-end camps run at Harrowden by Lts. Burton and Spencer of Wellingborough. These camps were very enjoyable and instructive, and were of a very good type. We slept under ground-sheet bivouacs slung between neighbouring trees in a spinney, we cooked our own meals, had a little lecture-demonstration, and plenty of thorough battle drills and exercises in which fieldcraft and camouflage were well taught and practised.

### USE OF "NOISES OFF"

Those concerned with instruction continued to attend refresher courses, and on one memorable occasion the Sub-District camouflage officers spent a week at the Army's No. 1

Camouflage Training and Development School at Farnham Castle. Officers and others from Northamptonshire made periodic visits to the No. 2 Group Camouflage School at Norwich, where the week-end courses run by Major Bull drew students from the whole of the Eastern Command. Here we learned, among other things, of the possibilities of "noises off" as a means of deceiving the enemy, and several people—notably in this district, Major Newton and Cadet-Lt. Smart—made interesting experiments in this technique and taught them at the school at Northampton.

Towards the end of the war we went "all natural", using only string, rubber bands, a garnished helmet cover, and natural and found materials exclusively, and the ability to use these intelligently and sensitively was generally well understood. We could prepare ourselves quickly and confidently, we knew how and where to move, and, to my mind, behaved in the field like well-trained troops.

It is interesting to survey our progress from the ashplant and armlet days of 1940. Then we had so little help from the Army, who, indeed, seemed to know so little themselves. There were times when the Army did give us fresh ideas and inspiration; but, in the main, I like to think and, I believe, rightly, that the greatest contributing factors to our efficiency in camouflage were first, that we realized all along that our Home Guard needs were special to us and that we must develop our own solutions to the problems, and, secondly, that we were a county of countrymen, none of us living far from the soil, and towards the end, at any rate, our countryman's awareness and sensitivity to our surroundings helped us considerably.

### "CHANGES IN THE 7TH"

It may seem strange in years to come to read that throughout 1942 and a large part of 1943 increased preparations were being made by the Home Guard to meet a large-scale invasion of this country. There was still, however, a possibility that Russia would have to capitulate, which would have enabled Hitler to turn about and strike at this island before American assistance became available, and, of course, all our own trained regular troops were more than ever needed overseas.

Thus, early in 1942, in common with other battalion commanders, the C.O. of the 7th was issuing fresh operational instructions and orders for the defence of his "defended places".

At Wellingborough a "keep" and five defended localities were provided for; at Irthlingborough a keep and a D.L. at the bridge; at Finedon a D.L. at the crossroads. Each of these places had its own reserves and patrols, and there were also village ambushes at Great Harrowden and Great Addington.

Fortunately, the summer of 1942 saw the arrival of some three hundred recruits under compulsion, while a complete platoon of air raid wardens voluntarily joined up under their chief warden (Mr. H. L. Shortland) at Irthlingborough. The Wellingborough recruits were given their basic training under battalion arrangements, and being largely active and fit men, enabled H.Q. Company there to be made into a strong infantry company, the specialists being drafted into the Keep (B) Company.

Thus in June 1942 the organization in Wellingborough was: B Company, the "keep" area; A Company, north and west, with two "D.L.s"; E Company, east, with one D.L.; F Company, south and southeast, with two D.L.s; H Company (formerly H.Q. Company), battalion reserve.

C Company was divided, Major Bennie taking the new G Company, comprising the Harrowden group of villages, and Capt. W. Bramham, shortly succeeded by Major R. D. Paterson, the new C Company at Finedon.

There followed three rapid changes of command of H Company. Capt. Smillie,

seconded to the A.C.F., was followed by Capt. H. C. Pearson, who three months later returned to London. Capt. Bramham, brought in from Finedon to replace him, left at the end of 1942 to take up a responsible Government post.

It thus came about that Major W. S. Solley was transferred to H Company from A Company, and that his second-in-command of A Company succeeded him. This was not all. Within a month Major E. Young, M.C., was transferred to Worcestershire where he soon became second-in-command of another battalion, while shortly afterwards Major A. E. S. Bayley, M.C., went to Cheshire and subsequently was given command of a battalion there.

The new company commanders were: A Company, Major G. M. Jones; E Company, Major V. L. Ward; F Company, Major L. F. Norman.

Twelve months later Major Ward and Major Bennie both left the district and were succeeded at the beginning of 1944 by Major E. H. L. Way and Major W. G. Gilbey respectively.

As an illustration of the difficulties encountered as roles were changed and different sites for H.Q. called for, it may be of interest to record how the 7th fared in this direction.

In 1940, battalion headquarters was at Wellingborough School, where the duty officer, battalion guard, and dispatch riders slept nightly from September 1940 until 1943. When the boys returned to school in September 1940, the battalion administrative H.Q. was moved to Capt. Barron's office in Sheep Street, and later to a flat over a draper's shop in Silver Street, the only approach to which was up a narrow outside wooden staircase. In September 1941, Evington House was secured and remained as Administrative H.Q. until the disbandment. Action H.Q. were first at

17

the police station, then at the School, and by the end of 1940 in a disused brewery known as "Dulley's Premises". With the introduction of a smaller keep in 1942 a move was made to the basement of the Regal Cinema, but by 1944 a very good Battle H.Q. had been furnished at the Priory in Church Street.

A Company H.Q. was for three years at Elm Street in the Church Room, but finally in a flat over the Conservative Club in High Street. B Company had rooms over a shop in Midland Road, next to the Volunteer Inn. When this company was fortunate enough in 1942 to get the old Drill Hall, the signallers and pioneers took over their quarters. C Company used throughout a hut at Finedon; D Company first used the old Salvation Army Hall at Irthlingborough and then two shops in the High Street. Their Action H.Q. was a room at the Council House. E Company functioned from the L.M.S. Control, then had a room in Silver Street, and finally the L.M.S. Railway presented them with two railway coaches. The companies used part of Dulley's premises until enemy action demolished this; then F Company moved to a disused dance hall, and H.Q. Company to the upper floor of a building at Croyland Road, the lower floor of which housed the llamas of the Wellingborough Zoo! G Company were fortunate in having the use of rooms at Harrowden Hall throughout the whole four years. In 1944 the Battalion was using over thirty requisitioned premises as H.Q. stores, or for training purposes.

In August 1943, the commander was asked by the Sub-District to provide a company of fit "List 1" men (i.e., those available at short notice for duty at a distance) to act as a "reinforcement company" for a garrison on the East Coast. The United Counties men of the M.T.

Company were detailed to provide transport.

To form this company, Lt.-Col. Allsopp transferred List 2 men from H Company, his battalion reserve, and replaced them by sufficient List 1 men there to make two strong infantry platoons. H Company was then given a List 1 platoon at Finedon and a support platoon at Irthlingborough, taken from C and D Companies respectively. This new company, with picked officers and men, under the command of Major W. S. Solley, was subsequently given an alternative role of mobile reserve for Sub-District.

To provide a new battalion reserve, B Company now seemed most suitable and handed over their role of defenders of the keep, as well as their specialist personnel, to A Company. It was with this main organization that the battalion commander hoped to face such an event as arose in the battle fought at the end of the "Megrim" exercise just before D-Day in 1944.

Such hopes, however, were dashed almost immediately.

In the autumn of 1943 it was decided by Eastern Command that the Battalion must provide a company of approximately 240 men at Irthlingborough for the purpose of decontamination work at the Command Laundry there. (This work had previously been done by the Royal Army Ordnance Corps, who were soon to go overseas.) It was also decided that a similar but smaller laundry at Wellingborough should be brought into use for the same purpose. Here one hundred men were needed, and, of course, there would have to be reliefs and reserves.

### IRTHLINGBOROUGH "TANKS"

This meant further reorganization. For example, at Irthlingborough the loss of a strong platoon to the reinforcement

Company had left D Company with barely enough men to do the job, which meant working in gas-proof clothing and respirators for two hours at a time, no task for weaklings. However, Irthlingborough had no weaklings. They quickly learned the job and then helped with instructing the men from Wellingborough, whose tanks were not yet ready. F Company now became

of 1943 the formation of four sector commands, each under the command of an officer with the rank of colonel. These sectors were established more or less on the lines of an infantry brigade command, with the view of co-ordinating the administration, training, and operational effectiveness of groups of battalions in the Northants Sub-District.

A scene from the Home Guard Play *Patrol Orders*, given by members of No. 6 Platoon of B Co. (Major A. McFarlane) of the 12th (Northampton) Battalion in March 1944. The producer was Lt. F. K. Thornton, who had as his collaborator Pte. J. E. Rice.

the Wellingborough decontamination company, with a further reshuffle of personnel, fortunately not so large this time.

Incidentally, this decontamination work gave rise to a joke not to be forgotten so long as a man from D Company of the 7th Battalion remains above ground, which was that the Irthlingborough company, who had produced their own armoured car in 1940, started their existence with one tank and finished with twenty-four—the number of tanks at the Command Laundry.

To these new and strange duties it is on record that the companies concerned adapted themselves with cheerful versatility.

**THE SECTOR COMMANDS**

We must now retrace our steps a few months to record in the spring and summer

In following the developments which led to the sectors, the story of No. 1 tells the story of its fellows.

In 1940, when Sir Hereward Wake was appointed Northants Organizer, six divisions were formed, corresponding with the County Police divisions, plus the Borough of Northampton and the Soke of Peterborough.

Lt.-Col. Burditt, M.C., T.D., of Desborough, was placed in command of the Kettering Division.

Sir F. Robinson, Bt., M.C., and Capt. R. C. Fowler ably assisted, and the Kettering area was divided into groups—Kettering, Desborough, Rothwell, Corby, Burton Latimer, Clipston, and Welford.

Eventually these groups were commanded by the Rev. G. Holborow, Capt.

Ginns, Canon Grimes, Capt. Lucas, Capt. B. Wright, Major Pelley, and Capt. Savill.

The organization became inevitably unwieldy and eventually battalions were formed. Lt.-Col. Burditt became C.O. of Kettering District Battalion, and Lt.-Col. Holborow C.O. of Kettering Town Battalion, while Lt.-Col. Menzies Wilson took command of the Corby Works Battalion.

Soon after it was decided to group the battalions in the county in two groups, and Lt.-Col. Burditt was appointed commander of the Northern Group, which consisted of battalions numbered 1 to 8. This was also found to be unwieldy, and the group idea was discarded.

When Col. Lester Reid succeeded Sir Hereward Wake as Zone Commander he had as his second-in-command Lt.-Col. Burditt, and then the group system was again introduced, but the number of battalions in each group was reduced. No. 1 Group was formed by the 3rd, 4th, 5th, and 6th battalions, and Lt.-Col. Burditt was promoted to Colonel to command it. Capt. C. E. Pierson, D.S.O., was appointed as Permanent Staff Adjutant to this group.

In August 1942, No. 1 Group H.Q. was at Desborough and Major W. H. Metcalfe, M.C. (King's Own Regiment) was posted to act as adviser to battalion commanders and to assist in training.

At this stage training began in earnest. Weapon training officers, with the help of the training officer, started extensive programmes to improve shooting throughout the Group.

In March 1943 No. 1 Group became No. 1 Sector of the four sectors into which Northants was then divided. Capt. Pierson was posted to Surrey to a similar position to that which he had held in Northants, and Capt. J. B. Green, of the Bedfordshire and Hertfordshire Regiment, then became

No. 4 Sector adjutant, with Miss Sheila Bennett as permanent Orderly Room clerk.

Capt. J. Ivans and Sgt. Bodimer ran the I. section, the signals were under Capt. L. M. Scott (including several women auxiliaries), and an administrative section (including the Assistant Adjutant, Capt. F. E. Francis, Staff-Sgt. Spencer, and C.Q.M.S. Donald) was also formed.

A sector school was started at Desborough for the training of H.G. officers and N.C.O.s.

The Intelligence Officer was Capt. J. R. Soanes, with Sgt. A. Bodimer and four O.R.s making up his staff.

Signals section was handled by Capt. L. M. Scott, with Sgt. Timpson and nine O.R.s.

Section liaison officers were drawn from each battalion and Lt. Bagshaw was detailed to act as Liaison to Sub-District.

Here a word must be said for the Women Home Guard Auxiliaries. These girls, recruited into a somewhat strange work, worked untiringly to gain a very high standard of efficiency, and in the months to follow were invaluable at the headquarters.

All through the summer of 1943 the sector paraded regularly on Tuesday and Thursday evenings and Sunday mornings; telephones were installed; an armoury was made, and sections trained to maintain an even higher standard of efficiency.

The Women Auxiliaries were awarded a small badge to wear—small compensation indeed for the work which they put in.

When on 22 and 23 January 1944 Exercise "Buzz", a full-scale exercise throughout Northants Sub-District, took place, the sector headquarters were manned by full staff, and meals were cooked for thirty in the H.Q.'s own cookhouse.

The morale of the cooks went considerably higher when the G.O.C. from East

Central District came over for breakfast and said he had had an excellent meal.

From then until 25 April, rifles, Sten guns, ammunition, motor-cycles for D.R.s, clothing, etc., started to flow in.

Exercises with battalions and Sub-District and special headquarters exercises, also assistance to the Army Cadet Force, kept time fully occupied.

On 25 April 1944, the sector was ordered to stand to for Exercise "Megrim". On 29 April the headquarters were mustered in full and personnel were called out of cinemas and dances and in a short time all were on duty. On 30 April one of the battalions brought in "the enemy"—seven American paratroopers—for interrogation and transmission to Sub-District H.Q.

The invasion of Europe at this stage was imminent, and the keenness and enthusiasm of all Home Guard personnel could be felt everywhere.

On 1 May, at 0230 hours, "Megrim" stood down, but at the same time the code word for the serious operation came through. At last the Sector was "at war", prepared for any counter-invasion by the enemy. The plans which had been so carefully worked out during the past months were now in actual operation.

Platoons had for weeks past been standing to on the East Coast, providing relief for the local Home Guard.

On 21 May, Headquarters were still being manned day and night, the permanent staff manning by day and the Home Guard taking over the night duty. This in addition to their normal day's work at their own factories or offices as the case might be. It was a tiring time for all, but no complaints were ever heard.

On 8 July 1944 the girls in this sector were awarded a uniform—khaki skirts, berets, and shirts, with brown belts—and very smart they looked.

On 17 August 1944 came the end of night duty—the scare was over—and from then on until 17 September the sector relaxed a little.

A Battle Platoon Competition was then contested at Sector level and won by a platoon of the 3rd Battalion.

Preparation was then in full swing for a large-scale shooting competition at Orton range, which was held on 23 September and the three following week-ends. Great interest was shown by G.O.C., E.C.D., and the Sub-District Commander.

On 6 October 1944 a happy party was held at the Rigid Container Factory Canteen, but for all the gaiety it was "farewell" and everyone there felt the wrench of leaving the organization which they had helped to build from nothing.

It was announced on 29 October 1944 that there would be no more compulsory parades and volunteers were called for in subsequent weeks to help clear the stores, etc., and close down. Everyone helped.

On 3 December voluntary parades had ceased, and by 12 December all secret documents had been burned and stores returned, and the adjutant and his clerk had left; on 16 December the commanding officer closed down No. 1 Sector Home Guard.

Early in 1945 Capt. F. E. Francis was awarded the Certificate of Merit.

### BATTLE H.Q. AT RECTORY

No. 2 Sector was formed on 24 March 1943—and consisted of the 10th, 13th, and 14th battalions. Its commanding officer was Col. J. G. Lowther, D.S.O., M.C., T.D., who brought first-class military experience to bear upon the post.

Col. Lowther, after a period with the Yorkshire Hussars, joined the 11th Hussars and served with the Northamptonshire Yeomanry during the 1914-18 war, when he was twice mentioned in dispatches and was awarded the D.S.O. and M.C.

After the war he continued with the Northamptonshire Yeomanry as Major, and from 1921 to 1924 was in command of the N.Y. Armoured Car Company. In 1924 he was promoted Lieutenant-Colonel, and took command of the 4th Battalion Northamptonshire Regiment. He became Colonel in 1928, and in 1931 was made Hon. Colonel. Home Guard sector officers were Major R. F. Sykes, M.A., Ll.B., the 5th (Hunts) Battalion the Northants Regiment, T.A., seconded to the Home Guard (Adjutant), Lt. M. S. Fatt (Assistant Adjutant), Lt. A. J. L. Knights (Signals Officer), Lt. C. T. Pettifer (Intelligence Officer), and Lt. E. A. Austin (Transport Officer and Quartermaster).

Col. J. G. Lowther.

There were twenty-six other ranks, two in the orderly room, seven on the intelligence section, sixteen on the signals section, and one on the transport section.

During the early summer of 1943 a battle headquarters for the sector was established at Everdon Rectory, and the first headquarters exercise in moving from Guilsborough to Everdon for action purposes took place on 24 and 25 July 1943. The headquarters did their own cooking and administration for the first time.

During the period 30 July to 2 August 1943 the headquarters moved into a tented camp at Denford, when the various headquarters sections performed some useful preliminary training. The sector was helped very considerably at this and other camps by the 8th Battalion (Lt.-Col. V. H. Sykes) and the Quartermaster (Capt. Pond).

On 8 August 1943 at 1400 hours the headquarters were inspected by the G.O.C. East Central District—and as a result of this visit the headquarters became self-accounting and published its own Part I and II orders.

A further week-end camp was held by the headquarters at Denford on 18 and 19 September 1943, when further specialist training was carried out.

## IN TYPICAL HOME GUARD WEATHER

During the summer and autumn of 1943 the headquarters made several visits to Brington range, and in addition several small exercises were held at Guilsborough, in which the various officers did excellent work in training their sections for battle.

On Sunday, 14 November 1943, all ranks of the sector marched to Elkington and back for battle practice. This march was undertaken in typical Home Guard weather —as it was the wettest day the headquarters had ever experienced.

The sector held its first dance and supper on 3 December 1943. The social event was followed by a surprise exercise arranged by the adjutant on 4 and 5 December, which entailed the moving of the whole headquarters to Everdon Rectory. During this exercise valuable work was done by C.Q.M.S. Edwards in arranging administrative details.

The first few weeks of 1944 were occupied by preparations for "Buzz", the large-scale exercise throughout Northamptonshire, which took place on 22 and 23 January. No. 2 Sector took up quarters in Everdon village and spent a very cold and damp night in the village hall.

From the beginning of April 1944 the sector staff were preparing for duty in the event of a counter-invasion when the Allies landed in Europe. A new battle headquarters was taken over at Farthingstone and the signals section spent many evenings laying telephone wires from Guilsborough to Farthingstone and the various battalion headquarters in the sector area. Intensive training was the order of the day. Headquarters went into camp again at Denford on 7 April and remained there until the 10th.

On 25 April a pre-invasion exercise began in the county, and headquarters were partially mustered.

**MANNED DAY AND NIGHT**

As from 0900 hours on 1 May 1944, headquarters was manned by at least one officer on duty, and throughout the summer months the headquarters was constantly manned day and night.

At 0020 hours on 15 July 1944 a message was received that sabotage was likely against the L.M.S. railway. The sector mobile platoon was moved from Middleton Cheney to Blisworth, but no action took place.

Denford was the scene of the last camp, which took place on 4–7 August 1944. Temporary communications with Sub-District were laid down by the signals officer and his men.

The manning of headquarters ceased on 17 August 1944.

In October 1944 the sector suffered a very heavy loss when Lt. Knights was killed near Hardingstone.

Headquarters held its farewell supper on the eve of Stand Down Sunday. This took place in the Grammar School at Guilsborough, and on the following day, 3 December 1944, the sector paraded for the last time at Guilsborough Court, its "peace" headquarters.

The sector awards included a Certificate of Merit to Lt. A. E. Austin in February 1945.

**NO. 3 SECTOR PLAYED FULL PART**

No. 3 Sector was no less fortunate than its fellows in point of the military standing of its command.

In its first function as No. 3 Group it was able to appoint as commander Col. R. P. A. Helps, O.B.E., M.C.

Col. Helps passed out of the Military College, Sandhurst, in 1910 and joined the Lancashire Fusiliers at Tidworth.

When the regiment was stationed at Dover he was A.D.C. to the General Commanding.

In August 1914 he went overseas with the regiment but was transferred to Brigade Headquarters, as brigade signals officer.

Wounded at Le Cateau, he returned to England, but in November 1914 went overseas again as brigade signals officer of the 9th Brigade, of which Major Archibald Wavell (later Viceroy of India) was Brigade Major.

Col. R. P. A. Helps.

In 1916 he commanded 3rd Division Signals and was then appointed General Staff Officer 3rd grade to 4th Army Corps, then commanded by Lt.-Gen. Sir Henry Wilson.

Invalided home in 1917, he was appointed Brigade Major of 207th Infantry Brigade, and in 1919 was appointed to General Staff Officer, training branch, General Headquarters, Horse Guards, Whitehall.

In 1921 he transferred to the Royal Corps of Signals and, after serving in various commands at home and abroad, he left the Army with the rank of Lieutenant-Colonel and entered industry.

In 1939 he was recalled and appointed to command A Depot Battalion Training Centre in North Wales, but temporarily released in November 1941 he resumed civil employment and was then appointed to command No. 3 Group in August 1942.

As his group staff officer, Col. Helps had the invaluable assistance of Col. F. J. Fulton, D.S.O., M.C., and on the change from group to sector, No. 34 Market Street, Wellingborough was acquired as H.Q. The sector consisted of the 7th, 8th, and 11th Battalions.

Late in 1943 a reshuffle of battalions took place to conform to the tactical requirements of the defence of the country, and the 11th Battalion left the sector to form part of a new sector grouped around Northampton Borough.

When the authorized staff of the Sector H.Q. eventually was completed it also included the following officers:

Intelligence Officer and G.S.O. III, Capt. H. G. Crawford-Jones; Staff Captains, Capts. J. R. Gammidge and W. O. Gibson; Signals Officer, Lt. A. R. Miller.

The sector operated for two and a half years and played a full and active part in the administration, training, and social activities of its battalions.

### NO. 4 SECTOR'S BUSY RECORD

When No. 4 Sector, comprising the 9th, 11th, 12th, and 15th Battalions, together with the East Central District mobile column, was first planned, Lt.-Col. G. S. Watson, then commanding the 9th Battalion, was asked by Col. P. Lester Reid to accept the command of the sector, and he agreed to do so.

A slight difficulty arose at the outset because the Northampton I.T.C. troops would then have come under the command of the sector commander, and the Sub-District commander was reluctant to place Lt.-Col. H. N. C. Wyburd, K.R.R.C., in a position which would have made him junior to a Home Guard officer.

This difficulty was temporarily overcome by Lt.-Col. Wyburd taking command of the sector with Lt.-Col. Watson as his second-in-command. This arrangement only lasted a few weeks, and during this period a sector headquarters was set up at 4 Lower Mounts, Northampton, and telephone, etc., installed.

Lt.-Col. J. A. Brawn, O.B.E. (Royal Norfolk Regiment) arrived as Sector Training Officer and made himself acquainted with all the troops in the sector area.

Lt.-Col Wyburd then left the district, and on 17 December 1943 Lt.-Col. Watson was gazetted to the command with the rank of colonel.

The original sector staff comprised Col. G. S. Watson, Commanding Officer; Lt.-Col. J. A. Brawn, O.B.E., Training Officer; Lt. (later Capt.) G. E. Dixon, Intelligence Officer, and when Capt. Dixon joined H.M. Forces his place was taken by Lt. (later Capt.) J. J. Wright; Capt. E. E. Barrs, O.B.E., Sector Adjutant; Capt. F. Toulson (9th Battalion), Staff Captain; and Lt. J. Mobbs, Signalling Officer.

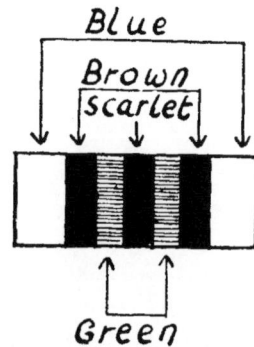

A 1943 suggestion for a Home Guard medal. Blue for the sky they scanned, brown for the earth they ranged, green for the woods they combed, and scarlet for the Army to which they belonged.

## A SHOWER OF COMPLIMENTS

Barely had the intelligence and signalling staffs been completed when Exercise Buzz 2 was started. No. 4 Sector was fighting on its own ground in this exercise, and all personnel greatly distinguished themselves. Special praise was awarded to the 9th Battalion by the East Central District Commander (Major-Gen. E. C.

The sector also provided relief platoons for East Coast duty in the months preceding D-Day, on the coast of Essex in the Bradwell–Quay area.

In the exercise Megrim much praise was gained by all ranks in the Sector for their work during a strenuous fortnight—especially as this strain was additional to their normal daily work. The greatest burden

The scene of the Northamptonshire Sub-District round in the East Central District 1943 Battle Platoon competition. A picture of a particularly complete and accurate sand table model made at Sub-District. Prominent landmarks are Brington Church (in foreground) and Little Brington Church to the S.S.W. at top right. The enemy post was in the barn indicated by an arrow. The starting-point was at the spot marked X.

Hayes) particularly to Capt. C. C. Oakey, M.C. (Adjutant of the 9th Battalion), and his runner, L.-Cpl. W. Faulkner. The sector commander and his staff also duly received their share of the commendations.

A complete sector defence scheme was prepared, and accepted by Sub-District. This arranged for mobile platoons with transport to act as duty troops daily in the event of an emergency—and in this connection "snap" exercises to practise the troops were held at least once during every week.

fell on sector and battalion staffs during the weeks before D-Day, but all duties were carried out cheerfully, and often at great personal inconvenience.

## "HIGHEST STANDARD OF TRAINING"

The most hotly contested event during the life of the sector was the Sector Battle Platoon Competition—an eliminating event for a competition open to the whole East Central District.

This was held in the autumn of 1943 (to which date in our chronological sequence

Drumhead Service of the 12th (Northampton) Battalion held at the County Ground, Northampton, on September 5, 1943, as part of the National Day of Prayer. The Battalion band played marches and accompanied the singing of the hymns.

we now return), and a particularly high compliment was gained in the sector final, won by No. 23 (Bugbrooke) Platoon (Lt. P. Campion) of F Company (Major W. G. Smith) of the 11th (Hardingstone) Battalion (Lt.-Col. W. J. Penn). They ran up a total of 67.1 marks, and the Chief Umpire (Major R. A. E. A. Wyzard, K.R.R.C.) stated that the Bugbrooke Platoon's work "reflected the highest standard of Home Guard training he had ever seen".

The same platoon then went on to compete as No. 4 Sub-District representatives in the final of the competition on Sunday, 10 October 1943.

There were two phases in this gruelling competition: (1) a march of three miles in forty-five minutes and (2) a tactical platoon in attack exercise.

It is on record that after the march, No. 23 Platoon looked as "fresh as paint".

In the second phase they chose a quick way to their objective and went for it with great dash in a frontal attack.

They thought they had the competition "in the pockets", but unfortunately they were beaten by the 11th Hertfordshire— only a decimal point robbing them of victory. The scores were—Hertfordshire Home Guard 54.49 points, Northamptonshire Home Guard 54.05 points. In turn, the Hertfordshire Home Guard were beaten by the 11th Buckinghamshire Battalion, whose score was 68.31 points. The Buckinghamshire Sub-District put up a magnificent display, and although the Bugbrooke lads finished the second phase in twenty minutes, the Buckinghamshire Home Guards took only eighteen.

However, Northamptonshire was rightly proud of its Champion Battle Platoon.

The competition was viewed by a company of senior Regular Army and Home Guard officers—including the General Officer Commanding Eastern Command.

### CZECHOSLOVAKS JOIN EXERCISE

In the same month the 11th Battalion also recorded another interesting item, that

The No. 23 (Bugbrooke) Platoon (Lt. P. Campion) of F Co. (Major W. G. Smith). They were Northamptonshire's champion Battle Platoon and are here relaxing for well-earned refreshment after the final of the October 1943 East Central District Battle Platoon Competition in which they were third to the 11th Bucks (1st) and 11th Herts (2nd). Left to right, standing in centre, can be identified Lt.-Col. W. J. Penn (C.O. 11th), Major H. Marland (Second-in-Command), Capt. G. B. Godson (Adjutant), Major W. G. Smith (F Co.), Major S. J. N. Bartley (Sub-District), and Lt.-Col. J. A. Brawn (Training Officer of No. 4 Sector).

of combination in the second stage of an A exercise on Sunday, 24 October 1943, with units of the Czechoslovak Armoured Brigade then stationed in Britain.

These fine soldiers had been in the

sidelight on the physical toll Home Guard duties were taking of numbers of its members.

Said extracts from this letter:

. . . where a man is working more than sixty

"Kamerad." This "Boche" was posted to trap attackers on the flank and did a lot of damage before he surrendered! An incident during the No. 2 Sector Battle Platoon finals in July 1943.

"What exactly are you firing at?" asks the umpire. An incident during No. 4 Sector Battle Platoon finals at Wootton in August 1943.

Middle East for over three years and during the exercise they put in some exemplary work. With characteristic generosity and sportsmanship they also placed themselves unreservedly under the command of the Home Guard officers engaged.

**"TO MINIMIZE FATIGUE"**

A significant and self-eloquent War Office letter, now issued, cast a revealing

hours a week at work of national importance and is in consequence unable to perform Home Guard duties, his Home Guard commander should consider discharging him if he requests. . . .

Everything is to be done to minimize fatigue to industrial workers.

Agricultural workers and railwaymen to be treated as industrial workers (i.e., railwaymen enrolled other than in railway units).

## C.O. FLEW WITH PARACHUTES

For novel realism, a parachute exercise, devised and carried out by the 10th (Daventry) Battalion on Sunday, 24 October 1943, was unique in Northamptonshire Home Guard records.

Most of the Battalion were at Action Stations for the greater part of the time, even including, to their credit, many railwaymen who had come off night shifts.

The platoon sent to deal with the invaders had to travel two miles in proper field order and then tackle an enemy strong-point. Their work can best be assessed from the fact that the final assault was delivered and the enemy captured before 1212 hours.

The Battalion Commander (Lt.-Col. G. W. M. Lees) flew with the plane and released the parachutes.

Men of Nos. 1 and 3 Platoons of D Company (Woodford Halse District) of the 10th (Daventry) Battalion celebrate the capture of their quarry in a parachute exercise. In centre is Lt. W. J. Preece.

And all were on their toes when, at a previously selected and secret hour, an aeroplane dived to 1,500 feet over Woodford Halse and at carefully timed intervals dropped weighted target parachutes, each of which represented ten enemy parachute troops.

Other villages were similarly targetted, but the action of D Company at Woodford Halse (Major T. Coy) can be selected as typical of the good work done throughout the exercise.

The first parachute dropped hit a point east of the village at 1134 hours. By 1135 an adjacent O.P. was informed, with exact map references, and, in turn, dispatched the information to Company Headquarters.

## DEATH OF MAJOR G. P. LANKESTER

In December 1943 all ranks of the 9th (Brixworth) Battalion, and many of his comrades in other Home Guard units, were saddened by the death of Major Guy Phillip Lankester, late officer commanding C Company of the 9th.

Major Lankester had been in failing health for some time, and eventually he was removed from his home at Church Brampton to the Northampton General Hospital, where, to the intense regret of all who knew him, he died at a comparatively early age.

Ample evidence of his great popularity and of the respect in which he was held in Home Guard circles was afforded at the funeral service at All Saints Church, North-ampton, on 9 December 1943, when his coffin, draped with the Union Jack, was escorted by a Guard of Honour of officers and N.C.O.s and men of the 9th.

Among those present were Lt.-Col. J. T. H. Pettitt (Commanding Officer of the 9th Battalion), Major H. St. John Browne (second-in-command of the 12th Battalion), Capt. C. C. Oakey (Adjutant of the 9th—representing Col. G. S. Watson, Commanding Officer of No. 4 Sector), and other officers, N.C.O.s, and men of the 9th.

Many tributes were paid to the late Major Lankester by old comrades, and perhaps the following extract from a fellow officer's tribute will serve to show the respect and affection in which he was held:

"All who served with him or under him never had anything but admiration for his inspiring leadership, particularly under the difficult conditions of the earlier months of the Guard."

No Home Guard could ask for a finer epitaph.

## Chapter XXX
## ATTACK ON EUROPE IMMINENT

1944 opened for the Home Guard, as for the British nation as a whole, in an atmosphere of electric expectancy.

Mr. Churchill had attended a conference with President Roosevelt and Marshal Stalin at Teheran in the preceding November, quickly followed in December by another conference with President Roosevelt and the President of Turkey at Cairo; the appointment of allied invasion commanders had been announced; the Russians were punching the enemy hard on the eastern front; and the Royal Air Force had for weeks been pounding the German capital in the Battle of Berlin which was still being pressed home with relentless and enormous power.

Everyone now felt in his heart that the long-awaited "Second Front", for which Britain had been yearning ever since the disastrous, if glorious, *débâcle* of Dunkirk, could not long be delayed.

The Home Guard keyed itself up to concert pitch and particularly in such areas as Northamptonshire, where it was known that, in any counter-invasion or diversion assault that the enemy might attempt by way of retaliation, he would almost certainly strike from the air and, almost equally certainly, strike at the heart centre of the country.

### PRACTICE WITH REGULAR
### PARACHUTISTS

In this connection the Guard was able to extract some first-class experience of the possibilities that faced them from a series of exercises organized in conjunction with members of the actual Regular forces who were to be detailed as parachute troops in the impending assault on the European mainland.

Training in gas warfare was also intensified in the Home Guard in 1944 under the supervision, in each unit, of a battalion gas officer, and practically everyone in the Command underwent an actual experience of gas by passing through one of a number of gas vans which toured the area.

The reason was obvious. No chances were being taken against the possibility that the now faltering enemy might resort to extremes in his desperation.

A reference to Exercise "Megrim" has been made elsewhere. This exercise, immediately preceding D-Day, was designed to test, on the one hand Special Service Troops destined for sabotage work behind the enemy lines in France, on the other, all "defence" organizations in Northamptonshire.

These men simulating enemy parachutists and saboteurs, etc., moved anywhere and everywhere throughout the area and a score of stories could be told of the really tough work that the Home Guard put in while, often successfully, seeking to effect their capture.

Later, when their "enemies" had actually landed in enemy territory the Home Guard were proud to know that, apart from the valuable training they themselves had received, these crack British troops, in their turn, also owed a lot to the Guard for the equally valuable experience they had thus been able to gain of concealed activities in a "hostile" countryside.

A joint meeting of H.G. commanders,

C.D. and Police officials from all over the county except Peterborough, was held at the Town Hall at Northampton and addressed by the Sub-District commander and the leader of the Special Service Troops. In view of the nature of the mission of the latter it was necessary that, although a very large number of people in the county would be involved, secrecy should be maintained as to what the "enemy" really was. For the Home Guard it was a very real test as they were now to be up against picked troops, trained to the last degree of efficiency.

The exercise was planned to last for fourteen days commencing on Sunday, 23 April 1944, during which the "enemy" saboteurs were to live as in hostile country and to carry out acts of sabotage (by token explosions) such as would seriously interfere with communications by rail and road throughout the county. H.G. and C.D. H.Q. were to be manned twenty-four hours each day with H.G. patrols and stand-by mobile troops on duty every night. Extra guards were placed on all vulnerable points.

The exercise started quietly, but after the first two days the sound of explosions by night brought into action the mobile platoons, and, it should be added, the U.S.A. troops co-operated in this. But, as the week went on, although in places the enemy had some narrow escapes and then only on occasion by leaving kits and meals behind them, flags found on the sites of explosions showed that the railways were being cut in many places.

At the end of the week the 7th Battalion had captured prisoners and they and the 8th had scoured the areas of the pits which marked their boundary near Irchester as well as the Nene valley. But, like other battalions, they found that rail communications would have been hampered if the saboteurs had used the real thing. So far

the roads had escaped, but the commanders now had an eye on the road bridges, lest they should be attacked.

The climax came on the evening of the second Sunday, and, as far as the 7th Battalion was concerned, began with the capture by the "enemy" of two men of the Battalion at Great Addington.

Within an hour the Battalion as a whole, and Irthlingborough in particular, were on the move. But in the meantime news of parties of troops in trucks passing through Wellingborough had led to the pursuit of these by battalion dispatch riders, and it was reported that these unknown troops had debussed and disappeared in the vicinity of the iron workings between Wellingborough, Finedon and Irthlingborough. Simultaneously a message came from Sub-District warning all battalions that the enemy had been strongly reinforced by troops wearing British uniforms. The pursuit was on. Immediately a message from the 7th Battalion to the U.S.A. troops in Wellingborough sent an American platoon along the southern road towards Irthlingborough and the Battalion Stand-by Platoon departed along the road through Finedon. Irthlingborough meanwhile reported the company rapidly turning out at full strength.

But the enemy had disappeared.

Now came the problem.

The point at which the reinforcements had last been seen was almost equidistant from the railway viaduct near Wellingborough and the main road viaduct at Irthlingborough and somewhat nearer the L.M.S. Control Centre, then still at Wellingborough, all vulnerable points. As darkness fell the area between Wellingborough and Irthlingborough was combed and negative reports began to come in. Then came news that enemy were *beyond* Irthlingborough and some prisoners were taken by

R.A.O.C. men of the Command Laundry who were under the command of Major Curtis, H.G. Commander at Irthlingborough.

Major Curtis, guarding the bridge, waited until about midnight and then set out with a strong fighting patrol in the direction from which enemy had been reported. By one of those accidents which could only happen at night when the enemy are wearing the same uniform as friendly troops the two bodies came into contact without realizing it. A portion of the "enemy", seeing the bridge guard reduced, stole up and carried out a rapid surprise demolition. How far they succeeded, for a battle immediately ensued in which the Home Guard on the spot must have been at least as strong as the attackers, was not disclosed. At that moment came through the order to stop the exercise—the period of special vigilance for the Home Guard throughout the country had begun and was to continue until our troops were firmly ashore in France. For the next few weeks the Home Guard as a whole stood prepared for real enemy interference of a kind such as they had been up against in "Megrim". That it never came we now know. How far the Home Guard acted as a deterrent we also do not know.

"Megrim" was the last full-scale exercise before the Home Guard stood down. As a test of co-operation between Civil Defence, Police, H.G., regular troops and Americans it gave full value. Subsequently company attacks supported by sub-artillery fire were practised, but the stage where those with urgent national civilian duties occupying long working hours, such as railwaymen and farmers, were to be given leave and even discharged, was rapidly approaching, and the actual "Stand Down", as is told elsewhere, came with an almost staggering suddenness.

18

## COASTAL DEFENCE REINFORCEMENT

Finally several units of Northamptonshire Home Guard now undertook rehearsals of coastal defence duty.

This duty had had its origin in the autumn of 1943 when the Home Forces Command decided that coastal reinforcement companies of the Home Guard were to be formed for the purpose of proceeding at once to the coast in the event of enemy landings by sea or air to reinforce the Regular Army and Home Guard units there.

These companies were to be self-contained units, complete with weapons, ammunition, cooking equipment, mess tins, water bottles, blankets and ground sheets, etc., and would come under the command of the local commander.

A Company of the 12th Battalion, commanded by Major Frank Jordan, was among those selected to represent the Northants Sub-District and it was decided that No. 2 Platoon from Kingsthorpe and No. 3 Platoon from Kingsley should comprise the new company (having four platoons, Nos. 14, 15, 16 and 17 with A Co. H.Q.) to be known as "D" (Reinforcement) Company.

Major Jordan was selected as its commander, with Capt. Beeston as his second-in-command.

Lt. Holland, Platoon Officer of No. 3 Platoon, was made Company Intelligence and Security Officer, and Lts. Howard and Griffin, Platoon Officers of No. 2 Platoon, were made Company Weapon Training Officer and O.C. No. 15 Platoon respectively. No. 14 was put in command of Lt. Wright, No. 16 of Lt. Lansman and No. 17 of Lt. Parker, with 2nd Lts. Bayley, Freeman and Cox as their platoon officers. 2nd Lt. Horwood was made Platoon Officer of No. 15 Platoon and 2nd Lt. Sharman became Company Ammunition Officer.

Platoon Sgt. Saunders of No. 3 Platoon was made Company Sergeant-Major.

The total maximum strength of the new company was put at 220, and it came into being on 15 December 1943 with a strength of twelve officers and 188 other ranks.

Accommodation was found for Co. H.Q. in a rather dilapidated old house at Kingsthorpe, known as "The Rosary", whose only advantage appeared to be that it was in close proximity to two houses of refreshment.

Everybody set to with a will, and soon the Company was hard at work training itself for its new role.

### HOLIDAY CAMP BILLET

Then, at last, came the day when it was necessary to send the whole of the Company to the coast for a full-dress rehearsal, and this was arranged for Easter week-end 1944.

If anyone thinks it is child's play to transport about 200 officers, N.C.O.s and men, together with their kit, some 140 miles to the coast, house and feed them while they are there, and bring them back, he is sadly mistaken.

Accommodation with cooking facilities was found in a former holiday camp at Hopton, between Gorleston and Lowestoft, right on the cliff edge in close proximity to the usual barbed wire and many coastal and ack-ack guns of various sizes.

Arriving on Easter Sunday afternoon the whole company went to their allotted positions in the defence area and became thoroughly acquainted with their terrain, which was singularly reminiscent of Holland, even to windmills. After tea and a break they then sallied forth again on night operations.

It was a lovely moonlight night, but cold, and in spite of their tiredness the men did their job well. When it was all over they once more returned to Hopton in the early hours to hot soup and to sleep the sleep of exhaustion on hard boards.

Easter Monday morning was spent on the cliff edge in carrying out Sten and Lewis gun firing practice and then, after a well-earned "rest", the return journey was made, Northampton being reached just before midnight.

### TRIAL WITH LANDING BARGES

Another report furnished by the O.C. of Kettering's Reinforcement Company tells of some lively moments at Bradwell-on-Sea.

Here is an excerpt:

On Wednesday at 0930 hours myself and nine men went by truck to Sandgate about eight miles away for what I was told was to be a trip on some landing barges.

There were seventy or eighty Home Guards there from different units and we embarked on five of these landing craft. We were taken out and were told we were to make a landing on Osea Island, which we did all right but not without getting a soaking as I fell all my length in the sea.

That was not enough, for we had to embark again and make another landing at another point. We landed dry this time, but some of the boats didn't and men had to wade ashore chest high in the water.

There were plenty of doodle-bugs (i.e., German fly-bombs) about every night and at 0130 hours on the Friday morning we saw one brought down in the sea while on patrol. On Thursday morning at 1000 hours we had a pay parade at which all men received £1 each.

I never heard any grumbling, but I think most of the men would have liked another week. We left Bradwell-on-Sea at 1515 hours on Sunday after handing over to the 14th Battalion Northants Home Guard and arrived back at Desborough at 2115 hours.

### N.C.O.s WENT AS PRIVATES

Further evidence of the popularity of these camps is contained in the records of

Although in the days of his victories Hitler had derided Britain's Home Guard, when the tide turned he hastily contrived to form a German Home Guard which was known as the Volkssturm—the People's Army. Here is a typical section on parade under a regular army instructor. The motley variety of uniforms are significant of the multiplicity of corps in Germany at that time whose members now found it necessary to unite as one force. Despite the fact that all were over 50 and armed only with rifles they proved a nuisance to the advancing Allies, particularly among the "rabbit warrens" of ruined cities.

the 4th (Kettering Town) Battalion which provided detachments to relieve the Essex Regiment on coast patrol.

"All ranks," says the record, "were so keen to go that warrant officers and N.C.O.s temporarily shed their badges of rank and went as private soldiers!"

The 4th's Reinforcement Company was provided for coastal defence and a sector of Great Yarmouth was allotted to the Battalion.

Throughout this tense period flashes from the battalion areas combined to reflect the prevailing high morale and enthusiasm of all ranks.

Here are a few such items recalled at random:

## A MODEL INDOOR RANGE

As an example of Home Guard resource and inventiveness the indoor rifle range

A splendid indoor range at Ector Hall, which was made by No. 6 (Ecton Platoon), (Lt. A. Barker) of C Company (Major J. C. Richardson) of the 8th (Wellingborough District) Battalion. Most of the cost of the range was borne by Lt.-Col. H. G. Sotheby, first Commander of the Battalion.

Officers and other ranks visited the area, T.E.W.T.s were held while there, and enjoyment and keenness were so obvious throughout that other companies strove hard to be detailed to go as well.

In addition to combining in providing against any contingency on the coast, the Home Guards' defence plans on their home ground were just as carefully interlocked with all adjacent Regular units including those of the United States of America whose Air Force now had a representation in the shire of many thousands.

designed and erected by the members of No. 6 (Ecton) Platoon (Lt. A. Barker) of C Company of the 8th (Wellingborough District) Battalion was a model.

This clever piece of work was made entirely by members of this platoon, and was a marvellous piece of realism.

Fields, churches, trees and other rural scenery were included all correctly scaled and coloured, while the whole was lit by floodlight and also by "daylight" Neon lighting.

Nor was this all. By a manipulation of

wires and pulleys enemy troops would suddenly pop up from behind cover, and at different levels. It was no wonder that the Platoon developed into a "hot" body of sharpshooters.

The range was of the normal length of twenty-five yards, and was erected and used in the old Riding School at Ecton Hall, lent by Lt.-Col. H. G. Sotheby, who with characteristic generosity also paid for all the lighting charges.

### 11TH BATTALION TAKES THE STAGE

No. 23 Platoon (Bugbrooke), the champion Northants Battle Platoon, were the guests of Lt.-Col. W. J. Penn (Commanding Officer of the Battalion) when they visited the Northampton Repertory Company's performance of *1066 and All That* in January 1944.

During the performance, Mr. Franklyn Davies, who was playing Richard I, wore a Home Guard armlet and "NN11" flash, and adroitly introduced "gags" referring to the achievements of No. 23 Platoon, which were made to include the Siege of Acre!

After the show the Platoon was welcomed on to the stage, where a photograph was taken including Crusaders in chain mail and Home Guardsmen in their prosaic modern battledress.

### A GUN-SITE EPISODE

The 11th Battalion were again humorously in the picture at this period when, during an evening exercise, No. 15 (Denton) Platoon (2nd Lt. R. Jacobs) had as their objective a body of A.A. troops, the A.A. Headquarters, a gun-site, and an approaching convoy. All these were gained by a right flanking attack, but the section detailed to make this attack discovered that they had to cross open ground in moonlight, and in full view of the enemy.

Accordingly three men hid under a couple of greatcoats and, imitating the shambling walk of a cow, approached the gun site. The ruse was successful for, as they got nearer they heard one of the enemy say: "What the —— is that over there?"

"Only a —— cow," came a growled reply.

The cow thereupon "mooed" and a self-satisfied voice said, "There, what did I tell you?"

There was no answer as, immediately afterwards, a bomb dispelled all illusions— together with the gun-site and its defenders!

### A FINE TRAINING SYLLABUS

There was no better-earned promotion in the whole fifteen battalions of the County than that of Lt. Frank Jordan to the rank of Major, and the command of D (Reinforcement) Company of the 12th (Northampton) Battalion to whose coastal defence rehearsal on the East Coast we have just referred. Major Jordan was one of the first volunteers in the L.D.V. in which he rapidly gained the rank of Section Sergeant, and one of his many notable pieces of work was the production of a perfect Home Guard Training Syllabus containing full programmes of every type of training, with an index, and with full cross-references to every relative Home Guard instruction, etc., a quite remarkable achievement which fully deserved the special commendation of the Sub-District Commander that it received, and one which was eagerly sought after by every commander who saw any chance of securing a copy.

### INVENTED SECRET WEAPONS?

A surprising revelation went the rounds of the Guard early in 1944 when a lance-corporal of the 4th (Kettering Town) Battalion—L./Cpl. J. W. Sharp—claimed that in December 1940 he had suggested to the War Office the use of two secret weapons which were almost identical with two later used by the enemy.

The weapons were (1) a rocket-like projectile which opened out in the air and had a canister attached to a parachute by a cable, and (2) a 12-ton rocket projectile which disintegrated the oxygen in the air over large areas, thus upsetting the carburation of aero engines.

The War Office had notified him, he said, that "it was regretted that nothing could be done" with his suggestions.

### SUBJECT OF A NATIONAL CARTOON

Another surprising revelation in the same month was of a different character but one with a national significance. It concerned the 8th (Wellingborough District) Battalion, one of whose members, it transpired, Pte. John Askham, a strapping six-footer, had been chosen by the famous cartoonist Bruce Bairnsfather as a model for a twelve-foot poster for the "Salute the Soldier" Savings Campaign then running.

Capt. Bairnsfather, it appeared, at a special parade of A Company of the 8th Battalion held at Raunds, had picked out Pte. Askham—had taken him into a nearby house, and had there immortalized him in a sketch!

No one (except the Battalion commanding officer) knew of the purpose of the parade, and when later the truth leaked out, it was a complete surprise and the source of a full sack of "chaff" for the central figure of the incident.

### THE "MEIN PAL" POSTER

While on the subject of cartoons we may recall here the widespread disgust which greeted the appearance of the official "Mein Pal" poster designed to combat absenteeism in the Home Guard.

(A fascimile of the poster appears in an accompanying illustration.)

"A crude effort" said a correspondent of this Home Guard poster which the Government later withdrew following strong protests.

The poster was short-lived, as it deserved to be, and its withdrawal drew many expressions of satisfaction both in letters to the Press and otherwise. Ran one of the former to the *Northampton Independent:* "The absentee problem is not so serious as would appear . . . we can do without the man who tries to avoid parades . . . and the man who cannot attend because of genuine national calls on his time deserves our sympathy and consideration."

### HOME GUARD A.A. REGIMENTED

With the gradual "pinning" of the Luftwaffe by the Royal Air Force and their own training perfected, the Home Guard anti-aircraftmen were now finding little to do, and only those who have known something of the deadly monotony of continuous manning of a gun-site unrelieved by action will know just what the "little to do" can mean.

The record of the Peterborough A.A. Battery confesses at this time that, although morale remained at a peak, the routine of weekly manning was beginning to tell. Those in charge of training, however, devised battle practices and basic infantry training and enthusiasm revived as the number of proficiency badges obtained slowly mounted up.

Interest was also maintained by exchanges of visits between the Cambridge and Leicester Batteries, and by the attendance at courses at the Regimental School at Chesterton. This was the regimental headquarters of Lt.-Col. E. B. Morison, T.D., R.A.

In February the Battery lost a very old and loyal member, with the death of Lt. James Woodward, who as administration clerk for the Territorial Army Association was in charge of the office.

Not too old at sixty-one to serve his country, he joined the Battery to carry on his work in the evenings, for which he received the first decoration in the Battery— a Certificate of Meritorious Service from the G.O.C.-in-Chief at A.A. Command.

March 1944 saw a further milestone for the Battery when the A.A. Home Guard were regimented and the 10th Home Guard A.A. Regiment, consisting of the batteries at Peterborough, Leicester and Cambridge, was formed. Lt.-Col. E. W. Bromige was appointed Regimental Commander.

At the same time the removal of the projector from the secret list brought the change in the name of the Battery to 101 Northants Home Guard Rocket A.A. Battery.

During the two years of co-operation with the Royal Artillery, a great effort on behalf of the Royal Artillery Prisoners of War Fund was made by Major C. R. Elwis, T.D., R.A., who, with the assistance of the Home Guard, raised over £2,000 during this period.

In particular may be mentioned the two gala nights when the revues *You've Z it* and *Watch the News* were performed at the Embassy Theatre, Peterborough.

Both revues were written and produced by Major Elwis.

### TOOK OVER FROM REGULARS

With the progress of the war demanding more and more from the Regular troops, the Regular personnel of the Battery was constantly diminished, but due to their training, the Home Guard were able to take over most of the duties and responsibilities on the site.

The Home Guard Officers serving at that time with the Battery were as follows:

Officer Commanding, Major W. A. Heighton; Capt. F. H. Martin, A. W. Ruddle, T. A. Irving, C. C. Fensome, H. Standen, H. G. Merchant, X. A. Halliday and A. Shallcross; Lts. A. N. Brand, G. Strickson, J. W. Clark, R. M. Hobbs, L. G. Bridgfoot, E. S. Slow, G. W. Keay, W. J. Launchbury, G. Fovargue, J. W. Haws, R. H. Pinder, W. E. R. Pulman, R. O. Warner, J. R. Ireland and M. C. Seago; 2nd Lts. B. S. Laxton, T. D. Ferrar, J. A. Deboo, Gratix, Falkinder, F. E. Long, H. B. Miller, W. G. James, W. Bishop, G. W. White, E. F. J. Rollins, J. R. Savage, C. J. W. Jessop and E. C. Pratt.

### NIGHT IN MINERAL WATER FACTORY

In conclusion of this mixed bag of 1944 side-lights let us add a typical "Buzz" exercise report in the diary of B Company of the 5th (Kettering District) Battalion. Three of these "Buzz" exercises were held in the East Central District as final tests of preparedness for D-Day. In one of these exercises in the Peterborough sector, B Company Battle Platoon made a six-mile approach across unknown country at night, capturing a guard on a railway bridge without a sound. Afterwards they lay up for the night in a mineral water factory!

For the final attack the way was barred by a wide stream four feet deep appearing on the map as a ditch! The Platoon Commander wanted to wade across but was stopped by an umpire as the men had a thirty-mile ride home afterwards. Feelings ran so high between attackers and defenders that fisticuffs nearly ensued. However, the first and *last* rum issued to B Company served to smooth matters and all ended happily.

## Chapter XXXI

## NO D-DAY MUSTER

FROM all of these diverse sidelights on the Home Guard life at this stage one may readily deduce the high sense of self-sufficiency which now animated the force.

They had received a high charge—nothing less than the sole responsibility for the defence of Britain—they were ready for anything and felt that they enjoyed the complete confidence of the highest commands.

Consequently, it was to the intense disappointment, not to say chagrin, of the entire personnel that there was no muster of the force either before or during the operation which resulted in the invasion of Normandy.

However, muster or no, they just grinned resignedly and continued to polish their preparedness. This "polishing" business was not merely a matter of practising well-mastered lessons but involved yet another change of operational role.

### BACK TO "MOBILE"

Writes Lt.-Col. Barnes of this period:

In 1944 the chances of invasion were much less than in the past. The Field Army had turned from its defensive role to a contemplated offensive overseas. When this came about the Home Guard had to assume the major responsibility of protecting these islands against seaborne and airborne raids. This was all that the enemy could hope to attempt at this stage; the landing of groups of men with the object of sabotage and destruction, and with the intention of dislocating communications and attacking vulnerable points. Looking back, it was astonishing that the enemy failed to interfere with the preparation and mounting of such a difficult operation as D-Day.

To meet this possible menace the role of the Home Guard was again altered and the principle of mobility extended. With the exception of a keep company all companies had to be prepared to take on a mobile role. During the weeks before D-Day, railways, roads, and vulnerable points were patrolled and guarded during the nights to prevent any sabotage of communications so necessary for the successful invasion of the Continent.

### INVASION OPERATIONAL ORDERS

Striking reflections of this preparedness, more or less typical of all battalions, were provided by the operational instructions issued to the 9th (Brixworth) Battalion and the 1st (Peterborough) Battalion. The 9th's battle headquarters were at Brixworth with administrative headquarters at 47 Overstone Road, Northampton. The alternative battle headquarters of the Battalion were at the Red Lion, Brixworth.

Battalion reserves were the East Haddon, Spratton, and Boughton platoons.

Company reserves were: A Company, Guilsborough Platoon; B Company, the Brixworth Platoon; C Company, the Brington Platoon; and D Company, the Moulton Platoon.

There were four defended places— Brixworth, the Northampton-Market Harborough road, 1 Platoon of B Company. Harlestone, the Rugby road, 1 Platoon of C Company; Chapel Brampton, Welford road, 1 Platoon of C Company and Moulton, the Kettering road, 1 Platoon of D Company.

### IN THE VULNERABLE NORTH

The Invasion Operational Orders issued to the 1st (Peterborough) Battalion provided for a strongly defended "keep" established on the north side of the Nene, covered by defended localities which were sited so that they could at all times give mutual fire support.

The "keep", which was manned by B Company under Major G. E. Hann, covered the crossings of the Nene by the main road and railway bridges, and included various important points, notably the electricity works.

In the defended localities, No. 1 A Company, under Major N. J. C. Donald, covered the approach to the keep, by the Market Place, Bridge Street, St. Mary Street, Vineyard Road, and the river meadows east of the omnibus station.

No. 2 D Company, under Major C. Taylor, D.C.M., were responsible for covering the approach to the keep by Crescent Bridge, River Lane, the line of the L.N.E. railway, and Cowgate.

No. 4 Company, under Major A. E. Stewart, covered the south end of Boroughbury, Westgate, Queen Street, and Wood Street.

C Company also furnished the garrison for No. 5 defended locality.

1 Platoon of D Company manned No. 3 defended locality and among other duties was responsible for holding the Spital road block in OUTPOST.

E Company, under Major F. H. Plaistowe, formed the garrison of No. 6 defended locality. Battalion headquarters was established at the new Town Hall.

### HAD THE NAZIS ARRIVED

Had reprisals or invasion in any large form materialized, the companies would have found themselves extremely busy, for there were numerous defended outposts, rail blocks, and road blocks to be manned, as it was the intention of the 1st Battalion to deny all communications to the enemy, to keep open for our own troops the main and alternative routes, and to hold the defended localities to the last man.

A garrison Mobile Reserve, consisting of Headquarters Company, with headquarters at the offices of Fox & Vergette, Priestgate, was formed to provide standing recce and fighting patrols intended to operate outside the areas of the defended localities.

The estimated strength on "mustering" was 1,200 of all ranks, and there can be no doubt that had the Nazis arrived they would have had a very hot reception in the ancient city.

The 10th (Daventry) Battalion, during this period, had its own special difficulties, owing to the scattered nature of the area.

In addition, there were the grave responsibilities for guarding the British Broadcasting Corporation's station at Daventry, and the two long tunnels on the L.M.S. main line.

### A VENERABLE PLATOON

During the pre-D-Day period there was no post throughout the Northamptonshire Home Guard area that was more alertly manned than the alarm post at the battalion headquarters of the 4th (Kettering Town) Battalion, located at the Rectory, Kettering.

It is a remarkable fact that this post was on duty throughout the whole life of the Battalion.

It was manned for twenty-four hours EVERY DAY from May 1940 to the "stand down".

The personnel consisted entirely of elderly volunteers, aged from sixty to seventy years—"old warriors", who formed a special platoon of the Headquarters Company.

Higher Command often congratulated the Battalion on the fact that the headquarters telephones were always manned night and day.

The Commanding Officer (Lt.-Col. A. Russell) wanted to cancel this arrangement soon after D-Day, but these old fellows begged to stay on until the job was finished.

The spirit of the old men was wonderful —on one occasion they received a message from the Northamptonshire Sub-District in cipher. It was only a routine message, but the excitement at the alarm post nearly resulted in the battalion being ordered to stand to!

## A ROYAL PARADE

For all the extra demands of 1944 the Guard found time to mount a creditable number of church and ceremonial parades whenever an occasion warranted.

One of the most impressive of these was that held by the 3rd (Oundle) Battalion on Sunday, 9 April 1944, when the occasion was honoured by the presence of the Duke and Duchess of Gloucester.

The Bishop of Peterborough (Dr. Claude Blagden) preached a stirring sermon and paid a fine tribute to the Home Guard. "The darkest days are now behind us," he said, "but we must never forget them—for out of them came the Home Guard . . . who had little equipment but who were armed with a noble enthusiasm."

H.R.H. the Duke of Gloucester.

After the service the Duke of Gloucester took the salute at a march past, and from the church porch the Duchess distributed prizes and certificates.

The parade was under the command of Lt.-Col. F. R. Berridge (Commanding Officer), and the band of the Northamptonshire Regiment was in attendance.

## "HUSH-HUSH" EXPERIMENTS

Some of the most "hush-hush" operations carried out in the whole of the Northamptonshire Area throughout the period of the force's existence were identified with the 13th (Towcester) Battalion during the pre-invasion period.

They consisted of experiments with radio-controlled explosives, following discussions between Lt. V. W. G. Chitty, the Battalion Signals Officer, and Capt. Rees, R.E., who was then stationed at Whittlebury.

Capt. Rees was interested in avoiding the very heavy casualty rate among Royal Engineers personnel during the laying of demolition charges and consequent reeling out of detonating cable during Commando raids on the Continent.

A method was worked out with Lt. Chitty, who was engaged on research work in the vicinity, whereby any explosive charge could be laid and then detonated at any convenient time by radio transmission from a land station or from aircraft.

Lt. Chitty had the necessary facilities to construct the apparatus, and the first experiments were conducted on the battalion range with the apparatus connected to, but not attached to, a small 1-lb. charge. The charge could be easily set off from a moving vehicle with a No. 18 set, from a distance of a mile or two.

Following this success, with very scratch apparatus, better and smaller models were built, incorporating coding devices to prevent accidental or intentional detonation by enemy or unauthorized transmissions. At this stage the Royal Air Force at Silverstone were contacted, and they very willingly agreed to assist in the experiments.

Various tests were made using aircraft flying at varied heights with great success.

Capt. Rees then suggested that a demonstration should be made, and this was done on the occasion of a visit of the General Officer Commanding Eastern Command to the Royal Engineers at Whittlebury.

Various charges were set off from aircraft and trucks and considerable interest was aroused. The War Office and the Ministry of Supply were then contacted and the results handed over to them. After more tests with the co-operation of the Royal Air Force, a small "box of tricks" was produced which could set off any charge buried underground, the control being from an aircraft flying high, or any powerful station hundreds of miles away.

These results were only obtained through the full co-operation of the Royal Engineers and the Royal Air Force at Silverstone—particularly Capt. Rees and Sqdn.-Ldr. Peel, who gave much valuable assistance.

### "HOME GUARD MUST CARRY ON"

How D-Day eventually came on 6 June 1944 and all that followed immediately afterwards is world history, but the Home Guard earned many tributes for the vigilant stand-by throughout the vital period.

One of the warmest came from the Commander-in-Chief Home Forces, Gen. Sir E. Franklyn, K.C.B., D.S.O., M.C., while visiting the 13th (Towcester) Battalion on Sunday, 25 June 1944.

The General saw incendiary bomb training on Tiffield range carried out by Lt. Moore, and then went to Blisworth and saw Spigot mortar indirect fire and platoon coming in to attack, carried out by B Company.

The Commander-in-Chief later expressed his appreciation to the Battalion.

The Home Guard, he said, had done and was doing a grand job of work. Their efficiency had enabled thousands of Regular troops to be sent abroad who would otherwise have had to remain in this country.

He considered that the likelihood of invasion was now extremely remote, and he doubted very much whether the enemy would now endeavour to land paratroops in this country, but one never knew what surprises he had in store, and therefore *the Home Guard must carry on.* They must not relax and say that now the Allies had landed in France the Home Guard could sit back and rest.

*The Home Guard must not die by inches.*

At the earliest possible date when he could do so he would give the order for the Home Guard to "stand down", but the end of the war would not necessarily mean the end of the Home Guard—it would continue in some form or other, but whether it would continue under the same name he could not say, but it would continue.

He asked all ranks to carry on as usual until he issued his "stand down" order so that it could be said that the Home Guard did its job efficiently to the end.

As events proved, the Home Guard did not continue as the Commander-in-Chief had so emphatically predicted, but it certainly "did its job efficiently to the end".

### "FOOLISH TO TAKE SLIGHTEST RISK"

A second tribute cast in similar terms was contained in a letter signed by Lt.-Gen. Kenneth Anderson, Commander-in-Chief Eastern Command, and circulated on 3 July 1944. Here is the text.

Now that Overlord has been successfully launched, I want to thank all ranks of the Home Guard for the really splendid way in which they rose to the calls made on them, and indeed are even now meeting the duties which are still required. . . .

The Home Guard can feel they have been, and still are, taking an important, though indirect part, in the invasion of Europe; though they were not put to the test of actual battle.

It is astonishing that the enemy failed to interfere with the mounting of such a difficult operation. It is unlikely that he will now attempt to do so, and raids or invasion are improbable. Some people, therefore, may think that the Home Guard is no longer required, and doubt whether it can serve any useful purpose in future.

I agree the time will come when the Home Guard (as at present constituted) will no longer be needed to defend this country. This may coincide with the end of the war in Europe or maybe earlier. The decision will rest with the War Cabinet. But it has not come yet, and in the meantime it would be foolish to take the slightest risk. So while there remains even a small danger, the Home Guard continues to be necessary for the defence of the country. Its continued presence acts as a potent insurance against the risk of raids. Therefore the Home Guard must continue its efforts to maintain and increase its efficiency.

I promise you there will be no delay in letting the Home Guard know when they are no longer required; but until then—carry on.

The enemy refrained from raids or invasion as Gen. Anderson had said, but they "stepped up" the bombardment of England by fly- and rocket-bombs.

### FLY-BOMB HITS CREATON

One of the former provided a surprise and busy diversion for units of the 9th (Brixworth) Battalion when, at 2252 hours on 22 July 1944, it passed over the east of

Major-General E. C. Hayes, G.O.C. East Central District, watching a wall-scaling demonstration by a section of Battle Platoon, H.Q. Co. of the 4th (Kettering) Battalion.

Northampton, "cut out" almost immediately afterwards, and then glided earthwards to land with a terrific explosion in the village of Creaton, and to spread havoc over a wide area around the crater.

Within three minutes of the explosion—even before the smoke had vanished or the debris had ceased to fall—Platoon-Sgt. J. J. Griffin, of No. 2 (Spratton) Platoon, reported in person to platoon headquarters, and then rushed to telephone his company commander.

The O.C. Company received the message at 2305 hours, but only partially, for the line was cut off before full details could be given.

In the meantime, another member of the Platoon (L.-Cpl. Adams) had reported to platoon headquarters at 2300 hours—eight minutes from the time the flying bomb had landed. This was prompt work.

Lt. E. Copson, Sgt. Griffin, and L.-Cpl. Adams then proceeded to the site at 2310 hours. Sgt. Griffin located the crater and remained on guard with L.-Cpl. Adams, while Lt. Copson returned to Spratton to telephone further information to his company commander. Unfortunately, this telephone was out of order!

At Cottesbrooke, L.-Cpl. Roy and Pte. Brown, of No. 3 Platoon, hastily got into uniform and were also on the scene almost immediately.

At 2305 hours (it will be noted that speedy action was the keynote throughout these Home Guard activities) Lt. D. S. Norman (A Company Intelligence Officer and also an air raid warden) arrived at Creaton, and managed to get a message through to the County A.R.P. Control before the line went dead.

Major A. H. Jackson, commanding A Company, arrived at Creaton at 2330 hours, after vain attempts to call Northampton telephone exchange with a view to contacting battalion headquarters. It was not until approximately 2400 hours that he managed to contact the Northamptonshire County Police and arranged for guards to be mounted on the site. These guards were detailed from Nos. 1, 2, and 3 Platoons, and were maintained until 2000 hours on 23 July.

The initiative displayed on this occasion earned the praise of the County Emergency Committee, and also that of the Chief Constable of Northamptonshire.

The officer commanding No. 4 Sector also added his appreciation in a letter to the commanding officer of the 9th, in which he said: "It is very gratifying to read that the Civil Defence authorities have meted out such unstinting praise to your battalion."

Happily, the bomb caused neither Home Guard nor civilian casualties.

### NOW CAME RELAXATION

With the successful progress of the Normandy invasion, the Home Guard shared in the national uplift of spirit and relief that not only had an anxious period ended but that, after many weary months, the first big step on the "road home" had been taken, and gloriously taken.

Thus it was hardly surprising that all Home Guard activities were now charged with rather less austerity than had prevailed for some months previously. The Guard wanted to "let themselves go" a little, and they did so whenever opportunity offered.

Evidence of this spirit was richly provided by an 8th Battalion tournament and by a memorable officers' camp of the 9th (Brixworth) Battalion.

The tournament arranged by the 8th Battalion on 23 September 1944 on the Sports Ground, The Hayway, Rushden, gave the numerous spectators a series of thrills they must have remembered long afterwards.

Among these were such diversified items as a competition for the quickest tent-pitching (won by G Company), bayonet training (won by B Company), marching by compass—the men in sacks to simulate night marching (won by C Company), first aid competition (won by E Company), a cooking competition (including making a fire and cooking a jam roll) (won by F Company), and a Spigot mortar competition which was won by C Company.

The judges were Cols. R. P. A. Helps, O.B.E., M.C., and J. D. Fulton, D.S.O., M.C., and Lt.-Col. V. H. Sykes. Prizes were presented by Col. J. D. Wyatt, M.C.

All of the camps of the 9th, as we have previously noted, were stimulating events, but this one was monumentally so.

The camp was held at Moulton Grange on 29 and 30 July 1944, and not only was it a huge success in point of training and inter-company liaison, but it was also honoured by the presence of Major-Gen. Sir Syme Drew, Director-General of the Home Guard, and the Sub-District Commander.

The General addressed all officers who were also individually introduced to him.

Part of Saturday evening was devoted to an engrossing description of the Normandy front by Major Trofimoff of the Royal Artillery, Light A.A., who had just returned to this country, and a T.E.W.T., consisting of a series of the trickiest problems that battalion headquarters could think up, occupied most of the following Sunday morning.

The commissariat arrangements were in the hands of Capt. A. Chappell, and were voted excellent, although, as somebody remarked, roast beef and Yorkshire pudding were found to be hardly the ideal diet for battle squads prior to demonstrating attack!

## COL. SHORT'S DEPARTURE

The end of July 1944 saw the departure from the Sub-District command of Col. J. L. Short almost exactly two years after he arrived.

He left to prepare for a command in the British Army of Occupation, to which, following the occupation of Germany, he was subsequently appointed.

For the last few months of its existence the Northamptonshire Home Guard had a Northampton man in the Sub-District command.

He was Col. J. D. Wyatt, M.C., who had joined the Northamptonshire Regiment in August 1914 and had gone to France with them in the same year to engage in the 1914–18 war.

Thereafter, he had put up a splendid record of service, and in view of his local association, it was unfortunate that his command of the "part-time army" of his home shire should have come at a time when the momentum of the force had almost ceased and there was no point in his devoting to it anything more than formal attention.

## A NINE-HOURS' RIFLE MEETING

Owing to the shortness of its life only sparse reference has been possible in these pages to the 15th (Northampton) Battalion, but this fact is no measure of the high reputation this battalion gained alike for its efficiency and keenness.

Thus, it is gratifying now to record, from the pen of the Battalion's own popular Commanding Officer (Lt.-Col. N. P. Andrews), a summary of the "high-lights" of the 15th's career. Here it is:

Probably the most outstanding event in the Battalion's history was the rifle meeting held at Brington Rifle Range on Thursday, 10 August 1944.

Those who participated will never forget it —the splendid organization of the competitions which went on for nine hours on end—the excellent team of butt markers provided by our friends of A Company of the 12th Battalion, the enjoyment of the wives and families, the smooth transport arrangements, all of these and many other details the work of Capts. Hubbard and Pack and the rest of the permanent staff.

Particularly should the battalion clerk, Miss Lack, be mentioned, for her untiring efforts on the memorable day.

Several most interesting inter-platoon miniature rifle competitions helped to maintain interest during the two winters of our existence, and added to these were the tests for the proficiency badge undertaken by a large proportion of the members of the Battalion.

When conditions were issued governing the award of the "marksman" badge, there was a keen desire on the part of many members to qualify for it, and the results were highly satisfactory.

Battle inoculation was another form of training always enjoyed.

**FORTY-NINE UMPIRES PROVIDED**

Very shortly after Major-Gen. Hayes took command of the East Central District a series of full-scale exercises were "laid on", and these were designed to test, under conditions as realistic as possible, the functioning of all formations from Sub-District level downwards.

In the first of these it was the Northampton Sub-District to be tested, and the 15th Battalion was called in to find no fewer than forty-nine umpires who were widely distributed over the "battle-field".

Beginning on the evening of Saturday, this exercise lasted throughout the night (a very bad one for weather) and the endurance of the troops taking part was severely tested.

This was also true of the umpires, who had a very difficult task to perform in checking all reports, observing the movement of troops, anticipating and moving to the possible scene of fighting, and rendering the reports very shortly after the "cease fire".

In all but the final "Buzz" Exercise, the Battalion provided a full complement of umpires, who travelled far and wide over the neighbouring counties.

In Buzz 3, one platoon of the Battalion was chosen to provide the "enemy" when the Hertfordshire Sub-District was tested.

When the invasion of the European continent was imminent the Battalion was closely concerned with the guarding of railway communications, and the battalion signals section laid a system of telephone lines connecting battalion headquarters with all important points, including a position as far away as Hunsbury Hill.

# Chapter XXXII

## THE STAND DOWN

IF, as we have indicated, the Home Guards' spirits rose after D-Day, they simply vaulted when it was announced on 16 September 1944 that compulsory parades were to cease.

The "old guard" of the Guard had never minded their parades and did not mind their continuance for as long as they were held to be necessary, but "compulsion" was anathema to them and their resentment of it throughout had only been lightly balanced by their recognition of its justice.

One magnificent parade at this period which needed no compulsion to attract a full muster was that mounted by the 1st (Peterborough City) Battalion in honour of Battle of Britain Sunday—an occasion that the Home Guard always delighted to salute, feeling that, even if in a far less glorious role, they were intimate comrades-in-arms with Britain's heroic young knights of the air in that both forces had the common responsibility of guarding the motherland.

The 1st Battalion attended service at Peterborough Cathedral and then marched past the Mayor to the King's School playing-fields where they were addressed by their Commanding Officer (Lt.-Col. R. J. C. Crowden, M.C.) before dismissal.

The spirit which had brought the Home Guard into being, he said, still permeated all ranks, and would not lapse, even though their services might not be called on to such a large extent in future. Service in the Home Guard was a great asset to citizenship . . . petty barriers of class distinction had been swept away.

The Home Guard had achieved ninety-five per cent of its service to the country. Although they had not met the enemy face to face they had several victories to their credit, and could feel that they had taken part with the Field Force in the victories on the Continent, and in the prevention of invasion earlier on.

One victory was when the Nazis thought twice about invading, owing to the strength of the Home Guard, and another was that the defence of the country could be safely entrusted to the Home Guard, which enabled the Field Force to undergo strenuous and uninterrupted training.

Members of the Home Guard might well be proud of what they had done . . . with a devotion to duty beyond praise. Now they were having a well-earned rest and, in future, action would be more on the social side. . . .

The Colonel concluded with a feeling expression of his high admiration of and thanks for their complete and splendid loyalty, to their battalion and to him.

### FIRST RUMOURS OF STAND DOWN

Although, once more, another of the inevitable crop of rumours now arose that the Home Guard was to be continued indefinitely on a reserve basis, or that its dispersal would not take place until, at least, peace was finally declared—this was generally desired—there came with the crop another report that Stand Down was imminent.

This report was inspired by the effects of a War Office letter to commands in the following terms:

During the last months the Home Guard has performed a vital service by enabling the Regular forces to leave this country and by providing protection against the danger of potential enemy interference. This danger has not yet disappeared.

The Home Guard has also given the most valuable service in assisting the Civil Defence organizations and the public in connection with the attack by flying missiles. This danger also has not yet passed.

It is, therefore, necessary that the Home Guard should continue to take the place of the Regular forces until, in the opinion of His Majesty's Government, all dangers are passed.

The success of the campaign on the Continent points to the likelihood of this date being near, and it is therefore necessary to have the machinery ready for the standing down of the Home Guard in order that the detail can be worked out and thus result in smooth and quick operation when the time comes.

The outline plan for the standing down has been prepared and will shortly be issued to enable formations, units, and Territorial Army Associations to draw up detailed plans ready for use when the actual orders are received.

## FOUR AND A HALF YEARS' SERVICE

"The Day" came, in fact, on 3 December 1944.

The Home Guard which, as the Local Defence Volunteers in 1940, thronged the police stations of the British Isles with an enthusiasm which has scarcely a parallel in all our rough island story, "stood down" after standing up to criticism (often uninformed), to ridicule, and to the puerile gibes of alleged comedians, for over four and a half long and toilsome years.

Their work was finished—and they laid their arms down quietly and returned almost unsung, if not unhonoured, to their various civilian occupations.

Their years of service—ungrudgingly given, often at the expense of much-needed leisure, and even of health and life itself—had been packed with interest, but intermingled with a sense of frustration that does not usually assail the Serviceman in war-time.

The thrill of battle was denied them to the last. With a few rare exceptions the opportunity to engage the enemy never came their way—although for years all their training and effort had been directed to that end.

Save for those few exceptions they never even saw a single enemy, and even in the dark days of 1940, and yet more exciting days before D-Day in 1944, they were not permitted by fate to take the field. The dreams they had dreamed, the hopes they had nursed, and the longing for some definite action which had marched with them through the years, were now dissolved and spent.

So, as the Allied armies rolled across Europe, and the Luftwaffe folded its wings, their arms were racked away.

## NOTHING MORE TO DO

It was only natural that the tenseness which had braced the network of the Home Guard now suddenly slackened, and the force realized, not without a little bitterness, that there was nothing more for it to do.

And yet how much it had done! There is no yardstick in all history by which the work of the Home Guard can ever be measured.

There are no words adequate to describe those early days, when men in armlets, and armed with domestic weapons, were ready to match their naked courage against an onslaught of fire and steel.

There is nothing in all the great stories of the world which remotely resembles the story of that fantastic force which thronged the police stations in 1940, and which included men in all walks of life and of all years, from callow youth to patriarchal age.

Posterity, which is often forgetful, should never be allowed to forget this.

For four and a half years some two million men sweated and trained in their leisure hours, surrendering cheerfully the ease and enjoyment which should have come after daily toil, and in many instances deliberately ignoring the toll of the years, with a self-sacrifice which can never be computed.

Most of their work had been done in hidden places, for they never courted popularity. Hence it was usually only the birds and the wild things of the woods that saw them in operation, save when, for a brief hour or two, they paraded through some city street or passed with cheerful jests along some village highway.

### A GREY DAY

The Stand Down was no glorious ceremony, such as it might, and should, have been. It was held, for one thing, in typical Home Guard weather, at the beginning of a wet, grey December that only seemed to throw the melancholy nature of the occasion into deeper and darker relief.

In spite of the fact that the musters generally were good, there was, it must be confessed, a prevailing listlessness which no showers of thanks from officials and officers could lift from the shoulders of those on parade.

The Home Guard had been "born" in a virile hour. It "died" quietly on a dark December Sunday, with only a few "mourners" present.

It died, in fact, while the rest of the armed forces were striving valiantly on the Continent, and the men of the Home Guard watched it die while most of them

longed for it to live until the hour when victory should arrive.

It was true that the work they had volunteered to do had been done. It was true that there was no longer any need for vigilance at home, but they *did* want to stay in uniform until the end. Actually they slipped out, as someone said, by a side door.

It was a bitter reflection. More bitter yet was the knowledge that they had not even been mustered. And, added to this douche, was the fact that they would now be out of harness when the guns ceased in Europe.

Yet there was one compensation which they took to their homes after the last salute.

They could look back—most of them—to over four and a half years of the finest comradeship that was ever inspired among any body of Britons in the history of their race.

Thousands of new and intimate friendships were made and kept—friendships forged by a shining bond of mutual service and mutual sacrifice for a common end.

### THE ROYAL STAND-DOWN MESSAGE

Space precludes reproduction of more than a selection of the orders and messages of appreciation which accompanied the Stand Down. One from the King had been issued some weeks previously. It came as a special Army Order from the War Office and ran as follows:

For more than four years you have borne a heavy burden. Most of you have been engaged for long hours in work necessary to the prosecution of the war or to maintaining the healthful life of the Nation; and you have given a great portion of the time which should have been your own to learning the skilled work of a soldier. By this patient, ungrudging effort you have built and maintained a force able to play an essential part in the defence of our threatened soil and liberty.

I have long wished to see you relieved of this burden; but it would have been a betrayal of all we owe to our fathers and our sons if any step had been taken which might have imperilled our country's safety. Till very recently a slackening of our defences might have encouraged the enemy to launch a desperate blow which could grievously have damaged us and weakened the power of our assault. Now, at last, the splendid resolution and endurance of the Allied Armies have thrust back that danger from our coasts. At last I can say you have fulfilled your charge.

The Home Guard has reached the end of its long tour of duty under arms. But I know that your devotion to our land, your comradeship, your power to work your hardest at the end of the longest day, will discover new outlets for patriotic service in time of peace.

History will say that your share in the greatest of all our struggles for freedom was a vitally important one. You have given your service without thought of reward. You have earned in full measure your Country's gratitude.

GEORGE R.I.
Colonel-in-Chief.

**AND A ROYAL BROADCAST**

On the Stand-Down Day itself His Majesty followed this up with a broadcast address to the Guard.

Here is a summary of its text:

Four years ago, in May 1940, our country was in mortal danger. The most powerful army the world had ever seen had forced its way to within a few miles of our coast. From day to day we were threatened with invasion. In those days our army had been gravely weakened.

A call went out for men to enrol themselves in a new citizen army—the Local Defence Volunteers—ready to use what weapons could be found to stand against the invader in every village and town.

Throughout Britain and Northern Ireland the nation answered that summons, as free men always will answer when freedom is in danger. From fields and hills, from factories and mills, from shops and offices, men of every age and every calling came forward to train themselves for battle. . . . In July 1940 the Local Defence Volunteers became the Home Guard. During those four years of continuing anxiety that civilian army grew in strength under the competent administration of the Territorial Army Associations, it soon became a well-equipped and capable force, able to take over many duties from the Regular soldiers preparing to go overseas.

I believe it is the voluntary spirit which has always made the Home Guard so splendid and so powerful a comradeship of arms.

The hope that this comradeship will long endure was strong in me this afternoon while many thousands of you marched past me in one of the most memorable and impressive parades I have ever seen.

. . . Your service in the Home Guard has not been easy . . . some of you have stood for many hours on the gun-sites in desolate fields and on wind-swept beaches. Many of you, after a long and hard day's work, scarcely had time for food before you changed into uniform for the evening parade. . . .

It was well known to the enemy that if he came to any part of our land he would meet determined opposition at every point in his advance from men who had good weapons, and better still, knew how to use them. In that way the existence of the Home Guard helped much to ward off the danger of invasion. . . .

As anti-aircraft and coastal gunners, as sentries at V.P.s, as units for dealing with unexploded bombs, and in many other ways the Home Guard have played a full part in the defence of their country.

Many will remember with special gratitude the unsparing help given to the Civil Defence services in days and nights of terror and destruction.

But you have gained something for yourselves. You have discovered in yourselves new capabilities. You have found how men from all kinds of homes and many different occupations, can work together in a great cause and how happy they can be with each other.

That is a memory and a knowledge which may help us all in the many peace-time problems that we shall have to tackle before long.

I am very proud of what the Home Guard have done and I give my heartfelt thanks to you all.

Officers, non-commissioned officers, and men, you have served your country with a steadfast devotion. I know your country will not forget that service.

### "VERY SPECIAL CONTRIBUTION"

A special Stand-down Order of the Day to the Home Guard was also issued by Gen. Sir Harold E. Franklyn, K.C.B., D.S.O., M.C., Commander-in-Chief Home Forces.

During the past few years [said the General] I have had many opportunities of seeing the Home Guard in most parts of the country, including Northern Ireland. A high standard of efficiency has been reached, which has been possible only by the keenness and devotion to duty of all ranks. I would like to emphasize the very special contribution of those who volunteered in 1940 and whose enthusiasm has never flagged since then; they have been the backbone of their units.

The Home Guard came into being at a time of acute crisis in our history, and for over four years has stood prepared to repel any invader of our shores. The reliance that has been placed on you during these years has been abundantly justified and it has enabled our Regular troops to go overseas in sufficient numbers to give battle to the enemy, with the magnificent results that we have seen.

And now as to the future. I hope that Home Guardsmen will take every opportunity of preserving the friendships and associations that you have formed during the past years. You can continue to be a real source of stability and strength to the country during what may be difficult years ahead. I hope also

that you will do all in your power to help the Cadets, even if only by encouragement. Here is a way by which you can continue to render valuable service for many years to come.

I am very proud to have had the Home Guard under my command. I have enjoyed meeting and speaking to thousands of you. Now you can stand down with every right to feel that you have done your duty and contributed very materially to victory.

The best of luck to every one of you.

Well done indeed the Home Guard.

### GUARANTEED HOME SHORES' DEFENCE

A farewell message that was received with particularly warm appreciation was that from the colonel of the Northamptonshire Regiment.

Major.-Gen. G. St. G. Robinson wrote:

The time has come for the final "stand down" of the Home Guard, and I therefore wish to send to you a message of thanks and goodwill on behalf of all ranks of the Northamptonshire Regiment.

Whilst the battalions of your county regiment have been away fighting the enemy in Africa, in Italy, in the Balkans, and in Burma, you, our comrades of the Home Guard, have guaranteed the defence of our home shores as a firm base.

I hope that the spirit of service and comradeship, which has been such a marked feature of the Home Guard, will be kept up and preserved for the future of our country.

Good-bye and good luck.

### TRIBUTES TO M.O.s

Finally, there should be recorded a special message sent to all battalion medical officers by Col. M. Wilson, East Central District A.D.M.S., through Lt.-Col. L. D. B. Cogan (Northants Sub-District Medical Adviser).

Col. Wilson wrote:

I would be grateful if you could convey to all your Home Guard medical officers my sincere thanks for the very efficient and willing co-operation they rendered in making the first aid training, and medical services organization in general of such a very high standard. I know the difficulties they encountered, and it speaks very highly of them that these were overcome.

Circulating this message, Lt.-Col. Cogan added the following covering letter to battalion M.O.s.

I have pleasure in sending you the following extract from a letter sent by the A.D.M.S. East Central District.

May I add to this my personal thanks to you for all the work you have done to make the medical side of the Home Guard training in the Sub-District the success it has been.

### STAND-DOWN PARADES

Every battalion staged stand-down parades in addition to a big national parade in London on 3 December 1944, at which the King took the salute.

In this great show, Northamptonshire was represented by the following:

Officer in charge: Lt. H. Willett, 9th (Brixworth) Battalion.

1 Sector: 3rd (Oundle) Battalion—L.-Cpl. Foster, H. E.; Pte. Hamp, W.; Pte. Davis, J. 4th (Kettering Town) Battalion—Sgt. Kerr, G.; Cpl. Warren, L.; Pte. Thorpe, W. 5th (Kettering District) Battalion—Cpl. Hodge, W. A.; Pte. Thomas, H.; Pte. Ovendon, C. 6th (Corby) Battalion—L.-Cpl. Kerfoot, H.; L.-Cpl. White, H.; Pte. Cowen, B.

2 Sector: 10th (Daventry) Battalion—Cpl. Tomalin, H.; Cpl. Cowell, J. H.; Pte. Major, A. 13th (Towcester) Battalion—Cpl. Kirton, J.; Cpl. Brown, A. E.; L.-Cpl. Faulkner, R. P. 14th (Brackley) Battalion—Sgt. Haynes, J. R.; Pte. Barrett, A. C.; Pte. Green, G.

3 Sector: 7th (Wellingborough) Battalion—Sgt. Negus, A. J.; Cpl. Drage,

R. H.; Cpt. Tibbenham, D. J. 8th (Wellingborough District) Battalion—Cpl. Fuddefoot, H.; Pte. Webb, E.; Pte. Wilson, J.

4 Sector: 9th (Brixworth) Battalion—Cpl. Haynes, A. B.; Cpl. Leak, T. H.; Cpl. Billingham, C. H. 11th (Hardingstone) Battalion—Cpl. Gateby, J. T.; Cpl. West, A.; Cpl. Harrison, A. W. 12th (Northampton) Battalion—Cpl. Barrett, H. H. E.; Cpl. Warren, A.; L.-Cpl. Tew, A. G. 15th (Northampton) Battalion—Cpl. Batterson, D.; Cpl. Loe, E. J.; Pte. Clapham, G.

The 1st and 2nd Battalions paraded with the Huntingdonshire County contingent, under Capt. J. R. Condie (1st Hunts Battalion). Their representatives were as follows:

1st (Peterborough City) Battalion—C.S.M. Gough, G.; Cpl. Wright, G.; Pte. Hands, R. 2nd (Peterborough District) Battalion—Cpl. Potter, W.; Pte. Pooley, E. D. J.; Pte. Good, G.

And here is a record of the parade as told by Lt. H. Willett, who led the Northamptonshire contingent.

Proceeding to London on the afternoon of Saturday, 2 December, we were billeted at a hotel in Marylebone, where everything possible was done for the comfort of the men. Excellent hot meals were provided and a concert in the hotel was specially arranged for their benefit on the Saturday evening.

Everywhere was the same that week-end; wherever one went in London one was welcomed as a Home Guard, and it made one realize exactly how much their services had been appreciated.

Out of the 7,000 Home Guards parading, about 300 were invited by the Lord Mayor of London (Sir Frank Alexander) to a memorable dinner at the Mansion House on the Saturday evening, and I was one of the fortunate ones.

In a brilliant toast-list our "ears burned" while tributes to the Home Guard were voiced by the Lord Mayor himself and then by distinguished officers of the Navy, Army, Air

Force, and Civil Defence services, an appreciative response being voiced by the then Director-General of the Home Guard (Major-Gen. Sir James Drew, K.B.E., C.B.). The Royal Marines added their praises musically by providing the accompanying band.

On the Sunday morning we paraded at 0930 in platoons and were given about an hour's foot drill and marching in the streets.

Then, after an early lunch, the troops fell in and marched to Hyde Park, where the whole parade was marshalled and formed up.

After a long wait, the march past began to the band of the Welsh Guards, the troops marching eight abreast, with the A.A. Command leading and the Eastern Command following.

The saluting base was near Marble Arch and the salute was taken by H.M. the King, who was accompanied by the Queen, the two Princesses, the First Lord of the Admiralty, the War Minister, and leading officers of all arms.

After passing the saluting base, the march continued through Marble Arch, Oxford Street, Regent Street, Piccadilly, Hyde Park Corner, into and round Hyde Park, and nearly to the Marble Arch again.

The whole march, without any break, took over ninety minutes, but the march discipline was excellent and no men fell out, which was a particularly good record seeing that steel helmets and greatcoats had to be worn the whole time.

The route was crowded with spectators in places nine to ten deep and there was cheering the whole of the way.

In the evening the troops were invited to a concert at the Albert Hall, specially arranged for their benefit, but as the seating accommodation was insufficient to allow everyone to attend lots were drawn for tickets.

The Northants contingent returned home by the 8.45 a.m. train on the Monday morning after a never-to-be-forgotten experience.

### THE BATTALION PARADES

Those who went to London had a far more exciting time than those who "stayed at home" for, as was, perhaps, inevitable, the Stand-down parades in the battalions were charged with too many sentimental elements to evoke either thrills or excitement.

Even the weather added to the greyness of the day.

A description of a few of the battalion parades typifies the many.

For that of the 4th (Kettering Town) Battalion large crowds turned out despite the wet and dismal weather.

The turnout was a splendid one of 930 of all ranks, and they were addressed in the Market Place at Kettering by the Mayor, Councillor G. B. Smith, J.P., C.C., and the Commanding Officer, Lt.-Col. A. Russell.

The Mayor said it was a great day for the Home Guard, made possible by the exploits of the Allied armies on the Continent. Although the Home Guard were going out by a side door, it was, nevertheless, a day on which they could rejoice. He then referred to the early days and spoke of the town's vulnerable points. The Home Guard, said the Mayor, had, by standing by at the critical moment, assisted in the invasion of Europe.

"You have done a grand job, and the town and country are proud of you," concluded His Worship.

The commanding officer then read several messages of farewell and good luck.

Many members of the Town Council were present, with their clerk and the electrical engineer.

Following this ceremony there was an impressive march round the town, when the Battalion was played round by the bands of the Salvation Army, the Sea Cadets, and the Air Training Cadets. Lt.-Col. Russell took the salute near the corner of St. Peter's Avenue.

The Battalion then reassembled on the Market Place, where the commanding officer presented service certificates to the company commanders, and then dismissed the companies, who dispersed to their own headquarters, where many farewells were said.

The second-in-command (Major A. Burns) led the march past, and the companies in their final parade were commanded by Major Bell (Headquarters Company), Major Newbould (A Company), Major G. D. Howard (B Company), Major H. W. Issitt (C Company), Major H. Davenport (D Company), Major J. W. Watt (E Company), and Major H. Green (G Company).

The Sector Commander (Col. H. Burditt) was represented by Major Metcalfe, and the arrangements for the parade were made by Capt. J. H. Banks (Adjutant) and Capt. H. Maidment (Quartermaster).

### 8TH BATTALION STAND DOWN

The 8th Battalion paraded 705 strong at the Stand Down at the Hall grounds, Rushden.

The ceremony was divided into three phases—a parade in Spencer Park before Col. R. P. A. Helps (Sector Commander), who told the Battalion it could well be proud of its four and a half years of unstinted, unselfish service.

The Battalion then marched through the town, where Col. Helps took the salute, accompanied by the chairman of the Urban District Council and other officials, and thence to a final parade, where Lt.-Col. Sykes bade them farewell.

"The ranks of this battalion have never been broken," he said. "It has been a privilege to command you. I thank you for your loyalty to the Battalion, your help to the country, and your service to the King. . . ."

After the National Anthem the officers fell out and faced the men in two ranks, and as the Battalion dismissed, the strains of "Auld Lang Syne" were echoing through the air.

The "Stand Down" Parade of the 4th (Kettering Borough) Battalion, December 3rd, 1944.

Some members of Mears Ashby Platoon (A Co. 7th Battalion), pictured on October 15, 1944. *Standing, left to right*, Ptes. W. Sandall, E. Knight, G. Knight, D. Goosey, E. Goosey, E. King, D. Murphy, O. Ebsworth, E. Roe, W. Kendrick. *Seated, left to right*, Pte. F. Boden, Cpl. F. Brown, Cpl. R. Vickers, Sgt. W. Smith, Lt. W. G. Callis, Sgt. H. Bazeley, Cpl. W. Collins and Pte. E. Bazeley.

### "IF WE HAD BEEN CALLED UPON"

The loyalty of the battalions to their commanders was an outstanding feature of the Home Guard and this quality was emphasized by Lt.-Col. J. T. H. Pettitt in his Stand-Down Special Order of the Day to the 9th (Brixworth) Battalion.

In this, my last message [he said] I wish to thank all ranks for their splendid loyalty. I am confident that if we had been called upon to face the enemy in action, we should have acquitted ourselves with valour and skill to the satisfaction of our superiors and to the discomfort of the enemy.

This efficiency has only been achieved at great sacrifice and only because of the keen spirit and enthusiasm that has prevailed. I send my most grateful thanks to you all with best wishes for the future.

### STAND DOWN IN A CINEMA

An original note was struck by the 10th (Daventry District) Battalion, whose Stand-Down parade was accompanied by an entertainment in the cinema at Daventry,

which was filled to capacity by members of the Battalion—some eight hundred of all ranks being crammed inside.

Two excellent films were shown, and a drum head service was then conducted by the battalion chaplain, the Rev. Mitcheson.

A marked feature was the inspiring community hymn singing, led by the battalion band, which was at full strength. The words of the hymns were thrown on the screen, and eight hundred lusty voices rendered them with an intensity of feeling that no one who was present will forget.

The Commanding Officer (Lt.-Col. G. W. M. Lees) then addressed the Battalion. He gave them a résumé of the Battalion's activities throughout its tour of duty, and concluded on a note of appreciation and thanks for the never-failing support he had received from all ranks, and for the hard work put in by everybody under his command. He said that, thanks

Their last war-time parade. The large drumhead service held on the County Ground, Northampton, by members of the 12th (Northampton) Battalion, under Lt.-Col. L. E. Barnes, on the fifth war anniversary Day of Prayer, held on September 3, 1944. Contingents of the British Legion and the old Contemptibles were also on parade, and those present included the Mayor and Mayoress (Councillor and Mrs. A. Weston), Major-Gen. Sir Hereward Wake, Lt.-Col. O. K. Parker, and other representative officers. The pictures above show, at top Major-Gen. E. Hayes taking the salute at the March Past which preceded the service. Below, the 12th Battalion dispatch riders are passing the saluting base, at which Colonel P. Lester Reid is seen on right.

to this, his duty as commanding officer had been made easy and enjoyable.

The Battalion then formed up outside and, with the band at its head, marched through the town, the salute being taken by the commanding officer in the main street.

The 7th Battalion also held their Stand-Down parade in a cinema, at Wellingborough, an eleventh-hour change of plan being made on account of early rain. Col. R. P. A. Helps, O.B.E., M.C. (Sector Commander), after thanking the officers and men, affirmed "The spirit of the Home Guard shall not die". The battalion chaplain, the Rev. H. C. Clutterbuck, H.C.F., then, for the last time, read the special battalion prayers, which for some time had been in normal use on Sunday parades, and reminded his listeners of the necessity for maintaining in peace the effort put out in war. The Battalion Commander, Lt.-Col. H. L. Allsopp, O.B.E., T.D., on behalf of the Battalion, thanked the Civil Defence services and Police and spoke of the comradeship which all had found in common effort. Councillor H. J. Harrison, Chairman, Wellingborough U.D.C., thanked the Battalion on behalf of the town and spoke of the value to morale of their example. Mr. F. H. Johnson referred to the co-operation which had taken place on the invasion committee and the C.D. Sub-Controller, Mr. F. E. Gadd, returned greetings from his organizations, while Supt. M. E. Williams added the thanks of the Police.

The Battalion then fell in and marched past, the battalion commander taking the salute.

The 11th (Hardingstone) Battalion held a Stand-Down service and parade at Hardingstone church, followed by a march past at Quebec Barracks, at which the Commanding Officer, Lt.-Col. W. J. Penn, took the salute.

The farewell message of the commanding officer of the 12th (Northampton) Battalion is reproduced almost in full because in addition to conveying a personal message it also serves the purpose of this history by recording the conditions of Stand Down as they related to the period of reserve which followed, and to the retention, or otherwise, of equipment.

## "WORTHY OF THE TOWN OF NORTHAMPTON"

Here is the message as issued by Lt.-Col. L. E. Barnes:

To-day the period of Stand Down commences, and our active work is almost finished.

After a time of doubt as to the future of the Home Guard, the position has now been made quite clear and should be understood by all. Stand Down means the end of all training and the collection of certain equipment, details of which have been issued down to platoons.

Battledress, greatcoat, cap and badge, respirators, boots, capes, A.G. and anklets will be retained, but a word of warning is necessary in regard to these. At the moment they should not be used in civilian life, for although the period of Stand Down finishes on 31 December we then go "on reserve". The reason for this is obvious; until the war with Germany is over, there is always the possibility, however slight, that the enemy may attempt some action in this country, necessitating the calling out of the Home Guard. Hence the necessity for the preservation of personal equipment. This is also the reason for the maintenance of company headquarters and the storage of rifles, Stens, and Lewis guns there. It is not likely that the Home Guard will be finally disbanded until the European conflict is over.

Sunday, 3 December, is being kept as the Stand Down Day of the Home Guard. On this day it is expected that His Majesty the King will broadcast a message to the Home Guard and farewell parades will be held throughout the British Isles. Like all other

"I am proud of what the Home Guard has done and I give my heartfelt thanks to you all. . . . You have served your country with a steadfast devotion. I know that your country will not forget that service." Thus did the King broadcast to the Home Guard on Sunday evening, December 3, 1944, following the final parades. At Northampton the salute at the parade of the 12th Battalion, commanded by Lt.-Col. L. E. Barnes (*in circle*), was taken by the Home Guard Adviser, Col. P. Lester Reid, seen on right of picture (1) with his Staff Officer, Major T. C. Shillito. In (2) is a view of the parade during Colonel Reid's address. Wootton Barracks parade ground was the venue of the 11th (Hardingstone District) Battalion and in picture (3) the C.O. Lt.-Col. W. J. Penn, is taking leave of his men. The 15th (Northampton) Battalion held their parade at Franklin's Gardens. In picture (4)—it might well be entitled "Oh, well, and that's that"— men of the 15th are breaking off after parading before their C.O. (Lt.-Col. N. P. Andrews) who in (5) is taking the salute at the March Past.

battalions, we shall hold a farewell parade on the afternoon of this day, assembling at the rear of the Drill Hall, where we fell in in those fateful times in 1940. I am particularly anxious that on this last occasion we shall have a 100 per cent turnout, not only of those in the Battalion now, but of all those old members who have had to retire on account of age, ill health, etc.

Reviewing the last four and a half years since the old L.D.V. days, I think we may safely say that the Battalion has been worthy of the town of Northampton, and that had we have been called upon to go into action, we should have done our damnedest.

All have worked hard and with enthusiasm, and our success (and I know this battalion is thought highly of by the authorities) is due to the spirit of comradeship which has always been present. I am particularly anxious that this spirit shall not be lost in the future. We have all made friendships in the Home Guard with people who were strangers to us before the war. Such friendships, I for one feel have been well worth the time and labour we have put in. I am particularly anxious that this comradeship shall not lapse with the passing of the Home Guard and I hope to announce before long plans for the formation of the 12th Battalion Old Comrades Association, so that we can keep alive, by means of gatherings and social events, that happy spirit of "fellowship" that has existed since 1940.

I wish to thank you all for the magnificent effort you made at the battalion fête. A gratifying sum of £1,513 was raised—which, I believe, is a record for a fête held in Northampton. This enables us to have a 12th Battalion bed at the General Hospital and another at the Manfield Hospital, so that our name will not be forgotten in the years to come.

I shall have the opportunity on December 3rd of saying a few last words to you, but I do most sincerely thank you all for the hard work and loyal support that you have given me. No commanding officer could have wished for a better lot of fellows.

## AN INSPIRING SCENE

The 12th's parade being held, the salute was taken by Col. P. Lester Reid, and afterwards there was a pleasant and inspiring scene when Lt.-Col. Barnes called Mr. Thomas Walton, of 8 Albion Crescent, Northampton, from the parade and presented him to Col. Reid.

Mr. Walton was eighty-eight years of age, and he was the oldest man in the Stand-Down parade of the 12th, and believed to be the oldest active Home Guard in the country.

Lt.-Col. Barnes said that he exemplified the spirit of the Force, for the "young devil" had knocked twenty years off his age to evade the sixty-five age limit, and at eighty-four had done all-night duty on Hunsbury Hill!

Another G.O.M. of Northamptonshire Home Guard was Pte. Charles William Ward, of Stoke Bruerne, who joined the 13th (Towcester) Battalion at the age of seventy-five and served up to the Stand Down.

## "A" AND "Q" TOILED ON

Stand Down *was* the end for the great mass of the Guard but not for "A" and "Q" personnel, and the Territorial Army Association, secretary, and staff, who had a prodigious task in closing down offices, winding up accounts, checking and handing over stores and ammunition, and so on, in accordance with a positive stream of instructions.

One of the best "pictures" of their Herculean labour is provided by the following order from Eastern Command, relating to Home Guard advisers and their staffs:

In common with instruction received from G.H.Q. that all sector headquarters should be closed down not later than 31 December 1944, all offices maintained by Home Guard advisers which may still remain should also be closed

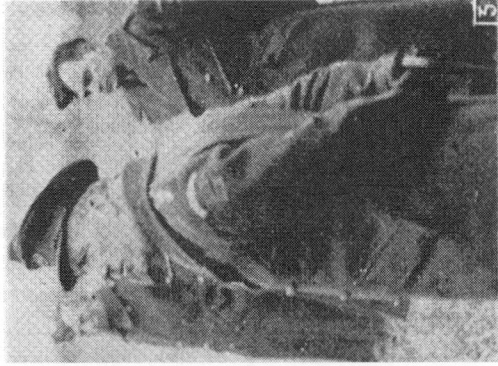

Scenes at three county battalion farewell parades in December 1944. (1) Lt.-Col. P. Y. Atkinson making his final inspection of the 13th (Towcester) Battalion. Following him (in trench coat) is Capt. Enos Lewin (Adjutant). (2) A section of a large audience of the 10th (Daventry) Battalion gathered in the Regal Cinema to hear an address by their C.O. (Lt.-Col. G. W. M. Lees). (3) The C.O. of the 9th (Brixworth) Battalion, Lt.-Col. J. T. H. Pettitt, addressing his men.

by that date—or, in view of the short notice, as soon after as possible. . . .

All operation instructions and other secret documents held by Home Guard advisers will be handed over to Sub-District Headquarters, who will dispose of them in due course in accordance with instructions which will be issued.

All training publications and papers connected with training, and maps should be taken over by a convenient Home Guard battalion headquarters if it is considered that they may be useful again. Otherwise, papers should be disposed of as salvage, except for those few files which Home Guard advisers may consider likely to be required for reference. These latter may also be stored by the nearest convenient battalion. It is obvious that these papers retained should be the minimum, as no doubt Sub-District and battalions will hold sufficient references to all matters except those more personal to the Home Guard adviser.

W.D. vehicles, weapons, ammunition, and equipment should be handed over to the local Home Guard battalion, who will dispose of the items in accordance with current instructions.

G licences still required may be retained in accordance with official requirements.

Like all such sweeping instructions, these orders were far, far "easier said than done" and the "Close Down" will be remembered even more vividly by those who had to carry it out than the "Stand Down".

## A LIVELY SUNDAY

The disposal of unwanted ammunition, bombs, etc., produced some thrilling effects, and at least one highly amusing one.

This was in the 5th (Kettering Town) area, where B Company decided to destroy their A.W. bombs in some ironstone workings near Desborough.

When the charge was fired an enormous cloud of black smoke arose.

At the identical moment a sentry at an adjacent aerodrome saw a large bomber disappear behind some trees and thought it had crashed.

At once the aerodrome fire brigade, rescue party, and S.B.s turned out pell-mell.

As this was during their Sunday afternoon "stand easy", the opinions the "rescuers" expressed concerning the Home Guard disposal squad are best imagined.

## THIS WAS THE NORTHAMPTONSHIRE HOME GUARD

Perhaps the most graphic idea of the immense task of dispersing the Home Guard is conveyed by the numbers under all heads of men in Northamptonshire alone.

Overleaf is the strength return at the date —a return which, incidentally, also provides a striking summary of the comprehensive character of the Home Guards' constitution and also how nearly all units approached their ceiling strengths:

| Batt. | Cos. | Plns. | Sectns. | Officers | O.R.s | Total | Ceiling | List II personnel | Civil Defence | Boys | Nominated Women Strength | Ceiling | Adjts. | Q.M.s | P.S.I.s |
|---|---|---|---|---|---|---|---|---|---|---|---|---|---|---|---|
| 1st | 6 | 29 | 110 | 103 | 1362 | 1465 | 1800 | 829 | — | — | — | 70 | 1 | 1 | 2 |
| 2nd | 6 | 29 | 101 | 92 | 1268 | 1360 | 1500 | 503 | — | 12 | 10 | 70 | 1 | 1 | 2 |
| 3rd | 8 | 28 | 88 | 80 | 1339 | 1419 | 1650 | 700 | 3 | — | 37 | 70 | — | 1 | 1 |
| 4th | 7 | 26 | 88 | 57 | 966 | 1023 | 1300 | 451 | — | — | 22 | 55 | 1 | 1 | 2 |
| 5th | 6 | 26 | 86 | 86 | 1356 | 1442 | 1500 | 425 | — | 15 | 41 | 60 | 1 | 1 | 2 |
| 6th | 5 | 17 | 71 | 72 | 1337 | 1409 | 1914 | — | 17 | — | 21 | 75 | 1 | 1 | 2 |
| 7th | 8 | 33 | 129 | 110 | 1538 | 1648 | 1933 | 674 | — | — | 62 | 80 | 2 | 1 | 2 |
| 8th | 7 | 36 | 120 | 83 | 1315 | 1398 | 1700 | — | — | — | — | — | 1 | 1 | 2 |
| 9th | 6 | 25 | 68 | 81 | 1134 | 1215 | 1350 | 321 | 4 | 11 | 11 | 58 | 1 | 1 | 3 |
| 10th | 6 | 21 | 84 | 64 | 1367 | 1431 | 1600 | 345 | 12 | 11 | 31 | 70 | 1 | 1 | 2 |
| 11th | 6 | 25 | 98 | 67 | 1208 | 1275 | 1600 | 178 | — | — | 24 | 70 | 1 | 1 | 2 |
| 12th | 7 | 23 | 79 | 92 | 1276 | 1368 | 1750 | 209 | — | — | 2 | 80 | 1 | 1 | 2 |
| 13th | 4 | 21 | 46 | 58 | 1090 | 1148 | 1300 | 29 | 9 | — | 25 | 55 | 1 | 1 | 2 |
| 14th | 5 | 24 | 72 | 47 | 817 | 864 | 900 | 230 | — | — | 12 | 30 | 1 | 1 | 2 |
| 15th | 6 | 16 | 45 | 60 | 960 | 1020 | 1266 | 613 | — | — | 6 | 55 | 1 | 1 | 2 |
| M.T. Cy. Rocket Bt. | 1 | 4 | 19 | 10 | 224 | 234 | 312 | 179 | — | — | — | — | — | — | — |
| A.A.R. | — | — | — | 40 | 1237 | 1277 | 1452 | 450 | — | — | — | — | — | — | — |
| H.Q. | — | — | — | 2 | — | 2 | 8 | — | — | — | — | — | — | — | — |
| *Totals* | 94 | 383 | 1304 | 1204 | 19794 | 20998 | 24835 | 6136 | 45 | 49 | 304 | 898 | 15 | 15 | 30 |

Included in 3rd Battalion total strength:    36 members of J.T.C.
Included in 5th Battalion, No. 1 Sector:    4 Officers; 21 O.Ranks; 6 nominated women.
Included in 7th Battalion, No. 3 Sector:    5 Officers; 32 O.Ranks; 1 Adjutant.
Included in 10th Battalion, No. 2 Sector:    4 Officers; 16 O.Ranks.

# Chapter XXXIII

## HONOURS AND AWARDS

This being a history of the Northamptonshire Home Guard, it is not within its

A member of the Northamptonshire Army Cadet Force shows how to take good cover during an exercise in conjunction with the Home Guard in May 1944.

terms of reference to include a history of the Northamptonshire Army Cadet Force.

Nevertheless, the early history of that force is closely bound up with the Guard, for from its inception in January 1942 Home Guards of all ranks readily responded to a request to "father" the junior organization and did so not only with advice and guidance but with much practical assistance in training exercises and in the organization of camps, lectures, etc.

By a fitting coincidence this close liaison was implemented from the outset, when in March 1942, Major-Gen. Sir Hereward Wake accepted the invitation to become County Colonel-Commandant of the Cadet Force, and how it developed was evidenced by the first full-scale camp of the cadets at Overstone Park in August 1943 which, incidentally, was visited on 5 August by Gen. Sir Harry Knox, K.C.B., D.S.O., Colonel of the Northamptonshire Regiment.

At that camp the commandant was Lt.-Col. H. L. Allsopp, T.D., 7th Northants

Col. P. Lester Reid (Home Guard Adviser), inspecting a County Cadet Unit. At its inception the Army Cadet Corps was largely trained by Home Guard instructors.

(Wellingborough Town) Battalion Home Guard, and the Quartermaster, Capt. W. E. Wetherall, 13th (Towcester) Battalion, while the attendant band was that of the 12th (Northampton) Battalion.

This association was continued after the Stand Down of the Home Guard by many officers, who took up new commissions in the Cadet Force, including the two battalion commanders, Lt.-Col. H. L. Allsopp, O.B.E., T.D., and Lt.-Col. J. T. H. Pettitt, who had commanded the 7th and 9th Home Guard Battalions respectively.

### HOME GUARD MUSIC

Throughout this record reference has been made to ceremonial parades, tournaments, and social occasions.

On most of these occasions Home Guard units managed with the willing aid of town or village bands, Salvation Army or youth organization bands, or those of school O.T.C.s and other bodies to grace their events with music of varying degrees of adequacy.

At least four battalions, however, were vastly fortunate in the possession of their own complete military bands for practically the whole period of their existence.

The first of these, as we have previously noted, was the 1st (Peterborough City) Battalion, which had a great stroke of luck in the first year of their being, when a patriotic lady made a gift of several hundred pounds to purchase band instruments.

An accomplished army bandmaster was "going spare", other subscriptions were forthcoming from the same and other sources, there were plenty of old bandsmen available, and the result was that the Battalion had a band of over forty capable performers, which ranked among the city's most important war-time institutions, apart from its value to its parent battalion.

The second full band, organized in September 1940, was that of the 7th (Wellingborough Town) Battalion, with Major A. E. S. Bayley, M.C., as first president and Mr. W. Groome bandmaster. From then until the summer of 1944 this band had its regular weekly parades, and in the

Long Buckby's Home Guard Band claimed to have been the first to be formed in the H.G. This picture was taken during the parade and march past before Admiral Sir Roger Keyes at Daventry in April 1943.

The first Home Guard band to be formed in Northampton (that of E Co. of the 12th Battalion) and the first railway Home Guard band in the country. The band was recruited from instrumentalists serving with the L.M.S. Railway Company plus members of the N.U.R. and the Northampton Silver Prize Bands. The Bandmaster was Mr. O. Mason, and the Band Sergeant Mr. W. J. Jenkinson.

early days functioned as stretcher-bearers for the town companies at Wellingborough.

Those who were present at the officers' dinner in December 1940 will, doubtless, remember the first-class way in which this band began—there have certainly been worse bands in Regular Army messes.

The instruments were held on loan from the L.M.S. railway, whose band was moribund, and many of the original players were drawn from ex-members of that band.

The loss of the cornet players into the Army was a severe blow for a time, but the presence of the band at the annual anniversary marches and other demonstrations was undoubtedly a tonic for the morale of the Battalion, and their concerts, given Sunday by Sunday in various parts of the county in 1942 and 1943, were much appreciated.

Unfortunately, the pressure of work on the railways very much interfered with practices in the first half of 1944, and in the summer of that year it was consequently disbanded.

The third band was that of the 12th (Northampton) Battalion.

Lt.-Col. L. E. Barnes, M.B.E. (C.O. of the 12th Battalion), records that it was in 1941 that Major E. W. Powell, commanding E Company, first formed a band, mainly from the remnants of the Northampton Silver Prize Band, which at the outbreak of war had been disbanded.

As a railway company band [says Col. Barnes] they had rendered good service, especially at the pageants at Franklin's Gardens. Early in 1943 I was approached with a view to their becoming a battalion band instead of a company one.

They certainly provided the 12th with something that many other battalions lacked, and on all our battalion parades gave invaluable assistance and contributed greatly to the success, especially on the drumhead services.

Besides their professional engagements, they gave voluntary service to Regular Army units in the town, to Army Cadets, to the British

Legion, to the Girl Guides, and many more organizations, as well as giving concerts for the troops at the Y.M.C.A. By their efforts in these directions they added prestige to the 12th Battalion, for which I thank them most sincerely.

I cannot close this account [adds Col. Barnes] without a personal note of thanks to the Bandmaster, Mr. O. Mason, to Band-Sgt. W. J. Jenkinson, and to Cpl. H. Cook, who did so much to make the band such a success.

The fourth band was claimed by the 10th (Daventry) Battalion, though this was, strictly speaking, a platoon unit rather than a battalion. The platoon which could thus claim its own band was that of Long Buckby, belonging to C Company of the 10th, commanded by Major C. T. Underwood.

Long Buckby Platoon held that theirs was the first Home Guard band in Northamptonshire, for it was formed in November 1940 and was entirely composed of Home Guardsmen.

During the life of the Home Guard, the band performed on eighty-one occasions, acting as the battalion band, and were in great demand for War Savings weeks, Red Cross fêtes, etc.

Transport was a problem, but it was overcome by the use of buses and of railway and builders' lorries, and on one occasion of a cattle truck!

Most of the players were drawn from the combined Long Buckby Town and Temperance Bands, and were fortunate in having as their bandmaster Sgt. E. J. Mason, who had given long service in the Temperance Band.

### HOW THE HOME GUARD REINFORCED THE ARMY

As we have repeatedly indicated, not the least of the recurrent problems of the Home Guard commanders was the constant drain on the personnel of their units as the result of calls to the Regular Services.

The anxiety and work these constant departures entailed was not lightened by the fact that, quite naturally, they always claimed the youngest, fittest and usually the most capable men, but the big compensation lay in the knowledge that in thus acting as a training "nursery" for the Regulars the Home Guard was performing, probably, its most valuable service and also identifying itself, directly, with the war as carried to the enemy.

It is impossible to reproduce a complete list of the whole of the men from all of the battalions who passed on to the wider sphere of service, most of them to gain rapid promotion as the result of their previous training with the Guard, and many to gain high honours and awards, but some idea of their volume may be gained from a few typical numbers sent by Northamptonshire battalions.

It should be emphasized that these numbers are in many cases incomplete since they do not include many men who joined the Services from the Guard in the early days of the Force when records were not kept.

| | |
|---|---|
| 1st (Peterborough City) Battalion | 1100 |
| 2nd (Soke of Peterborough) Battalion | 340 |
| 3rd (Oundle) Battalion | 297 |
| 5th (Kettering District) Battalion | 218 |
| 7th (Wellingborough) Battalion | 613 |
| 8th (Wellingborough District) Battalion | 660 |
| 12th (Northampton) Battalion | 1172 |
| 13th (Towcester) Battalion | 160 |
| 15th (Northampton) Battalion | 84 |

Among such large numbers there were, inevitably, many who made the supreme sacrifice—to their memory this history is dedicated — many others who were wounded, missing and taken prisoner. All of them were, and are, saluted by their old comrades as men who went to prove the worth of the Home Guard units they had left in the final test of all military training.

Here, too, old comrades salute the 193 members who died while serving with the Northamptonshire Home Guard.

## THE HOME GUARD AND CHARITY

Soon after the Northamptonshire Home Guard got into its real stride and was capable of staging really spectacular events it became evident that not only were numbers of the general public keenly interested in these events but that they were ready and willing to pay for the interest.

Thus units, from battalion level downwards, seized these opportunities on behalf of deserving charities of all types, and throughout the county very considerable sums were raised.

Among the finest efforts in this respect were those of the 1st (City of Peterborough) Battalion which raised over £1,000 for distribution to the Northamptonshire Old Comrades Association, Army Cadet Force, Merchant Navy Comforts Fund, and the Mayor's Troops Welfare Fund, etc., the 11th (Hardingstone) Battalion which, in addition to several donations to the Northamptonshire Regiment's Prisoners of War Fund, raised the splendid sum of £1,805 to endow beds at the Northamptonshire General Hospital and the Manfield Orthopaedic Hospital; the 12th (Northampton) Battalion, whose members raised another grand total of £1,512, which was devoted to the same purposes, and the 15th (Northampton) Battalion, which raised a donation of £601 to the Northampton General Hospital War Memorial Fund.

## HONOURS AND AWARDS

To serve as the subject of public controversy was no new experience to the Home Guard of 1944.

Thus, when the subject of medals for war service arose, they were not surprised when their rights to this, that, or the other war decoration were raised, debated, and bandied to and fro in Parliament and Press.

The great mass of the Guard were not deeply concerned in the controversy.

But, if anything *was* "coming to them" they would naturally have preferred to have had it while they were still in being and in uniform. They might then have "put up" the ribbon if only for a month or so. As it was, nothing arrived, but, after the Stand Down, all who had served not less than three years received the Defence Medal and the Colonel-in-Chief, H.M. the King, issued to all ranks an illuminated certificate, of which a facsimile is reproduced in this volume.

Of the 38,175 officers and men who served in the Northamptonshire Home Guard, 10,679 were entitled to the Defence Medal.

The task of distribution fell upon the Northamptonshire Territorial Army Association and, like all the Association's services to the Guard, was cheerfully undertaken by Lt.-Col. O. K. Parker (Secretary), Mr. P. W. Higgins (Assistant Secretary), Major R. E. Amos (officer-in-charge Northamptonshire Home Guard records), and their staffs.

There were also a number of special awards to individual members—awards derived from the Crown and from within the Guard itself or its Regular commands.

Of the former, Northamptonshire reveived twelve of the 808 Home Guard Honours awarded in December 1944 "in recognition of meritorious service", and in every case it can be said that they were well earned and richly deserved.

Here is the list:

### C.B.E. (MILITARY DIVISION)

Col. Percy Lester Reid (Sub-District Home Guard Adviser).

### O.B.E. (MILITARY DIVISION)

Lt.-Col. Herbert Leslie Allsopp (Officer Commanding the 7th (Wellingborough Town) Battalion.

### M.B.E. (MILITARY DIVISION)

Major Alfred Burns, 4th (Kettering Borough) Battalion; Lt. Phillip Campion, Bugbrooke Platoon of the 11th (Hardingstone District) Battalion, who was in command of the runners-up in the battle platoon competition for the East Central District; Major Reginald Kersey Green, 8th (Wellingborough District) Battalion; Major James Edwin Guy Hassall, 1st (Peterborough) Battalion; Major Harold Peter Hewett, 3rd (Oundle) Battalion.

### BRITISH EMPIRE MEDALS (MILITARY DIVISION)

Sgt. Arthur Ekin Briggs, 3rd (Oundle) Battalion; C.Q.M.S. John Reginald Ney, 13th (Towcester) Battalion; C.Q.M.S. Alfred Scholey Tattersall, 7th (Wellingborough Town) Battalion; L.-Cpl. John Walter Williams, 9th (Brixworth) Battalion; L.-Cpl. P. F. H. Hickman, 12th (Northampton) Battalion.

(Note: During the fourth birthday celebration of the 12th Battalion, L.-Cpl. P. F. H. Hickman, who was introduced by his commanding officer, Lt.-Col. L. E. Barnes, received the congratulations of Lt.-Gen. Sir John Brown on his award of the British Empire Medal. L.-Cpl. Hickman, although young in years, had a physical disability which debarred him from joining the Regular Army, and could also have disqualified him from joining the Home Guard had he wished. This Lance-Corporal chose to serve and proved to be one of the most enthusiastic members of the Battalion in spite of his disability. He was never absent from parade and he could march ten miles "with the best of them".)

### HOME GUARD CERTIFICATE FOR GALLANTRY

Major A. E. S. Bayley, M.C., Lt. W. D. Halton, C.S.M. Orton, Sgt. D. J. Evans, Sgt. T. E. Lloyd, all of 7th (Wellingborough Town) Battalion.

### HOME GUARD CERTIFICATES OF GOOD SERVICE

5th (Kettering District) Battalion—Capt. H. Barratt (B Company.

7th (Wellingborough Town) Battalion—Major T. R. Curtis (Commanding Irthlingborough Company), Capt. C. J. Chouler (Adjutant), R.S.M. A. J. Mason, Sgt. H. Bean (Battalion Intelligence Section). (Sgt. Bean, who attended parades for the first three years, normally three or four a week, was never once absent. In 1942 his son was killed and he asked for leave of absence, and although this was granted, he still attended.)

8th Battalion—Certificate for Gallantry or Good Service: C.S.M. H. S. T. Bassett (The Northamptonshire Regiment). Of this award a contemporary report stated: During a bombing class in the 8th (Wellingborough District) Battalion (Lt.-Col. V. H. Sykes) the prompt and sensible action of the Battalion's thirty-eight-year-old Permanent Staff Instructor saved one of the students from serious injury or more.

The man had taken a grenade and was about to throw it when it slipped from his hand. Realizing the danger, the instructor, Sgt.-Major H. S. T. Bassett, at once knocked the man over and so prevented his being hurt by the explosion.

Good Service Certificates—Lt. P. G. Whitney, Headquarters; C.Q.M.S. H. W. Clayton, B Company; C.Q.M.S. J. B. Smith, D Company; Sgt. A. Knight, Headquarters; Sgt. B. Matthews, F Company; Sgt. F. J. Murdon, G Company; Pte. G. Clayton, E Company.

9th (Brixworth Battalion—Major (later Lt.-Col.) J. T. H. Pettitt; Lt. H. Willett, M.B.E.; Lt. C. L. Robinson; C.S.M. Kirk; Sgt. J. Dicken; Cpl. E. W. K. Watts; L.-Cpl. J. W. Williams; L.-Cpl. W. Faulkner.

11th (Hardingstone District) Battalion —Lt. W. H. Clay (E Company); Lt. F. J. Frost, M.M. (C Company); C.S.M. H. B. Clifton (E Company); C.Q.M.S. A. Shaw (C Company); Sgt. F. Munroe (D Company); Sgt. G. Tamplin (D Company); Cpl. F. Espiner (F Company); Cpl. J. Thompson (H.Q. Company).

## HOME GUARD STAND DOWN CERTIFICATES

7th (Wellingborough Town) Battalion— C.S.M. C. G. Golbourn (B Company); C.Q.M.S. S. R. Clarke (A Company); Sgt. A. Bugby (C Company); Sgt. T. V. Hawker (Pioneers); Sgt. A. J. Negus (B Company); Sgt. J. Monaghan (Intelligence); Sgt. H. Sanders (G Company); Cpl. A. R. Pentelow (stretcher-bearer).

## MILITARY COMMENDATIONS, EAST CENTRAL DISTRICT

2nd (Soke of Peterborough) Battalion— Lt. J. G. Conington and Lt. A. G. Teesdale, of B Company, commended by East Central District for gallantry in rescuing a British airman from a blazing plane.

## ARMY COMMANDER'S COMMENDATION

15th (Northampton) Battalion—Lt. T. H. Bird, C.S.M. G. Busby, C.S.M.

S. B. Robinson, C.Q.M.S. H. J. Tite, Cpl. L. E. Bird, Cpl. H. T. Dalley.

## PARLIAMENT'S MOTION OF GRATITUDE

In a motion expressing gratitude to the Services on the victorious end of the war, which was submitted to both Houses of Parliament on 30 October 1945, the Home Guard received special mention in a passage devoted to the Army as follows:

"That the thanks of the House be accorded to all ranks of the Army . . . and to the Home Guard for the keenness and self-sacrifice with which they undertook voluntarily and in addition to their normal work the defence of these islands against the threat of imminent invasion."

The official "disbandment", as distinct from the Stand Down, was announced on 31 December 1945.

## IN THE VICTORY PARADE

But six months later, on 8 June 1946, the Guard emerged for a final and crowning scene in this "strange eventful drama" —the great Victory Parade of all arms of all Services before the King and Queen.

Here is the graphic story of a never-to-be-forgotten occasion as related, in his own words, by one of those who marched for Northamptonshire and who signs himself "A. H.".

Someone said that the Home Guard were dead but wouldn't lie down. They were certainly very much alive when 624 of them left their offices, workshops, factories, and farms to go to London for this great parade. They came from every part of the British Isles, from places as far apart as the Orkneys and Kent, the Shetlands and Cornwall, from Wales and Ulster, from Cheshire, Devonshire, Norfolk, from the Midlands, Manchester, Birmingham, and London; every part was represented.

The Northamptonshire contingent consisted of Lt. A. Holland (Northampton), C.S.M. B. W. Fisher (Peterborough), C.S.M. A.

Loughrey (Cosgrove), C.S.M. C. R. Wilson (Northampton), Sgt. W. T. Brown (Rushden), Sgt. G. S. Mayes (Thrapston), Cpl. B. M. Clarke (Daventry), Cpl. J. Drage (Arthingworth), and Pte. H. Cooper (Corby), and they met for the first time on the Friday evening in Kensington Gardens, dressed in familiar battledress but wearing web belts and gaiters and "berets", and medal ribbons, with the addition of the then new Defence ribbon.

We drew our blankets and were allocated to various tents. After tea there was a parade, and we were sorted into counties and then into ranks of twelve, with an officer as left-hand man; fifty-two ranks in all.

The Northamptonshires were rank No. 17 and their number was made up by three Scotties from Renfrewshire—grand fellows all. In the row behind us were the Norfolks and Dorsets.

There were 21,000 troops in Kensington Gardens, all of whom had been drilling and rehearsing for weeks, but the Home Guard, who had not handled a rifle or done any marching for over eighteen months, and had only worn their boots on the allotment, went "straight into battle", as it were, without any rehearsal apart from being told that when they came to the Cenotaph in Whitehall or to traffic islands along the route, the detachment would split into two columns, one going to the left, the other to the right; and that during the march, which would be at attention for the whole of the way, the order would be given to "change arms" at intervals along the route. That was all.

## GUARDS OFFICERS AS MARSHALS

Reveille next morning was at six o'clock, breakfast at seven, and after a final cleaning and polishing the Home Guard went on parade. What a grand sight they made with rifles cleaned, belts and gaiters "blancoed", brass gleaming like gold, boots polished, and "berets" at the correct angle. As far as the Northamptonshire men were concerned they were a credit to the county; and to C.S.M. Wilson, a Boer War veteran, who, in an incredibly short space of time, had, in a quiet spot behind the tents, "licked them into shape"; even the officer, a tartar for spit and polish on a ceremonial parade, could find no fault with them. Up came the Home Guard band, and with a final word and "good luck" from the officer commanding, we set off, accompanied by officers from the Guards regiments with their white arm-bands, who acted as marshals and shepherded us along the route.

From where we were in camp to the assembly point in Hyde Park near the Marble

FINALE. The Great Victory March in London on June 8, 1946. Northamptonshire Home Guard members are abreast of the Guards' officer pilot (with armlet) on left.

Arch was about one and a half miles, and by the time we arrived there we were getting into our stride. On the way we passed some German prisoners of war and we could well imagine what their thoughts were, remembering Hitler's boast in 1940. The troops were drawn up in long columns ready for the start, the Infantry of the line, whom the Home Guard were to follow, on our right, and the Royal Air Force, who would follow us, on our left. Our turn to move off came at last and the Royal Air Force gave us a rousing cheer which bucked us up no end. We went through the gates at Marble Arch and swung into Oxford Street, amid the greatest ovation the Home Guard has ever had. London loves a parade, and they really let themselves go. There were shouts from the crowd of "Good old Home Guard" and "Stick it, dad". The cheering was so great that there were times when we couldn't hear our own band, and we were only in the seventeenth rank. Policemen were struggling to hold back the crowds, and the St. John Ambulance Brigade were kept busy looking after those unfortunates who had temporarily lost interest in the proceedings, many of whom had waited for several hours to see the Services go by. Flags and bunting along both sides of the route presented a veritable kaleidoscope of colour. The pavements were packed tight with people, waving handkerchiefs and flags, and turning rattles as hard as they could. The noise was terrific. Every window was occupied, and many found precarious perches on roofs and at every vantage-point. It was evident that the Home Guard were expected for, curious to relate, every public house had a notice up "No beer".

**CIGARETTES THROWN FROM WINDOWS**

When the head of the marching column reached Parliament Square it halted for twenty minutes to allow the mechanized column, which had been traversing a different route, to precede it. The Home Guard, who were about three-quarters along the column, had only got as far as Lyon's Corner House in Oxford Street. It was here that the crowds showed their greatest appreciation, for as we waited, showers of cigarettes were thrown down from the windows, and quite a number of oranges and apples, too. An apple hit a policeman on his helmet close to us, much to the delight of the crowd. Some kind people passed trays of delicious-looking cakes, which, needless to say, were eagerly seized by those Home Guards fortunate enough to be near them. During all this, showers of torn-up paper descended upon us, and it is highly probable that there is still a scarcity of telephone directories in Oxford Street. To while away the time, our band played selections of music, but rather tactlessly included "We are far better off in a home".

Soon the order came to march again, the band struck up, and we continued down Oxford Street. Left, right; left, right; 116 steps to the minute, chins up, arms swinging, rifles at an angle of forty-five degrees; a glance along the line showed the men marching as though they had done nothing else all their lives. They were absolutely magnificent—there is no other word for it—and it made one feel intensely proud to be one of them. We were proud enough as it was, for weren't we all picked men, who had been given the honour of representing the various units of the Home Guard in the greatest parade in the history of London? Most of us had long left youth behind, many had been in two wars, and quite a number wore the Boer War medals and medals of other campaigns. Several of that gallant band were over sixty years of age and it was rumoured that two of them had turned seventy-four. And how they marched! Just as if they had come straight from Wellington Barracks; even the Regulars couldn't have done better.

On we went, amid frenzied bursts of cheering, down Charing Cross Road, past St. Martin-in-the-Fields, Trafalgar Square, with Nelson looking down at the splendid pageantry moving slowly beneath him, down Northumberland Avenue, Victoria Embankment to the Houses of Parliament, where Big Ben told us it was 12.35 p.m. Then swinging round Parliament Square, we went up Whitehall, paying our respects as we passed the Cenotaph, a column six deep on either side, joining up into twelves again as we proceeded towards Trafalgar Square, and turned left through the Admiralty Arch into The Mall. The Mall presented us with a wonderful sight with the trees in their dresses of green, interspersed with the splashes of colour from the flags of various nations, the sides thronged with cheering crowds as we marched on towards the saluting base. Now for it!

A swift word of warning—"Don't bunch" —followed by the order "Eyes left", and there on the dais decorated with clusters of hydrangeas, which gave an added touch of colour, stood their Majesties the King and Queen with the two Princesses, looking very fine and regal. The different coloured uniforms and the dresses of the ladies presented a very pretty picture, though it was impossible to take in the whole of the magnificent scene in such a short space of time. It was a great thrill to see their Majesties, but with a salute from the King and a gracious smile from the Queen we left the saluting base behind us and were on our way to the Queen Victoria Statue and Buckingham Palace, where a number of wounded soldiers, many of whose fathers probably served in the Home Guard, gave us a rousing cheer.

Up till now the weather had managed to keep fairly fine, with the sun occasionally peeping out of the clouds, but it started to rain, which steadily got worse, and by the time we got to Hyde Park it was coming down in real earnest. However, when we arrived back in camp at 1.45 p.m., tired but happy, a meal was waiting for us, and after that and a much-needed drink, we retired to our tents, the NAAFI canteen, and to the mess to enjoy a well-earned rest.

Let it be said without fear of contradiction, that the Home Guard fulfilled every expectation, and during that march of eight miles— marching at attention the whole of the way— without having done any for eighteen months, only two men out of that gallant band of 624 fell out—and then only as we were nearly back at camp. And just to show what they could do, many of them, after a meal and a rest, were ready to march round the route all over again. Even the marshals from the Guards were amazed at the way the Home Guard had stuck it out!

They were magnificent, and justly proud of their achievement. We all came back from London holding our heads a little higher.

The Home Guard may be "dead" but they will certainly never "lie down" while the old Home Guard spirit prevails.

Could this history close with a worthier valediction? We think not.

# INDEX

# TO ALL WHO HAVE SERVED

## IN THE

## NAVY—ARMY—AIR FORCE
## AND MERCANTILE MARINE

# HAVE YOU JOINED THE BRITISH LEGION?

---

THE LEGION wants the assistance of every ex-Serviceman and woman and of all who are interested in the ex-Service cause

---

If you are not a member you are asked to join the nearest Branch without delay. If no Branch exists in your district, kindly communicate with the

## NORTHANTS COUNTY COMMITTEE
## 15 WOOD STREET, NORTHAMPTON

who will put you in touch with the people in your own district who will advise you what to do.

PRINTED BY
JARROLD AND SONS LTD.
NORWICH

Printed in Great Britain
by Amazon